Lecture Notes in Computer Science 12042

More information about this series at http://www.springer.com/series/7407

Maurizio Gabbrielli (Ed.)

Logic-Based Program Synthesis and Transformation

29th International Symposium, LOPSTR 2019
Porto, Portugal, October 8–10, 2019
Revised Selected Papers

 Springer

Editor
Maurizio Gabbrielli ⓘ
University of Bologna
Bologna, Italy

ISSN 0302-9743 ISSN 1611-3349 (electronic)
Lecture Notes in Computer Science
ISBN 978-3-030-45259-9 ISBN 978-3-030-45260-5 (eBook)
https://doi.org/10.1007/978-3-030-45260-5

LNCS Sublibrary: SL1 – Theoretical Computer Science and General Issues

This Springer imprint is published by the registered company Springer Nature Switzerland AG
The registered company address is: Gewerbestrasse 11, 6330 Cham, Switzerland

Preface

This volume contains a selection of the papers presented at LOPSTR 2019, the 29th International Symposium on Logic-Based Program Synthesis and Transformation, held during September 7–10, 2019, in Porto, Portugal.

It was co-located with the 21th International ACM SIGPLAN Symposium on Principles and Practice of Declarative Programming (PPDP 2019), with the Symposium on Formal Methods (FM 2019), and with other events in the context of the FM Week. Previous LOPSTR symposia were held in Frankfurt am Main (2018) Namur (2017), Edinburgh (2016), Siena (2015), Canterbury (2014), Madrid (2013 and 2002), Leuven (2012 and 1997), Odense (2011), Hagenberg (2010), Coimbra (2009), Valencia (2008), Lyngby (2007), Venice (2006 and 1999), London (2005 and 2000), Verona (2004), Uppsala (2003), Paphos (2001), Manchester (1998, 1992 and 1991), Stockholm (1996), Arnhem (1995), Pisa (1994), and Louvain-la-Neuve (1993). More information about the symposium can be found at: http://www.cs.unibo.it/projects/lopstr19/.

The aim of the LOPSTR series is to stimulate and promote international research and collaboration on logic-based program development. LOPSTR is open to contributions on all aspects of logic-based program development, all stages of the software life cycle, and issues of both programming-in-the-small and programming-in-the-large. LOPSTR traditionally solicits contributions, in any language paradigm, in the areas of synthesis, specification, transformation, analysis and verification, specialization, testing and certification, composition, program/model manipulation, optimization, transformational techniques in software engineering, inversion, applications, and tools. This year, LOPSTR extended its traditional topics to include also logic-based program development based on integration of sub-symbolic and symbolic models, on machine learning techniques, and on differential semantics.

LOPSTR has a reputation for being a lively, friendly forum that allows for the presentation and discussion of both finished work and work in progress. Formal proceedings are produced only after the symposium so that authors can incorporate the feedback from the conference presentation and discussion. In response to the calls for papers, 32 contributions were submitted from 16 different countries. The Program Committee accepted 6 full papers for immediate inclusion in the formal proceedings, and 9 more papers presented at the symposium were accepted after a revision and another round of reviewing. Each submission was reviewed by at least three Program Committee members or external referees. The paper "On fixpoint/iteration/variant induction principles for proving total correctness of programs with denotational semantic" by Patrick Cousot won the Best Paper Award, sponsored by Springer. In addition to the 15 contributed papers, this volume includes the abstracts of the invited talks by two outstanding speakers whose talks where shared with PPDP: German Vidal (Universitat Politècnica de València) and John Gallagher (Roskilde University).

I would like to thank the Program Committee members, who worked diligently to produce high-quality reviews for the submitted papers, as well as all the external reviewers involved in the paper selection. We are very grateful to the local organizer, José Nuno Oliveira, and his team for the great job they did in managing the FM week. Many thanks also to Ekaterina Komendantskaya, the Program Committee chair of PPDP, with whom I interacted with for coordinating the events. I would also like to thank Andrei Voronkov for his excellent EasyChair conference management system that automates many of the tasks involved in chairing a conference, and Tong Liu for his work as publicity chair. Special thanks go to the invited speakers and to all the authors who submitted and presented their papers at LOPSTR 2019. We also thank our sponsor, Springer, for the cooperation and support in the organization of the symposium.

December 2019   Maurizio Gabbrielli

Organization

General Chair

José Nuno Oliveira   University of Minho, Portugal

Program Committee Chair

Maurizio Gabbrielli   University of Bologna, Italy, and Inria, France

Program Committee

Sabine Broda	University of Porto, Portugal
Manuel Carro	Technical University of Madrid and IMDEA, Spain
Ugo Dal Lago	University of Bologna, Italy, and Inria, France
Daniel De Schreye	KU Leuven, Belgium
Santiago Escobar	Polytechnic University of València, Spain
Moreno Falaschi	University of Siena, Italy
Laurent Fribourg	CNRS, France
Arnaud Gotlieb	SIMULA Research Laboratory, Norway
Gopal Gupta	The University of Texas at Dallas, USA
Andy King	University of Kent, UK
Herbert Kuchen	University of Münster, Germany
Jacopo Mauro	University of Southern Denmark, Denmark
Hernan Melgratti	University of Buenos Aires, Argentina
Maria Chiara Meo	University G.D'Annunzio of Chieti Pescara, Italy
Carlos Olarte	Federal University of Rio Grande do Norte, Brazil
Hirohisa Seki	Nagoya Institute of Technology, Japan
Caterina Urban	Inria, France
Herbert Wiklicky	Imperial College London, UK

Additional Reviewers

Jesus M. Almendros-Jimenez	Jan C. Dageförde
Gianluca Amato	Emanuele De Angelis
João Barbosa	Marco Eilers
Benoit Barbot	Fabio Fioravanti
Kinjal Basu	Andreas Fuchs
Guillaume Burel	Roberto Giacobazzi
Zhuo Chen	Saverio Giallorenzo
Federico Chesani	Line Jakubiec-Jamet
Marco Comini	Jean-Pierre Jouannaud

Invited Papers

Reversibilization in Functional and Concurrent Programming

Germán Vidal🆔

MiST, VRAIN, Universitat Politècnica de València, Spain
gvidal@dsic.upv.es

Landauer's seminal work [4] states that a computation principle can be made reversible by adding the history of the computation—a so-called Landauer embedding—to each state. Although it may seem impractical at first, there are several useful reversibilization techniques that are roughly based on this idea (e.g., [1, 8, 11, 13]).

In this talk, we first introduce a Landauer embedding for a simple (first-order) eager functional language [9, 11] and illustrate its usefulness to define an automatic *bidirectionalization* technique [12] in the context of bidirectional programming. This framework often considers two representations of some data and the functions that convert one representation into the other and vice versa (see, e.g., [3] for an overview). For instance, we may have a function called "get" that takes a *source* and returns a *view*. In turn, a function "put" takes a possibly updated view (together with the original source) and returns the corresponding, updated source. In this context, *bidirectionalization* [8] usually aims at automatically producing a function put from the corresponding function get (but the opposite approach is also possible, see, e.g., [2]).

Then, we extend the language with some primitives for message-passing concurrency and present an appropriate Landauer embedding to make its computations reversible [6, 10]. In this case, we consider *reversible debugging* as a promising application of reversible computing. Essentially, we allow the user to record an execution of a running program and, then, use the reversible semantics to reproduce some visible misbehavior inside the debugger. Here, the user can explore a computation back and forth in a *causal-consistent* way (i.e., so that an action is not undone until all the actions that depend on it have already been undone) until the source of a misbehavior is found [5, 7].

References

1. Danos, V., Krivine, J.: Reversible communicating systems. In: Gardner, P., Yoshida, N. (eds.) CONCUR 2004 - Concurrency Theory. CONCUR 2004. LNCS, vol. 3170, pp. 292–307. Springer, Heidelberg (2004). https://doi.org/10.1007/978-3-540-28644-8_19

This work has been partially supported by the EU (FEDER) and the *Spanish Ministerio de Ciencia e Innovación* under grant TIN2016-76843-C4-1-R, by the *Generalitat Valenciana* under grant Prometeo/ 2019/098 (DeepTrust), and by the COST Action IC1405 on Reversible Computation - extending horizons of computing.

2. Fischer, S., Hu, Z., Pacheco, H.: The essence of bidirectional programming. Sci. China Inf. Sci. **58**(5), 1–21 (2015)

3. Hu, Z., Schürr, A., Stevens, P., Terwilliger, J.F.: Bidirectional transformation "bx" (dagstuhl seminar 11031). Dagstuhl Reports **1**(1), 42–67 (2011)

4. Landauer, R.: Irreversibility and heat generation in the computing process. IBM J. Res. Dev. **5**, 183–191 (1961)

5. Lanese, I., Nishida, N., Palacios, A., Vidal, G.: CauDEr: A causal-consistent reversible debugger for erlang. In: Gallagher, J., Sulzmann, M. (eds.) Functional and Logic Programming. FLOPS 2018. LNCS, vol. 10818, pp. 247–263. Springer, Cham (2018). https://doi.org/10.1007/978-3-319-90686-7_16

6. Lanese, I., Nishida, N., Palacios, A., Vidal, G.: A theory of reversibility for Erlang. J. Log. Algebr. Methods Program. **100**, 71–97 (2018)

7. Lanese, I., Palacios, A., Vidal, G.: Causal-consistent replay debugging for message passing programs. In: Pérez, J., Yoshida, N. (eds.) Formal Techniques for Distributed Objects, Components, and Systems. FORTE 2019. LNCS, vol. 11535, pp. 167–184. Springer, Cham (2019). https://doi.org/10.1007/978-3-030-21759-4_10

8. Matsuda, K., Hu, Z., Nakano, K., Hamana, M., Takeichi, M.: Bidirectionalization transformation based on automatic derivation of view complement functions. In: Hinze, R., Ramsey, N. (eds.) Proceedings of the 12th ACM SIGPLAN International Conference on Functional Programming. ICFP 2007, pp. 47–58. ACM (2007)

9. Nishida, N., Palacios, A., Vidal, G.: Reversible term rewriting. In: Kesner, D., Pientka, B. (eds.) Proceedings of the 1st International Conference on Formal Structures for Computation and Deduction (FSCD'16). LIPIcs, vol. 52, pp. 28:1–28:18. Schloss Dagstuhl - Leibniz-Zentrum fuer Informatik (2016)

10. Nishida, N., Palacios, A., Vidal, G.: A reversible semantics for erlang. In: Hermenegildo, M., Lopez-Garcia, P. (eds.) Logic-Based Program Synthesis and Transformation. LOPSTR 2016. LNCS, vol. 10184, pp. 259–274. Springer, Cham (2017). https://doi.org/10.1007/978-3-319-63139-4_15

11. Nishida, N., Palacios, A., Vidal, G.: Reversible computation in term rewriting. J. Log. Algebr. Meth. Program. **94**, 128–149 (2018)

12. Nishida, N., Vidal, G.: Characterizing compatible view updates in syntactic bidirectionalization. In: Thomsen, M., Soeken, M. (eds.) Reversible Computation. RC 2019. LNCS, vol. 11497, pp. 67–83. Springer, Cham (2019). https://doi.org/10.1007/978-3-030-21500-2_5

13. Phillips, I.C., Ulidowski, I.: Reversing algebraic process calculi. J. Log. Algebr. Program. **73** (1–2), 70–96 (2007)

Horn Clauses and Tree Automata
for Imperative Program Verification

John P. Gallagher[1,2]

[1] Roskilde University, Denmark
[2] IMDEA Software Institute, Madrid, Spain

Automatic program verification is one of the oldest challenges in computer science. The formalism of constrained Horn clauses (CHCs) has emerged in recent years as a common representation language for the semantics of imperative programming languages and the modelling of sequential, concurrent and reactive systems. This has opened up possibilities for using CHCs in verification tools [1, 3, 7]. A number of software verification tools based on CHCs have been developed in recent years [2, 4, 8, 11, 12].

Since CHCs are syntactically and semantically the same as constraint logic programs (CLP) we look at how techniques for analysis and transformation of CLP can play a role in verification of imperative programs. These techniques include partial evaluation and abstract interpretation of logic programs, and the exploitation of the connection between tree automata and Horn clauses.

The talk summarises recent work exploiting tools, techniques and theory developed for the analysis of constraint logic programs. A set of CHCs corresponds directly to a finite tree automaton that recognises the set of derivation trees based on the CHCs. Well established properties and operations on tree automata can then be exploited to manipulate sets of CHCs. We examine how infeasible derivations can be pruned from a set of CHCs by computing the difference of tree automata. This leads to a refinement operation in a CHC verification tool [9, 11]. Secondly we show how partial evaluation can be used to specialise a set of CHCs with respect to a property to be verified. In this way, verification problems can be simplified by eliminating derivations that are irrelevant to the property being verified. Furthermore, CHCs that require disjunctive invariants can often be transformed by polyvariant specialisation [6] to CHCs that can be verified with simpler invariants [10].

The same technique is applied to achieve control flow refinement of CHCs; the resulting transformed CHCs often allow termination proofs that use simple ranking functions instead of requiring more complex ranking functions such as lexicographic ranking functions, and can improve the results of automatic complexity analysis [5].

References

1. Bjørner, N., Gurfinkel, A., McMillan, K., Rybalchenko, A.: Horn clause solvers for program verification. In: Beklemishev, L., Blass, A., Dershowitz, N., Finkbeiner, B., Schulte, W. (eds) Fields of Logic and Computation II. LNCS, vol. 9300, pp. 24–51. Springer, Cham (2015) .https://doi.org/10.1007/978-3-319-23534-9_2

2. Champion, A., Kobayashi, N., Sato, R.: HoIce: An ICE-based non-linear horn clause solver. In: Ryu, S. (eds.) Programming Languages and Systems. APLAS 2018. LNCS, vol. 11275, pp. 146–156. Springer, Cham (2018). https://doi.org/10.1007/978-3-030-02768-1_8

3. Angelis, E.De., Fioravanti, F., Pettorossi, A., Proietti, M.: Program verification via iterated specialization. Sci. Comput. Program. **95**, 149–175, (2014)

4. Dietsch, D., Heizmann, M., Hoenicke, J., Nutz, A., Podelski, A.: Ultimate Tree Automizer (CHC-COMP tool description). In: Angelis, E.D., Fedyukovich, G. Tzevelekos, N. Ulbrich, M., (eds.) Proceedings of the Sixth Workshop on Horn Clauses for Verification and Synthesis and Third Workshop on Program Equivalence and Relational Reasoning, HCVS/PERR@ETAPS 2019. vol. 296, pp. 42–47. EPTCS (2019)

5. Doménech, J.J., Gallagher, J.P., Genaim, S.: Control-flow refinement by partial evaluation, and its application to termination and cost analysis. TPLP **19**(5–6), 990–1005 (2019)

6. Gallagher, J.P.: Polyvariant program specialisation with property-based abstraction. In: Lisitsa, A., Nemytykh, A.P. (eds.) VPT-19, EPTCS, vol. 299 (2019)

7. Grebenshchikov, S., Lopes, N.P., Popeea, C., Rybalchenko, A.: Synthesizing software verifiers from proof rules. In: Vitek, J., Lin, H., Tip, F. (eds.) ACM SIGPLAN Conference on Programming Language Design and Implementation. PLDI 2012, pp. 405–416. ACM (2012)

8. Hojjat, H., Rümmer, P.: The ELDARICA Horn solver. In: Bjørner, N., Gurfinkel, A. (eds.) 2018 Formal Methods in Computer Aided Design. FMCAD 2018, Austin, TX, USA, October 30 - November 2, 2018, pp. 1–7. IEEE (2018)

9. Kafle, B., Gallagher, J.P.: Horn clause verification with convex polyhedral abstraction and tree automata-based refinement. Comput. Lang. Syst. Struct. **47**, 2–18 (2015)

10. Kafle, B., Gallagher, J.P., Gange, G., Schachte, P., Søndergaard, H., Stuckey, P.J.: An iterative approach to precondition inference using constrained Horn clauses. TPLP, **18**(3–4), 553–570 (2018)

11. Kafle, B., Gallagher, J.P., Morales, J.F.: RAHFT: A tool for verifying horn clauses using abstract interpretation and finite tree automata. In: Chaudhuri, S., Farzan, A. (eds.) Computer Aided Verification. CAV 2016. LNCS, vol. 9779, pp. 261–268. Springer, Cham (2016). https://doi.org/10.1007/978-3-319-41528-4_14

12. Komuravelli, A., Gurfinkel, A., Chaki, S.: SMT-based model checking for recursive programs. In: Biere, A., Bloem, R. (eds.) Computer Aided Verification. CAV 2014. LNCS, vol. 8559. Springer, Cham (2014). https://doi.org/10.1007/978-3-319-08867-9_2

Contents

Static Analysis

On fixpoint/iteration/variant induction principles for proving total correctness of programs with denotational semantics

Patrick Cousot

Courant Institute of Mathematical Sciences, New York University
and IMDEA Software Institute

Abstract. We study partial and total correctness proof methods based on generalized fixpoint/iteration/variant induction principles applied to the denotational semantics of first-order functional and iterative programs.

Keywords: Induction principles · Denotational semantics · Partial and total correctness · Verification

1 Introduction

Imperative and functional programming are very often separate worlds, even in languages like OCaml [18] which combines both styles. Most programmers definitely prefer one style to the other. This reflects in semantics mostly denotational for functional and operational for imperative. This also reflects on verification, mostly Turing/Floyd/Naur/Hoare for invariance and Turing/Floyd/Manna-Pnueli variant/convergence function for termination of imperative languages while Scott proof method is preferred for functional programming.

We show that after appropriate generalization the principles underlying the verification of these programming styles boils down to the same unified verification (hence analysis) methods.

2 Basic notions in denotational semantics

The denotational semantics of first-order functions $f \in \mathcal{D} \to \mathcal{D}_\perp$ uses a complete partial order (cpo) $\langle \mathcal{D}_\perp, \sqsubseteq, \perp, \sqcup \rangle$ where $\perp$ denotes non-termination and $\mathcal{D}_\perp = \mathcal{D} \cup \{\perp\}$ is the flat domain ordered by $\perp \sqsubseteq \perp \sqsubseteq d \sqsubseteq d$ for all $d \in \mathcal{D}$. $\sqcup$ is the least upper bound (lub) in $\mathcal{D}_\perp$. This is extended pointwise to $\langle \mathcal{D} \to \mathcal{D}_\perp, \dot{\sqsubseteq}, \dot{\perp}, \dot{\sqcup} \rangle$ by $f \dot{\sqsubseteq} g$ if and only if $\forall d \in \mathcal{D} . f(d) \sqsubseteq g(d)$, $\dot{\perp} \triangleq \lambda x \cdot \perp$, and $\dot{\bigsqcup}_{i \in \Delta} f_i \triangleq \lambda x \cdot \bigsqcup_{i \in \Delta} f_i(x)$. First-order functions f are defined recursively $f(x) = F(f)x$ as least fixpoints $f = \mathsf{lfp}^{\dot{\sqsubseteq}} F$ of continuous transformers $F \in (\mathcal{D} \to \mathcal{D}_\perp) \xrightarrow{uc} (\mathcal{D} \to \mathcal{D}_\perp)$. The iterates of F from f are $F^0(f) = f$ and $F^{i+1}(f) = F(F^i(f))$. F is continuous if and only iff for every denumerable increasing chain $f_0 \dot{\sqsubseteq} f_1 \dot{\sqsubseteq} ... \dot{\sqsubseteq} f_i \dot{\sqsubseteq} ...$, $\dot{\bigsqcup}_{i \in \mathbb{N}} F(f_i) = F(\dot{\bigsqcup}_{i \in \mathbb{N}} f_i)$. Continuity implies monotonically increasing ($f \dot{\sqsubseteq} g \Rightarrow F(f) \dot{\sqsubseteq} F(g)$). Since $F^0(\dot{\perp}) = \dot{\perp}$ and F is monotonically increasing, it follows that the iterates of F from $\dot{\perp}$ form an increasing chain. Then continuity guarantees that $\mathsf{lfp}^{\dot{\sqsubseteq}} F = \dot{\bigsqcup}_{i \in \mathbb{N}} F^i(\dot{\perp})$ is the limit of the iterates $F^i(\dot{\perp})$ of F from $\dot{\perp}$. By def. of $\dot{\sqsubseteq}$ and $\dot{\sqcup}$, $(\mathsf{lfp}^{\dot{\sqsubseteq}} F)x = y$ if and only if $\exists i \in \mathbb{N} . (\forall j < i . F^j(\dot{\perp})(x) = \perp) \wedge (\forall j \geqslant i . F^j(\dot{\perp})(x) = y)$.

M. Gabbrielli (Ed.): LOPSTR 2019, LNCS 12042, pp. 3–18, 2020.
https://doi.org/10.1007/978-3-030-45260-5_1

Example 1 (while iteration). The iteration $W = \textbf{while (B) S}$ operating on a vector $x \in \mathcal{D}$ of values of variables has denotational semantics $[\![W]\!] = \text{lfp}^{\sqsubseteq} F_W$ where $F_W(f)x = (\!|\, \neg B(x) \,?\, x \,\mathbf{?}\, f(S(x))\,|\!)$, $B \in \mathcal{D} \to \{\text{tt}, \text{ff}\}$ is the semantics of boolean expression B, $S \in \mathcal{D} \to \mathcal{D}_{\perp}$ that of statement S (which, by structural induction, may contain conditionals and inner loop), and $(\!|\, \text{tt} \,?\, a \,\mathbf{?}\, b\,|\!) = a$ and $(\!|\, \text{ff} \,?\, a \,\mathbf{?}\, b\,|\!) = b$ is the conditional. The iterates of F_W from $\perp$ are

$$F_W^0(\perp)x = \perp$$

$$F_W^1(\perp)x = F_W(F_W^0(\perp))x = (\!|\, \neg B(x) \,?\, x \,\mathbf{?}\, \perp\,|\!)$$

$$F_W^2(\perp)x = F_W(F_W^1(\perp))x = (\!|\, \neg B(x) \,?\, x \,\mathbf{?}\, F_W^1(\perp)(S(x))\,|\!) = (\!|\, \neg B(x) \,?\, x \,\mathbf{?}\, (\!|\, \neg B(S(x)) \,?\, S(x) \,\mathbf{?}\, \perp\,|\!)\,|\!)$$

$$= (\!|\, \neg B(x) \,?\, x \,\mathbf{?}\, \perp\,|\!) \sqcup (\!|\, B(x) \wedge \neg B(S(x)) \,?\, S(x) \,\mathbf{?}\, \perp\,|\!)$$

...

$$F_W^n(\perp)x = \bigsqcup_{i=0}^{n-1} (\!|\, (\bigwedge_{j=0}^{i-1} B(S^j(x)) \wedge \neg B(S^i(x)) \,?\, S^i(x) \,\mathbf{?}\, \perp\,|\!) \quad \langle\text{where } S^0(x) \triangleq x, \ S^{i+1}(x) \triangleq S(S^i(x)), \text{ and } \bigwedge \varnothing = \text{tt} \rangle$$

...

$$(\text{lfp}^{\sqsubseteq} F_W)x = \bigsqcup_{n \in \mathbb{N}} F_W^n(\perp)x = \bigsqcup_{n \in \mathbb{N}} \bigsqcup_{i=0}^{n-1} (\!|\, (\bigwedge_{j=0}^{i-1} B(S^j(x)) \wedge \neg B(S^i(x)) \,?\, S^i(x) \,\mathbf{?}\, \perp\,|\!) \qquad \langle\text{where } \bigsqcup \varnothing = \perp \rangle$$

$$= \bigsqcup_{n \in \mathbb{N}} (\!|\, (\bigwedge_{j=0}^{n-1} B(S^j(x)) \wedge \neg B(S^n(x)) \,?\, S^n(x) \,\mathbf{?}\, \perp\,|\!)$$

Note that in the lub, at most one condition is true, none if the iteration does not terminate. Moreover, if $(\text{lfp}^{\sqsubseteq} F_W)x \neq \perp$, then, by def. $\sqcup$, $\exists j \in \mathbb{N} \,.\, (\text{lfp}^{\sqsubseteq} F_W)x = F_W^j(\perp)x$ and so $\neg B(FW^j(\perp)x)$ holds proving $\neg B(\text{lfp}^{\sqsubseteq} F_W)$. □

3   Termination specification

The termination of function $f \in \mathcal{D} \to \mathcal{D}_{\perp}$ on a termination domain $T \in \wp(\mathcal{D})$ can be specified as $f \in \mathcal{P}_T$ where $\mathcal{P}_T \triangleq \{f \mid \forall x \in T \,.\, f(x) \neq \perp\}$. So $\mathcal{P}_T$ is the property of functions that terminate on domain T.

Example 2 (termination). For imperative program, the termination problem is usually solved by the Turing [29]/Floyd [12]/Manna-Pnueli [20] variant/convergence function method. For first-order functions, one can consider Jones size-change termination method [13,17]. □

4   Fixpoint induction principle

In case $\langle \mathcal{D}_{\perp}, \sqsubseteq, \perp, \sqcup, \sqcap \rangle$ is a complete lattice (*e.g.* by adding a supremum $\top$ as in Scott's original papers [27]), we can make proofs by fixpoint induction. [7, 3.4.1] and [23, (2.3)] observed that fixpoint induction directly follows from Tarski's fixpoint theorem [28].

Theorem 1 (Tarski fixpoint theorem [28]) *A monotonically increasing function* $F \in L \xrightarrow{\ \nearrow\ } L$ *on a complete lattice* $\langle L, \sqsubseteq, \perp, \top, \sqcap, \sqcup \rangle$ *has a least fixpoint* $\text{lfp}^{\sqsubseteq} F = \sqcap\{x \in L \mid F(x) \sqsubseteq x\}$.

Fixpoint induction relies on properties of F above its least fixpoint *i.e.* the $x \in L$ such that $F(x) \sqsubseteq x$ and therefore $\text{lfp}^{\sqsubseteq} F \sqsubseteq x$.

> **Theorem 2 (Fixpoint induction)** *Let $F \in L \xrightarrow{\scriptscriptstyle\nearrow} L$ be a monotonically increasing function on a complete lattice $\langle L, \sqsubseteq, \bot, \top, \sqcap, \sqcup \rangle$ and $P \in L$. We have*
>
> $$\mathsf{lfp}^{\sqsubseteq} F \sqsubseteq P \Leftrightarrow \exists I \in L \, . \, \begin{array}{l} F(I) \sqsubseteq I \\[2pt] \wedge \quad I \sqsubseteq P \end{array} \qquad\qquad \begin{array}{r}(2.a)\\[6pt](2.b)\end{array} \qquad \square$$

$J \in L$ is called an *invariant* of F when $\mathsf{lfp}^{\sqsubseteq} F \sqsubseteq J$ and an *inductive invariant* when satisfying $F(J) \sqsubseteq J$.

Soundness ($\Leftarrow$) states that if a statement is proved by the proof method then that statement is true. Completeness ($\Rightarrow$) states that the proof method is always applicable to prove a true statement.

Proof (of Th. 2). By Tarski fixpoint Th. 1, $\mathsf{lfp}^{\sqsubseteq} F = \sqcap \{x \in L \mid F(x) \sqsubseteq x\}$.

Soundness ($\Leftarrow$): If $I \in L$ satisfies $F(I) \sqsubseteq I$ then $I \in \{x \in L \mid F(x) \sqsubseteq x\}$ so by definition of the glb $\sqcap$, $\mathsf{lfp}^{\sqsubseteq} F = \sqcap \{x \in L \mid F(x) \sqsubseteq x\} \sqsubseteq I \sqsubseteq P$ by (2.b).

Completeness ($\Rightarrow$): If $\mathsf{lfp}^{\sqsubseteq} F \sqsubseteq P$ then take $I = \mathsf{lfp}^{\sqsubseteq} F$ then $I = F(I)$ so $F(I) \sqsubseteq I$ by reflexivity and $I \sqsubseteq P$ by hypothesis, proving $\exists I \in L . F(I) \sqsubseteq I \wedge I \sqsubseteq P$. $\qquad\square$

Usually, proofs are done using logics of limited expressive power so completeness is relative to the existence of a logic formula expressing the stronger invariant $I = \mathsf{lfp}^{\sqsubseteq} f$ [5,6]. In Th. 2, we consider invariants to be sets in order to make expressivity a separate problem.

The fixpoint induction principle Th. 2 has been used to justify invariance proof methods for small-step operational semantics/transition systems, including their contrapositive, backward, *etc.* variants [9]. It can also be used with a denotational semantics.

Example 3 (Partial correctness of the factorial). Define $F_!(f) \triangleq \lambda n \cdot (n = 0 \; ? \; 1 \; ⦂ \; n \times f(n-1))$. Let us prove that $\mathsf{lfp}^{\sqsubseteq} F_! \sqsubseteq \dot{} \, f_! \triangleq \lambda n \cdot (x \geqslant 0 \; ? \; n! \; ⦂ \; \bot)$ where $n!$ is the mathematical factorial function. Applying Th. 2 with $I = P = f_!$ so that (2.b) holds, we have

$$F_!(f_!)n$$

$$= (n = 0 \; ? \; 1 \; ⦂ \; n \times f_!(n-1)) \qquad\qquad\qquad (\text{def. } F_!($$

$$= (n = 0 \; ? \; f_!(n) \; ⦂ \; f_!(n)) \qquad\qquad\qquad (\text{def. } f_!($$

$$\sqsubseteq f_!(n) \qquad\qquad\qquad (\text{def. conditional and } \sqsubseteq \text{ reflexive}($$

so $F_!(f_!) \sqsubseteq \dot{} \, f_!$ by pointwise def. of $\sqsubseteq \dot{}$, proving (2.a). By definition of $\sqsubseteq \dot{}$, we have $\forall n \in \mathbb{Z} \, . \, (\mathsf{lfp}^{\sqsubseteq} F_!)n \neq \bot \Rightarrow \mathsf{lfp}^{\sqsubseteq} F_!(n) = f_!(n)$ *i.e.* if a call $(\mathsf{lfp}^{\sqsubseteq} F_!)n$ terminates then it returns $n!$. Obviously this is a partial correctness proof since *e.g.* the proof does not exclude that $\mathsf{lfp}^{\sqsubseteq} F_! = \lambda n \cdot \bot \sqsubseteq \dot{} \, f_!$. $\qquad\square$

Notice that if $P = \mathsf{lfp}^{\sqsubseteq} f$, fixpoint induction requires to prove that $f(\mathsf{lfp}^{\sqsubseteq} f) \sqsubseteq \mathsf{lfp}^{\sqsubseteq} f$ and $\mathsf{lfp}^{\sqsubseteq} f \sqsubseteq P$. So to prove $\mathsf{lfp}^{\sqsubseteq} f \sqsubseteq P$, we have to prove $\mathsf{lfp}^{\sqsubseteq} f \sqsubseteq P$! In that case fixpoint induction cannot help. In general, we have to prove $\mathsf{lfp}^{\sqsubseteq} F \subsetneqq P$ but nevertheless the only inductive invariant might be $\mathsf{lfp}^{\sqsubseteq} F$, as shown below where P is not inductive.

In such cases fixpoint induction is not useful but it is possible to reason on the iterates of F, as shown in Sect. 8.

5 Impossibility to prove termination by fixpoint induction with a denotational semantics

One can use a function $P \in \mathcal{D} \to \mathcal{D}_\bot$ to specify a termination domain $\mathrm{dom}(P) \triangleq \{x \in \mathcal{D} \mid P(x) \neq \bot\}$. However, by definition of $\sqsubseteq$, $\mathrm{lfp}^{\sqsubseteq} F \sqsubseteq P$ means that $\mathrm{lfp}^{\sqsubseteq} F$ terminates less often that P that is $\mathrm{dom}(\mathrm{lfp}^{\sqsubseteq} F) \subseteq \mathrm{dom}(P)$. This is not a specification of definite termination but of definite non-termination. So fixpoint induction can be used to prove non-termination but not termination. Of course $P \sqsubseteq \mathrm{lfp}^{\sqsubseteq} F$ would do but this is not what fixpoint induction is intended to prove. Considering the order-dual of Th. 2 will not work either (although it would work for greatest fixpoints) since, in general, $\mathrm{gfp}^{\sqsubseteq} F \neq \mathrm{lfp}^{\sqsubseteq} F$.

Example 4 (Termination/total correctness of the factorial). Continuing Ex. 3, termination of the factorial $\mathrm{lfp}^{\sqsubseteq} F_!$ where $F_!(f) \triangleq \lambda\, n \cdot (n = 0\ ?\ 1\ \text{\textsection}\ n \times f(n-1))$ is $f_! \sqsubseteq \mathrm{lfp}^{\sqsubseteq} F_!$ where $f_! \triangleq \lambda\, n \cdot (x \geqslant 0\ ?\ n!\ \text{\textsection}\ \bot)$ but this is not provable by fixpoint induction Th. 2. □

6 Iteration induction principle

As observed by [19,21,26], iteration induction directly follows from Kleene/Scott's fixpoint theorem below (which we used in Sect. 2 with $\mathcal{L} = \mathcal{D} \to \mathcal{D}_\bot$). (Th. 3 is often attributed to Stephen Cole Kleene, after its first recursion theorem [16, p. 348] and appears in [2].)

Theorem 3 (Kleene/Scott iterative fixpoint theorem [26]) *If $F \in \mathcal{L} \xrightarrow{uc} \mathcal{L}$ is an upper continuous function on a cpo $\langle \mathcal{L}, \sqsubseteq, \bot, \sqcup \rangle$ then F has a least fixpoint $\mathrm{lfp}^{\sqsubseteq} F = \bigsqcup_{n \in \mathbb{N}} F^n(\bot)$.*

Since $F^0(\bot) = \bot$ is the infimum and F is upper continuous hence monotonically increasing, the iterates $\langle F^n(\bot),\, n \in \mathbb{N} \rangle$ form a non-empty, infinite, denumerable, and maximally increasing chain which is either first strictly increasing and then stationary (when the iterates converge in finitely many steps) or else is strictly increasing.

Remark 1. Th. 3 generalizes to chain-α-complete posets (where every α-chain that is increasing chain of cardinality less than or equal to α has a lub) and α-continuous functions (preserving the lubs of α-chains), and to monotonically increasing functions on complete lattices, using transfinite iterations $F^0(\bot) = \bot$, $F^{\delta+1} = F(F^\delta)$ for successor ordinals and $F^\lambda = \bigsqcup_{\delta < \lambda} F^\delta$ for limit ordinals less than or equal to α [22], respectively all ordinals [8]. Th. 3 is then a corollary for the first infinite ordinal $\alpha = \omega$. □

Iteration induction relies on properties of F below its least fixpoint. It is usually referred to as Scott induction or De Bakker and Scott or computational induction and formalized as

$$\text{``If } \mathcal{P} \in \wp(\mathcal{D}) \text{ is an admissible predicate, } \bot \in \mathcal{P}, \text{ and } \forall d \in \mathcal{P} \,.\, F(d) \in \mathcal{P} \text{ then } \mathrm{lfp}^{\sqsubseteq} F \in \mathcal{P}\text{''}. \tag{4}$$

The predicate $\mathcal{P}$ is said to be admissible [19] or inclusive [25, p. 118] if and only if it holds for an increasing enumerable chain, it also holds for its limit, that is for all increasing enumerable chains $F_0 \sqsubseteq F_1 \sqsubseteq \ldots \sqsubseteq F_i \sqsubseteq \ldots$, if $\forall i \in \mathbb{N} \,.\, F_i \in \mathcal{P}$ then $\bigsqcup_{i \in \mathbb{N}} F_i \in \mathcal{P}$.

7 Impossibility to prove termination by iteration induction

The termination specification of functions $f \in \mathcal{D} \to \mathcal{D}_\perp$ is the set $\mathcal{P} \triangleq \{f \in \mathcal{D} \to \mathcal{D}_\perp \mid \forall x \in \mathcal{D} \ .$ $f(x) \in \mathcal{D}\} = \mathcal{D} \to \mathcal{D}$ of all functions that always terminate on the domain $\mathcal{D}$ of their argument. To prove $\mathsf{lfp}^{\sqsubseteq} F \in \mathcal{P}$ by structural induction (4) requires $\perp \in \mathcal{P}$, which is not true since, unless $\mathcal{D} = \varnothing$, $\forall x \in \mathcal{D} \ . \perp(x) = \perp \in \mathcal{D}$ is false. So Scott's iteration induction principle is incomplete since it cannot be used to prove termination.

8 Generalized iteration induction principle

This incompleteness calls for a generalization of iteration induction where the characterization Q of the iterations differs from that of their limit $\mathcal{P}$.

Example 5. For the factorial of Ex. 3, the iterates $F_!^n(\perp)$, $n \in \mathbb{N}$ are partial functions (characterized by Q) while the limit $f_!$ is a total function on $\mathcal{D} = \mathbb{N}$ (characterized by $\mathcal{P}$). □

Let $F \in S \to S$ and $\langle x_i, i \in \Delta \rangle$ be a family of elements of S. The family is *non-empty* if and only if $\Delta \neq \varnothing$. It is *infinite* when the cardinality of Δ is greater than or equal to that of $\mathbb{N}$. It is *denumerable* if and only if $\Delta \subseteq \mathbb{N}$ (up to an isomorphism). It is a $\sqsubseteq$-*increasing chain* if and only if $\forall i, j \in \Delta \ . (i \leqslant j) \Rightarrow (x_i \sqsubseteq x_j)$. It is a *strictly increasing chain* if and only if $\forall i, j \in \Delta \ . (i < j) \Rightarrow (x_i \subsetneq x_j)$. It is *in* $S' \subseteq S$ if and only if $\forall i \in \Delta \ . x_i \in S'$. The sequence $\langle x_i, i \in \mathbb{N} \rangle$ is F-*maximally increasing* when it is infinite (hence non-empty), denumerable, iterating F (*i.e.* $\forall i \in \mathbb{N} \ . x_{i+1} = F(x_i)$), and either strictly increasing (*i.e.* $\forall i, j \in \mathbb{N} \ . (i < j) \Rightarrow (x_i \subsetneq x_j)$) or is first strictly increasing and then stationary (*i.e.* $\exists k \in \mathbb{N} \ . \forall i, j \in \mathbb{N} \ . (i < j \leqslant k) \Rightarrow (x_i \subsetneq x_j) \wedge (k \leqslant i) \Rightarrow (x_k = x_i)$).

Theorem 5 (Iteration induction) *Let* $F \in L \xrightarrow{uc} L$ *be a continuous function on a cpo* $\langle L,$ $\sqsubseteq, \perp, \sqcup \rangle$ *and* $\mathcal{P} \in \wp(L)$.

$\mathsf{lfp}^{\sqsubseteq} F \in \mathcal{P} \Leftrightarrow \exists Q \in \wp(L) \ . \quad \perp \in Q$ (5.a)

$\wedge \quad \forall x \in Q \ . F(x) \in Q$ (5.b)

$\wedge \quad$ *for any* F-*maximally* $\sqsubseteq$-*increasing chain* $\langle x_i, i \in \mathbb{N} \rangle$ *in* Q,   (5.c)

$$\bigsqcup_{i \in \mathbb{N}} x_i \in \mathcal{P} \qquad \qquad \qquad □$$

The proof below shows that the hypotheses (a), (b), and (c) are necessary only for the iterates of F. The soundness proof shows that Q is a valid property of the iterates of F from $\perp$ while $\mathcal{P}$ is a property of their least upper bound, that is of the fixpoint. Offering the possibility of choosing $Q \neq \mathcal{P}$ is essential to solve the incompleteness problem of Scott induction (4) mentioned in the above Sect. 7. But of course Th. 5 can be used with $Q = \mathcal{P}$ so that it is a generalization of Scott induction (4) and a proof that (4) is sound.

Condition (5.c) corresponds to the "admissible predicates" in Scott induction. However, (5.c) is requested for maximally $\sqsubseteq$-increasing chains only since requiring it for all increasing chains would amount to Scott induction (4). The quantification over chains iterating F in (5.c) can be relaxed since this condition could also be imposed by an appropriate choice of Q.

Proof (of Th. 5). Soundness ($\Leftarrow$): Let $F^{i+1}(\perp) = F(F^i(\perp))$ be the iterates of F from $F^0(\perp) = \perp$. $F^0(\perp) \in Q$ by (5.a). By recurrence, $\forall i \in \mathbb{N} \ . F^i(\perp) \in Q$ by (5.b). F is continuous hence monotonically increasing so $\langle F^i(\bot) \in Q, i \in \mathbb{N}\rangle$ is a $\sqsubseteq$-increasing enumerable chain iterating F. If it is finite then $F^0(\bot) \sqsubseteq F^1(\bot) \sqsubseteq \dots \sqsubseteq F^{n-1}(\bot) = F^n(\bot) = \dots = \dots$ for some $n \in \mathbb{N}$ proving that the chain is F-maximally increasing in Q. So, by (5.c), $\mathsf{lfp}^{\sqsubseteq} F = F^{n-1}(\bot) = \bigsqcup_{i \in \mathbb{N}} F^i(\bot) \in \mathcal{P}$. Otherwise, the chain is infinite and strictly increasing so F-maximally increasing in Q. By Th. 3 and (5.c), we conclude that $\mathsf{lfp}^{\sqsubseteq} F = \bigsqcup_{i \in \mathbb{N}} F^i(\bot) \in \mathcal{P}$.

Completeness $(\Rightarrow)$: Let $F^{i+1}(\bot) = F(F^i(\bot))$ be the iterates of F from $F^0(\bot) = \bot$. Choosing $Q = \{F^i(\bot) \mid i \in \mathbb{N}\}$, we have (5.a) and (5.b). By Th. 3, $\langle F^i(\bot) \in Q, i \in \mathbb{N}\rangle$ is a $\sqsubseteq$-increasing chain in Q. It is enumerable and the only F-maximally increasing one so $\{x_i \in Q \mid i \in \mathbb{N}\} = \{F^i(\bot) \in Q \mid i \in \mathbb{N}\}$. By Th. 3, $\mathsf{lfp}^{\sqsubseteq} F = \bigsqcup_{i \in \mathbb{N}} F^i(\bot)$. By hypothesis, $\mathsf{lfp}^{\sqsubseteq} F \in \mathcal{P}$, and so $\bigsqcup_{i \in \mathbb{N}} F^i(\bot) = \bigsqcup_{i \in \mathbb{N}} x_i \in \mathcal{P}$, proving (5.c).   □

Remark 2. The same way that the inductive invariant in fixpoint induction need not necessarily be the strongest possible one, Q need not necessarily be the strongest possible one $Q = \{F^i(\bot) \mid i \in \mathbb{N}\}$ in Th. 5, as used in the completeness proof. An example is $\mathcal{L} = \{\bot, a, b, c\}$ with $\bot \sqsubsetneq a \sqsubsetneq b \sqsubsetneq c$, $F(\bot) = F(a) = a$, $F(c) = F(b) = b$, and $\mathcal{P} = \{a, b\}$. Take $Q = \{a, b, c\}$ so that the only F-maximally $\sqsubseteq$-increasing chains in Q are $\bot a^\omega$, a^ω, and b^ω which lubs a and b belong to $\mathcal{P}$, proving $\mathsf{lfp}^{\sqsubseteq} F \in \mathcal{P}$.   □

Remark 3. Following Rem. 1, Th. 5 generalizes to α-continuous functions on chain-α-complete posets and monotonically increasing functions on complete lattices, with Th. 5 holding for $\alpha = \omega$.   □

Example 6 (Hoare logic). Let $[\![\mathsf{W}]\!] = \mathsf{lfp}^{\sqsubseteq} F_{\mathsf{W}}$ be the denotational semantics of the iteration $\mathsf{W} = $ **while (B) S** where $F_{\mathsf{W}}(f)x = (\![\neg B(x) \mathbin{?} x \mathbin{\text{\textcent}} f(S(x))]\!)$ as defined in Ex. 1. Given $P, Q \in \wp(\mathcal{D})$, Hoare notation for partial correctness [14] is $\{\![P]\!\} \mathsf{W} \{\![Q]\!\}$ denoting $\forall x \in P . ([\![\mathsf{W}]\!]x \neq \bot) \Rightarrow ([\![\mathsf{W}]\!]x \in Q)$. Hoare partial correctness rule for the **while** iteration is

$$\frac{\{\![I \cap B]\!\} \mathsf{S} \{\![I]\!\}}{\{\![I]\!\} \mathsf{W} \{\![I \cap \neg B]\!\}} \tag{6}$$

[25, Sect. 6.6.6, p. 115] proves the soundness of the Hoare partial correctness rule for the **while** iteration based on its denotational semantics. The ad-hoc proof proceeds by induction on the semantics of the loop iterates and, assuming termination, passes to the limit. Formally, this consists in proving soundness by applying Th. 5, as follows.

- Take $Q \triangleq \{f \in \mathcal{D} \to \mathcal{D}_\bot \mid \forall x \in I . f(x) \neq \bot \Rightarrow f(x) \in I\}$.
- $\bot \in Q$ by def. Q, proving (5.a).
- Assume that $f \in Q$. To prove (5.b), we must show that the premiss of Hoare rule (6) implies that $F_{\mathsf{W}}(f) \in Q$.

   If $x \in I$ and $\neg B(x)$ then obviously $x \in I$. Otherwise if $x \in I \cap B(x)$ and $F_{\mathsf{W}}(f)x \neq \bot$ then $\{\![I \cap B]\!\} \mathsf{S} \{\![I]\!\}$ implies $S(x) \in I$ so if $S(x) \neq \bot$ then $f(S(x)) \in I$ since $f \in Q$ proving that $F_{\mathsf{W}}(f)x = f(S(x)) \in I$ that is $F_{\mathsf{W}}(f) \in Q$.
- Let $\langle f_i \in Q, i \in \mathbb{N}\rangle$ be any F_{W}-maximally $\sqsubseteq$-increasing enumerable chain. Assume that $x \in I$ and $(\bigsqcup_{i \in \mathbb{N}} f_i)x \triangleq \bigsqcup_{i \in \mathbb{N}} f_i(x) \neq \bot$. By def. lub $\sqsubseteq$, $\exists j \in \mathbb{N} . \bigsqcup_{i \in \mathbb{N}} f_i(x) = f_j(x) \neq \bot$. Since $f_j \in Q$, $f_j(x) \in I$, proving $\bigsqcup_{i \in \mathbb{N}} f_i(x) \in I$ that is $\bigsqcup_{i \in \mathbb{N}} f_i \in Q$ which is (5.c).
- By Th. 5, we conclude that $[\![\mathsf{W}]\!] = \mathsf{lfp}^{\sqsubseteq} F_{\mathsf{W}} \in Q$ so $\forall x \in I . [\![\mathsf{W}]\!](x) \neq \bot \Rightarrow [\![\mathsf{W}]\!](x) \in I$. Moreover, if $(\mathsf{lfp}^{\sqsubseteq} F_{\mathsf{W}})x \neq \bot$ then $\neg B(\mathsf{lfp}^{\sqsubseteq} F_{\mathsf{W}})$, as shown in Ex. 1, proving $\{\![I]\!\} \mathsf{W} \{\![I \wedge \neg B]\!\}$.

   Obviously, this rule is incomplete since I may not be inductive (so, for completeness, [5,6] has to ensure that I is inductive and use the consequence rule).   □

9 Proving total correctness by generalized iteration induction

By completeness, the termination of $\mathsf{lfp}^{\sqsubseteq} F$ on a termination domain $T \in \wp(\mathcal{D})$ can always be proved by generalized iteration induction Th. 5, if $\mathsf{lfp}^{\sqsubseteq} F \in \mathcal{P}_T$ does hold.

Example 7 (Total correctness II). Continuing Ex. 3, let us define $\mathcal{P}_{\mathbb{N}} \triangleq \{f \in \mathbb{N} \to \mathbb{N}_{\perp} \mid \forall n \in \mathbb{N} . f(n) \neq \perp\}$ and apply Th. 5 to prove that prove that $\mathsf{lfp}^{\sqsubseteq} F_! \in \mathcal{P}_{\mathbb{N}}$ (which, together with Ex. 3, shows that $\mathsf{lfp}^{\sqsubseteq} F_! = f_!$).

Let us define $\forall i \in \mathbb{N} . Q_i \triangleq \{f \in \mathbb{N} \to \mathbb{N}_{\perp} \mid \forall n \in [0, i[. f(n) \neq \perp \wedge \forall n \geq i . f(n) = \perp\}$ and $Q \triangleq \bigcup_{i \in \mathbb{N}} Q_i$.

- We have $\perp \in \{\perp\} = Q_0 \subseteq Q$, proving (5.a).

- Assume that $i \in \mathbb{N}$ and $f \in Q_i$. We have

$$F_!(f)$$
$$= \lambda n \cdot \left(n = 0 \;?\; 1 \;\S\; n \times f(n-1) \right) \qquad\qquad \text{\{def. } F_! \text{ in Ex. 3\}}$$
$$\Rightarrow F_!(f)0 \neq \perp \wedge \forall n - 1 \in [0, i[. F_!(f)(n) \neq \perp \qquad\qquad \text{\{} f \in Q_i \text{\}}$$
$$\Rightarrow F_!(f) \in Q_{i+1} \qquad\qquad \text{\{def. } Q_{i+1} \text{\}}$$

- It follows, by def. of Q, that if $f \in Q$ then $f \in Q_i$ for some $i \in \mathbb{N}$ and therefore $F_!(f) \in Q_{i+1} \subseteq Q$, so that (5.b) holds.

- Let $\langle f_n, n \in \mathbb{N} \rangle$ be $F_!$-maximally increasing chain of elements of Q. So, by def. Q, we have $f_0 \in Q_{j_0}, f_1 \in Q_{j_1}, ..., f_n \in Q_{j_n}, f_{n+1} \in Q_{j_{n+1}}, ...$

  Assume that the chain is stationary at some rank i such that $f_0 \subsetneq f_{i-1} \subsetneq ... \subsetneq f_i = f_{i+1} = ...$ Then $f_i \in Q_j$ for some $j \in \mathbb{N}$. So $f_{i+1} = f_i \in Q_j$ and $f_{i+1} = F_!(f_i) \in Q_{j+1}$, a contradiction since $Q_j \cap Q_{j+1} = \varnothing$.[1]

  It follows that the chain $f_0 \subsetneq f_1 \subsetneq ... \subsetneq f_n \subsetneq ...$ is strictly increasing and we have $j_0 < j_1 < ... < j_n < j_{n+1} < ...$ so $j_{n+1} > n + 1$. Since $f_{n+1} \in Q_{j_{n+1}}, f_{n+1}(n) \neq \perp$.

  To prove that $\bigsqcup_{i \in \mathbb{N}} f_i \in \mathcal{P}_{\mathbb{N}}$, assume by contradiction, that $\exists n \in \mathbb{N} . (\bigsqcup_{i \in \mathbb{N}} f_i)n = \perp$ so, by def. $\dot\sqcup$, $\exists n \in \mathbb{N} . \forall i \in \mathbb{N} . f_i(n) = \perp$. In particular $f_{n+1}(n) = \perp$, a contradiction.

  We have proved (5.c) hence $\mathsf{lfp}^{\sqsubseteq} F_! \in \mathcal{P}_{\mathbb{N}}$, that is $\forall n \in \mathbb{N} . (\mathsf{lfp}^{\sqsubseteq} F_!)n \neq \perp$. $\qquad\square$

A much simpler way of proving termination of $\mathsf{lfp}^{\sqsubseteq} F_!$ for positive parameters is to observe that parameters strictly decreases on recursive call and remains positive which can be done only a finite number of times since $\langle \mathbb{N}, < \rangle$ is well-founded. Such termination proofs using a variant/convergence function are formalized in Th. 10. Th. 11 shows that this proof is equivalent to the above proof based on Th. 5.

10 Parameter dependency

The fact that the evaluation of $f(x) = F(f)x$ for parameter $x \in \mathcal{D}$ where $f = \mathsf{lfp}^{\sqsubseteq} F$ makes a recursive call to $f(y)$ with parameter $y \in \mathcal{D}$, written $x \overset{F}{\longmapsto} y$, is usually defined syntactically.

---

[1] Notice that with our choice of Q, this is not necessarily true for chains that are not $F_{\mathbb{N}}$-iterations.

Example 8. Define $f(n) = F(f)n \triangleq (\!| n \in [0,1] \,?\, 0 \,\S\, f(n-1) + f(n-2) |\!)$. A call of f for $n \notin [0,1]$ will recursively call $f(n-1)$ and $f(n-2)$ in the expression $f(n-1) + f(n-2)$. So $\xmapsto{F} = \{\langle n, n-1\rangle, \langle n, n-2\rangle \mid n \in \mathbb{Z} \setminus [0,1]\}$:

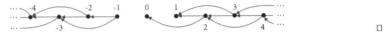

□

Since we don't want to provide a specific syntax for defining F, we have to define the call relation $\xmapsto{F}$ semantically. We let $f[y \leftarrow d] \in \mathcal{D} \rightarrow \mathcal{D}_\perp$ be the function f except for paramater y for which it has value $d \in \mathcal{D}_\perp$.

$$f[y \leftarrow d](y) \triangleq d$$
$$f[y \leftarrow d](z) \triangleq f(z) \quad \text{when} \quad z \neq y$$

The call relation is semantically defined as follows.

$$x \xmapsto{F} y \triangleq \text{let } f = \text{lfp}^{\sqsubseteq} F \text{ and } f'(z) = (\!| f(z) = \perp \,?\, 0 \,\S\, f(z) |\!) \text{ in} \tag{7}$$
$$F(f'[y \leftarrow \perp])x = \perp \wedge F(f')x \neq \perp$$

For simplicity, we assume F to be always well-defined so choosing $f'(z) = 0$ can never lead to a runtime error. The idea is that forcing f to terminate for all its parameters but for y for which f does not terminate, the main call to x will not terminate so this can only come from a recursive call to $f(y)$ (or the body of F does not terminate independently of its recursive calls to f, which we exclude by $F(f')x \neq \perp$).

Example 9. Continuing Ex. 8, let $f(n) = F(f)n \triangleq (\!| n \in [0,1] \,?\, 0 \,\S\, f(n-1) + f(n-2) |\!)$. The semantics is $f = \text{lfp}^{\sqsubseteq} F = \lambda n \cdot (\!| n \geqslant 0 \,?\, 0 \,\S\, \perp |\!)$ and $f' = \lambda n \cdot 0$. We have

$$F(f'[n-1 \leftarrow \perp])n$$
$= (\!| n \in [0,1] \,?\, 0 \,\S\, f'[n-1 \leftarrow \perp](n-1) + f'[n-1 \leftarrow \perp](n-2) |\!)$ ⟨def. F⟩
$= (\!| n \in [0,1] \,?\, 0 \,\S\, \perp + 0 |\!)$ ⟨def. $f'[n-1 \leftarrow \perp]$⟩
$= (\!| n \in [0,1] \,?\, 0 \,\S\, \perp |\!)$ ⟨def. + assumed to be strict⟩

Similarly $F(f'[n-2 \leftarrow \perp])n = (\!| n \in [0,1] \,?\, 0 \,\S\, \perp |\!)$. In conclusion, $\xmapsto{F} = \{\langle n, n-1\rangle, \langle n, n-2\rangle \mid n \in \mathbb{Z} \setminus [0,1]\}$.

□

11   Recursive non-termination

Since we are interested in the termination of recursive functions $f(x) = F(f)x$, we exclude non-termination of the function due to causes other than recursive calls in F:

Definition 1 (function body termination hypothesis).

$$\forall f \in \mathcal{D} \rightarrow \mathcal{D}_\perp . \forall x \in \mathcal{D} . (F(f)x = \perp) \Rightarrow (\exists y \in \mathcal{D} . x \xmapsto{F} y \wedge f(y) = \perp) \tag{8}$$

Example 10 (function body non-termination). Define $F(f)x = \textbf{if } (x = 0)\ 1\ \textbf{else while } (\text{tt})\ ; f(0)$, we have $F(f)1 = \bot$ since the iteration is entered and never exited so the function body termination hypothesis (8) is not satisfied. This is because the non-termination is not due to the recursive calls but only to the loop body.

For $F(f)x = f(f(x))$, if $\forall x \in \mathcal{D} . f(x) \neq \bot$ is assumed to always terminate then $F(f)x = f(f(x)) \neq \bot$ does terminate, so satisfies the function body termination hypothesis (8). □

A recursive function definition satisfying the function body termination hypothesis (8) does not terminate for a given parameter if and only if it makes a recursive call that does not terminate.

> **Lemma 9** *Let* $f = \textsf{lfp}^{\sqsubseteq} F$ *where* F *is continuous and satisfies the function body termination hypothesis* (8). *Then* $f(x) = \bot$ *if and only if* $\exists y \in \mathcal{D} . x \xmapsto{F} y \wedge f(y) = \bot$. □

Proof. – Let F satisfying the function body termination hypothesis (8) and $f = \textsf{lfp}^{\sqsubseteq} F$. We have $f(x) = \bot$ if and only if $F(f)x = \bot$ which, by (8), implies $\exists y \in \mathcal{D} . x \xmapsto{F} y \wedge f(y) = \bot$.
– Conversely, let $f'(z) = (f(z) = \bot ? 0 \mathbin{\S} f(z))$. Assume that $\exists y \in \mathcal{D} . x \xmapsto{F} y \wedge f(y) = \bot$. By (7), $x \xmapsto{F} y$ implies $F(f'[y \leftarrow \bot])x = \bot$. Since $\bot \sqsubseteq 0$ and $f(y) = \bot$, $f \sqsubseteq f'[y \leftarrow \bot]$ pointwise. Moreover, F is continuous hence monotonically increasing so $f(x) = F(f)x \sqsubseteq F(f'[y \leftarrow \bot]) = \bot$ so $f(x) = \bot$ since $\bot$ is the infimum. □

The function body termination hypothesis (8) is not restrictive. It simply means that, assuming that all recursive calls to f do terminate, the function body $F(f)$ must be proved to terminate. Depending on the considered programming language, this can be done *e.g.* by structural induction, using variant/convergence functions (as in Th. 10), etc. This may involve a preliminary partial correctness proof (*e.g.* using Th. 2) to restrict the values that can be taken by variables.

12   Proving termination by a variant/convergence function

Following Turing [29] and Floyd [12], most termination proofs are done using a variant/convergence function in a well-founded set which strictly decreases at each recursive call (or, equivalently, a well-founded relation). This is the case *e.g.* of the "size change principle" [13]. The variant/convergence function termination proof principle can be formulated as follows.

A relation $\langle D, \leqslant \rangle$ such that $\leqslant \in \wp(D \times D)$ is well-founded or Noetherian if and only if there is no infinite strictly $\geqslant$-decreasing chain of elements of D.

> **Theorem 10 (variant/convergence function proof principle for termination)** *Let* $F \in (\mathcal{D} \to \mathcal{D}_\bot) \xrightarrow{uc} (\mathcal{D} \to \mathcal{D}_\bot)$ *be a continuous function on the cpo* $\langle \mathcal{D} \to \mathcal{D}_\bot, \dot{\sqsubseteq}, \dot{\bot}, \dot{\sqcup} \rangle$ *satisfying the function body termination hypothesis* (8), $T \in \wp(\mathcal{D})$, *and* $\mathcal{P}_T \triangleq \{ f \in \mathcal{D} \to \mathcal{D}_\bot \mid \forall x \in T . f(x) \neq \bot \}$. *Then*
>
> $$\textsf{lfp}^{\sqsubseteq} F \in \mathcal{P}_T \Leftrightarrow \quad \exists D \in \wp(\mathcal{D}) . T \subseteq D \tag{10.a}$$
> $$\wedge \quad \exists \leqslant \in \wp(D \times D) . \langle D, \leqslant \rangle \text{ is well-founded} \tag{10.b}$$
> $$\wedge \quad \forall x \in D . \forall y \in \mathcal{D} . (x \xmapsto{F} y) \Rightarrow (y \in D \wedge x > y) \tag{10.c}$$
> □

Intuitively $\textsf{lfp}^{\sqsubseteq} F$ must terminate since, by contradiction, an infinite call sequence would create an infinite descent along the called parameters. Completeness follows from the fact that $>$ can be chosen as $\xmapsto{F}$, which is always well-founded for terminating programs. This is proved formally in Cor. 12.

Example 11. Continuing Ex. 8, the well-founded relation $\prec$ can be chosen as follows

Termination follows from the fact that $\overset{F}{\longmapsto}$ restricted to the naturals in included in $>$, which is well-founded.   □

The variant/convergence function proof principle remains sound when this semantic dependency relation is over-approximated syntactically (but maybe not complete, as shown by $F(f)x \triangleq (\!\!(\text{tt} \; ?\!\!\!\!\!\!\!\!\!\!\!\! $ $x \, \text{\textsf{?}} \, f(x))\!\!)$ where $x \overset{F}{\longmapsto} x$ syntactically, but not semantically because the recursive call $f(x)$ is not reachable).

13   Equivalence of the termination proof by generalized iteration induction and by variant/convergence function principle

> **Theorem 11** *Let $\mathcal{L} = \mathcal{D} \to \mathcal{D}_\perp$ and $F \in \mathcal{L} \overset{uc}{\longrightarrow} \mathcal{L}$ satisfying the function body termination hypothesis (8). There exists a termination proof by the generalized iteration induction of Th. 5 for F if and only if there exists one by the variant/convergence function principle of Th. 10.* □

The proof is constructive in that it shows how to construct a proof by one method knowing a proof by the other method.

Proof. — Let us first show that the existence of a termination proof of $\mathsf{lfp}^{\sqsubseteq} F$ by Th. 5 implies the existence of a termination proof of $\mathsf{lfp}^{\sqsubseteq} F$ by Th. 10.

– If $\mathsf{lfp}^{\sqsubseteq} F \in \mathcal{P}_T$ has been proved by Th. 5, then, as shown by the completeness proof of this theorem, this can also be done by Th. 5 with $\forall i \in \mathbb{N} . Q^i \triangleq \{F^i\}$ where $F^0 = \lambda x \cdot \perp$ and $F^{i+1} = F(F^i)$ are the iterates of F from $\lambda x \cdot \perp$ and $Q \triangleq \bigcup_{i \in \mathbb{N}} Q^i$ so that (5.a) and (5.b) are satisfied. The only F-maximal $\sqsubseteq$-increasing enumerable chain $\langle x_i \in Q, i \in \mathbb{N} \rangle$ is $\langle F^i, i \in \mathbb{N} \rangle$. By Th. 3, it is such that $\bigsqcup_{i \in \mathbb{N}} F^i = \mathsf{lfp}^{\sqsubseteq} F$, By hypothesis $\mathsf{lfp}^{\sqsubseteq} F \in \mathcal{P}_T$ and so $\bigsqcup_{i \in \mathbb{N}} F^i \in \mathcal{P}_T$, proving (5.c).

– Let us define $D^0 \triangleq \varnothing$, $D^i \triangleq \{x \mid F^{i-1}(x) = \perp \wedge F^i(x) \neq \perp\}$ for all $i > 0$, and $D \triangleq \bigcup_{i \in \mathbb{N}} D^i$. Let us prove that $T \subseteq D$.

By def. $\dot{\sqcup}$ and $\mathsf{lfp}^{\sqsubseteq} F = \bigsqcup_{i \in \mathbb{N}} F^i$, for all $n \in \mathcal{D}$, we have $(\mathsf{lfp}^{\sqsubseteq} F)n \neq \perp \Leftrightarrow \exists i \in \mathbb{N} . F^i(n) \neq \perp \Leftrightarrow$ $\exists i \in \mathbb{N} . n \in D^i \Leftrightarrow n \in D$. Since $\mathsf{lfp}^{\sqsubseteq} F \in \mathcal{P}_T$, for all $n \in T$, we have $(\mathsf{lfp}^{\sqsubseteq} F)n \neq \perp \Leftrightarrow n \in D$, proving $T \subseteq D$, that is (10.a).

– Let us define $x > y$ if and only if $\exists i \in \mathbb{N} . x \in D^{i+1} \wedge y \in D^i$. Let $>$ be the irreflexive transitive closure of $>$. Let us prove that $\langle D, \leqslant \rangle$ is well-founded. By def. of $\leqslant$, for an infinite strictly decreasing chain for $\leqslant$ there exists one $x_0 > x_1 > x_2 \ldots$ for $<$, and so there would exists $x_0 \in D^{i_0}$, $x_1 \in D^{i_1}$, $x_2 \in D^{i_2}$, ... with $i_0 > i_1 > i_2 > \ldots$ which is impossible since this chain on $\mathbb{N}$ cannot be infinite decreasing. This implies (10.b).

– Let x be any $x \in D$ and $y \in \mathcal{D}$ satisfies $x \overset{F}{\longmapsto} y$.

Since $x \in D$, there exists $i \in \mathbb{N}$ such that $x \in D^i$. Let i be the minimal such i. Since $x \overset{F}{\longmapsto} y$, we have $\mathsf{lfp}^{\sqsubseteq} F(x) \neq F(\mathsf{lfp}^{\sqsubseteq} F[y \leftarrow \perp])x$. Therefore $(\mathsf{lfp}^{\sqsubseteq} F)y \neq \perp$ since otherwise $F(\mathsf{lfp}^{\sqsubseteq} F[y \leftarrow \perp]) =$

$F(\mathsf{lfp}^{\sqsubseteq} F) = \mathsf{lfp}^{\sqsubseteq} F$, in contradiction with $F(\mathsf{lfp}^{\sqsubseteq} F[y \leftarrow \bot])x \neq \mathsf{lfp}^{\sqsubseteq} F(x)$. It follows that $\exists j \in \mathbb{N} \ . \ y \in D^j \subseteq D$.

- If $j < i$ then there exist $z_0 = y \in D^j$, $z_1 \in D^{j+1}$, ..., $z_{i-j} = x \in D^i$ such that, by def. of D^k, $\forall k \in [0, i - j] \ . \ F^{k-1}(z_k) = \bot \wedge F^k(z_k) \neq \bot$. By def. $<$, we have $y = z_0 < z_1 < ... < z_{i-j} = x$ proving that $x > y \in D$ i.e. (10.c).

- Else $j \geqslant i$. By def. $\sqsubseteq F_{i-1}(x) = \bot$, $F_i(x) = F_j(x) = (\mathsf{lfp}^{\sqsubseteq} F)x \neq \bot$, $F_{i-1}(y) = F_i(y) = F_{j-1}(y) = \bot$, and $F_j(y) = (\mathsf{lfp}^{\sqsubseteq} F)y \neq \bot$. Since $F_j(x) = F(F_{j-1}(x))$ and $F_{j-1}(y) = \bot$, we have $F_j(x) = F(F_{j-1}[y \leftarrow \bot](x))$ so $(\mathsf{lfp}^{\sqsubseteq} F)(x) = F((\mathsf{lfp}^{\sqsubseteq} F)[y \leftarrow \bot](x))$, a contradiction. This case is impossible and so (10.c) holds vacuously.

— Conversely, let us first show that the existence of a termination proof of $f = \mathsf{lfp}^{\sqsubseteq} F$ by Th. 10 implies the existence of a termination proof of $f = \mathsf{lfp}^{\sqsubseteq} F$ by Th. 5. So assume the existence of $D \in \wp(\mathcal{D})$ satisfying (10.a), (10.b), and (10.c).

— Define $Q_i = \{F^i(\bot)\}$ and $Q \triangleq \bigcup_{i \in \mathbb{N}} Q_i$ so (5.a) and (5.b) do hold. It remains to prove (5.c) that is $\bigsqcup_{i \in \mathbb{N}} F^i(\bot) \in \mathcal{P}_T$. By reductio ad absurdum, assume that $\exists x_0 \in T \ . \ (\bigsqcup_{i \in \mathbb{N}} F^i(\bot))x_0 = \bot$, that is, by (10.a) and Th. 3, $x_0 \in D$ and $(\mathsf{lfp}^{\sqsubseteq} F)x_0 = \bot$. Assume $\exists x_j \in D \ . \ f(x_j) = \bot$ where $f = \mathsf{lfp}^{\sqsubseteq} F$. Then, by the function body termination hypothesis (8), Lem. 9 implies that $\exists x_{j+1} \ . \ x_j \overset{F}{\longmapsto} x_{j+1} \wedge f(x_{j+1}) = \bot$. In this way, we can built an infinite sequence $x_0 \overset{F}{\longmapsto} x_1 \overset{F}{\longmapsto} x_2 \overset{F}{\longmapsto} ...$ such that $\forall j \in \mathbb{N} \ . \ (\mathsf{lfp}^{\sqsubseteq} F)x_j = \bot$. By recurrence and (10.c), this sequence is in D and $>$-decreasing. This is in contradiction with the well-foundness (10.b) of $\langle D, \leqslant \rangle$. $\qquad \square$

Corollary 12 *The variant/convergence function principle* (10) *is sound and complete for proving termination.* $\qquad \square$

Proof. By Th. 11 and Th. 5. $\qquad \square$

14   Extension to total correctness

The proof by [4] that Hoare logic does not exists for functional languages is based on the restriction of predicates to first-order logic with program variables only. But this is no longer the case without this restriction [11,24] and can be extended to total correctness.

Theorem 13 (The total correctness proof principle) *Let* $F \in \mathcal{D} \xrightarrow{uc} \mathcal{D}_\perp$ *satisfying the function body termination hypothesis* (8) *be a continuous function on the cpo* $\langle \mathcal{D}_\perp, \sqsubseteq, \perp, \sqcup \rangle$ *where* $\perp \notin \mathcal{D}$, $\mathcal{D}_\perp = \mathcal{D} \cup \{\perp\}$, $\forall x \in \mathcal{D} . \perp \sqsubseteq \perp \sqsubsetneq x \sqsubseteq x$, $P \in \wp(\mathcal{D})$, $Q \in \wp(\mathcal{D} \times \mathcal{D})$, *and* $\mathcal{P}_{P,Q} \triangleq \{ f \in \mathcal{D} \to \mathcal{D}_\perp \mid \forall x \in P . \langle x, f(x) \rangle \in Q \}$. *Then*

$$\mathsf{lfp}^\sqsubseteq F \in \mathcal{P}_{P,Q} \Leftrightarrow \exists D \in \wp(\mathcal{D}) . \exists I \in \wp(\mathcal{D} \times \mathcal{D}) .$$

$$\qquad P \subseteq D \tag{13.a}$$
$$\wedge \quad \{\langle x, y \rangle \in I \mid x \in P\} \subseteq Q \tag{13.b}$$
$$\wedge \quad \exists \leqslant \in \wp(\mathcal{D} \times \mathcal{D}) . \langle D, \leqslant \rangle \text{ is well-founded} \tag{13.c}$$
$$\wedge \quad \forall x, y \in \mathcal{D} . (x \in D \wedge x \xmapsto{F} y) \Rightarrow (y \in D \wedge x > y) \tag{13.d}$$
$$\wedge \quad \text{let } \mathcal{P}_{D,I} \triangleq \{ f \in \mathcal{D} \to \mathcal{D}_\perp \mid \forall x \in D . (f(x) \neq \perp \Rightarrow \langle x, f(x) \rangle \in I) \} \text{ in} \tag{13.e}$$
$$\qquad \forall f \in \mathcal{P}_{D,I} . F(f) \in \mathcal{P}_{D,I} \qquad\qquad \square$$

Example 12 (Total correctness of the factorial). Define $F_!(f) \triangleq \lambda n \cdot (n = 0 \,?\, 1 \,\natural\, n \times f(n-1))$, $P = \mathbb{N}$, $Q = \{\langle n, n! \rangle \mid n \in \mathbb{N}\}$ So that $\mathsf{lfp}^\sqsubseteq F \in \mathcal{P}_{P,Q}$ expresses that $F_!(f)n$ terminates for $n \in \mathbb{N}$ and returns the factorial $n!$ of n. Take $D = P$ and $I = Q$ so that (13.a), (13.b), (13.c) are trivially satisfied since $D = \mathbb{N}$ and $\langle \mathbb{N}, \leqslant \rangle$ is well-founded. If $n \in D$ and $n \xmapsto{F} y$ then $n \neq 0$ and $y = n - 1$ so $n > n - 1 \in D$, proving (13.d). If $f \in \mathcal{P}_{D,I}$ and $n \in D = \mathbb{N}$ then $f(n) = n!$. So $F_!(f)n = n!$ since either $n = 0$ and $F_!(f)0 = 1 = 0!$ or $n > 0$ so $n - 1 \in \mathbb{N}$, $f(n-1) = (n-1)!$ so $F_!(f)n = n \times (n-1)! = n!$. Therefore $F_!(f) \in \mathcal{P}_{D,I}$, proving (13.e). By Th. 13, $\mathsf{lfp}^\sqsubseteq F_! \in \mathcal{P}_{P,Q}$. $\square$

Proof (of Th. 13). Soundness ($\Leftarrow$): Take $T = D$ in Th. 10. Then (13.a) implies (10.a), (13.c) implies (10.b), and (13.d) implies (10.c). By Th. 10, this implies $\forall x \in P . (\mathsf{lfp}^\sqsubseteq F)x \neq \perp$.

Ta ke $\mathcal{L} = \mathcal{D} \to \mathcal{D}_\perp$, $\mathcal{P} = Q = \mathcal{P}_{D,I}$. By def. $\mathcal{P}_{D,I}$, $\perp \in Q$ proving (5.a). By (13.d), $\forall f \in Q . F(f) \in Q$, proving (5.b). Let $\{f_i \in Q \mid i \in \mathbb{N}\}$ be any F-maximal $\sqsubseteq$-increasing chain of elements of Q. If $x \in \mathcal{D}$ and $(\bigsqcup_{i\in\mathbb{N}} f_i)x \neq \perp$, then $(\bigsqcup_{i\in\mathbb{N}} f_i)x = d \in \mathcal{D}$ so, by def. lub $\bigsqcup$, there exists $j \in \mathbb{N} . (\bigsqcup_{i\in\mathbb{N}} f_i)x = f_j(x) = d$. But $f_j \in Q = \mathcal{P}_{D,I}$ so $\langle x, d \rangle = \langle x, (\bigsqcup_{i\in\mathbb{N}} f_i)x \rangle \in I$. If follows that $(\bigsqcup_{i\in\mathbb{N}} f_i) \in \mathcal{P}_{D,I} = \mathcal{P}$. By Th. 5, $\mathsf{lfp}^\sqsubseteq F \in \mathcal{P}_{D,I}$.

Since $\mathsf{lfp}^\sqsubseteq F \in \mathcal{P}_{D,I}$ and $\forall x \in P . (\mathsf{lfp}^\sqsubseteq F)x \neq \perp$, we conclude that $\mathsf{lfp}^\sqsubseteq F \in \mathcal{P}_{P,Q}$.

Completeness ($\Rightarrow$): Assume that $\mathsf{lfp}^\sqsubseteq F \in \mathcal{P}_{P,Q}$ so $\forall x \in P . (\mathsf{lfp}^\sqsubseteq F)x \neq \perp$. Applying Th. 10 with $T = P$, there exists $D \in \wp(\mathcal{D})$ satisfying (10.a), (10.b), and (10.c). Applying Th. 5 with $\mathcal{L} = \mathcal{D} \to \mathcal{D}_\perp$, there exists $Q \in \wp(\mathcal{D} \to \mathcal{D}_\perp)$ satisfying (5.a), (5.b), (5.c). Moreover, the completeness proof of Th. 5 shows that one can choose $Q = \{F^i(\perp) \mid i \in \mathbb{N}\}$.

Choose $I \triangleq \{\langle x, f(x) \rangle \in \mathcal{D} \times \mathcal{D} \mid f \in Q \vee f = \bigsqcup Q\}$, where, as shown in the completeness proof of Th. 5, $\bigsqcup Q$ is well-defined and equal to $\mathsf{lfp}^\sqsubseteq F$.

- We have $P = T \subseteq D$ by (10.a), proving (13.a);
- If $\langle x, y \rangle \in I$ then $y \neq \perp$ and $y = f(x)$ where $f \in Q$ or $f = \bigsqcup Q$. In both cases, by $Q = \{F^i(\perp) \mid i \in \mathbb{N}\}$ and $f(x) \neq \perp$, we have $y = \mathsf{lfp}^\sqsubseteq F)x$ so, by hypothesis $\mathsf{lfp}^\sqsubseteq F \in \mathcal{P}_{P,Q}$, if $x \in P$, then $\langle x, y \rangle \in Q$, proving (13.b);
- (10.b) is exactly (13.c);
- (10.c) is exactly (13.d);

– Assume that $f \in \mathcal{P}_{D,I} = \{f \in \mathcal{D} \to \mathcal{D}_\bot \mid \forall x \in D . (f(x) \neq \bot \Rightarrow \langle x, f(x) \rangle \in I)\}$. Then either $f \in Q$ so, by (5.b), $F(f) \in Q$ and therefore $F(f) \in \mathcal{P}_{D,I}$ or $f = \bigsqcup Q = \mathsf{lfp}^{\subseteq} F$ so $F(f) = f \in \mathcal{P}_{D,I}$, proving (13.e).   □

15 Application to the `while` iteration

Manna and Pnueli [20] generalized Hoare partial correctness rule for total correctness $(\!|P|\!)\ \mathsf{w}\ (\!|Q|\!)$ denoting $\forall x \in P . [\![\mathsf{w}]\!]x \in Q$ which is traditionally decomposed in partial correctness $\{\!|P|\!\}\ \mathsf{w}\ \{\!|Q|\!\}$ and termination $\forall x \in P . [\![\mathsf{w}]\!]x \neq \bot$. They rely on the idea of relating the initial and final values of variables in Q, writing $P(x)$ for $x \in P \in \wp(\mathcal{D})$ and $Q(x, x')$ for $\langle x, x' \rangle \in Q \in \wp(\mathcal{D} \times \mathcal{D})$, so that the rule are written in the form $(\!|P(x)|\!)\ \mathsf{w}\ (\!|Q(x, x')|\!)$ where x is the value before execution and x' that upon termination.

$(\!|P(x)|\!)\ \mathsf{w}\ (\!|Q(x, x')|\!)$ is equivalent to $\mathsf{lfp}^{\subseteq} F_\mathsf{w} \in \mathcal{P}_{P,Q}$. So, by the soundness and completeness of Th. 13, this is equivalent to the existence of $D \in \wp(\mathcal{D})$ and $I \in \wp(\mathcal{D} \times \mathcal{D})$ satisfying the conditions.

$$
\begin{array}{ll}
& P(x) \Rightarrow D(x) & (14.a) \\
\wedge & P(x) \wedge I(x, y) \Rightarrow Q(x, y) & (14.b) \\
\wedge & \exists \leqslant \in \wp(\mathcal{D} \times \mathcal{D}) . \langle D, \leqslant \rangle \text{ is well-founded} & (14.c) \\
\wedge & \forall x \in D . S(x) \in D \wedge x > S(x) & (14.d) \\
\wedge & \forall x \in D, x'' \in \mathcal{D} . (B(x) \wedge I(S(x), x'') \Rightarrow I(x, x'')) & (14.e) \\
\wedge & \forall x \in D . \neg B(x) \Rightarrow I(x, x) & (14.e')
\end{array}
$$

since for (13.d), $x \overset{F}{\longmapsto} y$ if and only if $y = S(x)$, by def. $F_\mathsf{w}(f)x = (\!| \neg B(x) \; ? \; x \; : \; f(S(x)) |\!)$ and for (13.e/e'), given $\mathcal{P}_{D,I} \triangleq \{f \in \mathcal{D} \to \mathcal{D}_\bot \mid \forall x \in D . f(x) \neq \bot \Rightarrow \langle x, f(x) \rangle \in I\}$, we have

$\forall f \in \mathcal{P}_{D,I} . F_\mathsf{w}(f) \in \mathcal{P}_{D,I}$

$\Leftrightarrow \forall f \in \mathcal{D} \to \mathcal{D}_\bot . (\forall x \in D . (f(x) \neq \bot) \Rightarrow (\langle x, f(x) \rangle \in I)) \Rightarrow (\forall x \in D . (\!| \neg B(x) \; ? \; \langle x, x \rangle \in I \; : \; (f(S(x)) \neq \bot) \Rightarrow (\langle x, f(S(x)) \rangle \in I) |\!))$ $(\text{def. } \mathcal{P}_{D,I} \text{ and } F_\mathsf{w})$

$\Leftrightarrow \forall f \in \mathcal{D} \to \mathcal{D} . (\forall x \in D . (\langle x, f(x) \rangle \in I)) \Rightarrow (\forall x \in D . (\!| \neg B(x) \; ? \; \langle x, x \rangle \in I \; : \; (\langle x, f(S(x)) \rangle \in I) |\!))$ $(\text{since the } \bot \text{ case is excluded})$

$\Leftrightarrow (\forall x \in D . \neg B(x) \Rightarrow \langle x, x \rangle \in I) \wedge (\forall x \in D . (B(x) \wedge \langle S(x), x'' \rangle \in I) \Rightarrow \langle x, x' \rangle \in I)$

$(\text{since } f \text{ is defined by } I \text{ and letting } x' = f(S(x)))$ □

Rewriting (14) in Manna-Pnueli style, we get the sound and complete rule (which incorporate the consequence rule):

$$
\begin{array}{ll}
P(x) \Rightarrow D(x), \quad P(x) \wedge I(x, y) \Rightarrow Q(x, y), & (15.a/b) \\
\exists \leqslant \in \wp(\mathcal{D} \times \mathcal{D}) . \langle D, \leqslant \rangle \text{ is well-founded,} & (15.c) \\
(\!|D(x)|\!)\ \mathsf{s}\ (\!|D(x') \wedge x > x'|\!), & (15.d) \\
(\!|D(x) \wedge B(x)|\!)\ \mathsf{s}\ (\!|I(x, x') \wedge \forall x'' . I(x', x'') \Rightarrow I(x, x'')|\!), & (15.e) \\
\forall x . D(x) \wedge \neg B(x) \Rightarrow I(x, x) & (15.e')
\end{array}
$$

$$\overline{(\!|P(x)|\!)\ \mathsf{w}\ (\!|Q(x, x') \wedge \neg B(x')|\!)}$$

(The conjunction with the post-condition $\neg B(x')$ is explained in Ex. 6).

The original Manna and Pnueli rule [20, Sect. 8.3] is slightly different, as follows.

$$(\!|\, P(x) \wedge B(x)\, |\!) \ \mathsf{S} \ (\!|\, P(x') \wedge Q(x, x') \wedge x \gtrless x'\, |\!), \qquad (16.\text{i})$$
$$\forall x, x', x'' \,.\, Q(x, x') \wedge Q(x', x'') \Rightarrow Q(x, x''), \qquad (16.\text{ii})$$
$$\forall x \,.\, P(x) \wedge \neg B(x) \Rightarrow Q(x, x) \qquad (16.\text{iii})$$

$$(\!|\, P(x)\, |\!) \ \mathsf{W} \ (\!|\, Q(x, x') \wedge \neg B(x')\, |\!)$$

As in [14], the proof rules are postulated so no soundness or completeness proof is given. A soundness and completeness proof is provided in [1] based on Scott induction (using transfinite iterates in absence of continuity due to the consideration of unbounded nondeterminism).

Assume the hypotheses of Manna-Pnueli inference rule (16), and define (with informal notations)

- $P' = D \triangleq P(x)$;
- $Q' = I(x, y) \triangleq Q(x, y)$;

so that

- (14.a) holds trivially by reflexivity;
- (14.b) holds trivially since $P(x) \wedge I(x, y) \Rightarrow Q'(x, y)$. Moreover, the conjunction with the term $B(x')$ follows from the semantics of the while iteration, as shown in Ex. 1;
- (14.c) is a side condition in Manna-Pnueli rule (there should be a convergence function u into a well-founded set $\langle W, \preceq \rangle$ with $x \leqslant y$ if and only if $u(x) \preceq u(y)$);
- Since $(\!|\, P'(x)\, |\!) \ \mathsf{S} \ (\!|\, Q'(x, x')\, |\!)$ denotes $\forall x \,.\, P'(x) \Rightarrow (Q'(x, S(x)) \wedge S(x) \neq \perp)$ where $S = [\![\mathsf{S}]\!]$ is the denotational semantics of S, (16.i) implies both
  - $\forall x \,.\, (P(x) \wedge B(x)) \Rightarrow (P(S(x)) \wedge x > S(x))$, which is (14.d);
  - and
    $$\forall x \,.\, (P(x) \wedge B(x)) \Rightarrow Q(x, S(x))$$
    which together with (16.ii)
    $$\forall x, x'' \,.\, (Q(x, S(x)) \wedge Q(S(x), x'') \Rightarrow Q(x, x'')$$
    yields
    $$\forall x \,.\, (P(x) \wedge B(x) \wedge Q(S(x), x'')) \Rightarrow Q(x, x''), \text{ which is (14.e)};$$
- (14.e') is exactly (16.ii).

By Th. 13, Moreover, if $(\mathsf{lfp}^{\subseteq} F_{\mathsf{w}})x \neq \perp$ then $\neg B(\mathsf{lfp}^{\subseteq} F_{\mathsf{w}})$, as shown in Ex. 1, we conclude that Manna-Pnueli rule is sound.

Obviously Manna-Pnueli rule (16) is not complete (since $Q(x, x')$ might not be inductive), but it can be applied to the strongest invariant and the conclusion derived by the consequence rule.

16   Conclusion

Park/fixpoint induction is useful to reason on post-fixpoints, above the least fixpoint. Scott/iteration induction is useful to reason on iterates, below the least fixpoint. Traditional Park/fixpoint induction can prove invariance/partial correctness but not termination (at least without introducing auxiliary variables such as bounded loop counters [15]). The traditional Scott/iteration induction cannot prove termination either. We generalized the iteration induction principles to prove termination/total correctness. For termination they are equivalent to the Turing/Floyd termination proof method using variant/convergence functions (which itself is equivalent [10] to Burstall's intermittent assertions induction principle [3]). This applies both to (first-order) functional and imperative programming. In particular, the Manna-Pnueli method for proving the total correctness of `while` loops is equivalent to Scott induction for the denotational semantics of these loops.

Acknowledgements

I thank Francesco Ranzato for comments and suggestions on earlier versions of the paper. Work supported in part by NSF Grant CCF-1617717.

References

1. Apt, K.R., Plotkin, G.D.: Countable nondeterminism and random assignment. J. ACM **33**(4), 724–767 (1986)
2. de Bakker, J.W., Scott, D.S.: A theory of programs (Aug 1969), IBM Seminar Vienna, Austria (Unpublished notes)
3. Burstall, R.M.: Program proving as hand simulation with a little induction. In: IFIP Congress. pp. 308–312. North-Holland (1974)
4. Clarke Jr., E.M.: Programming language constructs for which it is impossible to obtain good hoare axiom systems. J. ACM **26**(1), 129–147 (1979)
5. Cook, S.A.: Soundness and completeness of an axiom system for program verification. SIAM J. Comput. **7**(1), 70–90 (1978)
6. Cook, S.A.: Corrigendum: Soundness and completeness of an axiom system for program verification. SIAM J. Comput. **10**(3), 612 (1981)
7. Cousot, P.: Méthodes itératives de construction et d'approximation de points fixes d'opérateurs monotones sur un treillis, analyse sémantique de programmes (in French). Thèse d'État ès sciences mathématiques, Université de Grenoble Alpes, Grenoble, France (21 March 1978)
8. Cousot, P., Cousot, R.: Constructive versions of Tarski's fixed point theorems. Pacific Journal of Mathematics **82**(1), 43–57 (1979)
9. Cousot, P., Cousot, R.: Induction principles for proving invariance properties of programs. In: Néel, D. (ed.) Tools & Notions for Program Construction: an Advanced Course. pp. 75–119. Cambridge University Press, Cambridge, UK (Aug 1982)
10. Cousot, P., Cousot, R.: "a la burstall" intermittent assertions induction principles for proving inevitability properties of programs. Theor. Comput. Sci. **120**(1), 123–155 (1993)
11. Damm, W., Josko, B.: A sound and relatively* complete hoare-logic for a language with higher type procedures. Acta Inf. **20**, 59–101 (1983)
12. Floyd, R.W.: Assigning meaning to programs. In: Schwartz, J. (ed.) Proc. Symp. in Applied Math., vol. 19, pp. 19–32. Amer. Math. Soc. (1967)
13. Heizmann, M., Jones, N.D., Podelski, A.: Size-change termination and transition invariants. In: SAS. Lecture Notes in Computer Science, vol. 6337, pp. 22–50. Springer (2010)
14. Hoare, C.A.R.: An axiomatic basis for computer programming. Commun. ACM **12**(10), 576–580 (1969), http://doi.acm.org/10.1145/363235.363259
15. Katz, S., Manna, Z.: A closer look at termination. Acta Inf. **5**, 333–352 (1975)
16. Kleene, S.C.: Introduction to Meta-Mathematics. Elsevier North-Holland Pub. Co. (1952)
17. Lee, C.S., Jones, N.D., Ben-Amram, A.M.: The size-change principle for program termination. In: POPL. pp. 81–92. ACM (2001)
18. Leroy, X., Doligez, D., Frisch, A., Garrigue, J., Rémy, D., Vouillon, J.: The OCaml system, release 4.08, Documentation and user's manual (Feb 2019), http://caml.inria.fr/pub/docs/manual-ocaml/, copyright © 2013 Institut National de Recherche en Informatique et en Automatique

19. Manna, Z., Ness, S., Vuillemin, J.: Inductive methods for proving properties of programs. Commun. ACM **16**(8), 491–502 (1973)
20. Manna, Z., Pnueli, A.: Axiomatic approach to total correctness of programs. Acta Inf. **3**, 243–263 (1974)
21. Manna, Z., Vuillemin, J.: Fix point approach to the theory of computation. Commun. ACM **15**(7), 528–536 (1972)
22. Markowsky, G.: Chain-complete posets and directed sets with applications. Algebra Universalis **6**(1), 53–68 (Nov 1976)
23. Park, D.M.R.: On the semantics of fair parallelism. In: Abstract Software Specifications. Lecture Notes in Computer Science, vol. 86, pp. 504–526. Springer (1979)
24. Régis-Gianas, Y., Pottier, F.: A Hoare logic for call-by-value functional programs. In: MPC. Lecture Notes in Computer Science, vol. 5133, pp. 305–335. Springer (2008)
25. Schmidt, D.W.: Denotational Semantics: A Methodology for Language Development. William C. Brown Publishers, Dubuque, IA, USA (Jun 1988), `http://people.cs.ksu.edu/~schmidt/text/DenSem-full-book.pdf`
26. Scott, D.S.: Outline of a mathematical theory of computation. In: Proceedings of the Fourth Annual Princeton Conference on Information Sciences and Systems. pp. 169–176. Princeton University (Mar 1970)
27. Scott, D.S.: The lattice of flow diagrams. In: Symposium on Semantics of Algorithmic Languages, Lecture Notes in Mathematics, vol. 188, pp. 311–366. Springer (1971)
28. Tarski, A.: A lattice theoretical fixpoint theorem and its applications. Pacific J. of Math. **5**, 285–310 (1955)
29. Turing, A.: Checking a large routine. In: Report of a Conference on High Speed Automatic Calculating Machines, University of Cambridge Mathematical Laboratory, Cambridge, England. pp. 67–69 (1949), `http://www.turingarchive.org/browse.php/b/8`

A General Framework for Static Cost Analysis of Parallel Logic Programs

Maximiliano Klemen[1,2](✉) , Pedro López-García[1,3] , John P. Gallagher[1,4] ,
José F. Morales[1] , and Manuel V. Hermenegildo[1,2]

[1] IMDEA Software Institute, Madrid, Spain
{maximiliano.klemen,pedro.lopez,john.gallagher,
josef.morales,manuel.hermenegildo}@imdea.org
[2] ETSI Informáticos, Universidad Politécnica de Madrid (UPM), Madrid, Spain
[3] Spanish Council for Scientific Research (CSIC), Madrid, Spain
[4] Roskilde University, Roskilde, Denmark

Abstract. The estimation and control of *resource usage* is now an important challenge in an increasing number of computing systems. In particular, requirements on timing and energy arise in a wide variety of applications such as internet of things, cloud computing, health, transportation, and robots. At the same time, parallel computing, with (heterogeneous) multi-core platforms in particular, has become the dominant paradigm in computer architecture. Predicting resource usage on such platforms poses a difficult challenge. Most work on static resource analysis has focused on sequential programs, and relatively little progress has been made on the analysis of parallel programs, or more specifically on parallel logic programs. We propose a novel, general, and flexible framework for setting up cost equations/relations which can be instantiated for performing resource usage analysis of parallel logic programs for a wide range of resources, platforms, and execution models. The analysis estimates both lower and upper bounds on the resource usage of a parallel program (without executing it) as functions on input data sizes. In addition, it also infers other meaningful information to better exploit and assess the potential and actual parallelism of a system. We develop a method for solving cost relations involving the *max* function that arise in the analysis of parallel programs. Finally, we instantiate our general framework for the analysis of logic programs with Independent And-Parallelism, report on an implementation within the CiaoPP system, and provide some experimental results. To our knowledge, this is the first approach to the cost analysis of *parallel logic programs*.

Keywords: Resource usage analysis · Parallelism · Static analysis · Complexity analysis · (Constraint) Logic programming · Prolog

Research partially funded by Spanish MINECO TIN2015-67522-C3-1-R *TRACES* project, and the Madrid P2018/TCS-4339 *BLOQUES-CM* program. We are also grateful to the anonymous reviewers for their useful comments.

© Springer Nature Switzerland AG 2020
M. Gabbrielli (Ed.): LOPSTR 2019, LNCS 12042, pp. 19–35, 2020.
https://doi.org/10.1007/978-3-030-45260-5_2

1   Introduction

Estimating in advance the resource usage of computations is useful for a number of applications; examples include granularity control in parallel/distributed systems, automatic program optimization, verification of resource-related specifications and detection of performance bugs, as well as helping developers make resource-related design decisions. Besides *time* and *energy*, we assume a broad concept of resources as numerical properties of the execution of a program, including the number of *execution steps*, the number of *calls* to a procedure, the number of *network accesses*, number of *transactions* in a database, and other user-definable resources. The goal of automatic static analysis is to estimate such properties without running the program with concrete data, as a function of input data sizes and possibly other (environmental) parameters.

Due to the heat generation barrier in traditional sequential architectures, parallel computing, with (heterogeneous) multi-core processors in particular, has become the dominant paradigm in current computer architecture. Predicting resource usage on such platforms poses important challenges. Most work on static resource analysis has focused on sequential programs, and relatively little progress has been made on the analysis of parallel programs, or on parallel logic programs in particular. The significant body of work on static analysis of sequential logic programs has already been applied to the analysis of other programming paradigms, including imperative programs. This is achieved via a transformation into *Horn clauses* [22]. In this paper we concentrate on the analysis of parallel Horn clause programs, which could be the result of such a translation from a parallel imperative program or be themselves the source program. Our starting point is the well-developed technique of setting up recurrence relations representing resource usage functions parameterized by input data sizes [2, 7–9, 24–26, 29], which are then solved to obtain (exact or safely approximated) closed forms of such functions (i.e., functions that provide upper or lower bounds on resource usage). We build on this and propose a novel, general, and flexible framework for setting up cost equations/relations which can be instantiated for performing static resource usage analysis of parallel logic programs for a wide range of resources, platforms, and execution models. Such an analysis estimates both lower and upper bounds on the resource usage of a parallel program as functions on input data sizes. We have instantiated the framework for dealing with Independent And-Parallelism (IAP) [10, 14], which refers to the parallel execution of conjuncts in a goal. However, the results can be applied to other languages and types of parallelism, by performing suitable transformations into Horn clauses.

The main contributions of this paper can be summarized as follows:

- We have extended a general static analysis framework for the analysis of sequential Horn clause programs [24, 26], to deal with parallel programs.
- Our extensions and further generalizations support a wide range of resources, platforms, and parallel/distributed execution models, and allow the inference of both lower and upper bounds on resource usage. This is the first approach, to our knowledge, to the cost analysis of *parallel logic programs* that can deal

with features such as backtracking, multiple solutions (i.e., non-determinism), and failure.

– We have instantiated the developed framework to infer useful information for assessing and exploiting the potential and actual parallelism of a system.
– We have developed a method for finding closed-form functions of cost relations involving the *max* function that arise in the analysis of parallel programs.
– We have developed a prototype implementation that instantiates the framework for the analysis of logic programs with Independent And-Parallelism within the CiaoPP system [13,24,26], and provided some experimental results.

2 Overview of the Approach

Prior to explaining our approach, we provide some preliminary concepts. Independent And-Parallelism arises between two goals when their corresponding executions do not affect each other. For pure goals (i.e., without side effects) a sufficient condition for the correctness of IAP is the absence of variable sharing at run-time among such goals. IAP has traditionally been expressed using the &/2 meta-predicate as the constructor to represent the parallel execution of goals. In this way, the conjunction of goals (i.e., literals) p & q in the body of a clause will trigger the execution of goals p and q in parallel, finishing when both executions finish.

Given a program $\mathcal{P}$ and a predicate $p \in \mathcal{P}$ of arity k and a set Π of k-tuples of calling data to p, we refer to the *(standard) cost* of a call $p(\bar{e})$ (i.e., a call to p with actual data $\bar{e} \in \Pi$), as the resource usage (under a given cost metric) of the complete execution of $p(\bar{e})$. The *standard cost* is formalized as a function $\mathcal{C}_p : \Pi \rightarrow \mathcal{R}_\infty$, where $\mathcal{R}_\infty$ is the set of real numbers augmented with the special symbol ∞ (which is used to represent non-termination). We extend the function $\mathcal{C}_p$ to the powerset of Π, i.e., $\hat{\mathcal{C}}_p : 2^\Pi \rightarrow 2^{\mathcal{R}_\infty}$, where $\hat{\mathcal{C}}_p(E) = \{\mathcal{C}_p(\bar{e}) \mid \bar{e} \in E\}$. Our goal is to abstract (safely approximate, as accurately as possible) $\hat{\mathcal{C}}_p$ (note that $\mathcal{C}_p(\bar{e}) = \hat{\mathcal{C}}_p(\{\bar{e}\})$). Intuitively, this abstraction is the composition of two abstractions: a size abstraction and a cost abstraction. The goal of the analysis is to infer two functions $\hat{\mathcal{C}}_p^\downarrow$ and $\hat{\mathcal{C}}_p^\uparrow : \mathcal{N}_\top^m \rightarrow \mathcal{R}_\infty$ that give lower and upper bounds respectively on the cost function $\hat{\mathcal{C}}_p$, where $\mathcal{N}_\top^m$ is the set of m-tuples whose elements are natural numbers or the special symbol $\top$, meaning that the size of a given term under a given size metric is *undefined*. Such bounds are given as a function of tuples of data sizes (representing the concrete tuples of data of the concrete function $\hat{\mathcal{C}}_p$). Typical size metrics are the actual value of a number, the length of a list, the size (number of constant and function symbols) of a term, etc. [24,26].

We now enumerate different metrics used to evaluate the performance of parallel logic programs, compared against its corresponding sequential version [27]. Here, these metrics are parameterized with respect to the resource in which the cost is expressed (e.g., number of *resolution steps*, *execution time*, or *energy consumption*):

- **Sequential cost (*Work*):** It is the standard cost of executing a program, assuming no parallelism.
- **Parallel cost (*Depth*):** It is the cost of executing a program in parallel, considering an unbounded number of processors.
- **Maximum number of processes running in parallel:** It is the maximum number of processes that may run simultaneously in a program. This is useful to determine what is the minimum number of processors that are required to guarantee that all the processes run in parallel.

The following example illustrates our approach.

Example 1. Consider the predicate `scalar/3` below, and a calling mode to it with the first argument bound to an integer n and the second one bound to a list of integers $[x_1, x_2, \ldots, x_k]$. Upon success, the third argument is bound to the list of products $[n \cdot x_1, n \cdot x_2, \ldots, n \cdot x_k]$. Each product is recursively computed by predicate `mult/3`. The calling modes are automatically inferred by CiaoPP (see [13] and its references): the first two arguments of both predicates are input, and their last arguments are output.

```
scalar(_,[],[]).
scalar(N,[X|Xs],[Y|Ys]):-
    mult(N,X,Y) & scalar(N,Xs,Ys).
```

```
mult(0,_,0).
mult(N,X,Y):-
    N>1,
    N1 is N - 1,
    mult(N1,X,Y0),
    Y is Y0 + X.
```

The call to the parallel `&/2` operator in the body of the second clause of `scalar/3` causes the calls to `mult/3` and `scalar/3` to be executed in parallel. We want to infer the cost of such a call to `scalar/3`, in terms of the number of resolution steps, as a function of its input data sizes. We use the CiaoPP system to infer size relations for the different arguments in the clauses, as well as dealing with a rich set of size metrics (see [24, 26] for details). Assume that the size metrics used in this example are the *actual value* of N (denoted `int(N)`), for the first argument, and the *list-length* for the second and third arguments (denoted `length(X)` and `length(Y)`, respectively). Since size relations are obvious in this example, we focus only on the setting up of cost relations for the sake of brevity. Regarding the number of solutions, in this example all the predicates generate at most one solution. For simplicity we assume that all builtin predicates, such as `is/2` and the comparison operators have zero cost (in practice they have a "trust" assertion that specifies their cost as if it had been inferred by the system). As the program contains parallel calls, we are interested in inferring both total resolution steps, i.e., considering a sequential execution (represented by the `seq` identifier), and the number of parallel steps, considering a parallel execution, with an unbounded number of processors (represented by `par`). In the latter case, the definition of this resource establishes that the aggregator of the costs of the parallel calls that are arguments of the `&/2` meta-predicate is the `max/2` function. Thus, the number of resolution steps performed in parallel for `p & q` is the maximum between the parallel steps performed by `p` and the ones performed by `q`. However, for computing the *total resolution steps*, the aggregation operator we use is the addition, both for parallel and sequential calls. For brevity, in this example we only infer upper bounds on resource usages.

We now set up the cost relations for scalar/3 and mult/3. Note that the cost functions have two arguments, corresponding to the sizes of the input arguments.[1] In the equations, we underline the operation applied as cost aggregator for &/2.

For the sequential execution (seq), we obtain the following cost relations:

$$
\begin{aligned}
C_{\text{scalar}}(n, l) &= 1 & \text{if } l = 0 \\
C_{\text{scalar}}(n, l) &= 1 + C_{\text{mult}}(n)\underline{+}C_{\text{scalar}}(n, l - 1) & \text{if } l > 0 \\
C_{\text{mult}}(n) &= 1 & \text{if } n = 0 \\
C_{\text{mult}}(n) &= 1 + C_{\text{mult}}(n - 1) & \text{if } n > 0
\end{aligned}
$$

After solving these equations and composing the closed-form solutions, we obtain the following closed-form functions:

$$
\begin{aligned}
C_{\text{scalar}}(n, l) &= (n + 2) \times l + 1 & \text{if } n \geq 0 \wedge l \geq 0 \\
C_{\text{mult}}(n) &= n + 1 & \text{if } n \geq 0
\end{aligned}
$$

For the parallel execution (par), we obtain the following cost relations:

$$
\begin{aligned}
C_{\text{scalar}}(n, l) &= 1 & \text{if } l = 0 \\
C_{\text{scalar}}(n, l) &= 1 + \underline{max}(C_{\text{mult}}(n), C_{\text{scalar}}(n, l - 1)) & \text{if } l > 0 \\
C_{\text{mult}}(n) &= 1 & \text{if } n = 0 \\
C_{\text{mult}}(n) &= 1 + C_{\text{mult}}(n - 1) & \text{if } n > 0
\end{aligned}
$$

Similarly, we obtain the following closed-form functions:

$$
\begin{aligned}
C_{\text{scalar}}(n, l) &= n + l + 1 & \text{if } n \geq 0 \wedge l \geq 0 \\
C_{\text{mult}}(n) &= n + 1 & \text{if } n \geq 0
\end{aligned}
$$

By comparing the complexity order (in terms of resolution steps) of the sequential execution of scalar/3, $O(n \cdot l)$, with the complexity order of its parallel execution (assuming an ideal parallel model with an unbounded number of processors) $O(n+l)$, we can get a hint about the maximum achievable parallelization of the program.

Another useful piece of information about scalar/3 that we want to infer is the maximum number of processes that may run in parallel, considering all possible executions. For this purpose, we define a resource named sthreads. The operation count_process/3 aggregates the cost of both arguments of the meta-predicate &/2 for the sthreads resource, by adding the maximum number of processes for each argument plus one additional process, corresponding to the one created by the call to &/2. The sequential cost aggregator is now the *maximum* operator, in order to keep track of the maximum number of processes created along the different instructions of the program executed sequentially. Note that if the instruction p executes at most Pr_p processes in parallel, and

---

[1] For the sake of clarity, we abuse notation in the examples when representing the cost functions that depend on data sizes.

the instruction q executes at most Pr_q processes, then the program p, q will execute at most $max(Pr_p, Pr_q)$ processes in parallel, because all the parallel processes created by p will finish before the execution of q. Note also that for the sequential execution of both p and q, the cost in terms of the sthreads resource is always zero, because no additional process is created. The analysis sets up the following recurrences for the sthreads resource and the predicates scalar/3 and mult/3 of our example:

$$\begin{aligned}
&C_{\mathtt{scalar}}(n, l) = 0 &&\text{if } l = 0 \\
&C_{\mathtt{scalar}}(n, l) = C_{\mathtt{mult}}(n) + C_{\mathtt{scalar}}(n, l - 1) + 1 &&\text{if } l > 0 \\
&C_{\mathtt{mult}}(n) = 0 &&\text{if } n \geq 0
\end{aligned}$$

For which we obtain the following closed-form functions:

$$\begin{aligned}
&C_{\mathtt{scalar}}(n, l) = l \quad \text{if } n \geq 0 \wedge l \geq 0 \\
&C_{\mathtt{mult}}(n) = 0 \quad \text{if } n \geq 0
\end{aligned}$$

As we can see, this predicate will execute, in the worst case, as many processes as there are elements in the input list.

3   The Parametric Cost Relations Framework for Sequential Programs

The starting point of our work is the standard general framework described in [24] for setting up parametric relations representing the resource usage (and size relations) of programs and predicates.[2] The analysis infers size relations for each predicate in a program: arithmetic expressions that provide the size of output arguments of the predicate as a function of its input data sizes. It also infers size relations for each clause, which give the input data sizes of the body literals as functions of the input data sizes to the clause head. Such size relations are instrumental for setting up cost relations.

The framework is doubly parametric: first, the costs inferred are functions of input data sizes, and second, the framework itself is parametric with respect to the type of approximation made (upper or lower bounds), and to the resource analyzed. Each concrete resource r to be tracked is defined by two sets of (user-provided) functions, which can be constants, or general expressions of input data sizes:

1. *Head cost* $\varphi_{[ap,r]}(H)$: a function that returns an approximation of type ap of the amount of resource r used by the unification of the calling literal (subgoal) p and the head H of a clause matching p, plus any preparation for entering a clause (i.e., call and parameter passing cost).

---

[2] We give equivalent but simpler descriptions than in [24], which are allowed by assuming that programs are the result of a normalization process that makes all unifications explicit in the clause body, so that the arguments of the clause head and the body literals are all unique variables. We also change some notation for readability and illustrative purposes.

2. *Predicate cost* $\Psi_{[ap,r]}(\mathbf{p}, \bar{\mathbf{x}})$: it is also possible to define the *full cost* for a particular predicate $\mathbf{p}$ for resource r and approximation ap, i.e., the function $\Psi_{[ap,r]}(\mathbf{p}) : \mathcal{N}_\top^m \rightarrow \mathcal{R}_\infty$ (with the sizes of $\mathbf{p}$'s input data as parameters, $\bar{\mathbf{x}}$) that returns the usage of resource r made by a call to this predicate. This is especially useful for built-in or external predicates, i.e., predicates for which the source code is not available and thus cannot be analyzed, or for providing a more accurate function than analysis can infer. In the implementation, this information can be provided by the user to the analyzer through *trust assertions*.

For simplicity we only show the equations related to our standard definition of cost. However, our framework has also been extended to allow the inference of a more general definition of cost, called accumulated cost, which is useful for performing static profiling, obtaining more detailed information regarding how the cost is distributed among a set of user-defined *cost centers*. See [11,21] for more details. In order to infer the resource usage functions, all predicates in the program are processed in a single traversal of the call graph in reverse topological order. Consider a predicate $\mathbf{p}$ defined by clauses $C_1, \ldots, C_m$. Assume $\bar{\mathbf{x}}$ are the sizes of $\mathbf{p}$'s input parameters. Then, the resource usage (expressed in units of resource r with approximation ap) of a call to $\mathbf{p}$, for an input of size $\bar{\mathbf{x}}$, denoted as $C_{pred[ap,r]}(\mathbf{p}, \bar{\mathbf{x}})$, can be expressed as:

$$C_{pred[ap,r]}(\mathbf{p}, \bar{\mathbf{x}}) = \bigodot_{1 \le i \le m} (C_{cl[ap,r]}(C_i, \bar{\mathbf{x}})) \tag{1}$$

where $\bigodot = ClauseAggregator(ap, r)$ is a function that takes an approximation identifier ap and returns a function that applies over the cost of all the clauses, $C_{cl[ap,r]}(C_i, \bar{\mathbf{x}})$, for $1 \le i \le m$, in order to obtain the cost of a call to the predicate $\mathbf{p}$. For example, if ap is the identifier for approximation "upper bound" (ub), then a possible conservative definition for $ClauseAggregator(ub, r)$ is the $\sum$ function. In this case, and since the number of solutions generated by a predicate that will be demanded is generally not known in advance, a conservative upper bound on the computational cost of a predicate is obtained by assuming that all solutions are needed, and that all clauses are executed (thus the cost of the predicate is assumed to be the sum of the costs of all of its clauses). However, it is straightforward to take mutual exclusion into account to obtain a more precise estimate of the cost of a predicate, using the maximum of the costs of mutually exclusive groups of clauses, as done in [26].

Let us see now how to compute the resource usage of a clause. Consider a clause C of predicate $\mathbf{p}$ of the form $H :\!\!- L_1, \ldots, L_k$ where $L_j, 1 \le j \le k$, is a literal (either a predicate call, or an external or builtin predicate), and H is the clause head. Assume that $\psi_j(\bar{\mathbf{x}})$ is a tuple with the sizes of all the input arguments to literal L_j, given as functions of the sizes of the input arguments to the clause head. Note that these $\psi_j(\bar{\mathbf{x}})$ size relations have previously been computed during size analysis for all input arguments to literals in the bodies of all clauses. Then, the cost relation for clause C and a single call to $\mathbf{p}$ (obtaining all solutions), is:

$$C_{cl[ap,r]}(C,\bar{\mathbf{x}}) = \varphi_{[ap,r]}(H) + \sum_{j=1}^{lim(ap,C)} sols_j(\bar{\mathbf{x}}) \times C_{lit[ap,r]}(L_j, \psi_j(\bar{\mathbf{x}})) \qquad (2)$$

where $lim(ap, C)$ gives the index of the last body literal that is called in the execution of clause C, and $sols_j$ represents the product of the number of solutions produced by the predecessor literals of L_j in the clause body:

$$sols_j(\bar{\mathbf{x}}) = \prod_{i=1}^{j-1} s_{pred}(L_i, \psi_i(\bar{\mathbf{x}})) \qquad (3)$$

where $s_{pred}(L_i, \psi_i(\bar{\mathbf{x}}))$ gives the number of solutions produced by L_i, with arguments of size $\psi_i(\bar{\mathbf{x}})$. The number of solutions and size relations are both inferred automatically by the framework (we refer the reader to [7–9, 26] for a description).

Finally, $C_{lit[ap,r]}(L_j, \psi_j(\bar{\mathbf{x}}))$ is replaced by one of the following expressions, depending on L_j:

- If L_j is a call to a predicate q which is in the same strongly connected component as p (the predicate under analysis), then $C_{lit[ap,r]}(L_j, \psi_j(\bar{\mathbf{x}}))$ is replaced by the symbolic call $C_{pred[ap,r]}(\mathsf{q}, \psi_j(\bar{\mathbf{x}}))$, giving rise to a recurrence relation that needs to be bounded with a closed-form expression by the solver afterwards.
- If L_j is a call to a predicate q which is in a different strongly connected component than p, then $C_{lit[ap,r]}(L_j, \psi_j(\bar{\mathbf{x}}))$ is replaced by the closed-form expression that bounds $C_{pred[ap,r]}(\mathsf{q}, \psi_j(\bar{\mathbf{x}}))$. The analysis guarantees that this expression has been inferred beforehand, due to the fact that the analysis is performed for each strongly connected component, in a reverse topological order.
- If L_j is a call to a predicate q, whose cost is specified (with a trust assertion) as $\Psi_{[ap,r]}(q, \bar{\mathbf{y}})$, then $C_{lit[ap,r]}(L_j, \psi_j(\bar{\mathbf{x}}))$ is replaced by the expression $\Psi_{[ap,r]}(q, \psi_j(\bar{\mathbf{x}}))$.

4 Our Extended Resource Analysis Framework for Parallel Programs

In this section, we describe how we extend the resource analysis framework detailed above, in order to handle logic programs with Independent And-Parallelism, using the binary parallel &/2 operator. First, we introduce a new general parameter that indicates the execution model the analysis has to consider. For our current prototype, we have defined two different execution models: standard *sequential* execution, represented by seq, and an abstract parallel execution model, represented by $par(n)$, where $n \in \mathcal{N} \cup \{\infty\}$. The abstract execution model $par(\infty)$ is similar to the *work* and *depth* model, presented in [6] and used extensively in previous work such as [16]. Basically, this model is based on considering an unbounded number of available processors to infer bounds on the depth of the computation tree. The *work* measure is the amount of work to be performed considering a sequential execution. These two measures together give an idea on the impact of the parallelization of a particular program. The abstract execution model $par(n)$, where $n \in \mathcal{N}$, assumes a finite number n of processors.

In order to obtain the cost of a predicate, Eq. (1) remains almost identical, the only difference being the addition of the new parameter to indicate the execution model.

Now we address how to set up the cost for clauses. In this case, Eq. (2) is extended with the execution model ex, and also the default sequential cost aggregation, $\sum$, is replaced by a parametric associative operator $\bigoplus$, that depends on the resource being defined, the approximation, and the execution model. For $ex \equiv par(\infty)$ or $ex \equiv seq$, the following equation is set up:

$$C_{cl[ap,r,ex]}(C,\bar{x}) = \varphi_{[ap,r]}(H) + \bigoplus_{j=1}^{lim(ap,ex,C)} (sols_j(\bar{x}) \times C_{lit[ap,r,ex]}(L_j, \psi_j(\bar{x}))) \quad (4)$$

Note that the cost aggregation operators must depend on the resource r (besides the other parameters). For example, if r is *execution time*, then the cost of executing two tasks in parallel must be aggregated by taking the maximum of the execution times of the two tasks. In contrast, if r is *energy consumption*, then the aggregation is the addition of the energy of the two tasks.

Finally, we extend how the cost of a literal L_i, expressed as $C_{lit[ap,r,ex]}(L_i, \psi_i(\bar{x}))$, is set up. The previous definition is extended considering the new case where the literal is a call to the *meta-predicate* &/2. In this case, we introduce a new parallel aggregation associative operator, denoted by $\bigotimes$. Concretely, if $L_i = B_1 \& B_2$, where B_1 and B_2 are two sequences of goals, then:

$$C_{lit[ap,r,ex]}(B_1 \& B_2, \bar{x}) = C_{body[ap,r,ex]}(B_1, \bar{x}) \bigotimes C_{body[ap,r,ex]}(B_2, \bar{x}) \quad (5)$$

$$C_{body[ap,r,ex]}(B,\bar{x}) = \bigoplus_{j=1}^{lim(ap,ex,B)} (sols_j(\bar{x}) \times C_{lit[ap,r,ex]}(L_j^B, \psi_j(\bar{x}))) \quad (6)$$

where $B = L_1^B, \ldots, L_m^B$.

Consider now the execution model $ex \equiv par(n)$, where $n \in \mathcal{N}$ (i.e., assuming a finite number n of processors), and a recursive parallel predicate p that creates a parallel task q_i in each recursion i. Assume that we are interested in obtaining an upper bound on the cost of a call to p, for an input of size $\bar{x}$. We first infer the number k of parallel tasks created by p as a function of $\bar{x}$. This can be easily done by using our cost analysis framework and providing the suitable assertions for inferring a resource named "*ptasks*." Intuitively, the "counter" associated to such resource must be incremented by the (symbolic) execution of the &/2 parallel operator. More formally, $k = C_{pred[ub,ptasks]}(p, \bar{x})$. To this point, an upper bound m on the number of tasks executed by any of the n processors is given by $m = \lceil \frac{k}{n} \rceil$. Then, an upper bound on the cost (in terms of resolution steps, i.e., $r = steps$) of a call to p, for an input of size $\bar{x}$ can be given by:

$$C_{pred[ub,r,par(n)]}(\mathsf{p}, \bar{x}) = C^u + Spawn^u \tag{7}$$

where C^u can be computed in two possible ways: $C^u = \sum_{i=1}^{m} C_i^u$; or $C^u = m\, C_1^u$, where C_i^u denotes an upper bound on the cost of parallel task q_i, and $C_1^u, \ldots, C_k^u$ are ordered in descending order of cost. Each C_i^u can be considered as the sum of two components: $C_i^u = Sched_i^u + T_i^u$, where $Sched_i^u$ denotes the cost from the point in which the parallel subtask q_i is created until its execution is started by a processor (possibly the same processor that created the subtask), i.e. the cost of task preparation, scheduling, communication overheads, etc. T_i^u denotes the cost of the execution of q_i disregarding all the overheads mentioned before, i.e., $T_i^u = C_{pred[ub,r,seq]}(\mathsf{q}, \psi_q(\bar{x}))$, where $\psi_q(\bar{x})$ is a tuple with the sizes of all the input arguments to predicate q in the body of p. $Spawn^u$ denotes an upper bound on the cost of creating the k parallel tasks q_i. It will be dependent on the particular system in which p is going to be executed. It can be a constant, or a function of several parameters, (such as input data size, number of input arguments, or number of tasks) and can be experimentally determined.

4.1 Solving Cost Recurrence Relations Involving *max* Operation

We propose a method for finding closed-form functions for cost relations that use the parallel and sequential cost aggregation operators $\otimes$ and $\oplus$, which include the *max* function in their definitions.

Automatically finding closed-form upper and lower bounds for recurrence relations is an uncomputable problem. For some special classes of recurrences, exact solutions are known, for example for linear recurrences with one variable. For some other classes, it is possible to apply transformations to fit a class of recurrences with known solutions, even if this transformation obtains an appropriate approximation rather than an equivalent expression.

Particularly for the case of analyzing independent and-parallel logic programs, recurrences involving the *max* operator are quite common. For example, if we are analyzing elapsed time of a parallel logic program, a proper parallel aggregation operator is the maximum between the times elapsed for each literal running in parallel. To the best of our knowledge, no general solution exists for recurrences of this particular type. However, in this paper we identify some common classes of this type of recurrences, for which we obtain closed forms that are proven to be correct. In this section, we present these different classes, together with the corresponding method to obtain a correct bound.

Consider the following function $f : \mathcal{N}^m \to \mathcal{N}$, defined as a general form of a first-order recurrence equation with a *max* operator:

$$f(\bar{x}) = \begin{cases} max(C, f(\bar{x}_{|i} - 1)) + D & x_i > a \\ B & x_i \leq a \end{cases} \tag{8}$$

where $a \in \mathcal{N}$, and C, D, and B are arbitrary expressions possibly depending on $\bar{x}$. Note that $\bar{x} = x_1, x_2, \ldots, x_m$. We define $\bar{x}_{|i} - 1 = x_1, \ldots, x_i - 1, \ldots, x_m$, for a given i, $1 \leq i \leq m$. If C and D do not depend on x_i, then C and D do not change through the different recursive instances of f. In this case, an equivalent closed form is defined by the following theorem:

Theorem 1. *Given $f : \mathcal{N}^m \to \mathcal{N}$ as defined in (8), where C and D are functions of $\bar{x} \setminus x_i$ (i.e., they do not depend on x_i). Then, $\forall \bar{x}$:*

$$f(\bar{x}) = f'(\bar{x}) = \begin{cases} max(C, B) + (x_i - a) \cdot D & x_i > a \\ B & x_i \leq a \end{cases}$$

For the case where $C = g(\bar{x})$ and $D = h(\bar{x})$ are functions non-decreasing on x_i, then the upper bound is given by the following closed form:

Theorem 2. *Given $f : \mathcal{N}^m \to \mathcal{N}$ as defined in (8), where g and h are functions of $\bar{x}$, non-decreasing on x_i. Then, $\forall \bar{x}$:*

$$f(\bar{x}) \leq f'(\bar{x}) = \begin{cases} max(g(\bar{x}), B) + (x_i - a - 1) \times max(g(\bar{x}), h(\bar{x}_{|i} - 1)) + h(\bar{x}) & x_i > a \\ B & x_i \leq a \end{cases}$$

The proofs of both theorems are available in [18]. If the recurrence is not included in the classes defined by Theorems 1 and 2, we try to eliminate the max operator by simplification. Consider an expression $max(e_1, e_2)$ appearing in a recurrence relation. First, we use the function comparison capabilities of CiaoPP, presented in [19,20]. If an e_i contains non-closed recurrence function calls, we use an SMT solver [23] representing non-closed functions as uninterpreted functions, assuming that they are positive and non-decreasing. Concretely, for each non-closed function call $f(\bar{x})$ appearing in e_i, we add the properties $\forall \bar{x}. f(\bar{x}) \geq 0$ and $\forall \bar{x}, \bar{y}. \bar{x} \leq \bar{y} \iff f(\bar{x}) \leq f(\bar{y})$ to a set M. Then, we check if either $M \models e_1 \leq e_2$ or $M \models e_2 \leq e_1$ hold.[3]

Finally, if no proof is found, we replace the max operator with an addition, losing precision but still finding safe upper bounds.

Table 1. Description of the benchmarks.

map_add1/2	Parallel increment by one of each element of a list
fib/2	Parallel computation of the nth Fibonacci number
add_mat/3, mmatrix/3	Parallel matrix multiplication and addition
blur/2	Generic parallel image filter
intersect/3, union/3, diff/3	Set operations
dyade/3, dyade_map/3	Dyadic product of two vectors (and on a set of vectors)
append_all/3	Appends a prefix to each list of a list of lists

---

[3] As the algorithm used by SMT solvers in this case is not guaranteed to terminate, we set a timeout.

5   Implementation and Experimental Results

We have implemented a prototype of our approach, leveraging the existing resource usage analysis framework of CiaoPP. The implementation basically consists of the parameterization of the operators used for sequential and parallel cost aggregation, i.e., for the aggregation of the costs corresponding to the arguments of ,/2 and &/2, respectively. This allows the user to define resources in a general way, taking into account the underlying execution model. We use off-the-shelf Computer Algebra Systems, as well as a builtin recurrence solver extended with the techniques presented in this paper, in order to solve recurrence relations that arise during analysis. We also use an external SMT Solver (Z3 [23]), for the simplification of some recurrences with a max operator.

We selected a set of benchmarks that exhibit different common parallel patterns, briefly described in Table 1, together with the definition of a set of resources that help understand the overall behavior of the parallelization. Table 2 shows some results of the experiments that we have performed with our prototype implementation. Column **Bench** shows the main predicates analyzed for each benchmark. Set operations (intersect, union and diff), as well as the programs append_all, dyade and add_mat, are Prolog versions of the benchmarks analyzed in [16], which is the closest related work we are aware of. Column **Res** indicates the name of each of the resources inferred for each benchmark: *sequential resolution steps* (**SCost**), *parallel resolution steps* assuming an unbounded number of processors (**PCost**), and *maximum number of processes executing in parallel* (**SThreads**). The latter gives an indication of the maximum parallelism that can potentially be exploited. We are considering a resolution step as the overhead of spawning a new thread. Column **Bound Inferred** shows the upper bounds obtained for each of the resources indicated in Column **Res**. While in the experiments both upper and lower bounds were inferred, for the sake of brevity, we only show upper-bound functions. Column **BigO** shows the complexity order, in big O notation, corresponding to each resource. For all the benchmarks in Table 2 we obtain the exact complexity orders. We also obtain the same complexity order as in [16] for the Prolog versions of the benchmarks taken from that work. Finally, Column $\mathbf{T_A(ms)}$ shows the analysis times in milliseconds. The results show that most of the benchmarks have different asymptotic behavior in the sequential and parallel execution models. In particular, for fib(x), the analysis infers an exponential upper bound for sequential execution steps, and a linear upper bound for parallel execution steps. As mentioned before, this is an upper bound for an ideal case, assuming an unbounded number of processors. Nevertheless, such upper-bound information is useful for understanding how the cost behavior evolves in architectures with different levels of parallelism. In addition, this *dual* cost measure can be combined together with a bound on the number of processors in order to obtain a general asymptotic upper bound (see for example Brent's Theorem [12], which is also mentioned in [16]). The program map_add1(1) exhibits a different behavior: both sequential and parallel upper bounds are linear. This happens because we are considering *resolution steps*, i.e., we are counting each head unification produced from an initial call

Table 2. Resource usage inferred for independent and-parallel programs.

Bench	Res	Bound Inferred	BigO	T_A(ms)
map_add1(x)	SCost	$2 \cdot l_x + 1$	$\mathcal{O}(l_x)$	31.17
	PCost	$2 \cdot l_x + 1$	$\mathcal{O}(l_x)$	
	SThreads	l_x	$\mathcal{O}(l_x)$	
fib(x)	SCost	$F(i_x) + L(i_x) - 1$	$\mathcal{O}(2^{i_x})$	127.81
	PCost	$2 \cdot i_x + 1$	$\mathcal{O}(i_x)$	
	SThreads	$F(i_x) + L(i_x) - 1$	$\mathcal{O}(2^{i_x})$	
mmatrix(m_1, n_1, m_2, n_2)	SCost	$i_{n_2} \cdot i_{m_2} \cdot i_{m_1} + 2 \cdot i_{m_2} \cdot i_{m_1} + 2 \cdot i_{m_1} + 1$	$\mathcal{O}(i_{n_2} \cdot i_{m_2} \cdot i_{m_1})$	194.45
	PCost	$i_{n_2} + 2 \cdot i_{m_2} + 2 \cdot i_{m_1} + 1$	$\mathcal{O}(i_{n_1} + i_{m_1} + i_{m_2})$	
	SThreads	$i_{m_2} \cdot i_{m_1} + i_{m_1}$	$\mathcal{O}(i_{m_2} \cdot i_{m_1})$	
blur(m, n)	SCost	$2 \cdot i_m \cdot i_n + 2 \cdot i_n + 1$	$\mathcal{O}(i_m \cdot i_n)$	126.63
	PCost	$2 \cdot i_m + 2 \cdot i_n + 1$	$\mathcal{O}(i_m + i_n)$	
	SThreads	i_n	$\mathcal{O}(i_n)$	
add_mat(m, n)	SCost	$i_m \cdot i_n + 2 \cdot i_n + 1$	$\mathcal{O}(i_m \cdot i_n)$	128.93
	PCost	$i_m + 2 \cdot i_n + 1$	$\mathcal{O}(i_m + i_n)$	
	SThreads	i_n	$\mathcal{O}(i_n)$	
intersect(a, b)	SCost	$l_a \cdot l_b + 3 \cdot l_a + 3$	$\mathcal{O}(l_a \cdot l_b)$	233.14
	PCost	$l_b + 3 \cdot l_a + 3$	$\mathcal{O}(l_a + l_b)$	
	SThreads	l_a	$\mathcal{O}(l_a)$	
union(a, b)	SCost	$l_a \cdot l_b + 3 \cdot l_a + 3$	$\mathcal{O}(l_a \cdot l_b)$	218.31
	PCost	$2 \cdot l_b + 3 \cdot l_a + 3$	$\mathcal{O}(l_a + l_b)$	
	SThreads	l_a	$\mathcal{O}(l_a)$	
diff(a, b)	SCost	$l_a \cdot l_b + 3 \cdot l_a + 3$	$\mathcal{O}(l_a \cdot l_b)$	232.55
	PCost	$l_b + 3 \cdot l_a + 3$	$\mathcal{O}(l_a + l_b)$	
	SThreads	l_a	$\mathcal{O}(l_a)$	
dyade(a, b)	SCost	$l_a \cdot l_b + 2 \cdot l_a + 1$	$\mathcal{O}(l_a \cdot l_b)$	82.71
	PCost	$l_b + 2 \cdot l_a + 1$	$\mathcal{O}(l_a + l_b)$	
	SThreads	l_a	$\mathcal{O}(l_a)$	
dyade_map(l, m)	SCost	$i_{max(m)} \cdot l_m \cdot l_l + 2 \cdot l_m \cdot l_l + 2 \cdot l_m + 1$	$\mathcal{O}(i_{max(m)} \cdot l_m \cdot l_l)$	177.91
	PCost	$i_{max(m)} + 2 \cdot l_m + 2 \cdot l_l + 1$	$\mathcal{O}(i_{max(m)} + l_m + l_l)$	
	SThreads	$l_l \cdot l_m + l_l$	$\mathcal{O}(l_m \cdot l_l)$	
append_all(l, m)	SCost	$l_l \cdot l_m + 2 \cdot l_m + 1$	$\mathcal{O}(l_l \cdot l_m)$	81.97
	PCost	$l_l + 2 \cdot l_m + 1$	$\mathcal{O}(l_l + l_m)$	
	SThreads	l_m	$\mathcal{O}(l_m)$	

$F(n)$, $L(n)$ represent the nth. element of the Fibonacci sequence and the nth. Lucas number, respectively.
l_n, i_n represent the size of n in terms of the metrics *length* and *int*, respectively.

map_add1(l). Even under the parallel execution model, we have a chain of head unifications whose length depends linearly on the length of the input list. It follows from the results of this particular case that this simple, non-associative parallelization will not be useful for improving the number of resolution steps performed in parallel.

Another useful information inferred in our experiments is the maximum number of processes that can be executed in parallel, represented by the resource named **SThreads**. We can see that for most of our examples the analysis obtains a linear upper bound for this resource, in terms of the size of some of the inputs. For example, the execution of intersect(a,b) (parallel set intersection) will create *at most* l_a processes, where l_a represents the length of the list a. For other examples, the analysis shows a quadratic upper bound (as in mmatrix), or even exponential bounds (as in fib). The information about upper bounds

Table 3. Resource usage inferred for a bounded number of processors.

Bench	Bound Inferred	BigO	T_A(ms)
map_add1(x)	$2 \cdot \lceil \frac{l_x}{p} \rceil + 1$	$\mathcal{O}(\lceil \frac{l_x}{p} \rceil)$	54.36
blur(m, n)	$2 \cdot \lceil \frac{i_n}{p} \rceil \cdot i_m + 2 \cdot \lceil \frac{i_n}{p} \rceil + 1$	$\mathcal{O}(\lceil \frac{i_n}{p} \rceil \cdot i_m)$	205.97
add_mat(m, n)	$\lceil \frac{i_n}{p} \rceil \cdot i_m + 2 \cdot \lceil \frac{i_n}{p} \rceil + 1$	$\mathcal{O}(\lceil \frac{i_n}{p} \rceil \cdot i_m)$	185.89
intersect(a,b)	$\lceil \frac{l_a}{p} \rceil \cdot l_b + 2 \cdot \lceil \frac{l_a}{p} \rceil + l_a + 2$	$\mathcal{O}(\lceil \frac{l_a}{p} \rceil \cdot l_b)$	330.47
union(a,b)	$\lceil \frac{l_a}{p} \rceil \cdot l_b + 2 \cdot \lceil \frac{l_a}{p} \rceil + l_a + l_b + 2$	$\mathcal{O}(\lceil \frac{l_a}{p} \rceil \cdot l_b)$	311.3
diff(a,b)	$\lceil \frac{l_a}{p} \rceil \cdot l_b + 2 \cdot \lceil \frac{l_a}{p} \rceil + l_a + 2$	$\mathcal{O}(\lceil \frac{l_a}{p} \rceil \cdot l_b)$	339.01
dyade(a,b)	$\lceil \frac{l_a}{p} \rceil \cdot l_b + 2 \cdot \lceil \frac{l_a}{p} \rceil + 1$	$\mathcal{O}(\lceil \frac{l_a}{p} \rceil \cdot l_b)$	120.93
append_all(l,m)	$\lceil \frac{l_m}{p} \rceil \cdot l_l + 2 \cdot \lceil \frac{l_m}{p} \rceil + 1$	$\mathcal{O}(\lceil \frac{l_m}{p} \rceil \cdot l_l)$	117.8

p is defined as the minimum between the number of processors and SThreads.

on the maximum level of parallelism required by a program is useful for understanding its scalability in different parallel architectures, or for optimizing the number of processors that a particular call will use, depending on the size of the input data.

Finally, the results of our experiments considering a bounded number of processors are shown in Table 3.

6   Related Work

Our approach is an extension of an existing cost analysis framework for sequential logic programs [9,11,20], which extends the classical cost analysis techniques based on setting up and solving recurrence relations, pioneered by [29], with solutions for relations involving max and min functions. The framework handles characteristics such as backtracking, multiple solutions (i.e., non-determinism), failure, and inference of both upper and lower bounds including non-polynomial bounds. These features are inherited by our approach, and are absent from other approaches to parallel cost analysis in the literature.

The most closely-related work to our approach is [16], which describes an automatic analysis for deriving bounds on the worst-case evaluation cost of first order functional programs. The analysis derives bounds under an abstract *dual* cost model based on two measures: *work* and *depth*, which over-approximate the sequential and parallel evaluation cost of programs, respectively, considering an unlimited number of processors. Such an abstract cost model was introduced by [6] to formally analyze parallel programs. The work is based on type judgments annotated with a cost metric, which generate a set of inequalities which are then solved by linear programming techniques. Their analysis is only able to infer multivariate resource polynomial bounds, while non-polynomial bounds are left as future work. In [15] the authors propose an automatic analysis based on the *work* and *depth* model, for a simple imperative language with explicit parallel loops.

There are other approaches to cost analysis of parallel and distributed systems, based on different models of computation than the independent and-parallel model in our work. In [3] the authors present a static analysis which is able to infer upper bounds on the maximum number of *active* (i.e., not finished nor suspended) processes running in parallel, and the total number of processes created for imperative *async-finish* parallel programs. The approach described in [1] uses recurrence (cost) relations to derive upper bounds on the cost of concurrent object-oriented programs, with shared-memory communication and future variables. They address concurrent execution for loops with semi-controlled scheduling, i.e., with no arbitrary interleavings. In [4] the authors address the cost of parallel execution of object-oriented distributed programs. The approach is to identify the synchronization points in the program, use serial cost analysis of the blocks between these points, and then, exploiting the techniques mentioned, construct a graph structure to capture the possible parallel execution of the program. The path of maximal cost is then computed. The allocation of tasks to processors (called "locations") is part of the program in these works, and thus, although independent and-parallel programs could be modeled in this computation style, it is not directly comparable to our more abstract model of parallelism.

Solving, or safely bounding recurrence relations with `max` and `min` functions has been addressed mainly for recurrences derived from divide-and-conquer algorithms [5,17,28]. In [2] the authors present solutions for Cost Relation Systems by obtaining upper bounds for both the number of nodes and the cost added in each node in the derived evaluation tree. These bounds are then combined in order to obtain a closed-form upper-bound expression. This closed form possibly contains maximization operations to express upper bounds for a set of subexpressions. However, each cost relation is defined as a summatory of costs, while in our approach, in addition to summations, we also consider other operations for aggregating the costs, including `max` operators. The presence of these operators often produces recurrence relations where the recursive calls are under the scope of such a `max` operator, for which we present a method to obtain a closed-form bound. This class of recurrences are not handled by most of the current computer algebra systems, as the authors in [2] mention.

7   Conclusions

We have presented a novel, general, and flexible analysis framework that can be instantiated for estimating the resource usage of parallel logic programs, for a wide range of resources, platforms, and execution models. To the best of our knowledge, this is the first approach to the cost analysis of *parallel logic programs*. Such estimations include both lower and upper bounds, given as functions on input data sizes. In addition, our analysis also infers other information which is useful for improving the exploitation and assessing the potential and actual parallelism of a program. We have also developed a method for solving the cost relations that arise in this particular type of analysis, which involve the *max* function. Finally, we have developed a prototype implementation of our general framework, instantiated it for the analysis of logic programs with Independent And-Parallelism, and performed an experimental evaluation, obtaining encouraging results w.r.t. accuracy and efficiency.

References

1. Albert, E., Arenas, P., Genaim, S., Gómez-Zamalloa, M., Puebla, G.: Cost analysis of concurrent OO programs. In: Yang, H. (ed.) APLAS 2011. LNCS, vol. 7078, pp. 238–254. Springer, Heidelberg (2011). https://doi.org/10.1007/978-3-642-25318-8_19
2. Albert, E., Arenas, P., Genaim, S., Puebla, G.: Closed-form upper bounds in static cost analysis. J. Autom. Reason. **46**(2), 161–203 (2011)
3. Albert, E., Arenas, P., Genaim, S., Zanardini, D.: Task-level analysis for a language with async-finish parallelism. In: Proceedings of LCTES 2011, pp. 21–30. ACM Press (2011)
4. Albert, E., Correas, J., Johnsen, E., Pu, K., Román-Díez, G.: Parallel cost analysis. ACM Trans. Comput. Logic **19**(4), 1–37 (2018)
5. Alonso, L., Reingold, E., Schott, R.: Multidimensional divide-and-conquer maximin recurrences. SIAM J. Discret. Math. **8**(3), 428–447 (1995)
6. Blelloch, G.E., Greiner, J.: A provable time and space efficient implementation of NESL. In: ACM International Conference on Functional Programming, pp. 213–225, May 1996
7. Debray, S.K., Lin, N.W.: Cost analysis of logic programs. ACM TOPLAS **15**(5), 826–875 (1993)
8. Debray, S.K., Lin, N.W., Hermenegildo, M.V.: Task granularity analysis in logic programs. In: Proceedings of the PLDI 1990, pp. 174–188. ACM, June 1990
9. Debray, S.K., Lopez-Garcia, P., Hermenegildo, M.V., Lin, N.W.: Lower bound cost estimation for logic programs. In: ILPS 1997, pp. 291–305. MIT Press (1997)
10. Gupta, G., Pontelli, E., Ali, K., Carlsson, M., Hermenegildo, M.V.: Parallel execution of prolog programs: a survey. ACM TOPLAS **23**(4), 472–602 (2001)
11. Haemmerlé, R., López-García, P., Liqat, U., Klemen, M., Gallagher, J.P., Hermenegildo, M.V.: A transformational approach to parametric accumulated-cost static profiling. In: Kiselyov, O., King, A. (eds.) FLOPS 2016. LNCS, vol. 9613, pp. 163–180. Springer, Cham (2016). https://doi.org/10.1007/978-3-319-29604-3_11
12. Harper, R.: Practical Foundations for Programming Languages, 2 edn. Cambridge University Press (2016). https://doi.org/10.1017/CBO9781316576892
13. Hermenegildo, M., Puebla, G., Bueno, F., Garcia, P.L.: Integrated program debugging, verification, and optimization using abstract interpretation (and the Ciao system preprocessor). Sci. Comput. Program. **58**(1–2), 115–140 (2005)
14. Hermenegildo, M., Rossi, F.: Strict And non-strict independent and-parallelism in logic programs: correctness, efficiency, and compile-time conditions. J. Log. Program. **22**(1), 1–45 (1995)
15. Hoefler, T., Kwasniewski, G.: Automatic complexity analysis of explicitly parallel programs. In: 26th ACM Symposium on Parallelism in Algorithms and Architectures, SPAA 2014, pp. 226–235 (2014)
16. Hoffmann, J., Shao, Z.: Automatic static cost analysis for parallel programs. In: Vitek, J. (ed.) ESOP 2015. LNCS, vol. 9032, pp. 132–157. Springer, Heidelberg (2015). https://doi.org/10.1007/978-3-662-46669-8_6

17. Hwang, H., Tsai, T.H.: An asymptotic theory for recurrence relations based on minimization and maximization. Theoret. Comput. Sci. **290**(3), 1475–1501 (2003)
18. Klemen, M., Lopez-Garcia, P., Gallagher, J., Morales, J., Hermenegildo, M.V.: Towards a general framework for static cost analysis of parallel logic programs. Technical report CLIP-1/2019.0, The CLIP Lab, IMDEA Software Institute and T.U. Madrid, July 2019. http://arxiv.org/abs/1907.13272
19. Lopez-Garcia, P., Darmawan, L., Bueno, F.: A framework for verification and debugging of resource usage properties. In: Technical Communications of ICLP. LIPIcs, vol. 7, pp. 104–113. Schloss Dagstuhl, July 2010
20. Lopez-Garcia, P., Darmawan, L., Klemen, M., Liqat, U., Bueno, F., Hermenegildo, M.V.: Interval-based resource usage verification by translation into Horn clauses and an application to energy consumption. TPLP **18**, 167–223 (2018)
21. Lopez-Garcia, P., Klemen, M., Liqat, U., Hermenegildo, M.V.: A general framework for static profiling of parametric resource usage. TPLP **16**(5–6), 849–865 (2016)
22. Méndez-Lojo, M., Navas, J., Hermenegildo, M.V.: A flexible, (C)LP-based approach to the analysis of object-oriented programs. In: King, A. (ed.) LOPSTR 2007. LNCS, vol. 4915, pp. 154–168. Springer, Heidelberg (2008). https://doi.org/10.1007/978-3-540-78769-3_11
23. de Moura, L., Bjørner, N.: Z3: an efficient SMT solver. In: Ramakrishnan, C.R., Rehof, J. (eds.) TACAS 2008. LNCS, vol. 4963, pp. 337–340. Springer, Heidelberg (2008). https://doi.org/10.1007/978-3-540-78800-3_24
24. Navas, J., Mera, E., López-García, P., Hermenegildo, M.V.: User-definable resource bounds analysis for logic programs. In: Dahl, V., Niemelä, I. (eds.) ICLP 2007. LNCS, vol. 4670, pp. 348–363. Springer, Heidelberg (2007). https://doi.org/10.1007/978-3-540-74610-2_24
25. Rosendahl, M.: Automatic complexity analysis. In: Proceedings of FPCA 1989, pp. 144–156. ACM Press (1989)
26. Serrano, A., Lopez-Garcia, P., Hermenegildo, M.V.: Resource usage analysis of logic programs via abstract interpretation using sized types. TPLP **14**(4–5), 739–754 (2014). ICLP 2014 Special Issue
27. Shen, K., Hermenegildo, M.: High-level characteristics of or- and Independent and-parallelism in Prolog. Int. J. Parallel Prog. **24**(5), 433–478 (1996). https://doi.org/10.1007/BF02583023
28. Wang, B.F.: Tight bounds on the solutions of multidimensional divide-and-conquer maximin recurrences. Theoret. Comput. Sci. **242**(1), 377–401 (2000)
29. Wegbreit, B.: Mechanical program analysis. Comm. ACM **18**(9), 528–539 (1975)

Incremental Analysis of Logic Programs with Assertions and Open Predicates

Isabel Garcia-Contreras[1,2](✉) ⓘ, Jose F. Morales[1] ⓘ,
and Manuel V. Hermenegildo[1,2] ⓘ

[1] IMDEA Software Institute, Madrid, Spain
{isabel.garcia,josef.morales,manuel.hermenegildo}@imdea.org
[2] Universidad Politécnica de Madrid (UPM), Madrid, Spain

Abstract. *Generic* components are a further abstraction over the concept of modules, introducing dependencies on other (not necessarily available) components implementing specified interfaces. They have become a key concept in large and complex software applications. Despite undeniable advantages, generic code is also *anti-modular*. Precise analysis (e.g., for detecting bugs or optimizing code) requires such code to be instantiated with concrete implementations, potentially leading to expensive combinatorial explosion. In this paper we claim that *incremental*, whole program analysis can be very beneficial in this context, and alleviate the anti-modularity nature of generic code. We propose a simple Horn-clause encoding of generic programs, using *open* predicates and assertions, and we introduce a new *incremental, multivariant* analysis algorithm that reacts incrementally not only to changes in program clauses, but also to *changes in the assertions*, upon which large parts of the analysis graph may depend. We also discuss the application of the proposed techniques in a number of practical use cases. In addition, as a realistic case study, we apply the proposed techniques in the analysis of the LPdoc documentation system. We argue that the proposed traits are a convenient and elegant abstraction for modular generic programming, and that our preliminary results support our thesis that the new incrementality-related features added to the analysis bring promising advantages in this context.

Keywords: Incremental static analysis · Verification · Assertions · Generic code · Specifications · Abstract interpretation · Horn clauses · Logic programs

1 Introduction

When developing large, real-life programs it is important to ensure application reliability and coding convenience. An important component in order to achieve

Research partially funded by MINECO TIN2015-67522-C3-1-R *TRACES* project, FPU grant 16/04811, and the Madrid P2018/TCS-4339 *BLOQUES-CM* program. We are also grateful to the anonymous reviewers for their useful comments.

ⓒ Springer Nature Switzerland AG 2020
M. Gabbrielli (Ed.): LOPSTR 2019, LNCS 12042, pp. 36–56, 2020.
https://doi.org/10.1007/978-3-030-45260-5_3

these goals is the availability in the language (and use in the development process) of some mechanism for expressing specifications, combined with a way of determining if the program meets the specifications or locate errors. This determination is usually achieved through some combination of compile-time analysis and verification with testing and run-time assertion checking [7,9,12,22,23].

Another relevant aspect when developing large programs is modularity. In modern coding it is rarely necessary to write everything from scratch. Modules and interfaces allow dividing the program in manageable and interchangeable parts. *Interfaces*, including specifications and dependencies, are needed in order to connect with external code (including specifications of such code), to connect self-developed code that is common with other applications, and as a placeholder for different implementations of a given functionality, in general referred to as *generic code.*

Despite undeniable advantages, generic code is known to be in fact *anti-modular*, and the analysis of generic code poses challenges: parts of the code are unavailable, and the interface specifications may not be descriptive enough to allow verifying the specifications for the whole application. Several approaches are possible in order to balance separate compilation with precise analysis and optimization. First, it is possible to analyze generic code by *trusting* its interface specifications, i.e., analyzing the client code and the interface implementations independently, flattening the analysis information inferred at the boundaries to that of the interface descriptions. This technique can reduce global analysis cost significantly at the expense of some loss of precision. Some of it may be regained by, e.g., enriching specifications manually for the application at hand. Alternatively, for a closed set of interface implementations, it may be desirable to analyze the whole application together with these implementations, keeping different specialized versions of the analysis across the interfaces. This allows getting the most precise information, specializations, compiler optimizations, etc., but at a higher cost.

Multivariant analyses maintain different information for each predicate call, depending on the caller predicate and the sequence of calls to this call. For imperative programs this implies the notions of "context-" and "path-"sensitivity. We believe that this information is specially beneficial when dealing with generic code, both for precision of the analysis results and for efficiency of the algorithm. Thus, our starting point is a (whole program) analysis that is multivariant. To treat generic code we propose a simple Horn-clause encoding, using *open* predicates and assertions, and introduce a novel extension for logic programming (*traits*) that is translated using open predicates. This abstraction addresses typical use cases of generic code in a more elegant and analysis-friendly way than the traditional alternative in LP of using *multifile* predicates. Then, we introduce a new, multivariant analysis algorithm that, in addition to supporting and taking advantage of assertions during analysis, *reacts incrementally to changes* not only in the program clauses but also *in the assertions*, upon which large parts of the analysis graph may depend, while also *supporting natively open predicates*. Generic code offers many opportunities for the application of this new analysis technique. We study a number of use cases, including editing a client (of an interface), while keeping the interface unchanged (e.g., analyzing a program reusing the analysis of a –family of– libraries) and keeping the client code unchanged, but editing the interface implementation(s) (e.g., modifying one implementation of an interface). In addition, we provide experimental results in a realistic case study: the analysis of the LPdoc documentation system and its multiple backends for generating documentation in different formats. Related work is discussed in Sect. 7.

2   Background

Logic Programs. A *definite Logic Program*, or *program*, is a finite sequence of *Horn clauses* (*clauses* for short). A *clause* is of the form $H\text{:-}B_1, \ldots, B_n$ where H, the *head*, is an atom, and $B_1, \ldots, B_n$ is the *body*, a possibly empty finite conjunction of atoms. Atoms are also called *literals*. An *atom* is of the form $p(V_1, \ldots, V_n)$, where p is a symbol of arity n. It is *normalized* if the $V_1, \ldots, V_n$ are all distinct variables. Normalized atoms are also called *predicate descriptor*s. Each maximal set of clauses in the program with the same descriptor as head (modulo variable renaming) defines a *predicate* (or *procedure*). p/n refers to a predicate p of arity n. Body literals can be predicate descriptors, which represent *calls* to the corresponding predicates, or *built-ins*. A *built-in* is a predefined relation for some background theory. Note that built-ins are not necessarily normalized. In the examples we may use non-normalized programs. We denote with *vars*(A) the set of variables that appear in the atom A.

   For presentation purposes, the heads of the clauses of each predicate in the program will be referred to with a unique subscript attached to their predicate name (the clause number), and the literals of their bodies with dual subscript (clause number, body position), e.g., $P_k\text{:-}P_{k,1}, \ldots P_{k,n_k}$. The clause may also be referred to as clause k of predicate P. For example, for the predicate app/3:

```
1   app(X,Y,Z):- X=[],    Y=Z.
2   app(X,Y,Z):- X=[U|V], Z=[U|W], app(V,Y,W).
```

app/3$_1$ denotes the head of the first clause of app/3, app/3$_{2,1}$ denotes the first literal of the second clause of app/3, i.e., the unification X=[U|V].

Assertions. Assertions allow stating conditions on the state (current substitution) that hold or must hold at certain points of program execution. We use for concreteness a subset of the syntax of the **pred** assertions of [12,21], which allow describing sets of *preconditions* and *conditional postconditions* on the state for a given predicate. These assertions are instrumental for many purposes, e.g., expressing the results of analysis, providing specifications, and documenting [9,12,22]. A **pred** assertion is of the form:

$$\text{:- }\textbf{pred }\textit{Head }\text{[: }\textit{Pre}\text{] [=> }\textit{Post}\text{].}$$

where *Head* is a predicate descriptor that denotes the predicate that the assertion applies to, and *Pre* and *Post* are conjunctions of *property literals*, i.e., literals corresponding to predicates meeting certain conditions which make them amenable to checking, such as being decidable for any input [21]. *Pre* expresses properties that hold when *Head* is called, namely, at least one *Pre* must hold for each call to *Head*. *Post* states properties that hold if *Head* is called in a state compatible with *Pre* and the call succeeds. Both *Pre* and *Post* can be empty conjunctions (meaning true), and in that case they can be omitted.

Example 1. The following assertions describe different behaviors of an implementation of a hashing function `dgst`: (1) states that, when called with argument `Word` a string and `N` a variable, then, if it succeeds, `N` will be a number, (2) states that calls for which `Word` is a string and `N` is an integer are allowed, i.e., it can be used to check if `N` is the hash of `Word`.

```
1  :- pred dgst(Word,N) : (string(Word), var(N)) => num(N).   % (1)
2  :- pred dgst(Word,N) : (string(Word), int(N)).             % (2)
3  dgst(Word,N) :-
4  % implementation of the hashing function
```

Definition 1 (Meaning of a Set of Assertions for a Predicate). *Given a predicate represented by a normalized atom Head, and a corresponding set of assertions $\{a_1 \ldots a_n\}$, with $a_i = $ ":- **pred** Head : Pre_i => $Post_i$." the set of assertion conditions for Head is $\{C_0, C_1, \ldots, C_n\}$, with:*

$$C_i = \begin{cases} \mathtt{calls}(Head, \bigvee_{j=1}^{n} Pre_j) & i = 0 \\ \mathtt{success}(Head, Pre_i, Post_i) & i = 1..n \end{cases}$$

where $\mathtt{calls}(Head, Pre)$[1] states conditions on all concrete calls to the predicate described by *Head*, and $\mathtt{success}(Head, Pre_j, Post_j)$ describes conditions on the success substitutions produced by calls to *Head* if Pre_j is satisfied.

3 An Approach to Modular Generic Programming: *Traits*

In this section we present a simple approach to modular generic programming for logic programs without static typing. To that end we introduce the concept of *open* predicates. Then we show how they can be used to deal with generic code, by proposing a simple syntactic extension for logic programs for writing and using generic code (*traits*) and its translation to plain clauses.

Open vs. Closed Predicates. We consider a simple module system for logic programming where predicates are distributed in modules (each predicate symbol belongs to a particular module) and where module dependencies are explicit in the program [2]. An interesting property, specially for program analysis, is

---

[1] We denote the calling conditions with `calls` (plural) for historic reasons, and to avoid confusion with the higher order predicate in Prolog `call/2`.

that we can distinguish between *open* and *closed* predicates.[2] Closed predicates within a module are those whose complete definition is available in the module. In contrast, the definition of open predicates (traditionally declared as `multifile` in many Prolog systems) can be can be scattered across different modules, and thus not known until all the application modules are linked (note that programs still use the closed world assumption). Despite its flexibility, open predicates are "anti-modular" (in a similar way to typeclasses in Haskell).

Open as "multifile." The following example shows an implementation of a generic password-checking algorithm in Prolog:

```
1  :- multifile dgst/3.
2
3  check_passwd(User) :-
4      get_line(Plain),                     % Read plain text password
5      passwd(User,Hasher,Digest,Salt),     % Consult password database
6      append(Plain,Salt,Salted),           % Append salt
7      dgst(Hasher,Salted,Digest).          % Compute and check digest
```

The code above is generic w.r.t. the selected hashing algorithm (`Hasher`). Note that there is no explicit dependency between `check_passwd/1` and the different hashing algorithms. The special *multifile* predicate `dgst/3` acts as an *interface* between implementations of hashing algorithms and `check_passwd/1`. While this type of encoding is widely used in practice, the use of multifile predicates is semantically obscure and error-prone. Instead we propose *traits* as a syntactic extension that captures the essential mechanisms necessary for writing generic code.[3]

Traits. A *trait* is defined as a collection of predicate specifications (as predicate assertions). For example:

```
1  :- trait hasher { :- pred dgst(Str, Digest) : string(Str) => int(Digest). }.
```

defines a trait `hasher`, which specifies a predicate `dgst/2`, which must be called with an instantiated string, and obtains an integer in `Digest`.

As a minimalistic syntactic extension, we introduce a new head and literal notation $(X \text{ as } T).p(A_1, \ldots, A_n)$, which represents the predicate p for X implementing trait T. Basically, this is equivalent to $p(X, A_1, \ldots, A_n)$, where X is used to select the trait implementation. In literals, X is annotated with a trait, which can be different for each call due to dynamic typing and multiple trait implementations for the same data. When X (the implementation) is unknown

---

[2] For space reasons we only consider *static* predicates and modules. Predicates whose definition may change during execution, or modules that are dynamically loaded/unloaded at run time can also be dealt with, using various techniques, and in particular the incremental analysis proposed.

[3] In this paper we only focus on traits as interfaces. The actual design in Ciao supports default implementations, which makes them closer to traits in Rust.

at compile-time, this is equivalent to dynamic dispatch. The `check_passwd/1` predicate using the trait above is:

```
1  check_passwd(User) :-
2      get_line(Plain),
3      passwd(User,Hasher,Digest,Salt),
4      append(Plain,Salt,Salted),
5      (Hasher as hasher).dgst(Salted,Digest).
```

The following translation rules convert code using traits to plain predicates. Note that we rely on the underlying module system to add module qualification to function and trait (predicate) symbols. Calls to trait predicates are done through the interface (open) predicate, which also carries the predicate assertions declared in the trait definition:

```
1  % open predicates and assertions for each p/n in the trait
2  :- multifile 'T.p'/(n + 1).
3  :- pred 'T.p'(X, A_1,...,A_n) : ... => ... .
4  % call to p/n for X implementing T
5  ... :- ..., 'T.p'(X, A_1,...,A_n), ... % (X as T).p(A_1,...,A_n)
```

A trait *implementation* is a collection of predicates that implements a given trait, indexed by a specified functor associated with that implementation. E.g.:

```
1  :- impl(hasher, xor8/0).
2  (xor8 as hasher).dgst(Str, Digest) :- xor8_dgst(Xs, 0, Digest).
3
4  xor8_dgst([], D, D).
5  xor8_dgst([X|Xs], D0, D) :- D1 is D0 # X, xor8_dgst(Xs, D1, D).
```

declares that `xor8` implements a `hasher`. In this case `xor8` is an atom, but trait syntax allows arbitrary functors. The implementation for the `dgst/2` predicate is provided by `(xor8 as hasher).dgst(Str, Digest)`.

The translation rules to plain predicates are as follows:

```
1  % the implementation is a closed predicate (head renamed)
2  '<f/k as T>.p'(f(...), A_1,...,A_n) :- ... % (f(...) as T).p(A_1,...,A_n)
3
4  % bridge from interface (open predicate) to the implementation
5  'T.p'(X, A_1,...,A_n) :- X=f(...), '<f/k as T>.p'(X, A_1,...,A_n).
```

Adding new implementations is simple:

```
1  :- impl(hasher, sha256/0).
2  (sha256 as hasher).dgst(Str, Digest) :- ...
```

This approach still preserves some interesting modular features: trait names can be local to a module (and exported as other predicate/function symbols), and trait implementations (e.g., `sha256/0`) are just function symbols, which can also be made local to modules in the underlying module system.

4 Goal-Dependent Abstract Interpretation

We recall some basic concepts of abstract interpretation of logic programs.

Program Analysis with Abstract Interpretation. Our approach is based on *abstract interpretation* [4], a technique in which the execution of the program is simulated (over-approximated) on an *abstract domain* (D_α) which is simpler than the actual, *concrete domain* (D). Although not strictly required, we assume that D_α has a lattice structure with meet ($\sqcap$), join ($\sqcup$), and less than ($\sqsubseteq$) operators. Abstract values and sets of concrete values are related via a pair of monotonic mappings $\langle \alpha, \gamma \rangle$: *abstraction* $\alpha : D \to D_\alpha$, and *concretization* $\gamma : D_\alpha \to D$, which form a Galois connection. A description (or abstract value) $d \in D_\alpha$ *approximates* a concrete value $c \in D$ if $\alpha(c) \sqsubseteq d$ where $\sqsubseteq$ is the partial ordering on D_α.

Concrete Semantics. In out context, running a program consists of making a *query*. Executing (answering) a query is determining for which substitutions (answers) the query is a logical consequence of the program if any. A *query* is a pair $\langle G, \theta \rangle$ with G an atom and θ a substitution over the variables of G. For concreteness, we focus on top-down, left-to-right SLD-resolution. We base our semantics on the well-known notion of generalized AND trees [1]. The concrete semantics of a program P for a given set of queries $\mathcal{Q}$, $\llbracket P \rrbracket_{\mathcal{Q}}$, is the set of generalized AND trees that results from the execution of the queries in $\mathcal{Q}$ for P. Each node $\langle G, \theta^c, \theta^s \rangle$ in the tree represents a call to a predicate G (an atom), with the substitution (state) for that call, θ^c, and the success substitution θ^s (answer). The *calling_context*$(G, P, \mathcal{Q})$ of a predicate given by the predicate descriptor G defined in P for a set of queries $\mathcal{Q}$ is the set $\{\theta^c \mid \langle G', \theta'^c, \theta'^s \rangle \in T \ \forall \ T \in \llbracket P \rrbracket_{\mathcal{Q}} \wedge \exists \sigma, \sigma(G') = G \wedge \sigma(\theta'^c) = \theta^c\}$, where σ is a *renaming* substitution. I.e., a substitution that replaces each variable in the term with distinct, fresh variables. We denote by *answers*$(P, \mathcal{Q})$ the set of success substitutions computed by P for queries $\mathcal{Q}$.

Graphs and Paths. We denote by $G = (V, E)$ a finite *directed graph* (henceforward called simply a graph) where V is a set of nodes and $E \subseteq V \times V$ is an edge relation, denoted with $u \to v$. A *path* P is a sequence of edges $(e_1, \ldots, e_n)$ and each $e_i = (x_i, y_i)$ is such that $x_1 = u$, $y_n = v$, and for all $1 \leq i \leq n - 1$ we have $y_i = x_{i+1}$, we also denote paths with $u \rightsquigarrow v \in G$. We use $n \in P$ and $e \in P$ to denote, respectively, that a node n and an edge e appear in P.

4.1 Goal-Dependent Program Analysis

We perform goal-dependent abstract interpretation, whose result is an abstraction of the generalized AND tree semantics. This technique derives an analysis result from a program P, an abstract domain D_α, and a set of initial abstract queries $\mathcal{Q} = \{\langle A_i, \lambda^c_i \rangle\}$, where A_i is a normalized atom, and $\lambda^c_i \in D_\alpha$. An *analysis result* encodes an abstraction of the nodes of the generalized AND trees derived from all the queries $\langle G, \theta \rangle$ s.t. $\langle G, \lambda \rangle \in \mathcal{Q} \wedge \theta \in \gamma(\lambda)$.

Analysis Graphs. We use graphs to overapproximate all possible executions of a program given an initial query. Each node in the graph is identified by a pair (P, λ) with P a predicate descriptor and $\lambda \in D_\alpha$, an element of the abstract domain, representing the possibly infinite set of calls encountered. The analysis result defines a mapping function $ans : Pred \times D_\alpha \rightarrow D_\alpha$, denoted with $\langle P, \lambda^c \rangle \mapsto \lambda^s$ which over-approximates the answer to that abstract predicate call. It is interpreted as "*calls to predicate P with calling pattern λ^c have the answer pattern λ^s*" with $\lambda^c, \lambda^s \in D_\alpha$. The analysis graph is *multivariant*. Thus, it may contain a number of nodes for the same predicate capturing different call situations, for different contexts or different paths. As usual, $\bot$ denotes the abstract description such that $\gamma(\bot) = \emptyset$. A call mapped to $\bot$ ($\langle P, \lambda^c \rangle \mapsto \bot$) indicates that calls to predicate P with any description $\theta \in \gamma(\lambda^c)$ either fail or loop, i.e., they never succeed.

Edges in the graph represent a call dependency among two predicates. An edge is of the form $\langle P, \lambda_1 \rangle_{c,l} \xrightarrow[\lambda^r]{\lambda^p} \langle Q, \lambda_2 \rangle$, and is interpreted as "*calling predicate P with substitution λ_1 causes predicate Q (literal l of clause c) to be called with substitution λ_2*". Substitutions λ^p and λ^r are, respectively, the call and return context of the call. These values are introduced to ease the presentation of the algorithm, but they can be reconstructed with the identifiers of the nodes (i.e., predicate descriptor and abstract value) and the source code of the program. For simplicity, we may write $\bullet$ to omit the values when they are not relevant to the discussion. Note that the edges that represent the calls to a literal l and the following one $l+1$, $\langle P, \lambda_1 \rangle_{c,l} \xrightarrow[\bullet]{\lambda} \langle Q, \lambda_2 \rangle$ the result at the return of the literal is the call substitution of the next literal: $\langle P, \lambda_1 \rangle_{c,l+1} \xrightarrow[\bullet]{\lambda} \langle Q', \lambda_2' \rangle$. Figure 1 shows a possible analysis graph for a program that checks/computes the parity of a message. The following operations defined over an analysis result g allow us to inspect and manipulate analysis results to partially reuse or invalidate.

Graph Consultation Operations

$$\langle P, \lambda^c \rangle \in g : \text{there is a node in the call graph of } g \text{ with key } \langle P, \lambda^c \rangle.$$
$$\langle P, \lambda^c \rangle \mapsto \lambda^s \in g : \text{there is a node in } g \text{ with key } \langle P, \lambda^c \rangle \text{ and the answer}$$
$$\text{mapped to that call is } \lambda^s.$$
$$\langle P, \lambda^c \rangle_{c,l} \xrightarrow[\lambda^r]{\lambda^p} \langle Q, \lambda^{c'} \rangle \in g : \text{there are two nodes } (k = \langle P, \lambda^c \rangle \text{ and } k' = \langle Q, \lambda^{c'} \rangle) \text{ in } g$$
$$\text{and there is an annotated edge from } k \text{ to } k'.$$

Graph Update Operations

$\mathsf{add}(g, \{k_{c,l} \xrightarrow[\lambda^p]{\lambda^r} k'\})$: adds an edge from node k to k' (creating node k' if necessary) annotated with λ^p and λ^r for clause c and literal l.

$\mathsf{del}(g, \{k_{c,l} \xrightarrow[\bullet]{\bullet} k'\})$: removes the edge from node k to k' annotated for clause c and literal l.

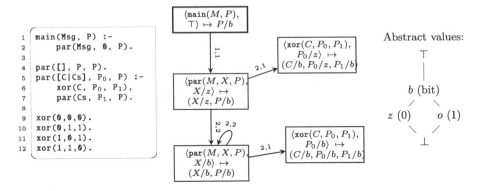

```
1   main(Msg, P) :-
2       par(Msg, 0, P).
3
4   par([], P, P).
5   par([C|Cs], P0, P) :-
6       xor(C, P0, P1),
7       par(Cs, P1, P).
8
9   xor(0,0,0).
10  xor(0,1,1).
11  xor(1,0,1).
12  xor(1,1,0).
```

Fig. 1. A program that implements a parity function and a possible analysis result for domain D_α.

5   Incremental Analysis of Programs with Assertions

Baseline Incremental Analysis Algorithm. We want to take advantage of the existing algorithms to design an analyzer that is sensible to changes in assertions also. We will use as a black box the combination of the algorithms to analyze incrementally a logic program [13], and the analyzer that is guided by assertions [8]. We will refer to it with the function $\mathscr{A}' =$ INCANALYZE$(P, \mathscr{Q}_\alpha, \Delta_{Cls}, \mathscr{A})$, where the inputs are:

- A program $P = (Cls, As)$ with Cls a set of clauses and As a set of assertions.
- A set of changes Δ_{Cls} in the form of added or deleted clauses.
- A set $\mathscr{Q}_\alpha$ of initial queries that will be the starting point of the analyzer.
- A previous result of the algorithm $\mathscr{A}$ which is a well formed analysis graph.

The algorithm produces a new $\mathscr{A}'$ that correctly abstracts the behavior of the program reacting incrementally to changes in the clauses. It is parametric on the abstract domain D_α, given by implementing (1) the domain-dependent operations $\sqsubseteq, \sqcap, \sqcup, \texttt{Aproj}(\lambda, Vs)$, which restricts the abstract substitution to the set of variables Vs, $\texttt{Aextend}(P_{k,n}, \lambda^p, \lambda^s)$ propagates the success abstract substitution over the variables of $P_{k,n}$, λ^s to the substitution of the variables of the clause λ^p, $\texttt{Acall}(\lambda, P, P_k)$ performs the abstract unification of predicate descriptor P with the head of the clause P_k, including in the new substitution abstract values for the variables in the body of clause P_k, and $\texttt{Ageneralize}(\lambda, \{\lambda_i\})$ performs the generalization of a set of abstract substitutions $\{\lambda_i\}$ and λ; and (2) *transfer functions* for program built-ins, that abstract the meaning of the basic operations of the language. Functions $\texttt{apply\_call}(P, \lambda^c, As)$ and $\texttt{apply\_succ}(P, \lambda^c, \lambda^s, As)$ abstract the meaning of the assertion conditions (respectively calls and success conditions). Further details of these functions are described in Appendix A and in [8]. These operations are assumed to be monotonic and to correctly overapproximate their correspondent concrete version.

Operation of the Algorithm. The algorithm is centered around processing events. It starts by queueing a *newcall* event for each of the call patterns that need to be recomputed. This triggers $\mathbf{process}(newcall(\langle P, \lambda^c \rangle))$, which processes the clauses of predicate P. For each of them an *arc* event is added for the first literal. The initial_guess function returns a guess of the λ^s to $\langle P, \lambda^c \rangle$. If possible, it reuses the results in $\mathscr{A}$, otherwise returns $\bot$. Procedure reanalyze_updated propagates the information of new computed answers across the analysis graph by creating *arc* events with the literals from which the analysis has to be restarted. $\mathbf{process}(arc(\langle P_k, \lambda^c \rangle_{l,c} \xrightarrow{\lambda^p} \langle P, \lambda^c \rangle))$ performs a single step of the left-to-right traversal of a clause body. First, the meaning of the assertion conditions of P is computed by apply_call. Then, if the literal $P_{k,i}$ is a *built-in*, its transfer function is computed; otherwise, an edge is added to $\mathscr{A}$ and the λ^s is looked up (a process that includes creating a *newcall* event for $\langle P, \lambda^c \rangle$ if the answer is not in the analysis graph). The answer is combined with the description λ^p from the literal immediately before $P_{k,i}$ to obtain the description (return) for the literal after $P_{k,i}$. This is used either to generate an *arc* event to process the next literal, or to update the answer of the predicate in insert_answer_info. This function combines the new answer with the semantics of any applicable assertions (in apply_succ), and the previous answers, propagating the new answer if needed.

Procedure add_clauses adds *arc* events for each of the new clauses. These trigger the analysis of each clause and the later update of $\mathscr{A}$ by using the edges in the graph.

The delete_clauses function selects the information to be kept in order to obtain the most precise semantics of the program, by removing all information which is potentially inaccurate (Fig. 2).

Definition 2 (Correct analysis). *Given a program P and initial concrete queries $\mathscr{Q}$, an analysis result $\mathscr{A}$ is correct for $P, \mathscr{Q}$ if:*

- *$\forall G, \theta^c \in calling\_context(G, P, \mathscr{Q}) \; \exists \langle G, \lambda^c \rangle \mapsto \lambda^s \in \mathscr{A} \; s.t. \; \theta^c \in \gamma(\lambda^c)$.*
- *$\forall \langle G, \lambda^c \rangle \mapsto \lambda^s \in \mathscr{A}, \forall \theta^c \in \gamma(\lambda^c) \; if \; \theta^s \in answers(P, \{\langle G, \theta^c \rangle\}) \; then \; \theta^s \in \gamma(\lambda^s)$.*

From [13] and [8] we have that:

Theorem 1 (Correctness of IncAnalyze from scratch). *Let P be a program, and $\mathscr{Q}_\alpha$ a set of abstract queries. Let $\mathscr{Q}$ be the set of concrete queries: $\mathscr{Q} = \{\langle G, \theta \rangle \mid \theta \in \gamma(\lambda) \wedge \langle G, \lambda \rangle \in \mathscr{Q}_\alpha\}$. The analysis result $\mathscr{A} = \text{INCANALYZE}(P, \mathscr{Q}_\alpha, \emptyset, \emptyset)$ for P with $\mathscr{Q}_\alpha$ is correct for $P, \mathscr{Q}$.*

Additionally, assertions ensure that certain executions never occur. This information is included in the analysis in the following way (adapted from [8]):

Theorem 2 (Applied assertion conditions). *Let P be a program, and $\mathscr{Q}_\alpha$ a set of abstract queries. Let $\mathscr{A} = \text{INCANALYZE}(P, \mathscr{Q}_\alpha, \emptyset, \emptyset)$.*

(a). The call assertion conditions cover all the inferred states:
$$\forall \langle P, \lambda^c \rangle \mapsto \lambda^s \in \mathscr{A}.\lambda^c \sqsubseteq \text{apply\_call}(P, \top, As).$$

29: **procedure** process($newcall(\langle P, \lambda^c \rangle)$)

INCANALYZE($P, \mathcal{Q}_\alpha, \Delta_{Cls}, \mathscr{A}$)

30: **for all** P_k :- $P_{k,1}, \ldots, P_{k,n_k} \in Cls$ **do**

1: **for all** $\langle P, \lambda^c \rangle \in \mathcal{Q}_\alpha$ **do**

31:    $\lambda^p :=$ Acall(λ^c, P, P_k)

2:    add_event($newcall(\langle P, \lambda^c \rangle)$)

32:    $\lambda^c{}_0 :=$ Aproj($\lambda^p, vars(P_{k,1})$)

3: **if** $\Delta_{Cls} = (Dels, Adds) \neq (\emptyset, \emptyset)$ **then**

33:    $Calls := \{\lambda \mid \langle P, \lambda \rangle \in \mathscr{A}\}$

4:    delete_clauses($Dels$)

34:    $\lambda^c{}_1 :=$ Ageneralize($\lambda^c{}_0, Calls$)

5:    add_clauses($Adds$)

35:    add_event($arc(\langle P, \lambda^c \rangle_{k,1} \xrightarrow{\lambda^p} \langle P_{k,1}, \lambda^c{}_1 \rangle)$)

6: analysis_loop()

36: $\lambda^s :=$ initial_guess($\langle P, \lambda^c \rangle$)

7: **procedure** analysis_loop()

37: **if** $\lambda^s \neq \perp$ **then**

8:   **while** $E :=$ next_event() **do**

38:    reanalyze_updated($\langle P, \lambda^c \rangle$)

9:     process(E)

39: upd($\mathscr{A}, \langle P, \lambda^c \rangle \hookleftarrow \lambda^s$)

10: **procedure** add_clauses(Cls)

40: **procedure**   process($arc(\langle P, \lambda^c{}_0 \rangle_{k,i} \xrightarrow{\lambda^p}$

11: **for all** P_k :- $P_{k,1}, \ldots, P_{k,n_k} \in Cls$ **do**

$\langle Q, \lambda^c{}_1 \rangle)$)

12:   **for all** $\langle P, \lambda^c \rangle \mapsto \lambda^s \in \mathscr{A}$ **do**

41: $\lambda^a :=$ apply_call($Q, \lambda^c{}_1, As$)

13:    $\lambda^p :=$ Acall(λ^c, P, P_k)

42: **if** $P_{k,i}$ is a *built-in* **then**

14:    $\lambda^c{}_1 :=$ Aproj($\lambda^p, vars(P_{k,1})$)

43:    $\lambda^s{}_0 := f^\alpha(P_{k,i}, \lambda^a)$ ▷ Apply transfer

15:    add_event($arc(\langle P, \lambda^c \rangle_{k,1}$ function

$\xrightarrow{\lambda^p}$ 44: **else** $\lambda^s{}_0 :=$ lookup_answer($\langle Q, \lambda^a \rangle$)

$\langle P_{k,1}, \lambda^c{}_1 \rangle)$)

45: $\lambda^r :=$ Aextend($\lambda^p, \lambda^s{}_0$)

16: **procedure** delete_clauses(Cls)

46: upd($\mathscr{A}, \langle P, \lambda^c{}_0 \rangle_{k,i} \xrightarrow{\lambda^p}{}_{\lambda^r} \langle Q, \lambda^a \rangle$)

17: $Calls := \{\langle P, \lambda^c \rangle | \langle P, \lambda^c \rangle \in \mathscr{A}, (P_k$:- $\ldots) \in$

47: **if** $\lambda^r \neq \perp$ and $i \neq n_k$ **then**

$Cls\}$

48:    $\lambda^c{}_2 :=$ Aproj($\lambda^r, vars(P_{k,i+1})$)

18: $Ns := \{N \in \mathscr{A} | N \rightsquigarrow C \in \mathscr{A}, C \in Calls\}$

49:    add_event($arc(\langle H, \lambda^c{}_0 \rangle_{k,i+1} \xrightarrow{\lambda^r} \langle B, \lambda^c{}_2 \rangle)$)

19: del($\mathscr{A}, Ns$)

50: **else if** $\lambda^r \neq \perp$ and $i = n_k$ **then**

20: **function** lookup_answer($\langle P, \lambda^c \rangle$)

51:    $\lambda^s :=$ Aproj($\lambda^r, vars(P_k)$)

21: **if** $\langle P, \lambda^c \rangle \mapsto \lambda^s \in \mathscr{A}$ **then**

52:    insert_answer_info($\langle P, \lambda^c{}_0 \rangle, \lambda^s$)

22:   **return** λ^s

53: **procedure** insert_answer_info($\langle P, \lambda^c \rangle, \lambda^s$)

23: **else**

54: $\lambda^a :=$ apply_succ($P, \lambda^c, \lambda^s, As$)

24:   add_event($newcall(\langle P, \lambda^a \rangle)$)

55: **if** $\langle P, \lambda^c \rangle \mapsto \lambda^s{}_0 \in \mathscr{A}$ **then**

25:   **return** $\perp$

56:    $\lambda^s{}_1 :=$ Ageneralize($\lambda^a, \{\lambda^s{}_0\}$)

26: **procedure** reanalyze_updated($\langle P, \lambda^c \rangle$)

57: **else** $\lambda^s{}_1 := \perp$

27: **for all** $E := \langle Q, \lambda^c{}_0 \rangle_{k,i} \xrightarrow{\lambda^p} \langle P, \lambda^c \rangle \in \mathscr{A}$ **do**

58: **if** $\lambda^s{}_0 \neq \lambda^s{}_1$ **then**

28:   add_event($arc(E)$)

59:    upd($\mathscr{A}, \langle P, \lambda^c \rangle \hookleftarrow \lambda^s{}_1$)

60:    reanalyze_updated($\langle P, \lambda^c \rangle$)

Fig. 2. The generic context-sensitive, incremental fixpoint algorithm using (not changing) assertion conditions.

6: **function** PREPROCESS($Cls, As, \mathscr{A}$)

1: **function** IAwAC($(Cls, As), \Delta_{Cls}, \Delta_{As}, \mathcal{Q}_\alpha, \mathscr{A}$) 7: $R := \emptyset$

2: $R :=$ PREPROCESS($Cls, As, \mathscr{A}$)

8: **for each** $P \in Cls$ **do**

3: $\mathscr{A}' :=$ INCANALYZE($(Cls, As), \mathcal{Q}_\alpha \cup$ 9:   **if** $\Delta_{As}[P] \neq \emptyset$ **then**

R, Δ_{Cls}) 10: $R := R \cup$ update_calls_pred($P, As, \mathscr{A}$)

4: del ($\mathscr{A}', \{E \mid E \in \mathscr{A}' \wedge Q \not\rightarrow E \wedge Q \in \mathcal{Q}_\alpha\}$) 11: R := R $\cup$

5: **return** $\mathscr{A}'$ update_success_pred($P, As, \mathscr{A}$)

12:   **return** R

Fig. 3. High-level view of the proposed algorithm

(b). *The inferred abstract success states are covered by the success assertion conditions:* $\forall \langle P, \lambda^c \rangle \mapsto \lambda^s \in \mathscr{A}. \lambda^s \sqsubseteq$ apply_succ($P, \lambda^c, \top, As$)

We introduce a new proposition about the algorithm that will be of use later.

Proposition 1 (Correctness starting from a partial analysis). *Let P be a program, $\mathcal{Q}_\alpha$ a set of abstract queries, and $\mathcal{A}_0$ any analysis graph. Let $\mathcal{A} = \text{INCANALYZE}(P, \mathcal{Q}_\alpha, \Delta_{Cls}, \mathcal{A}_0)$. $\mathcal{A}$ is correct for P and a query $Q \in \mathcal{Q}_\alpha$ if for any node $N \in \mathcal{A}_0$ such that there is a path $Q \rightsquigarrow N$ in $[\![P]\!]_{\gamma(Q)}$, $N \in \mathcal{Q}_\alpha$.*

Proof. This follows from the creation of a *newcall* event for each of the queries, which will trigger the recomputation and later update of all the nodes of the analysis graph that are potentially under the fixpoint.

Note that here we are not assuming that $\mathcal{A}_0$ is the (correct) output of a previous analysis, it can be any partial analysis (below the fixpoint).

5.1   The Incremental Analyzer of Programs with Assertions

We propose to inspect and update the analysis graph to guarantee that a call to INCANALYZE produces results that are correct and precise. We call this new analyzer IAwAC, short for INCANALYZE-w/ASSRTCHANGES (Fig. 3). The PRE-PROCESS phase consists in inspecting all the literals affected by the changes in the assertions, collecting which call patterns need to be reanalyzed by the incremental analysis, i.e., it may be different from the set of initial queries $\mathcal{Q}$ originally requested by the user. In addition, after the analysis phase, the unreachable abstract calls that were safe to reuse may not be reachable anymore, so they need to be removed from the analysis result.

Detecting the Affected Parts in the Analysis Results. The steps to find potential changes in the analysis results when assertions are changed are detailed in Fig. 4 with procedures `update_calls_pred` and `update_successes_pred`. The goal is to identify which edges and nodes of the analysis graph are not precise or correct. Since assertions may affect the inferred call or the inferred success of predicates, we have split the procedure into two functions. However, the overall idea is to obtain the current substitution, which encodes the semantics of the assertions in the previous version of the program, and the abstract substitution that would have been inferred if no assertions were present. Then functions `apply_call` and `apply_success` obtain the meaning of the new assertions. Finally, we call a general procedure to treat the potential changes, `treat_change` (see Fig. 5). Specifically, in the case of `call` conditions, we review all the program points from which it is called, by checking the incoming edges of the nodes of that predicate. For each node we project the substitution of the clause (λ^p) to the variables of the literal to obtain the call patterns if no assertions would be specified (line 4). We then detect if the call pattern produced by the new meaning of the assertions already existed in the analysis graph to reuse its result, and, last, we call the procedure to treat the change. In the case of `success` conditions we obtain the substitution including the new meaning of the assertion by joining the return substitution at the last literal of each of the clauses of the predicate, previously projected to the variables of the head (line 16).

Amending the Analysis Results. The procedure `treat_change` (Fig. 5), given an edge that points to a literal whose success potentially changed, updates the

```
 1: function update_calls_pred(P, As, 𝒜)              11: function update_successes_pred(P, As, 𝒜)
 2:    Q := ∅                                          12:    Q := ∅
 3:    for each ⟨P′,λ⟩_{c,l} --λᵖ/•--> ⟨P,λᶜ_{old}⟩ ∈ 𝒜 do   13:    for each ⟨P,λᶜ⟩ ↦ λˢ ∈ 𝒜 do
 4:       λᶜ := σ(Aproj(λᵖ, vars(P′_{c,l})) s.t. σ(P′_{c,l}) =   14:       λ := ⊥
          P                                            15:       for each ⟨P,λᶜ⟩_{c,last} --•/λʳ--> ⟨Q,λ⟩ ∈ 𝒜 do
 5:       λᶜ_{new} := apply_call(P, λᶜ, As)            16:          λ := λ ⊔ apply_succ(P, λᶜ, Aproj(λʳ, vars(P_c)), As)
 6:       if ∃⟨P′,λᶜ_{new}⟩ ↦ λˢ ∈ 𝒜 then
 7:          λˢ′ := λˢ                                  17:       for each E = N_{•,•} --•/•--> ⟨P,λᶜ⟩ ∈ 𝒜 do
 8:       else λˢ′ := ⊥                                 18:          Q := Q ∪ treat_change (E, λ, 𝒜)
 9:       Q := Q ∪ treat_change(⟨P′,λ⟩_{c,l} --λᵖ/λʳ--> 19:    return Q
          ⟨P,λᶜ_{new}⟩,λˢ′, 𝒜)
10:    return Q
```

Fig. 4. Changes in assertions (split by assertion conditions)

analysis result, and decides which predicates and call patterns need to be recomputed. After updating the annotation of the edge (line 4), we study how the abstract substitution changed. If the new substitution ($\lambda^{r'}$) is more general than the previous one (λ^r), this means that the previous assertions where pruning more concrete states than the new one, and, thus, this call pattern needs to be reanalyzed. Else, if $\lambda^r \not\sqsubseteq \lambda^{r'}$, i.e., the new abstract substitution is more concrete or incompatible, some parts of the analysis graph may not be accurate. Therefore, we have to eliminate from the graph the literals that were affected by the change (i.e., the literals following the program point with a change) and all the dependent code from this call pattern. Also, the analysis has to be restarted from the original entry points that were affected by the deletion of these potentially imprecise nodes. In the last case (line 3) the old and the new substitutions are the same, and, thus, nothing needs to be reanalyzed (the $\emptyset$ is returned).

```
 1: function treat_change(⟨P,λ⟩_{c,l} --λᵖ/λʳ--> ⟨Q,λᶜ⟩, λˢ, 𝒜)

 2:    λ^{r′} := Aextend(λᵖ, λˢ)                    ▷ Obtain new abstraction at literal return
 3:    if λʳ = λ^{r′} then return ∅
 4:    del(𝒜, ⟨P,λ⟩_{c,l} --•/•--> •)
 5:    add(𝒜, ⟨P,λ⟩_{c,l} --λᵖ/λ^{r′}--> ⟨Q,λᶜ⟩)      ▷ Update the analysis graph

 6:    if λʳ ⊏ λ^{r′} then return {⟨P,λ⟩}
 7:    else if λʳ ⋢ λ^{r′} then                     ▷ Analysis is potentially imprecise
 8:       Lits := {E | E = ⟨P,λ⟩_{c,i} ⟶ N ∈ 𝒜 ∧ i > l}
 9:       IN := {E | E ⤳ L ∈ 𝒜 ∧ L ∈ Lits}        ▷ Potentially imprecise nodes
10:       del(𝒜, IN)
11:       return IN
```

Fig. 5. Procedure to determine how the analysis result needs to be recomputed.

Correctness of the Algorithm

Proposition 2 (IAwAC from scratch). *Let P be a program, $\mathcal{Q}_\alpha$ a set of abstract queries. Let $\mathcal{Q}$ be the set of concrete queries: $\mathcal{Q} = \{\langle G, \theta \rangle \mid \theta \in \gamma(\lambda) \wedge \langle G, \lambda \rangle \in \mathcal{Q}_\alpha\}$. The analysis $\mathcal{A} = \mathrm{IAwAC}(P, \mathcal{Q}_\alpha, \emptyset, \emptyset, \emptyset)$ for P with $\mathcal{Q}_\alpha$ is correct for $P, \mathcal{Q}$.*

Proof. Since the preprocessing phase only modifies information that is already in the initial analysis and it is empty, correctness follows from Theorem 1.

In terms of precision, we want to ensure that the meaning of the new assertions is precisely included in the analysis result.

Proposition 3 (Precision after update_calls_pred). *Let Cls be a set of clauses, As be a set of assertions, and $\mathcal{A}$ any analysis graph. For any predicate G of Cls, let $\mathcal{A}'$ be the state of $\mathcal{A}$ after update_calls_pred$(G, As, \mathcal{A})$. Then, for any $\langle G, \lambda^c \rangle \mapsto \lambda^s \in \mathcal{A}'.\lambda^c \sqsubseteq$ apply_call$(G, \top, As)$.*

Proof. Given a predicate G, the function update_calls_pred looks at each edge that finishes in a node G, and obtains the new meaning of the conditions (line 5). Then, in line 4 of treat_change, the node is removed if it is different. Because apply_call is assumed to be monotonic, for any λ^c. apply_call$(G, \lambda^c, As) \sqsubseteq$ apply_call$(G, \top, As)$.

Proposition 4 (Precision after update_successes_pred). *Under the conditions of Proposition 3, for any predicate G of Cls, let $\mathcal{A}'$ be the state of $\mathcal{A}$ after update_successes_pred$(G, As, \mathcal{A})$. Then, for any $\langle G, \lambda^c \rangle \mapsto \lambda^s \in \mathcal{A}'.\lambda^s \sqsubseteq$ apply_succ$(G, \lambda^c, \top, As)$.*

Proof. Given a predicate G, the function update_successes_pred looks at the last literal of each clause of G, and obtains the new meaning of the conditions (line 16). Then, in line 4 of treat_change, the node is removed if it is different. Because apply_call is assumed to be monotonic, for any pair (λ^c, λ^s). apply_succ$(G, \lambda^c, \lambda^s, As) \sqsubseteq$ apply_call$(G, \lambda^c, \lambda^s, As)$.

As shown in Proposition 1, given any partial analysis result, we can ensure correctness of the reanalysis if we guarantee that all literals that need to be reanalyzed are included in $\mathcal{Q}_\alpha$. We want to show that the set Q of queries collected in treat_change is enough to guarantee the correctness of the result.

Proposition 5 (Queries collected in preprocess). *Let $P = (Cls, As_0)$ be a program, $\mathcal{Q}_\alpha$ a set of abstract queries. Let $\mathcal{Q}$ be the set of concrete queries: $\mathcal{Q} = \{\langle G, \theta \rangle \mid \theta \in \gamma(\lambda) \wedge \langle G, \lambda \rangle \in \mathcal{Q}_\alpha\}$. Let $\mathcal{A} = \mathrm{IAwAC}(P, \mathcal{Q}_\alpha, \emptyset, \emptyset, \emptyset)$ be the correct analysis for $P, \mathcal{Q}$. If P changes to $P' = (Cls, As)$, $\mathcal{Q}_\alpha' = \mathrm{PREPROCESS}(Cls, As, \mathcal{A})$ guarantees that $\mathcal{A}' = \mathrm{INCANALYZE}((Cls, As), \mathcal{Q}_\alpha', \emptyset, \mathcal{A})$ is correct for P' and $\mathcal{Q}$.*

Proof. We split the proof into two cases: (a) The assertions change only for one predicate: because $\mathscr{A}$ is correct, by Theorem 1, since $\mathscr{A}$ is an over-approximation of $[\![P]\!]_\mathscr{Q}$, and Proposition 1 is true.

(b) The assertions change for more than one predicate: after processing the first predicate $\mathscr{A}$ may not be correct, as `treat_change` removes nodes. However, every node that is removed is added to the set of queries. This means that the nodes that are unreachable when processing the following predicates were already stored before, and therefore, Proposition 1 also holds.

Theorem 3 collects all correctness and precision properties of the algorithm.

Theorem 3 (Correctness of IAwAC). *Let P_0 and $P = (Cls, As)$ be programs that differ in Δ_{Cls} and Δ_{As}, $\mathscr{Q}_\alpha$ be a set of abstract queries. Let $\mathscr{Q}$ be the set of concrete queries $\mathscr{Q} = \{\langle G, \theta \rangle \mid \theta \in \gamma(\lambda) \wedge \langle G, \lambda \rangle \in \mathscr{Q}_\alpha\}$. Given $\mathscr{A}_0 =$ IAwAC$(P_0, \mathscr{Q}_\alpha, \emptyset, \emptyset, \emptyset)$, and the analysis $\mathscr{A} = $ IAwAC$(P, \mathscr{Q}_\alpha, \Delta_{Cls}, \Delta_{As}, \mathscr{A}_0)$.*

(a). $\mathscr{A}$ is correct *or P and $\mathscr{Q}$.*
(b). $\forall \langle G, \lambda^c \rangle \mapsto \lambda^s \in \mathscr{A}.\lambda^c \sqsubseteq$ apply_call$(G, \top, As)$.
(c). $\forall \langle G, \lambda^c \rangle \mapsto \lambda^s \in \mathscr{A}. \ \lambda^s \sqsubseteq$ apply_succ$(G, \lambda^c, \top, As)$

Proof. (a) follows from Theorem 2 and Proposition 5. (b) and (c) follow from Lemma 2 and Propositions 3 and 4.

5.2   Use Cases

We show some examples of the algorithm. We assume that we analyze with a shape domain in which the properties in the assertions can be exactly represented.

Example 2 (Reusing a preanalyzed generic program). Consider a slightly modified version the program that checks a password as shown earlier, that only allows the user to write passwords with *lowercase* letters. Until we have a concrete implementation for the hasher we will not be able to analyze precisely this program. However, we can preanalyze it by using the information of the assertion of the trait to obtain the following simplified analysis graph:

```
1   :- trait hasher { :- pred dgst(Str, Digest)
2         : lowercase(Str) => int(Digest). }.
3
4   check_passwd(User) :-
5         get_line(Plain),
6         passwd(User,Hasher,Digest,Salt),
7         append(Plain,Salt,Salted),
8         (Hasher as hasher).dgst(Salted,Digest).
9
10  passwd(don,xor8,0x6d,"eNfwuBhtN9CUHxg==").
```

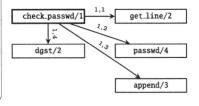

The node for `dgst/2` represents the call $\langle$dgst$(S, D), (S/$lowercase$, D/$num$)\rangle \mapsto (S/$lowercase$, D/$int$)$, in this case, D was inferred to be a *number* because of the success of `passwd/4`. If we add a very naive implementation that consists on counting the number of some letters in the password, reanalyzing will cause adding to the graph some new nodes, shown with a dashed line:

```
1  :- impl(hasher, naive/0).
2  (naive as hasher).dgst(Str, Digest) :-
3      naive_count(Xs, 0, Digest).
4
5  naive_count(L, D0, D) :-
6      count(L,'a',Na), D1 is D0 + Na*1,
7      count(L,'b',Nb), D2 is D1 + Nb*2,
8      count(L,'c',Nc), D3 is D2 + Nc*3,
```

We detect that none of the previous nodes need to be recomputed due to tracking dependencies for each literal. The analysis was performed by going directly to the program point of **dgst/2** and inspecting the new clause (that was generated automatically by the translation) that calls **naive_count/2**. By analyzing **naive_count/2** we obtain nodes $\langle$naive_count$(S,D), (S/$lowercase$, D/$num$)\rangle \mapsto (S/$lowercase$, D/$int$)$, and $\langle$count$(L,C,N), (S/$lowercase$, C/$char$)\rangle \mapsto (S/$lowercase$, C/$char$, N/$int$)$. As no information needs to be propagated because the head does not contain any of the variables of the call to digest, we are done, and we avoided reanalyzing any caller to **check_passwd/2**, if existed.

Example 3 (Weakening assertion properties). Consider the program and analysis result of Example 2. We realize that allowing the user to write a password only with lowercase letters is not very secure. We can change the assertion of the trait to allow any string as a valid password.

```
1  :- trait hasher { :- pred dgst(Str, Digest) : string(Str) => int(Digest). }.
```

When reanalyzing, node $\langle$dgst$(S,D), (S/$lowercase$, D/$num$)\rangle$ will disappear to become $\langle$dgst$(S,D), (S/$string$, D/$num$)\rangle$, and the same for **naive_count/3**. A new call pattern will appear for **count/3** $\langle$count$(L,C,N), (S/$string$, C/$char$)\rangle \mapsto (S/$string$, C/$char$, N/$int$)$, leading to the same result for **dgst/2**. I.e., we only had to partially analyze the library, instead of the whole program.

Table 1. Analysis time for LPdoc adding one backend at a time (time in seconds).

Domain	No backend	+ texinfo	+ man	+ html
reachability	1.7	2.1	3.4	3.9
reachability *inc*	1.7	1.2	1.0	1.6
gr	2.1	2.2	2.3	2.6
gr *inc*	2.1	1.4	0.9	1.8
def	6.0	7.1	7.8	9.7
def *inc*	6.0	2.2	1.3	3.5
sharing	27.2	28.1	24.2	28.5
sharing *inc*	27.2	3.9	1.4	5.1

6 Experiments

We have implemented the proposed analysis algorithm within the CiaoPP system [9] and performed some preliminary experiments to test the use case described in Example 2. Our test case is the LPdoc documentation generator tool [10,11], which takes a set of Prolog files with assertions and machine-readable comments and generates a reference manual from them. LPdoc consists of around 150 files, of mostly (Ciao) Prolog code,with assertions (most of which, when written, were only meant for documentation generation), as well as some auxiliary scripts in Lisp, JavaScript, bash, etc. The Prolog code analyzed is about 22 K lines. This is a tool in everyday use that generates for example all the manuals and web sites for the Ciao system (http://ciao-lang.org, http://ciao-lang.org/documentation.html) and as well as for all the different *bundles* developed internal or externally, processing around 20 K files and around 1M lines of Prolog and interfaces to another 1M lines of C and other miscellaneous code). The LPdoc code has also been adapted as the documentation generator for the XSB system [24].

LPdoc is specially relevant in our context because it includes a number of backends in order to generate the documentation in different formats such as texinfo, Unix man format, html, ascii, etc. The front end of the tool generates a documentation tree with all the content and formatting information and this is passed to one out of a number of these backends, which then does the actual, specialized generation in the corresponding typesetting language. We analyzed all the LPdoc code with a reachability domain, a groundness domain (gr), a domain tracking dependencies via propositional clauses [6] (def), and a sharing domain with cliques [19]. The experiment consisted in preanalyzing the tool with no backends and then adding incrementally the backends one by one. In Table 1 we show how much time it took to analyze in each setting, i.e., for the different domains and with the incremental algorithm or analyzing from scratch. The experiments were run on a MacBook Pro with an Intel Core i5 2.7 GHz processor, 8GB of RAM, and an SSD disk. These preliminary results support our hypothesis that the proposed incremental analysis brings performance advantages when dealing with these use cases of generic code.

7 Related Work

Languages like C++ require specializing all parametric polymorphic code (e.g., templates [25]) to monomorphic variants. While this is more restrictive than *runtime polymorphism* (variants must be statically known at compile time), it solves the analysis precision problem, but not without additional costs. First, it is known to be slow, as templates must be instantiated, reanalized, and recompiled for each compilation unit. Second, it produces many duplicates which must be removed later by the linker. Rust [15] takes a similar approach for *unboxed* types.

Runtime polymorphism or dynamic dispatch can be used in C++ (virtual methods), Rust (boxed traits), Go [5] (interfaces), or Haskell's [14] type classes.

However, in this case compilers and analyzers do not usually consider the particular instances, except when a single one can be deduced (e.g., in C++ devirtualization [18]).

Mora et al. [17] perform modular symbolic execution to prove that some (versions of) libraries are equivalent with respect to the same client. Chatterjee et al. [3] analyze libraries in the presence of callbacks incrementally for data dependence analysis. I.e., they preanalyze the libraries and when a client uses it reuses the analysis and adds incrementally possible calls made by the client. We argue that when using our Horn clause encoding, both high analysis precision and compiler optimizations can be achieved more generally by combining the incremental static global analysis that we have proposed with abstract specialization [20].

8   Conclusions

While logic programming can intrinsically handle generic programming, we have illustrated a number of problems that appear when handling generic code with the standard solutions provided by current (C)LP module systems, namely, using multifile predicates. We argue that the proposed traits are a convenient and elegant abstraction for modular generic programming, and that our preliminary results support the conclusion that the novel incremental analysis proposed brings promising analysis performance advantages for this type of code. Our encoding is very close to the underlying mechanisms used in other languages for implementing dynamic dispatch or run-time polymorphism (like Go's interfaces, Rust's traits, or a limited form of Haskell's type clases), so we believe that our techniques and results can be generalized to other languages. This also includes our proposed algorithm for incremental analysis with assertion changes, which can be applied to different languages through the standard technique of translation to Horn-clause representation [16]. Traits are also related to higher-order code (e.g., a "callable" trait with a single "call" method). We also claim that our work contributes to the specification and analysis of higher-order code.

A   Assertions

Assertions may not be exactly represented in the abstract domain used by the analyzer. We recall some definitions (adapted from [22]) which are instrumental to correctly approximate the properties of the assertions during the analysis (Fig. 6).

Definition 3 (Set of Calls for which a Property Formula Trivially Succeeds (Trivial Success Set)). *Given a conjunction L of property literals and the definitions for each of these properties in P, we define the trivial success set of L in P as:*

$$TS(L, P) = \{\theta | Var(L) \ s.t. \ \exists \theta' \in answers(P, \{\langle L, \theta \rangle\}), \theta \models \theta'\}$$

global flag: speed-up
1: **function** apply_call(P, λ^c)
2:    **if** $\exists \sigma, \lambda^t = \lambda^+_{TS(\sigma(Pre),P)}$ s.t. **calls**$(H, Pre) \in C, \sigma(H) = P$ **then**
3:       **if** speed-up **return** λ^t **else return** $\lambda^c \sqcap \lambda^t$
4:    **else return** λ^c
5: **function** apply_succ$(P, \lambda^c, \lambda^{so})$
6:    $app = \{\lambda \mid \exists \ \sigma, \mathbf{success}(H, Pre, Post) \in C, \sigma(H) = P,$
7:       $\lambda = \lambda^+_{TS(\sigma(Post),P)}, \lambda^-_{TS(\sigma(Pre),P)} \sqsupseteq \lambda^c\}$
8:    **if** $app \neq \emptyset$ **then**
9:       $\lambda^t := \sqcap app$
10:       **if** speed-up **return** λ^t **else return** $\lambda^t \sqcap \lambda^{so}$
11: secbeg **else return** λ^{so}

Fig. 6. Applying assertions.

where $\theta|Var(L)$ above denotes the projection of θ onto the variables of L, and $\models$ denotes that θ' is a more general constraint than θ (entailment). Intuitively, $TS(L, P)$ is the set of constraints θ for which the literal L succeeds without adding new constraints to θ (i.e., without constraining it further). For example, given the following program P:

```
1  list([]).
2  list([_|T]) :- list(T).
```

and $L = list(X)$, both $\theta_1 = \{X = [1, 2]\}$ and $\theta_2 = \{X = [1, A]\}$ are in the trivial success set of L in P, since calling $(X = [1, 2], list(X))$ returns $X = [1, 2]$ and calling $(X = [1, A], list(X))$ returns $X = [1, A]$. However, $\theta_3 = \{X = [1|\_]\}$ is not, since a call to $(X = [1|Y], list(X))$ will further constrain the term $[1|Y]$, returning $X = [1|Y], Y = []$. We define abstract counterparts for Definition 3:

Definition 4 (Abstract Trivial Success Subset of a Property Formula). *Under the same conditions of Definition 3, given an abstract domain D_α, $\lambda^-_{TS(L,P)} \in D_\alpha$ is an abstract trivial success subset of L in P iff $\gamma(\lambda^-_{TS(L,P)}) \subseteq TS(L, P)$.*

Definition 5 (Abstract Trivial Success Superset of a Property Formula). *Under the same conditions of Definition 4, an abstract constraint $\lambda^+_{TS(L,P)}$ is an abstract trivial success superset of L in P iff $\gamma(\lambda^+_{TS(L,P)}) \supseteq TS(L, P)$.*

I.e., $\lambda^-_{TS(L,P)}$ and $\lambda^+_{TS(L,P)}$ are, respectively, safe under- and over-approximations of $TS(L, P)$. These abstractions come useful when the properties expressed in the assertions cannot be represented exactly in the abstract domain.

References

1. Bruynooghe, M.: A practical framework for the abstract interpretation of logic programs. J. Logic Program. **10**, 91–124 (1991)

2. Cabeza, D., Hermenegildo, M.: A new module system for prolog. In: Lloyd, J., et al. (eds.) CL 2000. LNCS (LNAI), vol. 1861, pp. 131–148. Springer, Heidelberg (2000). https://doi.org/10.1007/3-540-44957-4_9

3. Chatterjee, K., Choudhary, B., Pavlogiannis, A.: Optimal Dyck reachability for data-dependence and alias analysis. PACMPL **2**(POPL), 1–30 (2018)

4. Cousot, P., Cousot, R.: Abstract interpretation: a unified lattice model for static analysis of programs by construction or approximation of fixpoints. In: Proceedings of POPL 1977, pp. 238–252. ACM Press (1977)

5. Donovan, A.A.A., Kernighan, B.W.: The Go Programming Language, Professional Computing. Addison-Wesley, Boston (2015)

6. Dumortier, V., Janssens, G., Simoens, W., García de la Banda, M.: Combining a definiteness and a freeness abstraction for CLP languages. In: Workshop on LP Synthesis and Transformation (1993)

7. Flanagan, C.: Hybrid type checking. In: 33rd ACM Symposium on Principles of Programming Languages (POPL 2006), pp. 245–256, January 2006

8. Garcia-Contreras, I., Morales, J.F., Hermenegildo, M.V.: Multivariant assertion-based guidance in abstract interpretation. In: Mesnard, F., Stuckey, P.J. (eds.) LOPSTR 2018. LNCS, vol. 11408, pp. 184–201. Springer, Cham (2019). https://doi.org/10.1007/978-3-030-13838-7_11

9. Hermenegildo, M., Puebla, G., Bueno, F., Lopez-Garcia, P.: Integrated program debugging, verification, and optimization using abstract interpretation (and The Ciao System Preprocessor). Sci. Comput. Program. 58(1–2), 115–140 (2005)

10. Hermenegildo, M.: A documentation generator for (C)LP systems. In: Lloyd, J., et al. (eds.) CL 2000. LNCS (LNAI), vol. 1861, pp. 1345–1361. Springer, Heidelberg (2000). https://doi.org/10.1007/3-540-44957-4_90

11. Hermenegildo, M.V., Morales, J.: The LPdoc documentation generator. Ref. Manual (v3.0). Technical report, July 2011. http://ciao-lang.org

12. Hermenegildo, M.V., Puebla, G., Bueno, F.: Using global analysis, partial specifications, and an extensible assertion language for program validation and debugging. In: Apt, K.R., Marek, V.W., Truszczynski, M., Warren, D.S. (eds.) The Logic Programming Paradigm, pp. 161–192. Springer, Heidelberg (1999). https://doi.org/10.1007/978-3-642-60085-2_7

13. Hermenegildo, M.V., Puebla, G., Marriott, K., Stuckey, P.: Incremental analysis of constraint logic programs. ACM TOPLAS **22**(2), 187–223 (2000)

14. Hudak, P., et al.: Report on the programming language Haskell. Haskell special issue. ACM SIGPLAN Not. **27**(5), 1–164 (1992)

15. Klabnik, S., Nichols, C.: The Rust Programming Language. No Starch Press, San Francisco (2018)

16. Méndez-Lojo, M., Navas, J., Hermenegildo, M.V.: A flexible, (C)LP-based approach to the analysis of object-oriented programs. In: King, A. (ed.) LOPSTR 2007. LNCS, vol. 4915, pp. 154–168. Springer, Heidelberg (2008). https://doi.org/10.1007/978-3-540-78769-3_11

17. Mora, F., Li, Y., Rubin, J., Chechik, M.: Client-specific equivalence checking. In: 33rd ACM/IEEE International Conference on Automated Software Engineering, pp. 441–451. ASE (2018)

18. Namolaru, M.: Devirtualization in GCC. In: Proceedings of the GCC Developers' Summit, pp. 125–133 (2006)

19. Navas, J., Bueno, F., Hermenegildo, M.: Efficient top-down set-sharing analysis using cliques. In: Van Hentenryck, P. (ed.) PADL 2006. LNCS, vol. 3819, pp. 183–198. Springer, Heidelberg (2005). https://doi.org/10.1007/11603023_13

20. Puebla, G., Albert, E., Hermenegildo, M.: Abstract interpretation with specialized definitions. In: Yi, K. (ed.) SAS 2006. LNCS, vol. 4134, pp. 107–126. Springer, Heidelberg (2006). https://doi.org/10.1007/11823230_8

21. Puebla, G., Bueno, F., Hermenegildo, M.: An assertion language for constraint logic programs. In: Deransart, P., Hermenegildo, M.V., Małuszynski, J. (eds.) Analysis and Visualization Tools for Constraint Programming. LNCS, vol. 1870, pp. 23–61. Springer, Heidelberg (2000). https://doi.org/10.1007/10722311_2

22. Puebla, G., Bueno, F., Hermenegildo, M.: Combined static and dynamic assertion-based debugging of constraint logic programs. In: Bossi, A. (ed.) LOPSTR 1999. LNCS, vol. 1817, pp. 273–292. Springer, Heidelberg (2000). https://doi.org/10.1007/10720327_16

23. Siek, J.G., Taha, W.: Gradual typing for functional languages. In: Scheme and Functional Programming Workshop, pp. 81–92 (2006)

24. Swift, T., Warren, D.: XSB: extending prolog with tabled logic programming. TPLP **12**(1–2), 157–187 (2012). https://doi.org/10.1017/S1471068411000500

25. Vandevoorde, D., Josuttis, N.M.: C++ Templates. Addison-Wesley Longman Publishing Co. Inc., Boston (2002)

Computing Abstract Distances in Logic Programs

Ignacio Casso[1,2]([envelope]) [ID], José F. Morales[1] [ID], Pedro López-García[1,3] [ID],
Roberto Giacobazzi[1,4] [ID], and Manuel V. Hermenegildo[1,2] [ID]

[1] IMDEA Software Institute, Madrid, Spain
{ignacio.decasso,josef.morales,pedro.lopez,manuel.hermenegildo}@imdea.org
[2] T. University of Madrid (UPM), Madrid, Spain
[3] Spanish Council for Scientific Research (CSIC), Madrid, Spain
[4] University of Verona, Verona, Italy

Abstract. Abstract interpretation is a well-established technique for performing static analyses of logic programs. However, choosing the abstract domain, widening, fixpoint, etc. that provides the best precision-cost trade-off remains an open problem. This is in a good part because of the challenges involved in measuring and comparing the precision of different analyses. We propose a new approach for measuring such precision, based on defining distances in abstract domains and extending them to distances between whole analyses of a given program, thus allowing comparing precision across different analyses. We survey and extend existing proposals for distances and metrics in lattices or abstract domains, and we propose metrics for some common domains used in logic program analysis, as well as extensions of those metrics to the space of whole program analyses. We implement those metrics within the CiaoPP framework and apply them to measure the precision of different analyses on both benchmarks and a realistic program.

Keywords: Abstract interpretation · Static analysis · Logic programming · Metrics · Distances · Complete lattices · Program semantics

1 Introduction

Many practical static analyzers for (Constraint) Logic Programming ((C)LP) are based on the theory of Abstract Interpretation [8]. The basic idea behind this technique is to interpret (i.e., execute) the program over a special abstract domain to obtain some abstract semantics of the program, which will over-approximate every possible execution in the standard (concrete) domain. This

Research partially funded by MINECO TIN2015-67522-C3-1-R *TRACES* project, and the Madrid P2018/TCS-4339 *BLOQUES-CM* program. We are also grateful to the anonymous reviewers for their useful comments.

M. Gabbrielli (Ed.): LOPSTR 2019, LNCS 12042, pp. 57–72, 2020.
https://doi.org/10.1007/978-3-030-45260-5_4

makes it possible to reason safely (but perhaps imprecisely) about the properties that hold for all such executions. As mentioned before, abstract interpretation has proved practical and effective for building static analysis tools, and in particular in the context of (C)LP [4,5,12,16,21,26,30,32,40]. Recently, these techniques have also been applied successfully to the analysis and verification of other programming paradigms by using (C)LP (Horn Clauses) as the intermediate representation for different compilation levels, ranging from source to bytecode or ISA [2,3,10,17,19,25,27,29,31,35].

When designing or choosing an abstract interpretation-based analysis, a crucial issue is the trade-off between cost and precision, and thus research in new abstract domains, widenings, fixpoints, etc., often requires studying this trade-off. However, while measuring analysis cost is typically relatively straightforward, having effective precision measures is much more involved. There have been a few proposals for this purpose, including, e.g., probabilistic abstract interpretation [13] and some measures in numeric domains [28,39],[1] but they have limitations and in practice most studies come up with ad-hoc measures for measuring precision. Furthermore, there have been no proposals for such measures in (C)LP domains.

We propose a new approach for measuring the precision of abstract interpretation-based analyses in (C)LP, based on defining *distances in abstract domains* and extending them to *distances between whole analyses of a given program*, which allow comparison of precision across different analyses. Our contributions can be summarized as follows: We survey and extend existing proposals for distances in lattices and abstract domains (Sect. 3). We then build on this theory and ideas to propose distances for common domains used in (C)LP analysis (Sect. 3.2). We also propose a principled methodology for comparing quantitatively the precision of different abstract interpretation-based analyses of a whole program (Sect. 4). This methodology is parametric on the distance in the underlying abstract domain and only relies in a unified representation of those analysis results as AND-OR trees. Thus, it can be used to measure the precision of new fixpoints, widenings, etc. within a given abstract interpretation framework, not requiring knowledge of its implementation. Finally, we also provide experimental evidence about the appropriateness of the proposed distances (Sect. 5).

2   Background and Notation

Lattices: A *partial order* on a set X is a binary relation $\sqsubseteq$ that is reflexive, transitive, and antisymmetric. The *greatest lower bound* or *meet* of a and b, denoted by $a \sqcap b$, is the greatest element in X that is still lower than both of them ($a \sqcap b \sqsubseteq a$, $a \sqcap b \sqsubseteq b$, ($c \sqsubseteq a \wedge c \sqsubseteq b \implies c \sqsubseteq a \sqcap b$)). If it exists, it is unique. The *least upper bound* or *join* of a and b, denoted by $a \sqcup b$, is

---

[1] Some of these attempts (and others) are further explained in the related work section (Sect. 6).

the smallest element in X that is still greater than both of them ($a \sqsubseteq a \sqcup b$, $b \sqsubseteq a \sqcup b$, ($a \sqsubseteq c \wedge b \sqsubseteq c \implies a \sqcup b \sqsubseteq c$)). If it exists, it is unique. A partially ordered set (poset) is a couple $(X, \sqsubseteq)$ such that the first element X is a set and the second one is a partial order relation on X. A *lattice* is a poset for which any two elements have a meet and a join. A lattice L is complete if, extending in the natural way the definition of supremum and infimum to subsets of L, every subset S of L has both a supremum $sup(S)$ and an infimum $inf(S)$. The maximum element of a complete lattice, $sup(L)$ is called *top* or $\top$, and the minimum, $inf(L)$ is called *bottom* or $\bot$.

Galois Connections: Let $(L_1, \sqsubseteq_1)$ and $(L_2, \sqsubseteq_2)$ be two posets. Let $f : L_1 \longrightarrow L_2$ and $g : L_2 \longrightarrow L_1$ be two applications such that:

$$\forall x \in L_1, y \in L_2 : f(x) \sqsubseteq_2 y \iff x \sqsubseteq_1 g(y)$$

Then the quadruple $\langle L_1, f, L_2, g \rangle$ is a *Galois connection*, written $L_1 \xrightarrow[f]{g} L_2$. If $f \circ g$ is the identity, then the quadruple is called a *Galois insertion*.

Abstract Interpretation and Abstract Domains: Abstract interpretation [8] is a well-known static analysis technique that allows computing sound over-approximations of the semantics of programs. The semantics of a program can be described in terms of the *concrete domain*, whose values in the case of (C)LP are typically sets of variable substitutions that may occur at runtime. The idea behind abstract interpretation is to interpret the program over a special abstract domain, whose values, called *abstract substitutions*, are finite representations of possibly infinite sets of actual substitutions in the concrete domain. We will denote the concrete domain as D, and the abstract domain as D_α. We will denote the functions that relate sets of concrete substitutions with abstract substitutions as the *abstraction* function $\alpha : D \longrightarrow D_\alpha$ and the *concretization* function $\gamma : D_\alpha \longrightarrow D$. The concrete domain is a complete lattice under the set inclusion order, and that order induces an ordering relation in the abstract domain herein represented by "$\sqsubseteq$." Under this relation the abstract domain is usually a complete lattice and $(D, \alpha, D_\alpha, \gamma)$ is a Galois insertion. The abstract domain is of finite height or alternatively it is equipped with a *widening operator*, which allows for skipping over infinite ascending chains during analysis to a greater fixpoint, achieving convergence in exchange for precision.

Metric: A metric on a set S is a function $d : S \times S \to \mathbb{R}$ satisfying:

- Non-negativity: $\qquad\qquad\qquad\qquad\qquad \forall x, y \in S, \; d(x, y) \geq 0.$
- Identity of indiscernibles: $\qquad\quad \forall x, y \in S, \; d(x, y) = 0 \iff x = y.$
- Symmetry: $\qquad\qquad\qquad\qquad\qquad \forall x, y \in S, \; d(x, y) = d(y, x).$
- Triangle inequality: $\qquad \forall x, y, z \in S, \; d(x, z) \leq d(x, y) + d(y, z).$

A set S in which a metric is defined is called a metric space. A pseudometric is a metric where two elements which are different are allowed to have distance

0. We call the left implication of the identity of indiscernibles, weak identity of indiscernibles. A well-known method to extend a metric $d : S \times S \longrightarrow \mathbb{R}$ to a distance in 2^S is using the Hausdorff distance, defined as:

$$d_H(A, B) = \max \left\{ \sup_{a \in A} \inf_{b \in B} d(a,b), \sup_{b \in B} \inf_{a \in A} d(a,b) \right\}$$

3 Distances in Abstract Domains

As anticipated in the introduction, our distances between abstract interpretation-based analyses of a program will be parameterized by a distance in the underlying abstract domain, which we assume to be a complete lattice. In this section we propose a few such distances for relevant logic programming abstract domains. But first we review and extend some of the concepts that arise when working with lattices or abstract domains as metric spaces.

3.1 Distances in Lattices and Abstract Domains

When defining a distance in a partially ordered set, it is necessary to consider the compatibility between the metric and the structure of the lattice. This relationship will suggest new properties that a metric in a lattice should satisfy. For example, a distance in a lattice should be *order-preserving*, that is, $\forall a, b, c \in D$ with $a \sqsubseteq b \sqsubseteq c$, then $d(a,b), d(b,c) \leq d(a,c)$. It is also reasonable to expect that it fulfills what we have called the diamond inequality, that is, $\forall a, b, c, d \in D$ with $c \sqcap d \sqsubseteq a \sqcap b$, $a \sqcup b \sqsubseteq c \sqcup d$, then $d(a,b) \leq d(c,d)$. But more importantly, this relationship will suggest insights for constructing such metrics.

One such insight is precisely defining a partial metric $d_\sqsubseteq$ only between elements which are related in the lattice, which is arguably easier, and to extend it later to a distance between arbitrary elements x, y, as a function of $d_\sqsubseteq(x, x \sqcap y)$, $d_\sqsubseteq(y, x \sqcap y)$, $d_\sqsubseteq(x, x \sqcup y)$, $d_\sqsubseteq(x, x \sqcup y)$ and $d_\sqsubseteq(x \sqcap y, x \sqcup y)$. Ramon et al. [38] show under which circumstances $d_\sqsubseteq(x, x \sqcup y) + d_\sqsubseteq(y, x \sqcup y)$ is a distance, that is, when $d_\sqsubseteq$ is order-preserving and fulfills $d_\sqsubseteq(x, x \sqcup y) + d_\sqsubseteq(y, x \sqcup y) \leq d_\sqsubseteq(x, x \sqcap y) + d_\sqsubseteq(y, x \sqcap y)$.

In particular, one could define a monotonic size $size : L \to \mathbb{R}$ in the lattice and define $d_\sqsubseteq(a, b)$ as $size(b) - size(a)$. Gratzer [18] shows that if the size fulfills $size(x) + size(y) = size(x \sqcap y) + size(x \sqcup y)$, then $d(x, y) = size(x \sqcup y) - size(x \sqcap y)$ is a metric. De Raedt [11] shows that $d(x, y) = size(x) + size(y) - 2 \cdot size(x \sqcup y)$ is a metric iff $size(x) + size(y) \leq size(x \sqcap y) + size(x \sqcup y)$, and an analogous result with $d(x, y) = size(x) + size(y) - 2 \cdot size(x \sqcup y)$ and $\geq$ instead of $\leq$. Note that the first distance is the equivalent of the *symmetric difference distance* in finite sets, with $\sqsubseteq$ instead of $\subseteq$ and *size* instead of the cardinal of a set. Similar distances for finite sets, such as the Jaccard distance, can be translated to lattices in the same way. Another approach to defining $d_\sqsubseteq$ that follows from the idea of using the lattice structure, is counting the steps between two elements (i.e., the number of edges between both elements in the Hasse diagram of the lattice). This was used by Logozzo [28].

When defining a distance not just in any lattice, but in an actual abstract domain (*abstract distance* from now on), it is also necessary to consider the relation of the abstract domain with the concrete domain (i.e., the Galois connection), and how an abstract distance is interpreted under that relation. In that sense, we can observe that a distance $d_{D_\alpha} : D_\alpha \times D_\alpha \to \mathbb{R}^+$ in an abstract domain will induce a distance $d_D^\alpha : D \times D \to \mathbb{R}^+$ in the concrete one, as $d_D^\alpha(A, B) = d_{D_\alpha}(\alpha(A), \alpha(B))$, and the other way around: a distance $d_D : D \times D \to \mathbb{R}^+$ in the concrete domain induces an abstract distance $d_{D_\alpha}^\gamma : D_\alpha \times D_\alpha \to \mathbb{R}^+$ in the abstract one, as $d_{D_\alpha}^\gamma(a, b) = d_D(\gamma(a), \gamma(b))$. Thus, an abstract distance can be interpreted as an abstraction of a distance in the concrete domain, or as a way to define a distance in it, and it is clear that it is when interpreted that way that an abstract distance makes most sense from a program semantics point of view.

It is straightforward to see (and we show in [6]) that these induced distances inherit most metric and order-related properties. In particular, if a distance d_D in the concrete domain is a metric, its abstraction d_{D_α} is a pseudo-metric in the abstract domain, and a full metric if the Galois connection between D and D_α is a Galois insertion. This allows us to define distances d_α in the abstract domain from distances d the concrete domain, as $d_\alpha(a, b) = d(\gamma(a), \gamma(b))$. This approach might seem of little applicability, due to the fact that concretizations will most likely be infinite and we still need metrics in the concrete domain. But in the case of logic programs, such metrics for Herbrand terms already exist (e.g., [23,36,38]), and in fact we show later a distance for the *regular types* domain that can be interpreted as an extension of this kind, of the distance proposed by Nienhuys-Cheng [36] for sets of terms.

Finally, recall that a metric in the Cartesian product of lattices can be easily derived from existing distances in each lattice, for example as the 2-norm or any other norm of the vector of distances component to component. This is relevant because many abstract domains, such as those that are combinations of two different abstract domains, or non-relational domains which provide an abstract value from a lattice for each variable in the substitution, are of such form (modulo equivalent abstract values, i.e., those with the same concretization). It is straightforward to see that in this case those classical extensions of distances to the Cartesian product will still be metrics and will also inherit lattice-related properties such as being *order-preserving*.

3.2   Distances in Logic Programming Domains

We now propose some distances for two well-known abstract domains used in (C)LP, following the considerations presented in the previous section.

Sharing Domain: The `sharing` domain [24,32] is a well-known domain for analyzing the sharing (aliasing) relationships between variables and grounding in logic programs. It is defined as $2^{2^{Pvar}}$, that is, an abstract substitution for a clause is defined to be *a set of sets of program variables* in that clause, where each set indicates that the terms to which those variables are instantiated at run-time might share a free variable. More formally, we define $Occ(\theta, U) = \{X | X \in dom(\theta), U \in vars(X\theta)\}$, the set of all program variables $X \in Pvar$ in the clause such that the variable $U \in Uvar$ appears in $X\theta$. We define the abstraction of a substitution θ as $\mathcal{A}_{sharing}(\theta) = \{Occ(\theta, U) \mid U \in Uvar\}$, and extend it to sets of substitutions. The order induced by this abstraction in $2^{2^{Pvar}}$ is the set inclusion, the join, the set union, and the meet, the set intersection. As an example, $\top = 2^{Pvar}$, a program variable that does not appear in any set is guaranteed to be ground, or two variables that never appear in the same set are guaranteed to not share. The complete definition can be found in [24,32].

Following the approach of the previous section, we define this monotone size in the domain: $size(a) = |a| + 1, size(\bot) = 0$. It is straightforward to check that $\forall a, b \in 2^{2^{Pvar}}$, $size(a) + size(b) = size(a \sqcap b) + size(a \sqcup b)$. Therefore the following distance is a metric and order-preserving:

$$d_{share}(Sh_1, Sh_2)$$
$$= size(Sh_1 \cup Sh_2) - size(Sh_1 \cap Sh_2) = |Sh_1 \cup Sh_2| - |Sh_1 \cap Sh_2|$$

We would like our distance to be in a normalized range $[0, 1]$, and for that we divide it between $d(\bot, \top) = 2^n + 1$, where $n = |V|$ denotes the number of variables in the domain of the substitutions. This yields the following final distance, which is a metric by construction:

$$d_{share}(Sh_1, Sh_2) = (|(Sh_1 \cup Sh_2)| - |size(Sh_1 \cap Sh_2)|)/(2^n + 1)$$

Regular-Type Domain: Another well-known domain for logic programs is the *regular types* domain [9], which abstracts the shape or type of the terms to which variables are assigned at run time. It associates each variable with a deterministic context free grammar that describes its shape, with the possible functors and atoms of the program as terminal symbols. A more formal definition can be found in [9]. We will write abstract substitutions as tuples $\langle G_1, \ldots, G_n \rangle$, where $G_i = (\mathcal{T}_i, \mathcal{F}_i, \mathcal{R}_i, S_i)$ is the grammar that describes the term associated to the i-th variable in the substitution. We propose to use as a basis the Hausdorff distance in the concrete domain, using the distance between terms proposed in [36], i.e.,

$$d_{term}(f(x_1, \ldots, x_n), g(y_1, \ldots, y_m)) = \begin{cases} 1 & if \quad f/n \neq g/m \\ else: & p\sum_{i=1}^{n} \frac{1}{n} d_{term}(x_i, y_i) \end{cases}$$

where p is a parameter of the distance. As the derived abstract version, we propose the following recursive distance between two types or grammars G_a, G_b, where $G|_T$ is the grammar G with initial symbol T instead of S:

$$d'(G_a, G_b) = \begin{cases} 1 \ if \ \exists \ (S_a \to f(T_1, \ldots, T_n)) \in \mathcal{R}_a \wedge \nexists(S_b \to f(T_1', \ldots, T_n')) \in \mathcal{R}_b \\ 1 \ if \ \exists \ (S_b \to f(T_1, \ldots, T_n)) \in \mathcal{R}_b \wedge \nexists(S_a \to f(T_1', \ldots, T_n')) \in \mathcal{R}_a \\ else: max\{p\sum_{i=1}^{n} \frac{1}{n} d'(G_a|_{T_i}, G_b|_{T_i'}) \mid (S_a \to f(T_1, \ldots, T_n)) \in \mathcal{R}_a, \\ \qquad\qquad\qquad\qquad\qquad\qquad (S_b \to f(T_1', \ldots, T_n')) \in \mathcal{R}_b\} \end{cases}$$

We also extend this distance between types to distance between substitutions in the abstract domain as follows: $d(\langle T_1, \ldots, T_n \rangle, \langle T'_1, \ldots, T'_n \rangle) = \sqrt{d'(T_1, T'_1)^2 + \ldots + d'(T_n, T'_n)^2}$. Since d' is the abstraction of the Hausdorff distance with d_{term}, which it is proved to be a metric in [36], d' is a metric too.[2] Therefore d is also a metric, since it is its extension to the cartesian product.

4   Distances Between Analyses

We now attempt to extend a distance in an abstract domain to distances between results of different abstract interpretation-based analyses of the same program over that domain. In the following we will assume (following most "top-down" analyzers for (C)LP programs [4,16,26,32]) that the result of an analysis for a given entry (i.e., an initial predicate P, and an initial call pattern or abstract query λ_c), is an AND-OR tree, with root the OR-node $\langle P, \lambda_c, \lambda_s \rangle_\vee$, where λ_s is the abstract substitution computed by the analysis for that predicate given that initial call pattern. An AND-OR tree alternates AND-nodes, which correspond to clauses in the program, and OR-nodes, which correspond to literals in those clauses. An AND-node is a triplet $\langle C, \beta_{entry}, \beta_{exit} \rangle_\wedge$, with C a clause $Head : -L_1, \ldots, L_n$ and with $\beta_{entry}, \beta_{exit}$ the abstract entry and exit substitutions for that clause. It has an OR-node $\langle L_i, \lambda_c^i, \lambda_s^i \rangle_\vee$ as child for each literal L_i in the clause, where $\lambda_c^1 = \beta_{entry}$, $\lambda_c^{i+1} = \lambda_s^i$ for $i = 2 \ldots n$, and $\beta_{exit} = \lambda_s^n$. An OR-node is a triplet $\langle L, \lambda_c, \lambda_s \rangle_\vee$, with L a literal in the program, which is a call to a predicate P, and λ_c, λ_s the abstract call and success substitutions for that goal. It has one AND-node $\langle C_j, \beta_{entry}^j, \beta_{exit}^j \rangle_\wedge$ as child for each clause C_j in the definition of P, where β_{entry}^j is derived from λ_c by projecting and renaming to the variables in the clause C_j, and λ_s is obtained from $\{\beta_{exit}^j\}$ by extending and renaming each exit substitution to the variables in the calling literal L and computing the least upper bound of the results. This tree is the abstract counterpart of the resolution trees that represent concrete top-down executions, and represents a possibly infinite set of those resolution trees at once. The tree will most likely be infinite, but can be represented as a finite cyclic tree. We denote the children of a node T as $ch(T)$ and its triplet as $val(T)$.

Example 1. Let us consider as an example the simple quick-sort program (using difference lists) in Fig. 1, which uses an *entry* assertion to specify the initial abstract query of the analysis [37]. If we analyze it with a simple *groundness* domain (with just two values g and ng, plus $\top$ and $\bot$), the result can be represented with the cyclic tree shown in Fig. 1. That tree is a finite representation of an infinite abstract AND-OR tree. The nodes in layers 1, 3 and 5 represent OR-nodes, and the ones in layers 2,4 and 6, AND-nodes, where p/i/j corresponds to the j-th clause of predicate p/i. The actual values of the nodes are specified above the tree.   □

---

[2] Actually that only guarantees that d' is a pseudo-metric. Proving that it is indeed a metric is more involved and not really relevant to our discussion.

We propose three distances between AND-OR trees S_1, S_2 for the same entry, in increasing order of complexity, and parameterized by a distance d_α in the underlying abstract domain. We also discuss which metric properties are inherited by these distances from d_α. Note that a good distance for measuring precision should fulfill the identity of indiscernibles.

Top Distance. The first consists in considering only the roots of the top trees, $\langle P, \lambda_c, \lambda_s^1 \rangle_\vee$ and $\langle P, \lambda_c, \lambda_s^2 \rangle_\vee$, and defining our new distance as $d(S_1, S_2) = d_\alpha(\lambda_s^1, \lambda_s^2)$. This distance ignores too much information (e.g., if the entry point is a predicate `main/0`, the distance would only distinguish analyses that detect failure from analysis which do not), so it is not appropriate for measuring analysis precision, but it is still interesting as a baseline. It is straightforward to see that it is a pseudometric if d_α is, but will not fulfill the identity of indiscernibles even if d_α does.

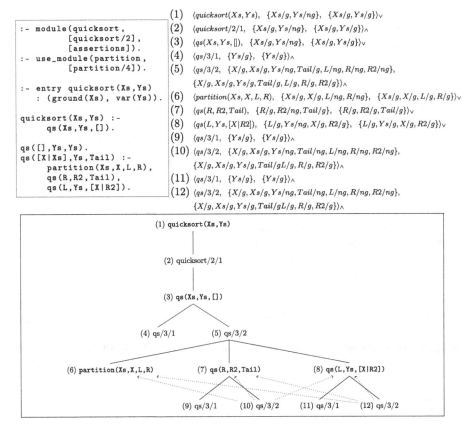

Fig. 1. Analysis of `quicksort/2` (using difference lists).

Flat Distance. The second distance considers all the information inferred by the analysis for each program point, but forgetting about its context in the AND-OR tree. In fact, analysis information is often used this way, i.e., considering only the substitutions with which a given literal in the program can be called or succeeds, and not which traces lead to those calls (path insensitivity). We define a distance between a program point or literal PP in two analysis S_1, S_2

$$d_{PP}(S_1, S_2) = \frac{1}{2}(d_\alpha(\bigsqcup_{\lambda \in PP_c^1} \lambda, \bigsqcup_{\lambda \in PP_c^2} \lambda) + d_\alpha(\bigsqcup_{\lambda \in PP_s^1} \lambda, \bigsqcup_{\lambda \in PP_s^2} \lambda))$$

where $PP_c^i = \{\lambda_c \mid \langle PP, \lambda_c, \lambda_s \rangle_\vee \in S_i\}$, $PP_s^i = \{\lambda_s \mid \langle PP, \lambda_c, \lambda_s \rangle_\vee \in S_i\}$. If we denote P as the set of all program points in the program, that distance can later be extended to a distance between analyses as $d(S_1, S_2) = \frac{1}{|P|} \sum_{PP \in P} d_{PP}(S_1, S_2)$, or any other combination of the distances $d_{PP}(S_1, S_2)$ (e.g, weighted average, $\| \cdot \|_2$). This distance is more appropriate for measuring precision than the previous one, but it will still inherit all metric properties except the identity of indiscernibles. An example of this distance can be found in [6].

Tree Distance. For the third distance, we propose the following recursive definition, which can easily be translated into an algorithm:

$$d(T_1, T_2) = \begin{cases} \mu \frac{1}{2}(d_\alpha(\lambda_c^1, \lambda_c^2) + d_\alpha(\lambda_s^1, \lambda_s^2)) + (1 - \mu)\frac{1}{|C|} \sum_{(c_1, c_2) \in C} d(c_1, c_2) & if\ C \neq \emptyset \\ else\ \ \frac{1}{2}(d_\alpha(\lambda_c^1, \lambda_c^2) + d_\alpha(\lambda_s^1, \lambda_s^2)) \end{cases}$$

where $T_1 = \langle P, \lambda_c^1, \lambda_s^1 \rangle$, $T_2 = \langle P, \lambda_c^2, \lambda_s^2 \rangle$, $\mu \in (0, 1]$ and $C = \{(c_1, c_2) \mid c_1 \in ch(T_1), c_2 \in ch(T_2), val(c_1) = \langle X, -, - \rangle, val(c_2) = \langle Y, -, - \rangle, X = Y\}$.

This definition is possible because the two AND-OR trees, when considering their infinite, non cyclic representation, will necessarily have the same shape, and therefore we are always comparing a node with its correspondent node in the other tree. That shape could only differ for real analysis if one of them detects and unreachable trace (e.g., a clause not applicable or a literal after another that fails), but not the other, thus having one subtree in the second not occurring in the first. But that can also be modelled as that subtree occurring also in the first with every abstract substitution being $\bot$.

This distance is well defined, even if the trees, and therefore the recursions, are infinite, since the expression above always converges. To back up that claim we provide the following argument, which also shows how that distance can be easily computed in finite time. Since the AND-OR trees always have a finite representation as cyclic trees with n and m nodes respectively, there are at most $n * m$ different pairs of nodes to visit during the recursion. Assigning a variable to each pair that is actually visited, the recursive expression can be expressed as a linear system of equations. That system has a unique solution since there is an equation for each variable and the associated matrix, which is therefore squared, has strictly dominant diagonal. An example of this can be found in [6].

The idea of this distance is that we consider more relevant the distance between the upper nodes than the distance between the deeper ones, but we still consider all of them and do not miss any of the analysis information. As a result, this distance will directly inherit the identity of indiscernibles (apart from all other metric properties) from d_α.

5   Experimental Evaluation

To evaluate the usefulness of the program analysis distances, we set up a practical scenario in which we study quantitatively the cost and precision tradeoff for several abstract domains. We propose the following methodology to measure that precision:

Base Domain. Recall that in the distances defined so far, we assume that we compare two analyses using the same abstract domain. We relax this requirement by translating each analysis to a common *base domain*, rich enough to reflect a particular program property of interest. An abstract substitution λ over a domain D_α is translated to a new domain $D_{\alpha'}$ as $\lambda' = \alpha'(\gamma(\lambda))$, and the AND-OR tree is translated by just translating any abstract substitution occurring in it. The results still over-approximates concrete executions, but this time all over the same abstract domain.

Program Analysis Intersection. Ideally we would compare each analysis with the actual semantics of a program for a given abstract query, represented also as an AND-OR tree. However, this semantics is undecidable in general, and we are seeking an automated process. Instead, we approximated it as the *intersection* of all the computed analyses. The intersection between two trees, which can be easily generalized to n trees, is defined as $inter(T_1, T_2) = T$, with

$$val(T_1) = \langle X, \lambda_c^1, \lambda_s^2 \rangle, \ val(T_2) = \langle X, \lambda_c^2, \lambda_s^2 \rangle, \ val(T) = \langle X, \lambda_c^1 \sqcap \lambda_c^2, \lambda_s^1 \sqcap \lambda_s^2 \rangle$$
$$ch(T) \ = \{ \ inter(c_1, c_2) \mid c_1 \in ch(T_1), \ c_2 \in ch(T_2), \ val(c_1) = \langle X, \_, \_ \rangle,$$
$$val(c_2) = \langle Y, \_, \_ \rangle, \ X = Y \}$$

That is, a new AND-OR tree with the same shape as those computed by the analyses, but where each abstract substitution is the greatest lower bound of the corresponding abstract substitutions in the other trees. The resulting tree is the least general AND-OR tree we can obtain that still over-approximates every concrete execution. We can now use that tree to measure the (loss of) precision of an analysis as its distance to the tree, being that distance 0 is the analysis is as precise as the intersection, and growing up to 1 as it gets more imprecise.

Case Study: Variable Sharing Domains. We have applied the method above on a well known set of (micro-)benchmarks for CLP analysis, and a number of modules from a real application (the LPdoc documentation generator). The programs are analyzed using the CiaoPP framework [20] and the domains *shfr* [33],

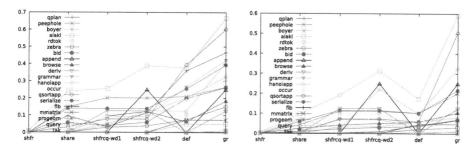

Fig. 2. (a) Precision using flat distance and (b) tree distance (micro-benchmarks)

share [24,32], *def* [1,15], and *sharefree_clique* [34] with different widenings. All these domains express sharing between variables among other things, and we compare them with respect to the base *share* domain. All experiments are run on a Linux machine with Intel Core i5 CPU and 8 GB of RAM.

Figures 2 and 3 show the results for the micro-benchmarks. Figures 4 and 5 show the same experiment on LPdoc modules. In both experiments we measure the precision using the flat distance, tree distance, and top distance. In general, the results align with our a priori knowledge: that *shfr* is strictly more precise than all other domains, but can sometimes be slower; while *gr* is less precise and generally faster. As expected, the flat and tree distances show that *share* is in all cases less precise than *shfr*, and not significantly cheaper (sometimes even more costly). The tree distance shows a more pronounced variation of precision when comparing *share* and widenings. While this can also be appreciated in the top distance, the top distance fails to show the difference between *share* and *shfr*. Thus, the tree distance seems to offer a good balance. For small programs where analysis requires less than 100 ms in *shfr*, there seems to be no advantage in using less precise domains. Also as expected, for large programs widenings provide significant speedups with moderate precision lose. Small programs do not benefit in general from widenings. Finally, the *def* domain shows very good precision w.r.t. the top distance, representing that the domain is good enough

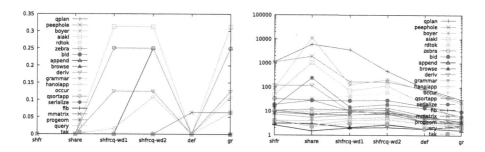

Fig. 3. (a) Precision using top distance and (b) Analysis time (micro-benchmarks)

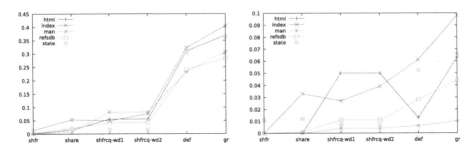

Fig. 4. (a) Precision using flat distance and (b) tree distance (LPdoc benchmark)

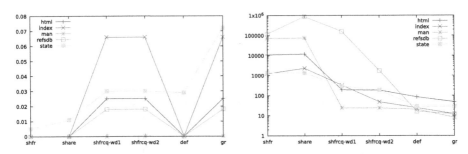

Fig. 5. (a) Precision using top distance and (b) Analysis time (LPdoc benchmarks)

to capture the behavior of predicates at the module interface for the selected benchmarks.

Figure 6 reflects the size of the AND-OR tree and experimentally it is correlated with the analysis time. The size measures the cost of representing abstract substitutions as Prolog terms (roughly as the number of functor and constant symbols).

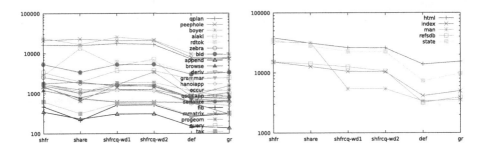

Fig. 6. (a) Analysis size (micro-benchmarks) and (b) Analysis size (LPdoc benchmark)

6   Related Work

Distances in lattices: Lattices and other structures that arise from order relations are common in many areas of computer science and mathematics, so it is not surprising that there have been already some attempts at proposing metrics in them. E.g., [18] has a dedicated chapter for metrics in lattices, Horn and Tarski [22] studied measures in boolean algebras. *Distances among terms:* Hutch [23], Nienhuys-Cheng [36] and Ramon [38] all propose distances in the space of terms and extend them to distances between sets of terms or clauses. Our proposed distance for *regular types* can be interpreted as the abstraction of the distance proposed by Nienhuys-Cheng. Furthermore, [38] develop some theory of metrics in partial orders, as also does De Raedt [11]. *Distances among abstract elements and operators:* Logozzo [28] proposes defining metrics in partially ordered sets and applying them to quantifying the relative loss of precision induced by numeric abstract domains. Our work is similar in that we also propose a notion of distance in abstract domains. However, they restrict their proposed distances to finite or numeric domains, while we focus instead on logic programming-oriented, possible infinite, domains. Also, our approach to quantifying the precision of abstract interpretations follows quite different ideas. They use their distances to define a notion of error induced by an abstract value, and then a notion of error induced by a finite abstract domain and its abstract operators, with respect to the concrete domain and concrete operators. Instead, we work in the context of given programs, and quantify the difference of precision between the results of different analyses for those programs, by extending our metrics in abstract domains to metrics in the space of abstract executions of a program and comparing those results. Sotin [39] defines measures in $\mathbb{R}^n$ that allow quantifying the difference in precision between two abstract values of a numeric domain, by comparing the size of their concretizations. This is applied to guessing the most appropriate domain to analyse a program, by under-approximating the potentially visited states via random testing and comparing the precision with which different domains would approximate those states. Di Pierro [13] proposes a notion of probabilistic abstract interpretation, which allows measuring the precision of an abstract domain and its operators. In their proposed framework, abstract domains are vector spaces instead of partially ordered sets, and it is not clear whether every domain, and in particular those used in logic programming, can be reinterpreted within that framework. Cortesi [7] proposes a formal methodology to compare qualitatively the precision of two abstract domains with respect to some of the information they express, that is, to know if one is strictly more precise that the other according to only part of the properties they abstract. In our experiments, we compare the precision of different analyses with respect to some of the information they express. For some, we know that one is qualitatively more precise than the other in Cortesi's paper's sense, and that is reflected in our results.

7   Conclusions

We have proposed a new approach for measuring and comparing precision across different analyses, based on defining distances in abstract domains and extending them to distances between whole analyses. We have surveyed and extended previous proposals for distances and metrics in lattices or abstract domains, and proposed metrics for some common (C)LP domains. We have also proposed extensions of those metrics to the space of whole program analysis. We have implemented those metrics and applied them to measuring the precision of different sharing-related (C)LP analyses on both benchmarks and a realistic program. We believe that this application of distances is promising for debugging the precision of analyses and calibrating heuristics for combining different domains in portfolio approaches, without prior knowledge and treating domains as black boxes (except for the translation to the *base* domain). In the future we plan to apply the proposed concepts in other applications beyond measuring precision in analysis, such as studying how programming methodologies or optimizations affect the analyses, comparing obfuscated programs, giving approximate results in semantic code browsing [14], program synthesis, software metrics, etc.

References

1. Armstrong, T., Marriott, K., Schachte, P., Søndergaard, H.: Boolean functions for dependency analysis: algebraic properties and efficient representation. In: Le Charlier, B. (ed.) SAS 1994. LNCS, vol. 864, pp. 266–280. Springer, Heidelberg (1994). https://doi.org/10.1007/3-540-58485-4_46
2. Banda, G., Gallagher, J.P.: Analysis of linear hybrid systems in CLP. In: Hanus, M. (ed.) LOPSTR 2008. LNCS, vol. 5438, pp. 55–70. Springer, Heidelberg (2009). https://doi.org/10.1007/978-3-642-00515-2_5
3. Bjørner, N., Gurfinkel, A., McMillan, K., Rybalchenko, A.: Horn clause solvers for program verification. In: Beklemishev, L.D., Blass, A., Dershowitz, N., Finkbeiner, B., Schulte, W. (eds.) Fields of Logic and Computation II. LNCS, vol. 9300, pp. 24–51. Springer, Cham (2015). https://doi.org/10.1007/978-3-319-23534-9_2
4. Bruynooghe, M.: A practical framework for the abstract interpretation of logic programs. J. Logic Program. **10**, 91–124 (1991)
5. Bueno, F., García de la Banda, M., Hermenegildo, M.V.: Effectiveness of global analysis in strict independence-based automatic program parallelization. In: International Symposium on Logic Programming, pp. 320–336. MIT Press, November 1994
6. Casso, I., Morales, J.F., Lopez-Garcia, P., Hermenegildo, M.V.: Computing abstract distances in logic programs. Technical report CLIP-2/2019.0, The CLIP Lab, IMDEA Software Institute and T.U., Madrid, July 2019. http://arxiv.org/abs/1907.13263
7. Cortesi, A., Filé, G., Winsborough, W.: Comparison of abstract interpretations. In: Kuich, W. (ed.) ICALP 1992. LNCS, vol. 623, pp. 521–532. Springer, Heidelberg (1992). https://doi.org/10.1007/3-540-55719-9_101
8. Cousot, P., Cousot, R.: Abstract interpretation: a unified lattice model for static analysis of programs by construction or approximation of fixpoints. In: Proceedings of POPL 1977, pp. 238–252. ACM Press (1977)

9. Dart, P., Zobel, J.: A Regular type language for logic programs. In: Pfenning, F. (ed.) Types in Logic Programming, pp. 157–187. MIT Press, Cambridge (1992)
10. De Angelis, E., Fioravanti, F., Pettorossi, A., Proietti, M.: VeriMAP: a tool for verifying programs through transformations. In: Ábrahám, E., Havelund, K. (eds.) TACAS 2014. LNCS, vol. 8413, pp. 568–574. Springer, Heidelberg (2014). https://doi.org/10.1007/978-3-642-54862-8_47
11. De Raedt, L., Ramon, J.: Deriving distance metrics from generality relations. Pattern Recogn. Lett. **30**(3), 187–191 (2009). https://doi.org/10.1016/j.patrec.2008.09.007
12. Debray, S.K.: Static inference of modes and data dependencies in logic programs. ACM Trans. Program. Lang. Syst. **11**(3), 418–450 (1989)
13. Di Pierro, A., Wiklicky, H.: Measuring the precision of abstract interpretations. LOPSTR 2000. LNCS, vol. 2042, pp. 147–164. Springer, Heidelberg (2001). https://doi.org/10.1007/3-540-45142-0_9
14. Garcia-Contreras, I., Morales, J.F., Hermenegildo, M.V.: Semantic code browsing. TPLP (ICLP 2016 Special Issue) **16**(5–6), 721–737 (2016)
15. García de la Banda, M., Hermenegildo, M.V.: A practical application of sharing and freeness inference. In: 1992 Workshop on Static Analysis, WSA 1992, pp. 118–125. No. 81–82 in BIGRE. IRISA, Beaulieu, September 1992
16. de la Banda, M.G., Hermenegildo, M.V., Bruynooghe, M., Dumortier, V., Janssens, G., Simoens, W.: Global analysis of constraint logic programs. ACM TOPLAS **18**(5), 564–614 (1996)
17. Grebenshchikov, S., Gupta, A., Lopes, N.P., Popeea, C., Rybalchenko, A.: HSF(C): a software verifier based on Horn clauses. In: Flanagan, C., König, B. (eds.) TACAS 2012. LNCS, vol. 7214, pp. 549–551. Springer, Heidelberg (2012). https://doi.org/10.1007/978-3-642-28756-5_46
18. Grätzer, G.: General Lattice Theory, 2nd edn. (1998). https://doi.org/10.1007/978-3-0348-7633-9
19. Gurfinkel, A., Kahsai, T., Komuravelli, A., Navas, J.A.: The SeaHorn verification framework. In: Kroening, D., Pǎsǎreanu, C.S. (eds.) CAV 2015. LNCS, vol. 9206, pp. 343–361. Springer, Cham (2015). https://doi.org/10.1007/978-3-319-21690-4_20
20. Hermenegildo, M., Puebla, G., Bueno, F., Lopez-Garcia, P.: Integrated program debugging, verification, and optimization using abstract interpretation (and the Ciao system preprocessor). Sci. Comput. Progr. **58**(1–2), 115–140 (2005)
21. Hermenegildo, M., Warren, R., Debray, S.K.: Global flow analysis as a practical compilation tool. JLP **13**(4), 349–367 (1992)
22. Horn, A., Tarski, A.: Measures in Boolean algebras. Trans. Am. Math. Soc. **64**(3), 467–497 (1948)
23. Hutchinson, A.: Metrics on terms and clauses. In: van Someren, M., Widmer, G. (eds.) ECML 1997. LNCS, vol. 1224, pp. 138–145. Springer, Heidelberg (1997). https://doi.org/10.1007/3-540-62858-4_78
24. Jacobs, D., Langen, A.: Accurate and efficient approximation of variable aliasing in logic programs. In: North American Conference on Logic Programming (1989)
25. Kafle, B., Gallagher, J.P., Morales, J.F.: RAHFT: a tool for verifying horn clauses using abstract interpretation and finite tree automata. In: Chaudhuri, S., Farzan, A. (eds.) CAV 2016. LNCS, vol. 9779, pp. 261–268. Springer, Cham (2016). https://doi.org/10.1007/978-3-319-41528-4_14

26. Kelly, A.D., Macdonald, A., Marriott, K., Søndergaard, H., Stuckey, P.J., Yap, R.H.C.: An optimizing compiler for CLP $\mathscr{R}$. In: Montanari, U., Rossi, F. (eds.) CP 1995. LNCS, vol. 976, pp. 222–239. Springer, Heidelberg (1995). https://doi.org/10.1007/3-540-60299-2_14

27. Liqat, U., et al.: Energy consumption analysis of programs based on XMOS ISA-level models. In: Gupta, G., Peña, R. (eds.) LOPSTR 2013. LNCS, vol. 8901, pp. 72–90. Springer, Cham (2014). https://doi.org/10.1007/978-3-319-14125-1_5

28. Logozzo, F., Popeea, C., Laviron, V.: Towards a quantitative estimation of abstract interpretations (extended abstract). In: Workshop on Quantitative Analysis of Software, June 2009

29. Madsen, M., Yee, M., Lhoták, O.: From Datalog to FLIX: a declarative language for fixed points on lattices. In: PLDI, pp. 194–208. ACM (2016)

30. Marriott, K., Søndergaard, H., Jones, N.: Denotational abstract interpretation of logic programs. ACM Trans. Program. Lang. Syst. **16**(3), 607–648 (1994)

31. Méndez-Lojo, M., Navas, J., Hermenegildo, M.V.: A flexible, (C)LP-based approach to the analysis of object-oriented programs. In: King, A. (ed.) LOPSTR 2007. LNCS, vol. 4915, pp. 154–168. Springer, Heidelberg (2008). https://doi.org/10.1007/978-3-540-78769-3_11

32. Muthukumar, K., Hermenegildo, M.: Determination of variable dependence information at compile-time through abstract interpretation. In: NACLP 1989, pp. 166–189. MIT Press, October 1989

33. Muthukumar, K., Hermenegildo, M.: Combined determination of sharing and freeness of program variables through abstract interpretation. In: ICLP 1991, pp. 49–63. MIT Press, June 1991

34. Navas, J., Bueno, F., Hermenegildo, M.: Efficient top-down set-sharing analysis using cliques. In: Van Hentenryck, P. (ed.) PADL 2006. LNCS, vol. 3819, pp. 183–198. Springer, Heidelberg (2005). https://doi.org/10.1007/11603023_13

35. Navas, J., Méndez-Lojo, M., Hermenegildo, M.V.: User-definable resource usage bounds analysis for Java bytecode. In: BYTECODE 2009. ENTCS, vol. 253. Elsevier, March 2009

36. Nienhuys-Cheng, S.-H.: Distance between Herbrand interpretations: a measure for approximations to a target concept. In: Lavrač, N., Džeroski, S. (eds.) ILP 1997. LNCS, vol. 1297, pp. 213–226. Springer, Heidelberg (1997). https://doi.org/10.1007/3540635149_50

37. Puebla, G., Bueno, F., Hermenegildo, M.: An assertion language for constraint logic programs. In: Deransart, P., Hermenegildo, M.V., Małuszynski, J. (eds.) Analysis and Visualization Tools for Constraint Programming. LNCS, vol. 1870, pp. 23–61. Springer, Heidelberg (2000). https://doi.org/10.1007/10722311_2

38. Ramon, J., Bruynooghe, M.: A framework for defining distances between first-order logic objects. In: Page, D. (ed.) ILP 1998. LNCS, vol. 1446, pp. 271–280. Springer, Heidelberg (1998). https://doi.org/10.1007/BFb0027331

39. Sotin, P.: Quantifying the precision of numerical abstract domains. Research report, INRIA, February 2010. https://hal.inria.fr/inria-00457324

40. Van Roy, P., Despain, A.: High-performance logic programming with the aquarius prolog compiler. IEEE Comput. Mag. **25**, 54–68 (1992)

Program Synthesis

Synthesizing Imperative Code from Answer Set Programming Specifications

Sarat Chandra Varanasi$^{(\boxtimes)}$ (ID), Elmer Salazar (ID), Neeraj Mittal (ID),
and Gopal Gupta (ID)

Department of Computer Science, The University of Texas at Dallas,
Richardson, TX, USA
{sxv153030,elmer.salazar,neerajm,gupta}@utdallas.edu

Abstract. We consider the problem of obtaining an implementation of an algorithm from its specification. We assume that these specifications are written in answer set programming (ASP). ASP is an ideal formalism for writing specifications due to its highly declarative and expressive nature. To obtain an implementation from its specification, we utilize the operational semantics of ASP implemented in the s(ASP) system. This operational semantics is used to transform the declarative specification written in ASP to obtain an equivalent efficient program that uses imperative control features. This work is inspired by our overarching goal of automatically deriving efficient concurrent algorithms from declarative specifications. This paper reports our first step towards achieving that goal where we restrict ourselves to simple sequential algorithms. We illustrate our ideas through several examples. Our work opens up a new approach to logic-based program synthesis not explored before.

Keywords: Program synthesis · Program transformation · Answer Set Programming · Partial evaluation · Symbolic execution

1 Introduction

Program synthesis concerns generating programs according to given specifications. This problem has been tackled in various ways. One of the earliest approaches was to use theorem proving to generate imperative programs from a given logical input-output specification [10]. Extensive work using logical approaches are surveyed [2]. More recently synthesis has been reduced to the task of verification [15]. In this paper, we provide a method to extract programs from executable specifications written in a particular class of datalog answer set programs, by means of program transformation. Answer Set Programming (ASP) is a declarative, logic-based programming paradigm for solving combinatorial search and knowledge representation problems [6]. In ASP, specification and

Work partially supported by US NSF grants IIS 1718945, CNS-1115733 and CNS-1619197.

M. Gabbrielli (Ed.): LOPSTR 2019, LNCS 12042, pp. 75–89, 2020.
https://doi.org/10.1007/978-3-030-45260-5_5

computation are synonymous, which is highly desirable to rapidly prototype systems [4]. However the implementations of ASP are quite complex [5]. It is rather difficult to justify why a specification computes what it computes. On the other hand, imperative programs are relatively easier to trace and in general enjoy faster run-times than their declarative program counterparts. This is because imperative programs often represent computationally faster implementations of a specification without directly being concerned about the specification. This makes deriving imperative programs from ASP specifications highly desirable. Our main insight is to employ the recently-developed operational semantics for ASP realized in the s(ASP) system [1,11]. s(ASP) is a query-driven answer set programming system which computes the (partial) stable models of a query of an answer set program without grounding the program first. Traditional implementations of ASP are based on grounding the program to its propositional equivalent and then using SAT solvers to compute the *answer sets*. Using the operational semantics of s(ASP), one can follow how the stable models are computed for a query in a step-by-step manner. This provides us the right playground to extract an imperative program while simplifying all the machinery that makes s(ASP) work.

Our key contribution is the following. We demonstrate how program transformation, based on s(ASP)-style operational semantics, can be used to realize efficient imperative programs from their declarative ASP specifications. We illustrate our approach through several sequential algorithms. Our major contribution is the novel use of the *forall* mechanism that is part of s(ASP)'s operational semantics. The *forall* directly translates into a *for-loop* in the derived imperative program. Eventually, we plan to employ partial evaluation obeying the s(ASP) operational semantics to further improve efficiency.

Answer set programming is essentially logic programming with negation as failure (NAF) under the stable model semantics [6]. Answer set programs consist of *even loops* that act as *generators of worlds* and *odd loops* (or *constraints*) that act as *destroyer of worlds*. ASP provides a paradigm where each rule can be written and understood in isolation from others. Due to presence of negation as failure, ASP permits specification of a concept by stating what it is not. ASP thus serves as a very high-level and expressive specification language.

Our main idea is as follows: Programs are written as abstractions over certain allowed primitives and there could be more abstractions built on top of existing abstractions. This applies to specifications as well, particularly for the specifications we are interested in this paper. In logic programs, a specification contains either positive terms or negated terms. However, in a corresponding imperative program, there are only function-calls and constraints (if-checks). We eliminate negated terms in the imperative program by making them implicit. In doing so, the meaning of negated terms is propagated downward from the abstractions to the primitives. In ASP, combinations of possibilities or situations that are not permitted are expressed as constraints that a consistent world (answer set) must obey; those that are permitted or desired are represented through simple rules, even loops, etc. Our insight behind obtaining an imperative algorithm from an

ASP specification involves simply following the s(ASP) operational semantics, to orchestrate the calls to predicates so that constraints end up as if-then-else checks in the imperative execution. In addition, s(ASP) semantics creates universally quantified variables in the body of negated rules that translate directly into an imperative *for-loop*. These ideas are illustrated in more detail later.

Our ultimate goal is to synthesize efficient concurrent algorithms from their declarative specifications. Concurrent algorithms are notoriously difficult to design. They are also equally difficult to verify. ASP provides the right formalism to represent concepts of concurrency in an elegant, straightforward way. For instance, the ASP program that describes the behaviour of a concurrent linked list is no different than the ASP program for blocks world planning [6]. Thus, to be able to synthesize imperative code from a concurrent specification, will greatly aide designers of concurrent algorithms. Further, our work corroborates the idea of writing programs that are *correct by construction*.

Rest of the paper is organized as follows: We give an overview of s(ASP) and its features used for synthesis in Sect. 2. We then provide two examples, one in Sect. 3 for motivating the idea of synthesis and the second in Sect. 4 to elaborate in detail. Section 5 describes the assumptions on which our technique is based. Section 6 outlines the entire algorithm followed by concluding remarks in Sect. 7.

2   Background

The ASP Paradigm: We assume basic familiarity with ASP syntax [6] and its applications in building intelligent systems [3,6]. The sets of satisfiable truth assignments to the propositional variables of an answer set program constitute its *answer sets* under the stable model semantics [6,8]. In general, ASP programs have predicates with variables. Most of the ASP solvers [5] ground the predicated program into propositions and find stable models by SAT solving. The s(ASP) system takes a different path by finding stable models relevant to a given query such as ?- p(X). s(ASP) finds the stable models for the issued query operationally without grounding the program. In short, stable models are solved in traditional ASP solvers, whereas the models are proved in s(ASP). For every answer set, there is a justification tree (proof tree) produced by the s(ASP) system describing all the sub-goals that lead up to the query. The s(ASP) system employs coinductive SLD Resolution [14] to execute even loops in a top down manner. Odd loops and constraints (NMR checks) serve as an extension of the top-level query in order to constrain the answers. For instance, a query ?- p(X) issued by the user is extended with a constraint {chk :- ...} as ?- p(X), chk. The goal-directed s(ASP) algorithm can be found elsewhere [11].

Prominent Features of s(ASP): We next summarize the salient features of the s(ASP) system that are relevant to our work here. The operational semantics of s(ASP) is a Prolog style execution of an issued query adhering to the stable model semantics. The query triggers a search where all clauses that are consistent are resolved and backtracking happens when inconsistent goals are encountered. All the terms encountered in the consistent goals constitute the "partial" stable model associated with the query. At a basic level, the current resolvent is invalid when during expansion it leads to a stable model that has both a goal and its negation. This is, in fact, how stable models are constructed in the propositional variant of s(ASP), namely Galliwasp [13]. Note that the execution algorithm of s(ASP) relies on *corecursion* [14] to handle even loops [11], but this feature is not as important for the work reported here.

Handling Negation with Dual Rules: In s(ASP), negated goals are executed through dual rules. The dual rule of a predicate p systematically negates the literals in a rule body defining p. Dual rules of all predicates together with the rules in the original program represent its *completion* [9]. For instance, the dual rule of the predicate p with the following definition is shown below:

```
%definition of p      %dual of p/0
p :- not q.           not p :- np1, np2
p :- r, not s.        %negating of not q yields q
                      np1 :- q.
                      %negating r, not s yields
                          disjunction (not r) ∨ s
                      np2 :- not r.
                      np2 :- s.
```

Forall Mechanism: We have just shown dual rules for propositions which are simple enough. However, writing dual rules for predicates is more involved. One complication is due to implicit quantifiers in predicate rules. For a rule such as:

$$p(X) \; :- \; q(Y), \; r(X).$$

X is universally quantified over the whole formula, whereas Y is existentially quantified in the body only. Therefore, negating $p(X)$ results in Y being universally quantified in the body as follows:

```
not p(X) :- np1(X) ;  np2(X).
np1(X) :- forall(Y, not q(Y)).
np2(X) :- not r(X).
```

Notice that the universal quantifier for Y in *not* $q(Y)$ is enclosed within a *forall*(...). The *forall* represents a proof procedure that runs through all values in the domain of Y and verifies if the goal enclosed within it is satisfied. In our example, the *forall* checks that *not* $q(Y)$ holds for all values in the domain of Y. No such mechanism existed in prior Prolog based systems. It is this *forall* mechanism coupled with dual rules that we make extensive use of in our synthesis procedure. Because they treat negated predicates *constructively* [11], we turn them into computations in our synthesis procedure.

3   Motivating Example

Consider the program that finds the maximum of n numbers, which is naturally specified in ASP as shown below:

```
max(X) :- num(X), not smaller(X).
smaller(X) :- num(X), num(Y), X < Y.
```

$num(X)$ provides the domain of numbers over which the input values range. $smaller(X)$ defines when a number X is dominated by another number Y. $max(X)$ gives the definition for X to be the maximum. The main predicate from where the computation to decide whether a given number X is the maximum begins with $max(X)$. The negation of $smaller(X)$ can be translated to a *forall* as shown below:

```
not smaller(X) :- forall(Y, not (num(X), num(Y), X < Y)).
```

Assuming that $num(X)$ and $num(Y)$ are true, the negation only applies to $X < Y$. Therefore, replacing the definition of *not smaller(X)* in $max(X)$ gives us the following:

```
max(X) :- forall(Y, num(X), num(Y), not (X < Y)).
```

The *forall* definition of $max(X)$ makes apparent the operational flavor involved in finding the maximum of n numbers: enumerate all numbers Y and compare them with X. If X is not smaller than any Y, i.e., $X < Y$ is false for all Y, then X is maximum. The *forall* can be translated to a *for-loop* in imperative languages if the domains of the variables involved in the scope of *forall* are finite. From an Answer Set Programming point of view, $max(X)$ is present in the answer set if the *forall* succeeds (if X is the maximum), otherwise it is not present in the answer set. The abstract code synthesized through program transformation, thus looks like:

```
def max(x):
    for y in num:
        if x < y:
            return False
    return True
```

The interpretation shown above is not sufficient to translate ASP programs written to solve graph-coloring or sorting an array. We illustrate our idea further in the following section taking the example of graph-coloring.

4   Synthesizing Code for Graph Coloring

We first provide an ASP program and then provide an operational interpretation which is still a logic program. Finally, we show how the various fragments of the "intermediate" logic program[1] can be transformed into an imperative program.

The Graph Coloring Problem: Graph coloring involves selecting a color c for every node v in an input graph such that no two adjacent (edge-connected) nodes (x, y) have the same color c. The ASP program is shown below:

---

[1] Both intermediate logic program and intermediate ASP program are used interchangeably.

```
color(X, C) :- node(X), color(C), not another_color(X,C),
               not conflict(X,C).
another_color(X, C) :- node(X), color(C), color(C1), C != C1,
                       color(X, C1).
conflict(X, C) :- node(X), color(C), node(Y), X != Y, edge(X, Y),
                  color(X, C), color(Y, C).
```

The domain of nodes and colors come from the predicates node/1 and color/1. The predicate color(X, C) provides the definition of what it means to color a node X with color C: Color X with C provided there is no other choice for X other than C and, the choice of color C does not conflict with the color C′ of all nodes Y edge-connected to X. The two conditions stated now are represented by predicates another_color/2 and conflict/2, respectively.

Operational Interpretation for Predicates in Graph Coloring: Considering color(X, C) to start off a computation for coloring node X (and subsequently the entire graph), we follow the definition of color(X, C) in a top-down, left-right manner while simplifying all intervening negations until we either reach an assertion about a domain variable (or) reach a recursive definition of color/2.

In the definition of color(X, C), the dual clause synthesized by s(ASP) for another_color(X, C) will be used for the call not another_color(X, C). This clause contains a *forall* with disjunction of negated terms as follows:

```
not another_color(X, C) :-
forall(C1,node(X),color(C),(not (C!= C1) or not color(X,C1)).
```

Operationally, not another_color(X, C) checks two constraints over all colors C1. For the first constraint we check if C != C1 is false, an assertion on the domain variables C and C1. The second constraint checks if the negation of not color(X, C1) is true, which is the negation of the predicate that started the computation, but with a possibly different binding for C1 than C. In order to compute the negation of color(X, C1) we generate the following dual rule:

```
not color(X, C) :- node(X), color(C), another_color(X, C).
not color(X, C) :- node(X), color(C), conflict(X, C).
```

Similarly, not conflict(X, C) is translated in terms of *forall* :

```
not_conflict(X, C) :-  forall(Y,node(X),color(C),node(Y),
                       (not (X != Y)) or not edge(X,Y) or
                       not color(Y,C)).
```

Notice that the negation is not applied to node(X), color(C) and node(Y) as we are not concerned about bindings for X, C, Y that are neither nodes nor colors. Further, not color(X, C) is skipped in the disjunction. This is because expanding negation of color(X, C) in the expansion of color(X, C) leads to a direct contradiction.

Once we have the intermediate logic program generated by the s(ASP) compiler (s(ASP) automatically generates dual rules), we have to transform the program further in a top-down, left-right manner, using s(ASP) semantics, starting from `color(X, C)` while generating imperative code for each of the predicates found in the body of `color(X, C)` (while excluding domain predicates). For our current research, the language of choice is Python. The choice could as well be any other imperative language as long as it supports recursion. Again, support for recursion is also not strictly necessary as the lack of it thereof would increase the size of the generated code to explicitly handle it.

Translating Graph Coloring to Imperative Code: The intermediate ASP program for graph coloring is broken down into its constituent syntactic parts and the translation for each of them is discussed in turn:

1. ***Main Rule-Head maps to Function call (Abstraction):*** `color(X, C)` is our starting point which is in fact the rule-head defining `color(X, C)`. Rule heads represent abstractions in Logic Programming [9], and hence an obvious choice is to map them to a function prototype such as: `def color(x, c)`. But it is not clear what the "function" `color(x, c)` should compute. At this point we can treat the call to `color(x, c)` as a query in the s(ASP) system: `?- color(X, C)`. The query immediately finds bindings for node X, color C and also relevant bindings `color(X', C')` for other node, color pairs X', C' that are consistent with `color(X, C)` in the ASP program.

   In other words, the s(ASP) system finds the first answer set (partial stable model) of the program. If s(ASP) cannot find an answer set, it returns false. Further, imperative languages can only operate on ground values (unlike logic program queries). Thus, the call `color(x, c)` in Python has ground values for parameters `x, c` at run-time. With these arguments, it makes sense that `def color(x, c)` should return all "terms" consistent with the choice `x, c` taken at run-time. Also, at run-time, the function should be able to track the consistent terms computed thus far. Therefore every function call `color(x, c)` is designated an additional parameter named *context*, which stores set of the consistent terms. Thus the complete function prototype is: `def color(x, c, context)` with the initial context being the empty set `{}`. In addition to returning consistent terms, the function should also report failure. Therefore, the function `color(x, c, {})` returns a pair (*success, set*). *success* is a boolean variable taking the value *True* upon success and *False* upon failure. *set* is the set of consistent terms found.

2. ***Domains map to Dictionary objects (Domain mapping):*** Domains are represented by Dictionary objects. A dictionary object can be viewed as a set of key-value pairs and it is iterable over the keys. If the colors in the coloring problem are `color(red)`, `color(green)` and `color(blue)` then the corresponding domain of colors is represented as:

   ```
   colors = {'red' : True, green' : True, 'blue' : True}
   ```

   Domains in rule-bodies, such as `color(X)` translate to `if color[x]: ...`
3. ***Predicates in the rule-body map to a sequence of statements (Sequencing):*** As stated previously, we follow the intermediate logic program in a top-down, left-right manner. For graph coloring, the *forall* for **not** `another_color(X, C)` is followed by the *forall* for **not** `conflict(X, C)` in

the body of the function color(x, c, context). Note that there are recursive calls to color in both the *foralls*. Now that there are a sequence of statements following other statements, the *context* is passed and returned from any recursive calls to color. The *context* is always passed-by-value because we might have to backtrack if any recursive call fails for some reason. Although dictionary objects are always passed-by-reference, we emulate this by use of a copy function which always copies the value of the *context* before passing it to a recursive call.

4. **Assertions on domain variables map to if-else conditions (Constraint checking):** From the intermediate logic program, we can identify three assertions on the domain variables. The first one is the check not (C != C1) in not another_color(X, C) and the other two are not (X != Y) and not edge(X, Y) in not conflict(X, C). All these constraints are trivially translated into simple if-conditions. For example, the check not edge(X, Y) is translated to if not edge(x, y):.... Failure to satisfy this assertion would explore any other assertion in the disjunction. If all assertions are not satisfied, then the program returns (*false, context*) where *context* is the set of consistent terms explored upto failure.

5. **Forall maps to a for-loop on the domain variable (Forall transformation):** At first glance, it is easy to see the *forall* map exactly to the *for-loop* (this is in fact the case for max(X) as shown in Sect. 3). However, this is not always the case. There needs to be additional code added to handle recursive calls within the *forall*. For graph coloring, consider the following input graph:

```
node(a). node(b). node(c). edge(a,b). edge(b,c).edge(c,a).
color(red). color(green). color(blue).
```

It is clear that all the colors assigned to the nodes should be unique as the graph is a complete graph. If we translated the *forall* for not conflict(X, C) exactly to a *for-loop*, then the *for-loop* would look like:

```
1   def color(x, c, context):
2     ...
3   # forall corresponding to not conflict(X, C)
4   for y in node:
5     if(not (x != y):
6       # nothing else to check, continue
7     else:
8       if not edge(x, y):
9         # again nothing to check, continue
10      else:
11        ctx = not_color(y, c, copy(context))
12        if ctx['success']:
13          context = ctx
14        else:
15          return {'success': False, 'context': context}
16    ...
```

The above *for-loop*, starting at line 5 and ending at line 15, checks for nodes y that are consistent with the choice of color(x, c). Say the choice is x = a, c = green, the iteration for y = a succeeds with the not (x != y) succeeding. The iteration for y = b fails the check at line 4 and the check at line 8 resulting in the execution of line 11. The dual not_color(y, c, copy(context)) selects the first color c' which is not c = green. Say the first color that is not green is c' = red. Then, not_color(y, c, context)[2] adds color(b, red) to ctx. Similary, for y = c the color selected would be red. The entire context is now {color(a, green), color(b, red), color(c, red)}. It is clear that the constraints are satisfied locally but are inconsistent globally.

To address this and thus to ensure global consistency, we check y with all pairs of choices (x',c') which are in the current context. If there is no violation, we proceed. Otherwise, there must be some choice (x'', c'') in the current context that is globally inconsistent and the recursive program reports failure while making another choice c''' for x'' upon backtracking. The rectified code now looks like:

```
1    def color(x, c, context):
2        ...
3    # forall corresponding to not conflict(X, C)
4    for y in node:
5      for(color(x1,c1) in context):
6        if(not (x1 != y)):
7          # nothing else to check, continue
8        else:
9          if not edge(x1, y):
10           # again nothing to check, continue
11         else:
12           ctx = not_color(y, c, copy(context))
13           if ctx['success']:
14             context = ctx
15           else:
16             return {'success': False, 'context': context
                   }
17       ...
```

Notice that line 5 now ensures the variable y is checked against all terms in the current context. Since we are in the scope of color(x, c), it is assumed that color(x, c) is already added to the context. This is done in the first statement of color(x, c, context){...} as def color(x, c, context){ context['color(x, c)'] = true ... }.

5 Synthesis Assumptions

The program synthesis process we have illustrated is confined to a class of answer set programs. The source ASP program should be a safe program (datalog

---

[2] not_color(y, c, copy(context)).

program) and cannot have head-less rules (constraints). Further, the program should consist of a unique *main predicate*. The program structure is as follows:

```
%main_predicate is defined in terms of abstractions
main_predicate(X1,..,Xn)  :-
   dom₁(X1),..,domₙ(Xn), abstraction₁(..),..,abstractionₘ(..)
   .

%abstractions define constraints on domain variables
abstraction1(X1,..,Xp) :- domα₁(X1),..,domαₚ(Xp),constraintα₁
   .

%or, abstractions can recursively call main_predicate
abstraction1(X1,..,Xp)  :-
     domα₁(X1),..domαₚ(Xp),constraintα₂,main_predicate(..).
  ...

abstractionₘ(X1,..,Xq) :- domμ₁(X1),..,domμq(Xq),constraintμ₁
   .

abstractionₘ(X1,..,  Xq) :-
     domμ₁(X1),..,  domμq(Xq),constraintμ₂,main_predicate(..).
```

Abstractions can be either positive literals or NAF literals (dual rules). Constraints are traditional relational operators found in most imperative languages. Notice that the abstractions do not call other abstractions directly. This is required of the source ASP program. Because if they do call other abstractions directly, constraint propagation through negation becomes non-trivial and most of the s(ASP) machinery would have to be exposed in the imperative program. These restrictions are discussed more in Sect. 7.

6   Synthesis Task

Every rule-head in the ASP program stands for an abstraction and defines more abstractions that eventually reduce to constraints on domain variables. For the synthesis algorithm, it is useful to see the intermediate ASP program as a grammar with associated attributes for each of the non-terminal symbols. Each rule-head represents its own non-terminal symbol including the dual rules. Every rule-head (non-terminal symbol) has a set of attributes which are relevant for translation. If the rule-head is R, then R.arity and R.arglist represent the number of arguments and the list of arguments with their associated domains. R.callsMain is a boolean attribute that signifies R directly calls the main predicate. This helps us in adding extra code required for global consistency checking within a *forall* as illustrated in the graph coloring example. R.bodyVariables represents the set of body variables that appear in the definition of the rule represented by the rule-head R. Body variables give rise to choice-points and R.bodyVariables enables us to add backtracking code. Constraints on domain variables such as $X < Y$ are treated as terminal symbols in the grammar. We assume the rule-head R stands for its own name. This is useful when R represents a domain or an input fact (such as edge relation for graphs). Next, we give a syntax-directed translation of all syntactic fragments found in the intermediate logic program.

6.1 Syntax-Directed Translation

We provide a top-down translation of ASP code (grammar symbols at this juncture) into imperative code. The translation function T maps syntax of intermediate ASP to Python code. Letters $p, q, ..$ are used to denote predicates. Predicates get mapped to function-calls. Letters $X_i, Y_j, ...$ denote arguments of predicates. The arguments get translated to variables $x_i, y_j, ...$ with their respective associated domains $D_{x_i}, D_{y_j}, ...$ and so on. The notation $\bar{X}$ stands for an arbitrary list of arguments. It is also used in the Python translation as $\bar{x}$, representing an arbitrary list of arguments in a function-call. The *context*, which is the set of consistent terms of the main predicate, is taken to be visible in all code fragments and is universally passed as the last argument at every function-call. The call associated with the predicate $q(\bar{Y})$ would be $q(\bar{y}, context)$. Dual rules are prefixed with $not\_$. For instance, if $p(\bar{x}, context)$ is a function-call associated with the predicate $p(\bar{X})$, then $not\_p(\bar{x}, context)$ stands for the call associated with the dual rule $not\ p(\bar{X})$. We list important rules for translation and explain the ones that are not obvious. More general rules can be found elsewhere [17].

6.2 Synthesis Procedure

The procedure *Gen_Intermediate* generates the dual rules and foralls on body variables (if any). This procedure is quite straightforward and not further elucidated. Likewise, *Gen_Attribute_Grammar* associates the intermediate program with grammar symbols and annotates them with appropriate attributes. Again, it is easy to determine the body variables of a rule, to check if an abstraction calls the main predicate directly. The algorithm is given below:

Algorithm 1. Synthesizing Imperative code from source ASP

1: $Code \leftarrow \emptyset$
2: $\mathscr{P}_{int} \leftarrow Gen\_Intermediate(\mathscr{P}_{input})$ ▷ generate dual rules and foralls
3: $\mathscr{G} \leftarrow Gen\_Attribute\_Grammar(\mathscr{P}_{int})$
4: **for** *every fact* $\mathscr{F} \in \mathscr{P}_{input}$ **do**
5:      $Code \leftarrow Code \cup T[\![\mathscr{F}]\!]$ ▷ add code for input facts and domains
6: **end for**
7: **for** *every rule* $R \in \mathscr{G}$ **do**
8:      $Code \leftarrow Code \cup T[\![R]\!]$ ▷ where T is the translation function
9: **end for**

6.3 Transformation Rules

I. Domain mapping:
$$T[\![domain(constant)]\!] = \quad \texttt{domain[str(constant)] = True}$$

II. Constraint Checking:
$$T[\![X\ relop\ Y]\!] = \begin{cases} \texttt{if not x relop y:} \\ \quad \texttt{return \{'success':False,'context':ctx\}} \end{cases}$$

where *relop* is relational operator

III. Sequencing:

$$T[\![\, p_1(\bar{X}_1), p_2(\bar{X}_2)\,]\!] = \begin{cases} \text{ctx\_p1 = } p_1(x_1,..,\text{copy(ctx))} \\ \text{if ctx['success']:} \\ \quad \text{ctx = ctx\_p1} \\ \quad T[\![p_2(\bar{X}_2)]\!] \\ \text{else:} \\ \quad \text{return\{'success':False,'context':ctx\_p1\}} \end{cases}$$

IV. Double negations cancel out:

$$T[\![\, not\ not\_p(\bar{X})\,]\!] = \ T[\![\, p(\bar{X})\,]\!]$$

V. Forall transformation (global consistency):

$$T[\![forall(Y, p(X_1,..,Y,..,X_n)]\!] = \begin{cases} \text{for y in } D_y: \\ \quad \text{for main\_pred}(x_{\alpha_1},..,x_{\alpha_m}) \text{ in ctx:} \\ \quad \quad \text{ctx\_p = p}(x_{\beta_1},..\text{y},..,x_{\beta_m},\text{copy(ctx))} \\ \quad \quad \text{if ctx\_p['success']:} \\ \quad \quad \quad \text{ctx = ctx\_p} \\ \quad \quad \text{else:} \\ \quad \quad \quad \text{return \{'success':False'context':ctx\}} \end{cases}$$

where p.callsMain is *true*, $X_{\beta_1},..,X_{\beta_m}$ are some variables in $p(X_1,..,$ $Y,..,X_n)$ which unify with main_pred$(X_{\alpha_1},..,X_{\alpha_m})$. Also, the choice $p(x_1,..,x_n, ctx)$ is checked against all terms in the context explored thus far.

VI. Disjunction translates to nested if-else condition:

$$T[\![\, p_1(\bar{X}_1) \vee p_2(\bar{X}_2)\,]\!] = \begin{cases} \text{context = } p_1(x_1, \ ...,\ \text{copy(context))} \\ \text{if not context['success']:} \\ \quad T[\![p_2(\bar{X}_2)]\!] \\ \text{else:} \\ \quad \text{pass} \end{cases}$$

VII. Abstraction (positive rule-heads):

$$T[\![p(\bar{X}) : - q_1(\bar{X}_1),..,q_m(\bar{X}_m)]\!] = \begin{cases} \text{def p}(\bar{x},\text{ctx}): \\ \quad \text{if ctx[p}(\bar{x})]: \\ \quad \quad \text{return \{'success': True, 'context': ctx\}} \\ \quad \text{ctx[p}(\bar{x})] \text{ = true} \\ \quad T[\![q_1(\bar{X}_1), q_2(\bar{X}_2), ..., q_m(\bar{X}_m)]\!] \\ \quad \text{return \{'success': False, 'context': ctx\}} \end{cases}$$

The if-check in the beginning signals the function to report success if it already part of the context. Otherwise, it is added to the context contingent on the success of the rule body.

VIII. Abstraction (dual rule-heads):

$$T[\![not\_p(\bar{X}) : -q_1(\bar{X}_1),..,q_m(\bar{X}_m)]\!] = \begin{cases} \text{def not\_p}(\bar{x},\text{ctx}): \\ \quad \text{if ctx[p}(\bar{x})]: \\ \quad \quad \text{return \{'success':False,'context':ctx\}} \\ \quad T[\![q_1(\bar{X}_1),..,q_m(\bar{X}_m)]\!] \\ \quad \text{return \{'success': False,'context':ctx\}} \end{cases}$$

If the positive term corresponding to the dual is already part of the context, then we report failure. Else, it would be a contradiction to have both the positive term and its NAF term in the same answer set (context).

6.4 Efficiency of the Synthesized Code

Since the synthesized code has the s(ASP) logic encoded within and due to the fact that it is imperative in nature, the execution time is expected to be faster. This is, in fact, the case. We ran the synthesized graph coloring code on complete graphs of size 3, 4, 5 respectively. A complete graph of size n is labelled K_n. The running times are shown in the table below. The programs were run on an Intel i7 Processor at 2.90 GHz with 8 GB RAM. Average of 10 runs is shown:

K_n	Graph colorable				Graph not colorable			
	Python basic	Python optimized	s(ASP)	Speedup optimized	Python basic	Python optimized	s(ASP)	Speedup optimized
K_3	0.109 s	0.043 s	1.14 s	26.51	0.109 s	0.039 s	0.359 s	9.21
K_4	0.135 s	0.05 s	4.80 s	96	0.129 s	0.046 s	3.330 s	72.39
K_5	0.334 s	0.071 s	34.63 s	487.64	0.444 s	0.074 s	62.295 s	841.82
K_{10}	≈3 h	772.05 s	>15 h	Large	≈3 h	79.78 s	>15 h	Large

The speedup as the graph sizes increase is significant. Although asymptotically both the synthesized code and the s(ASP) execution suffer from the same exponential time complexity (in the size of the input graph), the improvement in the constant factor cannot be ignored. This echoes the idea that program transformation by partial evaluation results in program speedup [7]. Although we have very minimal partial evaluation, we eliminate the NMR checks that s(ASP) appends to every query. The NMR checks are implicitly handled by reducing them to a simple check of asserting whether both a proposition and its negation are present in the same context (partial stable model). For larger graph sizes such as K_{10}, the imperative program found a solution in 3 h in whereas s(ASP) did not produce even after 15 h. This again confirms the effectiveness of our program transformation. Nonetheless, it should also be noted that s(ASP) is still experimental and can handle any answer set program. Another point that should be highlighted is that the imperative program just produces one stable model as opposed to producing all stable models. This is well suited for ASP programs that have at most one answer set. The top-down translation can admit optimization in the imperative program by having the program maintain a set of inconsistent models in its computation. It can also be improved by user-provided heuristics. We leave this for future work. An optimization of the graph-coloring and n-queens can be found elsewhere [17]. The entire transformation is automated in our tool called **PySasp** [16].

6.5   Proof of Correctness

The first proof obligation is to ensure that the synthesized program is adherent to the stable model semantics. For this, we need to ensure that the steps taken by the imperative algorithm correspond to the steps taken by s(ASP) given a query. The imperative program represents on-the-fly grounding. This is stated in the following theorem as follows:

Theorem 1. Goal-directed on-the-fly grounding is equivalent to goal-directed grounded execution.

Proof Outline. The proof can be found in the paper on s(ASP) [11]. □

Next we state two lemmas. The first lemma justifies having just the *main predicate* in the *context*, the second lemma proves the equivalence of the *forall* and *for-loop*. Let $\mathscr{P}$ represent the class of answer set programs from Sect. 5.

Lemma 1. For every program $\Pi \in \mathscr{P}$ that is satisfiable, every partial stable model consists of at least one grounded term of the *main predicate*. □

Lemma 2. The translated *for-loop* is equivalent to the *forall* . □

Theorem 2. For every query Q of *main predicate* of every program $\Pi \in \mathscr{P}$, the synthesized imperative program returns a *context* corresponding to some partial stable model of Q in Π. The program returns an empty context if Q is unsatisfiable in Π.

Proof Outline. Follows directly from Theorem 1, Lemmas 1 and 2. □
Note: The proofs of Lemmas 1, 2 can be found elsewhere [17].

7   Conclusion

In this paper, we described a way to synthesize imperative code from (a class of) ASP program specification under the goal-directed operational semantics of s(ASP). The work reported here is the first step towards obtaining efficient implementation from high level specifications. Our eventual goal is to specify algorithms for concurrent data structures as answer set programs and automatically be able to obtain the efficient, imperative versions of those algorithms. Achieving such a goal requires making extensive use of partial evaluation and semantics-preserving re-arrangement of goals in the current resolvent. It is part of our future work. Essentially, we should be able to take constraints and move them up in the resolvent to the earliest point where this constraint can be executed. Note that this is essential for efficiency since constraints could be specified globally as in this different version of the graph-coloring answer set program below:

```
color(X, C) :- node(X), color(C), not another_color(X, C).
another_color(X, C) :- node(X), color(C), node(Y), X != Y, color(Y,C).
:- color(X, C), color(Y, C), edge(X, Y).
```

Handling global constraints is closely related to dynamic consistency checking (DCC) in goal-directed answer set programs [12,13]. DCC ensures only the necessary constraints, that are relevant to a rule and the possible bindings variables could take, are checked along with the rule-body. All other constraints not relevant to the rule can be ignored. This would also enable synthesis of programs specifying data structures and planning problems.

References

1. Arias, J., et al.: Constraint answer set programming without grounding. Theory Pract. Logic Program. **18**(3–4), 337–354 (2018)
2. Basin, D., Deville, Y., Flener, P., Hamfelt, A., Fischer Nilsson, J.: Synthesis of programs in computational logic. In: Bruynooghe, M., Lau, K.-K. (eds.) Program Development in Computational Logic. LNCS, vol. 3049, pp. 30–65. Springer, Heidelberg (2004). https://doi.org/10.1007/978-3-540-25951-0_2
3. Chen, Z., et al.: A physician advisory system for chronic heart failure management. TPLP **16**(5–6), 604–618 (2016)
4. Eiter, T.: Data integration and answer set programming. In: Baral, C., Greco, G., Leone, N., Terracina, G. (eds.) LPNMR 2005. LNCS (LNAI), vol. 3662, pp. 13–25. Springer, Heidelberg (2005). https://doi.org/10.1007/11546207_2
5. Gebser, M., Kaufmann, B., Neumann, A., Schaub, T.: *clasp*: a conflict-driven answer set solver. In: Baral, C., Brewka, G., Schlipf, J. (eds.) LPNMR 2007. LNCS (LNAI), vol. 4483, pp. 260–265. Springer, Heidelberg (2007). https://doi.org/10.1007/978-3-540-72200-7_23
6. Gelfond, M., Kahl, Y.: Knowledge Representation, Reasoning, and the Design of Intelligent Agents: The Answer-set Programming Approach. Cambridge University Press, New York (2014)
7. Jones, N.: Constant time factors do matter. In: STOC 1993. 6-2-611
8. Leone, N., et al.: The DLV system. In: Flesca, S., Greco, S., Ianni, G., Leone, N. (eds.) JELIA 2002. LNCS (LNAI), vol. 2424, pp. 537–540. Springer, Heidelberg (2002). https://doi.org/10.1007/3-540-45757-7_50
9. Lloyd, J.W.: Foundations of Logic Programming. Symbolic Computation. Springer, Cham (1987). https://doi.org/10.1007/978-3-642-83189-8
10. Manna, Z., Waldinger, R.J.: Towards automatic program synthesis. In: Engeler, E. (ed.) Symposium on Semantics of Algorithmic Languages. LNM, vol. 188, pp. 270–310. Springer, Heidelberg (1971). https://doi.org/10.1007/BFb0059702
11. Marple, K., Salazar, E., Gupta, G.: Computing stable models of normal logic programs without grounding. arXiv:1709.00501 (2017)
12. Marple, K., Gupta, G.: Dynamic consistency checking in goal- directed answer set programming. TPLP **14**(4–5), 415–427 (2014)
13. Marple, K., et al.: Goal-directed execution of answer set programs. In: Proceedings of the 14th PPDP Symposium, pp. 35–44. ACM (2012)
14. Simon, L., Mallya, A., Bansal, A., Gupta, G.: Coinductive logic programming. In: Etalle, S., Truszczyński, M. (eds.) ICLP 2006. LNCS, vol. 4079, pp. 330–345. Springer, Heidelberg (2006). https://doi.org/10.1007/11799573_25
15. Srivastava, S., Gulwani, S., Foster, J.S.: From program verification to program synthesis. ACM SIGPLAN Not. **45**(1), 313–326 (2010)
16. Varanasi, S.C.: PySasp (2019). https://github.com/sarat-chandra-varanasi/pysasp
17. Varanasi, S.C., et al.: Synthesizing imperative code from answer set programming specifications (extended). UT Dallas CS Technical report (2019). www.utdallas.edu/~gupta/aspsynthesis.pdf

Verified Construction of Fair Voting Rules

Karsten Diekhoff, Michael Kirsten$^{(\boxtimes)}$ (ID), and Jonas Krämer

Karlsruhe Institute of Technology (KIT), Karlsruhe, Germany
{karsten.diekhoff,jonas.kraemer}@student.kit.edu, kirsten@kit.edu

Abstract. Voting rules aggregate multiple individual preferences in order to make collective decisions. Commonly, these mechanisms are expected to respect a multitude of different fairness and reliability properties, e.g., to ensure that each voter's ballot accounts for the same proportion of the elected alternatives, or that a voter cannot change the election outcome in her favor by insincerely filling out her ballot. However, no voting rule is fair in all respects, and trade-off attempts between such properties often bring out inconsistencies, which makes the construction of arguably practical and fair voting rules non-trivial and error-prone. In this paper, we present a formal and systematic approach for the flexible and verified construction of voting rules from composable core modules to respect such properties by construction. Formal composition rules guarantee resulting properties from properties of the individual components, which are of generic nature to be reused for various voting rules. We provide a prototypical logic-based implementation with proofs for a selected set of structures and composition rules within the theorem prover Isabelle/HOL. The approach can be readily extended in order to support many voting rules from the literature by extending the set of basic modules and composition rules. We exemplarily construct the well-known voting rule *sequential majority comparison* (SMC) from simple generic modules, and automatically produce a formal proof that SMC satisfies the fairness property monotonicity. Monotonicity is a well-known social-choice property that is easily violated by voting rules in practice.

Keywords: Social choice · Higher-order logic · Modular verification

1 Introduction

In an election, voters cast ballots to express their individual preferences about eligible alternatives. From these individual preferences, a collective decision, i.e., a set of winning alternatives, is determined using a *voting rule*. Throughout the literature and in practice, there are many different voting rules each of which exhibit different behaviors and properties. Depending on the specific applications and regulations, voting rules are devised for a variety of different design goals towards carefully selected behaviors and properties. Imagine, for instance, one situation where a village wants to elect a local council, or another one where a group of friends wants to choose a destination to go on vacation based on each

© Springer Nature Switzerland AG 2020
M. Gabbrielli (Ed.): LOPSTR 2019, LNCS 12042, pp. 90–104, 2020.
https://doi.org/10.1007/978-3-030-45260-5_6

of the friend's preferences. In the former case, the village might prefer to be represented by a larger council rather than having only few representatives who are elected by a majority, but are strongly disliked by everybody else. For the latter, it is clearly undesirable to choose multiple destinations, but rather settle for one so that the group can spend the vacation together.

Indeed, there is no general rule which caters for every requirement, and any voting rule shows paradoxical behavior for some voting situation [1]. Therefore, an approach to analyze voting rules for their behavior by clear-cut formal properties, the so-called *axiomatic method*, has emerged. The axiomatic method advocates the use of rules that provide rigorous guarantees (which we call *properties*), and compares them based on guarantees that they do, or do not, satisfy. These properties capture very different requirements of fairness or reliability, e.g., principles that each vote is counted equally, that the electees proportionally reflect the voters' preferences, or that they are preferred by a majority of the voters. Devising voting rules towards such properties is generally cumbersome as their trade-off is inherently difficult and error-prone. Attempting to prove properties for specific voting rules often exhibits design errors, but is cumbersome as well [4]. As of yet, there exists no general formal approach to systematically devise voting rules towards formal properties without being either error-prone or extremely cumbersome.

Contribution. In this paper, we present a formal systematic approach for the flexible and verified construction of voting rules from compact composable modules with guaranteed formal properties. Indeed, when taking an abstract view, many voting rules share similar structures, e.g., aggregating the individual votes by calculating the sum or some other aggregator function. Based on this observation, our approach enables flexible, intuitive and verified construction of interesting voting rules from a small number of compositional structures. These structures exhibit precise and general interfaces such that their scope may easily be extended with further modules. We devise a general component type as well as special types, e.g., for aggregation functions, and compositional structures, e.g., for sequential, parallel and loop composition. The resulting properties, e.g., common social choice properties from the literature, are guaranteed from composing modules with given individual properties by rigorous composition rules.

We demonstrate the logic-based application with proofs for a selected set of composition structures and rules, and composable modules within the theorem prover Isabelle/HOL [13]. Thereby, the approach is amenable both for external scrutiny as compositions are rigorously and compactly defined, and for an integration in larger automatic voting rule design or verification frameworks. As case study, we define composition rules for the common social choice property *monotonicity*, and demonstrate a formal correct-by-construction verification of the rule *sequential majority comparison* (SMC). The construction produces a proof that SMC fulfills the monotonicity property using a set of basic modules.

Outline. The rest of this paper is structured as follows: Sect. 2 introduces formal concepts and definitions from social choice theory for our construction approach. We present the core framework in Sect. 3 and demonstrate the verified construction framework within Isabelle/HOL in Sect. 4. In Sect. 5, we apply our approach to the case study of constructing the monotone voting rule sequential majority comparison, and give an overview of related work to our approach in Sect. 6. We finally conclude and discuss future work in Sect. 7.

2   Concepts and Definitions from Social Choice Theory

We consider a fixed finite set $\mathcal{A}$ of eligible *alternatives* and a finite (possibly ordered) set $\mathcal{K}$ of *voters* (with cardinality k). In an election, each voter i casts a *ballot* $\succsim_i \in \mathcal{L}(\mathcal{A})$, which is a linear order[1], ranking the alternatives $\mathcal{A}$ according to i's preference. We collect all votes in a *profile*, i.e., a sequence $\succsim = (\succsim_1, \ldots, \succsim_k)$ of k ballots. Given the set $\mathcal{L}(\mathcal{A})$ of linear orders on $\mathcal{A}$, $\mathcal{L}(\mathcal{A})^k$ defines the set of all profiles on $\mathcal{A}$ of length k, i.e., for all voters. Hence, we have $\mathcal{L}(\mathcal{A})^+ = \bigcup_{k \in \mathbb{N}^+} \mathcal{L}(\mathcal{A})^k$, the set of all finite, nonempty profiles on $\mathcal{A}$, i.e., the input domain for a voting rule. Voting rules (see Definition 1) elect a nonempty subset $\mathcal{C}(\mathcal{A})$ of the alternatives as (possibly tied) winners, given $\mathcal{C}(X)$ denotes the set of all nonempty subsets of a set X.

Definition 1 (Voting Rule). *Given a finite set of alternatives $\mathcal{A}$, a voting rule f maps each possible profile $\succsim \in \mathcal{L}(\mathcal{A})^+$ to a nonempty set of winning alternatives in $\mathcal{C}(\mathcal{A})$:*

$$f : \mathcal{L}(\mathcal{A})^+ \to \mathcal{C}(\mathcal{A}).$$

In practice and in literature, a multitude of voting rules are in use. A common example is the function that returns all alternatives that are ranked at first position by a plurality of the voters, hence called *plurality voting*. Another common kind of voting rules assigns values for every ballot to each alternative according to her position occupied on the ballot, and elects the alternatives with the maximal score, i.e., the sum of all such values for her. Such rules are called scoring rules, e.g., the *Borda rule*, where the value of an alternative on a ballot is the number of alternatives ranked below her on that ballot.

Social Choice Properties. Within social choice theory, the axiomatic method has established a number of general fairness and reliability properties called (*axiomatic*) *social choice properties*. They formally capture intuitively desirable or in other ways useful properties to compare, evaluate, or characterize voting rules. Such properties are applicable in a general way as they are defined on abstract voting rules only with respect to profiles and returned sets of winning alternatives. For the sake of simplicity, the examples illustrated in this paper only address properties of universal nature, i.e., they require that all mappings of a given voting rule belong to some set of admissible ways, as formally described by the property of interest, for associating sets of winners to profiles. Besides properties which *functionally* limit the possible sets of winning alternatives for any one given profile, properties may also *relationally* limit combinations (of finite arity) of mappings, e.g., certain (hypothetical) changes of a profile may

---

[1] A linear order is a transitive, complete, and antisymmetric relation.

only lead to certain changes of the winning alternatives. Relational properties capture a voter's considerations such as how certain ways of (not) filling out her ballot may or may not affect the chances of winning for some alternatives.

Within this paper, we use *Condorcet consistency* and *monotonicity* as running examples. The functional property *Condorcet consistency* (see Definition 3) requires that if there is an alternative w that is the *Condorcet winner* (see Definition 2), the rule elects w as unique winner. A Condorcet winner is an alternative that wins every pairwise majority comparison against all other alternatives, i.e., for any other alternative, there is a majority of voters who rank the Condorcet winner higher than that alternative.

Definition 2 (Condorcet Winner). *For a set of alternatives A and a profile $\succsim \in \mathcal{L}(A)^+$, an alternative $w \in A$ is a* Condorcet winner *iff the following holds:*

$$\forall a \in A \setminus \{w\} : |\{i \in \mathcal{K} : a \succsim_i w\}| < |\{i \in \mathcal{K} : w \succsim_i a\}|.$$

Note that, if a Condorcet winner exists, it is unique by the above definition.

Definition 3 (Condorcet Consistency). *For a set of alternatives A, a voting rule f is* Condorcet consistent *iff for every profile $\succsim \in \mathcal{L}(A)^+$ and (if existing) the respective Condorcet winner $w \in A$, the following holds:*

$$w \text{ is Condorcet winner for } \succsim \quad \Rightarrow \quad f(\succsim) = \{w\}.$$

Note here that for profiles for which no Condorcet winner exists, the property imposes no requirements on the election outcome. The relational property *monotonicity* expresses that if a voter were to change her vote in favor of some other alternative, the outcome could never change to the disadvantage of that alternative. Monotone voting rules are resistant to some forms of strategic manipulation where a voter could make their preferred alternative the (unique) winner by misrepresenting her actual preferences and assigning a higher rank to another alternative on her ballot. A voting rule is monotone (see Definition 5) iff for any two profiles $\succsim$ and $\succsim'$ which are identical except for one alternative a that is ranked higher in $\succsim'$ (while preserving all remaining pairwise-relative rankings), the election of a for $\succsim$ always implies her election for $\succsim'$. We define this "ranking higher" as *lifting* an alternative (see Definition 4).

Definition 4 (Lifting). *For a set of alternatives A and two profiles $\succsim, \succsim' \in \mathcal{L}(A)^k$, $\succsim'$ is obtained from $\succsim$ by* lifting *an alternative $a \in A$ iff there exists a ballot $i \in [1, k]$ such that $\succsim_i \neq \succsim'_i$ and for each such i the following holds:*

i. *There exists some alternative $x \in A$ such that $x \succsim_i a$ and $a \succsim'_i x$, and*
ii. *we have $y \succsim_i z \Leftrightarrow y \succsim'_i z$ for all other alternatives $y, z \in A \setminus \{a\}$.*

We may thus define the monotonicity property as follows.

Definition 5 (Monotonicity). *For a set of alternatives A and an alternative $a \in A$, a voting rule f is* monotone *iff for all profiles $\succsim, \succsim' \in \mathcal{L}(A)^+$ where $\succsim'$ is obtained from lifting a in $\succsim$, the following implication holds:*

$$a \in f(\succsim) \Rightarrow a \in f(\succsim').$$

3 Composable Modules and Compositional Structures

The verified construction approach consists of two structural and two semantic concepts, namely (i) *component types* that specify structural interfaces wherein components can be implemented, and (ii)*compositional structures* that specify structural contracts which combine components to create new components that are again composable. Moreover, semantic aspects for constructing concrete voting rules are addressed by (iii) *composition rules* that define semantic rules which compositions can contractually depend on, i.e., if components fulfill a rule's requirements, the composition guarantees the rule's semantics, as well as (iv) *composable modules* that define concrete semantics of either directly implemented or constructed modules from which other modules can be composed using the composition rules. In the following, we give details on component types and compositional structures for composing voting rules based on the ideas in [9].

3.1 Electoral Modules

The structural foundation of our approach are *electoral modules*, a generalization of voting rules as in Definition 1. We define electoral modules (see Definition 6) so that they act as the principal component type (cf. (i)) within our framework. In contrast to a voting rule, an electoral module does not need to make final decisions for all the alternatives, i.e., partition[2] them (only) into winning and losing alternatives, but can instead defer the decision for some or all of them to other modules. Hence, electoral modules partition the received (possibly empty) set of alternatives $A \subseteq \mathcal{A}$ into *elected*, *rejected* and *deferred* alternatives. In particular, any of those sets, e.g., the set of winning (elected) alternatives, may also be left empty, as long as they collectively still hold all the received alternatives. Just like a voting rule, an electoral module also receives a profile which holds the voters' preferences, which, unlike a voting rule, consider only the (sub-)set of alternatives that the module receives. We take this into account by the following definition of our input domain $\mathcal{D}_{\mathrm{mod}}^{\mathcal{A}}$:

$$\mathcal{D}_{\mathrm{mod}}^{\mathcal{A}} := \{(A, \succsim) \mid A \subseteq \mathcal{A}, \succsim \in \mathcal{L}(A)^{+}\}$$

$\mathcal{D}_{\mathrm{mod}}^{\mathcal{A}}$ contains all subsets of $\mathcal{A}$ paired with matching profiles. We can hence define electoral modules as follows:

Definition 6 (Electoral Module). *For eligible alternatives $\mathcal{A}$ and a (sub-)set $A \subseteq \mathcal{A}$, we define an* electoral module *as a function m with*

$$m : \mathcal{D}_{\mathrm{mod}}^{\mathcal{A}} \to \mathcal{P}(\mathcal{A})^{3}.$$

The function m maps a set of alternatives with a matching profile to the set-triple (e, r, d) of sets of elected *(e), rejected (r), and* deferred *(d) alternatives such that*

$$(A, \succsim) \in \mathcal{D}_{\mathrm{mod}}^{\mathcal{A}} \Rightarrow (m(A, \succsim) = (e, r, d) \text{ partitions } A).$$

---

[2] We say that a sequence of sets $s_1, \ldots, s_n$ partitions a set S if and only if S equals the union $\bigcup_{i \in [1,n]} s_i$ over all sets s_i for $i \in [1, n]$ and all their pairwise intersections are empty, i.e., $\forall i \neq j \in [1, n] : s_i \cap s_j = \emptyset$.

In the following, we denote the set of electoral modules by $\mathcal{M}_\mathcal{A}$, as well as $m_e(A, \succsim)$, $m_r(A, \succsim)$, and $m_d(A, \succsim)$ for the elected, rejected and deferred alternatives, respectively, of an electoral module m for $(A, \succsim)$.

Moreover, we can easily translate voting rules to electoral modules by returning a triple of empty sets in case the module receives an empty set. Otherwise, we return an empty deferred set, an elected set with exactly the winning alternatives, and a rejected set with the complement of the winning alternatives (we remove the alternatives which are not contained in the received set of alternatives). Note that, as a consequence, social choice properties can also be easily translated in order to conform to electoral modules.

3.2   Sequential Composition

Sequential composition (see Definition 7) is a compositional structure (cf. (ii)) for composing two electoral modules m, n into a new electoral module $(m \rhd n)$ such that the second module n only decides on alternatives which m defers and cannot reduce the set of alternatives already elected or rejected by m. In this composition, n receives only m's deferred alternatives $m_d(A, \succsim)$ and a profile $\succsim_{|(m_d(A,\succsim))}$ which only addresses alternatives contained in $m_d(A, \succsim)$.

Definition 7 (Sequential Composition). *For any set of alternatives $\mathcal{A}$ and a (sub-)set $A \subseteq \mathcal{A}$, electoral modules $m, n \in \mathcal{M}_\mathcal{A}$ and input $(A, \succsim) \in \mathcal{D}_{\mathrm{mod}}^\mathcal{A}$, we define the sequential composition function $(\rhd) : \mathcal{M}_\mathcal{A}^2 \to \mathcal{M}_\mathcal{A}$ as*

$$(m \rhd n)(A, \succsim) := \quad \begin{aligned} & (m_e(A, \succsim) \cup n_e(m_d(A, \succsim), \succsim_{|(m_d(A,\succsim))}), \\ & m_r(A, \succsim) \cup n_r(m_d(A, \succsim), \succsim_{|(m_d(A,\succsim))}), \\ & n_d(m_d(A, \succsim), \succsim_{|(m_d(A,\succsim))})) \end{aligned}$$

3.3   Revision Composition

Mostly for convenience, we define a revision composition (see Definition 8) for situations in which we want to revise the alternatives already elected by a prior module, e.g., for enabling sequential composition with a tie-breaking module. For an electoral module m, the revision composition removes m's elected alternatives and attaches them to the previous deferred alternatives, while the rejected alternatives are kept unchanged. Whereas this composition can also be achieved by parallel composition, this dedicated structure turns out to be beneficial in our implementation due to its frequent uses.

Definition 8 (Revision Composition). *For any set of alternatives $\mathcal{A}$ and a (sub-)set $A \subseteq \mathcal{A}$, electoral module $m \in \mathcal{M}_\mathcal{A}$, and input $(A, \succsim) \in \mathcal{D}_{\mathrm{mod}}^\mathcal{A}$, we define the revision composition $(\downarrow) : \mathcal{M}_\mathcal{A} \to \mathcal{M}_\mathcal{A}$ as*

$$(m \downarrow)(A, \succsim) := (\emptyset, \ m_r(A, \succsim), \ m_e(A, \succsim) \cup m_d(A, \succsim)).$$

3.4 Parallel Composition

The parallel composition (see Definition 11) lets two electoral modules make two independent decisions for the given set of alternatives. Their two decisions are then aggregated by an *aggregator* (see Definition 9), which is another component type that combines two set-triples of elected, rejected and deferred alternatives (as well as the set of alternatives) into a single such triple (we define the input domain $\mathcal{D}_{\mathrm{agg}}^{\mathcal{A}}$ accordingly).

Definition 9 (Aggregator). *For a set of alternatives $\mathcal{A}$, a (sub-)set $A \subseteq \mathcal{A}$ and input $(A, p_1, p_2) \in \mathcal{D}_{\mathrm{agg}}^{\mathcal{A}}$, an aggregator is a function*

$$agg : \mathcal{D}_{\mathrm{agg}}^{\mathcal{A}} \to \mathcal{P}(\mathcal{A})^3 \text{ such that } agg(A, p_1, p_2) \text{ partitions } A.$$

A useful instance of such an aggregator is the max-aggregator agg_{max}:

Definition 10 (Max-Aggregator). *Given two set-triples (e_1, r_1, d_1), $(e2, r2, d2)$ of elected (e), rejected (r) and deferred (d) alternatives, agg_{max} picks, for each alternative a and the sets containing a, the superior one of the two sets (assuming the order $e > d > r$).*

$$
\begin{aligned}
agg_{\mathrm{max}}&((e_1, r_1, d_1),\ (e_2, r_2, d_2)) \\
&= (e_1 \cup e_2, (r_1 \cup r_2) \setminus (e_1 \cup e_2 \cup d_1 \cup d_2), (d_1 \cup d_2) \setminus (e_1 \cup e_2))
\end{aligned}
$$

Based on the notion of aggregators, we can now define the parallel composition as a function mapping two electoral modules m, n and an aggregator $agg \in \mathcal{G}_{\mathcal{A}}$ (the set of all aggregators) to a new electoral module $(m \,||_{agg}\, n)$:

Definition 11 (Parallel Composition). *For a set of alternatives A and a (sub-)set $A \subseteq \mathcal{A}$, electoral modules m, n, and an aggregator agg we define the parallel composition $(||) : (\mathcal{M}_{\mathcal{A}} \times \mathcal{G}_{\mathcal{A}} \times \mathcal{M}_{\mathcal{A}}) \to \mathcal{M}_{\mathcal{A}}$ as*

$$(m \,||_{agg}\, n)(A, \succsim) := agg(A,\ m(A, \succsim),\ n(A, \succsim)).$$

3.5 Loop Composition

Based on sequential composition (Sect. 3.2) for electoral modules, we define the more general loop composition for sequential compositions of dynamic length. A loop composition $(m \circlearrowright_t)$ repeatedly composes an electoral module m sequentially with itself until either a fixed point is reached or a *termination condition* t is satisfied. Within our framework, termination conditions, technically another component type, are boolean predicates on set-triples such that they are suitable for electoral modules. The full definition can be found within the Isabelle/HOL theories provided with this paper.

3.6   A Simple Example

As a simple example, we illustrate the construction of a voting rule using structures from above. Consider the well-known *Baldwin's rule*, which is a voting rule based on sequential elimination [2]. The rule repeatedly eliminates the alternative with the lowest Borda score (see Sect. 2) until only one alternative remains.

As basic modules (cf. (iv)), we use (a) a module that computes the Borda scores, rejects the alternative with the lowest such score, and defers the rest, as well as (b) a module that attaches all deferred alternatives to the elected set.

Moreover, we choose a termination condition such that the loop of interest stops when the set of (deferred) alternatives has reached size one.

Therefore, Baldwin's rule can be obtained by

1. composing (a) by a loop structure with above mentioned termination condition, and
2. sequentially composing the loop composition with (b).

Moreover, loop composition can be directly used for many voting rules of a category called *tournament solutions*. Tournament solutions typically consist of multiple rounds, in each comparing a pair of alternatives based on their profile rankings, and the winner of a comparison advances to the next round.

4   Verified Modular Construction Framework

In the following, we describe how we model the concepts defined in Sect. 3 within a modular proof framework for the verified construction of voting rules.

4.1   Isabelle and Higher-Order Logic (HOL)

We implemented and proved our logical concepts within the interactive theorem prover Isabelle/HOL [13]. The Isabelle/HOL system provides a generic infrastructure for implementing deductive systems in higher-order logics and enabling to write tactics for human-readable and machine-checked proofs to show that the deductive conclusions are indeed correct. We decided to use Isabelle/HOL, because higher-order logic (HOL) allows to define very expressive, rigorous and general theorems. By this means, a theorem is –once proven correct within Isabelle– re-checked and confirmed by Isabelle/HOL within a few seconds every time the theorem is loaded. Proofs within Isabelle/HOL are based on the employed theories at the core of the Isabelle system. We made use of the possibility to define very general theorems to be reused for the construction of various voting rules and sorts of composition. Moreover, the framework allows for easy application and extension potentially within a larger framework for the automatic discovery and construction of voting rules, provided that the voting rule of interest can be composed from the given compositional rules and composable modules using the given composition structures and component types.

The definitions and theorems within our framework are mostly self-contained, i.e., for the most part they only rely on basic set theory as well as the theories of finite lists, relations, and order relations for defining the profiles and linear orders used within our notion of profiles and modules as seen in Listing 1. Therein, we introduce a handy type abbreviation (Line 1) for profiles which are lists of relations and therefrom define profiles on alternatives (Lines 3 to 4) based on the theory of order relations, and moreover finite profiles (Lines 5 to 6) which we use in a number of structures and concepts. Moreover, type abbreviations for results of electoral modules (Line 8), i.e., set-triples, are introduced, and electoral modules (Line 10) as defined in Sect. 3. We capture the partitioning with the two functions to express disjointness of the three sets in an electoral module result (Lines 20 to 21) and that their union yields the set of alternatives of the input (Lines 17 to 18). Finally, at the end of Listing 1, we can essentially define electoral modules on finite profiles and partitionings of the alternatives (Lines 23 to 25). We did not require any additional theories besides the ones provided off-the-shelf with the Isabelle system.

```
1  type_synonym 'a Profile = "('a rel) list"
2
3  definition profile_on :: "'a set ⇒ 'a Profile ⇒ bool" where
4    "profile_on A p ≡ (∀ b ∈ (set p). linear_order_on A b)"
5  abbreviation finite_profile :: "'a set ⇒ 'a Profile ⇒ bool" where
6    "finite_profile A p ≡ finite A ∧ profile_on A p"
7
8  type_synonym 'a Result = "'a set * 'a set * 'a set"
9
10  type_synonym 'a Electoral_module = "'a set ⇒ 'a Profile ⇒ 'a Result"
11
12  fun disjoint :: "'a Result ⇒ bool" where "disjoint (e, r, d) =
13    ((e ∩ r = {}) ∧
14     (e ∩ d = {}) ∧
15     (r ∩ d = {}))"
16
17  fun unify_to :: "'a set ⇒'a Result ⇒ bool"
18    where "unify_to A (e, r, d) ↔ (e ∪ r ∪ d = A)"
19
20  definition partition_of :: "'a set ⇒ 'a Result ⇒ bool" where
21    "partition_of A result ≡ disjoint result ∧ unify_to A result"
22
23  definition electoral_module :: " 'a Electoral_module ⇒ bool"
24    where "electoral_module m ≡
25    ∀A p. finite_profile A p → partition_of A (m A p)"
```

Listing 1. Central Isabelle/HOL definitions for electoral modules.

As of yet, our verified construction framework comprises concepts and proofs for 18 composition rules with ten reusable auxiliary properties and eight properties which translate directly to common social choice properties from the literature. Thereof, we implemented the auxiliary properties and the monotonicity property with respective proofs within the Isabelle/HOL framework.

4.2 Verified Construction Based on Composition Rules

From devising composition rules and properties as described in the beginning of this section together with the component types and structures as described in Sect. 3, our framework now only requires a small set of basic components in order to construct interesting voting rules for the desired social choice properties which have been defined as properties and included in the rules for composing electoral modules. The power of our approach lies both in the generality of the composition rules and compositional structures such that various voting rules may be constructed for various properties, and in the reduction of complexity such that compositions for complex social choice properties can be defined by predominantly local composition rules in a step-by-step manner.

In general, the verified construction using composition rules works as follows: When we want to obtain a voting rule with a set of properties p from some basic components c and d which satisfy sets of properties p_c and p_d respectively, we might make use of a compositional structure X which guarantees that a composed module $m_c X m_d$ satisfies the properties p. Hence, we can get a desired voting rule by instantiating m_c and m_d by c and d respectively, which gives us the induced voting rule f_{cXd}. Note that, when we specify a set of target properties p, any voting rule induced by our framework (if a suitable one can be induced) from a set of basic components and compositional structures, necessarily comes with an Isabelle proof which establishes the validity of p for the induced voting rule. By design, these proofs are short and can in most cases be automatically inferred. Hence, given the soundness of the Isabelle/HOL theorem prover, we obtain a formal proof that the resulting voting rule indeed satisfies the required properties without the need to re-check the obtained rule.

Example. One such example using structures from Sect. 3 and properties defined in this section is that p consists of the property Condorcet consistency, X is the sequential composition, p_c also consists of Condorcet consistency, and p_d is empty. Thus, we have no requirements for properties of any component d, since sequential composition cannot revoke any alternatives that are already elected. If a Condorcet winner exists, this alternative is already elected by the first module, and if not, Condorcet consistency trivially holds. On its own, this composition rule might not be very sensible, but may be used in combination with other rules to preserve Condorcet consistency of composed voting rules. A voting rule from the literature which is constructed in such a manner is *Black's rule*. Black's rule is a sequential composition of (a component which induces) the Condorcet rule and (a component which induces) the Borda rule.

5 Case Study

As a case study for demonstrating the applicability of our approach to existing voting rules and the merits of composition, we constructed the voting rule *sequential majority comparison* (SMC) from the literature (e.g., from Brandt et al. [5]), thereby producing a compositional proof that the rule is monotone.

Sequential Majority Comparison (SMC). The voting rule of sequential majority comparison, also known as sequential pairwise majority, is simple enough for understanding, but still complex enough such that it demonstrates interesting properties such as monotonicity. Essentially, SMC fixes some (potentially arbitrary) order on all alternatives and then consecutively performs pairwise majority elections. We start by doing pairwise comparisons of the first and the second alternative, then compare the winner of this pairwise comparison to the third alternative, whose winner is then compared to the fourth alternative, and so on. SMC belongs to a category of voting rules called *tournament solutions*, for which we outline a possible construction pattern in the following.

Verified Construction of Tournament Solution. As indicated in Sect. 3, loop composition appears sensible for *tournament solutions*, as a list of alternatives is processed by multiple rounds, whereof in each, the previously chosen alternative is compared to the next alternative on the list regarding their rankings in the profile, and the winner of a comparison advances to the next round.

To compare alternatives, we use any electoral module m which elects one alternative and rejects the rest (for example via plurality voting). To limit comparisons to two alternatives, we use the electoral module $pass^2_>$, which defers the two alternatives ranked highest in some fixed order $>$ and rejects the rest. Similarly, $drop^2_>$ rejects these two alternatives and defers the rest.

We can now describe a single comparison in our tournament as

$$c = (pass^2_> \triangleright m) \,||_{agg_{max}} drop^2_>$$

The first part of the parallel composition elects the winner of the current comparison and rejects all other alternatives. The second part defers all alternatives which are not currently being compared and therefore stay in the tournament.

The termination condition $t_{|d|=0}$ is satisfied iff the set of deferred alternatives passed to it is empty. Then we describe a single round of our tournament as

$$r = (c \circlearrowleft_{t_{|d|=0}}) \downarrow$$

Now, for the case of sequential majority comparison (SMC), we proceed as follows.

Verified Construction of SMC. Every single comparison elects a single alternative to advance to the next round and rejects the other. As long as alternatives are left, the next c compares the next two alternatives. If there ever is only a single alternative left, it advances to the next round automatically. At the end of the round, we need to revise to defer all winners to the next round instead of electing them.

Let m_{elect} be the electoral module which elects all alternatives passed to it and $t_{|d|=1}$ the termination condition that is satisfied when exactly one alternative is deferred. We can now define the whole tournament as

$$t = (r \circlearrowleft_{t_{|d|=1}}) \triangleright m_{elect}.$$

t repeats single rounds as long as there is more than one alternative left and then elects the single survivor.

Implementing the Construction of SMC in Isabelle/HOL. After having described a general pattern for the verified construction of tournament solutions and sequential majority comparison, we give only structural information on the implemented construction proofs for SMC as the details are rather lengthy, but instead refer the reader to the Isabelle/HOL proofs.

We can construct SMC by combining six different basic components by using all of our composition structures, i.e., the sequential, parallel, loop, and revision structure, and thereby produce a proof that SMC is a monotone voting rule.

```
1  definition SMC :: "'a rel ⇒ 'a Electoral_module" where
2    "SMC x ≡ let a = Max_aggregator; t = Defer_eq_condition 1 in
3      ((((Pass_module 2 x) ▷ ((Plurality_module↓) ▷ (Pass_module 1 x))) ||a
4        (Drop_module 2 x)) ↻t) ▷ Elect_module"
5
6  theorem SMC_sound:
7    assumes order: "linear_order x"
8    shows "electoral_module (SMC x)"
9
10 theorem SMC_monotone:
11   assumes order: "linear_order x"
12   shows "monotone (SMC x)"
```

Listing 2. The modular construction of SMC in Isabelle/HOL.

The high-level modular construction can be seen in Listing 2, where SMC stands for sequential majority comparison composed of a number of simple components. Each component, the largest of which is an electoral module inducing plurality voting (see Sect. 2), consists of not more than three lines in higher-order logic and we provided proofs within our Isabelle/HOL framework for easy reuse and modification for similar voting rules.

Moreover, Listing 2 shows the simplicity of the abstract proof obligations both that SMC is again an electoral module and satisfies the monotonicity property. Both tasks are proven fully modularly and are hence a direct result of SMC's composition, and is apt for an automated integration within a potential future logic-based synthesis tool. We omit the proofs at this point, but they are available for download[3] and can be inspected and re-played for inspection and automatically checked using Isabelle/HOL. The full proof comprises 26 compositions using a set of six basic components within the theorem prover Isabelle/HOL.

6   Related Work

We base the core component type in our verified construction framework on the electoral modules from the unified description of electoral systems in [7]. Therein,

---

[3] https://github.com/VeriVote/verifiedVotingRuleConstruction/.

Grilli di Cortona et al. devise a complex component structure for describing hierarchical electoral systems with a focus on proportional voting rules including notions for electoral districts and concepts of proportionality. Note, however, that the component type within this work is already quite different from the structures in [7]. In the current state, essentially, both concepts only share the concept of reducing and partitioning the set of alternatives.

General informal advice on voting rule design is given by Taagepera [15]. Moreover, a first approach for composing voting rules in a limited setting is given by Narodytska et al. [12] that is readily expressible by our structures. Other work designs voting rules less modularly for statistically guaranteeing social choice properties by machine learning [17]. Prior modular approaches also target verification [10,16] or declarative combinations of voting rules [6], but ignore the social choice or fairness properties targeted by our work.

We have defined our compositional approach within Isabelle/HOL [13], a theorem prover for higher-order logic. Isabelle/HOL provides interactive theorem proving for rigorous systems design. Further work on computer-aided verification of social choice properties for voting rules using HOL4 has been done by Dawson et al. [8]. More light-weight approaches with some loss of generality, but the merit of generating counterexamples for failing properties has been devised by Beckert et al. [3] and Kirsten and Cailloux [11]. Therein, techniques for relational verification of more involved social choice properties have been applied. Another interesting approach has been followed by Pattinson and Schürmann [14], where voting rules are directly encoded into HOL rules within tactical theorem provers.

7 Conclusion

Within this work, we introduced an approach to systematically construct voting rules from compact composable modules to satisfy formal social choice properties. We devised composition rules for a selection of common social choice properties, such as monotonicity or Condorcet consistency, as well as for reusable auxiliary properties. By design, these composition rules give formal guarantees, in the form of an Isabelle proof based on the properties satisfied by the component properties, that a constructed voting rule fulfills the social choice property of interest as long as its components satisfy specific properties, which we have proved within Isabelle/HOL for the scope of our case study.

Currently, the construction capabilities of our framework are not fully automatic, as in order to construct a voting rule with a specific property, the concrete assembly structure (in the form of a chain of composition structures and core modules) needs to be given. However, this can already be easily turned into a (simple) synthesis tool by a simple Prolog program. This program holds (only) a collection of which core components satisfy (as proven in Isabelle/HOL within the framework presented in this paper) which individual properties, together with the composition rules, i.e., how the composition of components requires and establishes formal properties). As a result, this program comes up with (albeit simple) proposals for concrete compositions in order to obtain a voting rule which (provenly) satisfies the requested properties, with the proofs provided by our framework within Isabelle/HOL.

Our approach is applicable to the construction of a wide range of voting rules which use sequential or parallel modular structures, notably voting rules with tie-breakers, elimination procedures, or tournament structures. This includes well-known rules such as instant-runoff voting, Nanson's method, or sequential majority comparison (SMC). We constructed SMC from simple components, which we presume to be reusable for the construction of further rules, and automatically by construction produced a proof that SMC satisfies monotonicity from basic formal proofs for the structures, compositions and components which we compositionally constructed. This case study and all required definitions were implemented and verified with the theorem prover Isabelle/HOL. Finally, our approach can be safely extended with additional modules, compositional structures, and rules, for integration into voting rule design or verification frameworks.

Outlook. So far, composition is realized mostly by transferring sets of deferred alternatives between modules. We also intend to inspect the more involved modular structures already incorporated in some more complicated voting rules, in order to achieve a more flexible notion of composition. This, however, also involves making more detailed assumptions on how exactly information is passed between modules, which might come with a loss of generality. This however, seems to be necessary for voting rules such as Single-Transferable Vote (STV), which are not composable for sensible social choice properties with our strong notion of locality in composition rules.

Moreover, it would be interesting to make use of the code generation functionality of Isabelle/HOL in order to, besides the abstract specifications of the components and composition structures, produce actual executable program code for the constructed voting rules. Furthermore, we envision an automatic synthesis tool built on top of the provided framework such that construction can be provided fully automatically. This could be done by, e.g., a Prolog program as described above, together with SMT or Horn solvers to manage larger and more complex compositions.

References

1. Arrow, K.J.: Social Choice and Individual Values, 3rd edn. Yale University Press, New Haven (2012)
2. Baldwin, J.M.: The technique of the Nanson preferential majority system of election. Trans. Proc. R. Soc. Vic. **39**, 42–52 (1926)
3. Beckert, B., Bormer, T., Kirsten, M., Neuber, T., Ulbrich, M.: Automated verification for functional and relational properties of voting rules. In: Sixth International Workshop on Computational Social Choice (COMSOC 2016) (2016)
4. Beckert, B., Goré, R., Schürmann, C.: Analysing vote counting algorithms via logic. In: Bonacina, M.P. (ed.) CADE 2013. LNCS (LNAI), vol. 7898, pp. 135–144. Springer, Heidelberg (2013). https://doi.org/10.1007/978-3-642-38574-2_9
5. Brandt, F., Conitzer, V., Endriss, U., Lang, J., Procaccia, A.D.: Handbook of Computational Social Choice. Cambridge University Press, Cambridge (2016)

6. Charwat, G., Pfandler, A.: Democratix: a declarative approach to winner determination. In: Walsh, T. (ed.) ADT 2015. LNCS (LNAI), vol. 9346, pp. 253–269. Springer, Cham (2015). https://doi.org/10.1007/978-3-319-23114-3_16

7. Grilli di Cortona, P., Manzi, C., Pennisi, A., Ricca, F., Simeone, B.: Evaluation and optimization of electoral systems. In: SIAM (1999)

8. Dawson, J.E., Goré, R., Meumann, T.: Machine-checked reasoning about complex voting schemes using higher-order logic. In: Haenni, R., Koenig, R.E., Wikström, D. (eds.) VOTELID 2015. LNCS, vol. 9269, pp. 142–158. Springer, Cham (2015). https://doi.org/10.1007/978-3-319-22270-7_9

9. Diekhoff, K., Kirsten, M., Krämer, J.: Formal property-oriented design of voting rules using composable modules. In: Venable, K., Pekec, S. (eds.) 6th International Conference on Algorithmic Decision Theory (ADT 2019). LNAI (2019)

10. Ghale, M.K., Goré, R., Pattinson, D., Tiwari, M.: Modular formalisation and verification of STV algorithms. In: Krimmer, R., et al. (eds.) E-Vote-ID 2018. LNCS, vol. 11143, pp. 51–66. Springer, Cham (2018). https://doi.org/10.1007/978-3-030-00419-4_4

11. Kirsten, M., Cailloux, O.: Towards automatic argumentation about voting rules. In: Bringay, S., Mattioli, J. (eds.) 4ème conférence sur les Applications Pratiques de l'Intelligence Artificielle (APIA 2018), Nancy, France, 2–6 July 2018 (2018)

12. Narodytska, N., Walsh, T., Xia, L.: Combining voting rules together. In: De Raedt, L., et al. (eds.) 20th European Conference on Artificial Intelligence (ECAI 2012), vol. 242. IOS Press (2012)

13. Nipkow, T., Wenzel, M., Paulson, L.C.: Isabelle/HOL. LNCS, vol. 2283. Springer, Heidelberg (2002). https://doi.org/10.1007/3-540-45949-9

14. Pattinson, D., Schürmann, C.: Vote counting as mathematical proof. In: Pfahringer, B., Renz, J. (eds.) AI 2015. LNCS (LNAI), vol. 9457, pp. 464–475. Springer, Cham (2015). https://doi.org/10.1007/978-3-319-26350-2_41

15. Taagepera, R.: Designing electoral rules and waiting for an electoral system to evolve. The Architecture of Democracy: Institutional Design, Conflict Management, and Democracy in the Late Twentieth Century (2002)

16. Verity, F., Pattinson, D.: Formally verified invariants of vote counting schemes. In: Australasian Computer Science Week Multiconference (ACSW 2017). ACM (2017)

17. Xia, L.: Designing social choice mechanisms using machine learning. In: Gini, M.L., et al. (eds.) International Conference on Autonomous Agents and Multi-Agent Systems (AAMAS 2013). IFAAMAS (2013)

Constraints and Unification

Solving Proximity Constraints

Temur Kutsia[(✉)] and Cleo Pau

Research Institute for Symbolic Computation, Johannes Kepler University Linz,
Linz, Austria
kutsia@risc.jku.at

Abstract. Proximity relations are binary fuzzy relations that satisfy reflexivity and symmetry properties, but are not transitive. They
induce the notion of distance between function symbols, which is further
extended to terms. Given two terms, we aim at bringing them "sufficiently close" to each other, by finding an appropriate substitution. We
impose no extra restrictions on proximity relations, allowing a term in
unification to be close to two terms that themselves are not close to each
other. Our unification algorithm works in two phases: first reducing the
equation solving problem to constraints over sets of function symbols,
and then solving the obtained constraints. Termination, soundness and
completeness of both algorithms are shown. The unification problem has
finite minimal complete set of unifiers.

1 Introduction

Proximity relations are reflexive and symmetric fuzzy binary relations. Introduced in [2], they generalize similarity relations (a fuzzy version of equivalence),
by dropping transitivity. Proximity relations help to represent fuzzy information in situations, where similarity is not adequate, providing more flexibility in
expressing vague knowledge. For unification, working modulo proximity or similarity means to treat different function symbols as if they were the same when
the given relation asserts they are "close enough" to each other.

Unification for similarity relations was studied in [3,4,11] in the context of
fuzzy logic programming. In [1], the authors extended the algorithm from [11]
to full fuzzy signature (permitting arity mismatches between function symbols)
and studied also anti-unification, a dual technique to unification.

A constraint logic programming schema with proximity relations has been
introduced in [10]. The similarity-based unification algorithm from [11] was generalized for proximity relations in [5], where the authors introduced the notion
of proximity-based unification under a certain restriction imposed on the proximity relation. The restriction requires that the same symbol can not be close to
two symbols at the same time, when those symbols are not close to each other.
One of them should be chosen as the proximal candidate to the given symbol.

Supported by Austrian Science Fund (FWF) under project 28789-N32 and by the
strategic program "Innovatives OÖ 2020" by the Upper Austrian Government.

M. Gabbrielli (Ed.): LOPSTR 2019, LNCS 12042, pp. 107–122, 2020.
https://doi.org/10.1007/978-3-030-45260-5_7

Essentially, proximal neighborhoods of two function symbols are treated as being either identical or disjoint. Looking at the proximity relation as an undirected graph, this restriction implies that maximal cliques in the graph are disjoint. From the unification point of view, it means that $p(x,x)$ can not be unified with $p(a,c)$ when a and c are not close to each other, even if there exists a b which is close both to a and c. Anti-unification for such kind of proximity relations, and its subalgorithm for computing all maximal partitions of a graph into maximal cliques have been considered in [7,8].

In this paper we consider the general case of unification for a proximity relation without any restrictions, and develop an algorithm which computes a compact representation of the set of solutions. Considering neighborhoods of function symbols as finite sets, we work with term representation where in place of function symbols we permit neighborhoods or names. The latter are some kind of variables, which stand for unknown neighborhoods. The algorithm is split into two phases. In the first one, which is a generalization of syntactic unification for proximity relations, we produce a substitution together with a constraint over neighborhoods and their names. A crucial step in the algorithm is variable elimination, which is done not with a term to which a variable should be unified, but with a copy of that term with fresh names and variables. This step also introduces new neighborhood constraints to ensure that the copy of the term remains close to its original.

In the second phase, the constraint is solved by a constraint solving algorithm. Combining each solution from the second phase with the substitution computed in the first phase, we obtain a compact representation of the minimal complete set of unifiers of the original problem. We prove termination, soundness and completeness of both algorithms. To the best of our knowledge, this is the first detailed study of full-scale proximity-based unification.

In the rest of the paper, the necessary notions and terminology are introduced in Sect. 2, and both algorithms are developed and studied in Sect. 3. Some proofs, which are only sketched here, can be found in the technical report [9].

2   Preliminaries

Proximity Relations. We define basic notions about proximity relations following [5]. A binary *fuzzy relation* on a set S is a mapping from $S \times S$ to the real interval $[0,1]$. If $\mathcal{R}$ is a fuzzy relation on S and λ is a number $0 \leq \lambda \leq 1$, then the λ-*cut* of $\mathcal{R}$ on S, denoted $\mathcal{R}_\lambda$, is an ordinary (crisp) relation on S defined as $\mathcal{R}_\lambda := \{(s_1, s_2) \mid \mathcal{R}(s_1, s_2) \geq \lambda\}$. In the role of T-norm $\wedge$ we take the minimum.

A fuzzy relation $\mathcal{R}$ on a set S is called a *proximity relation* on S iff it is reflexive and symmetric. The λ-*proximity class of* $s \in S$ (a λ-*neighborhood* of s) is a set $\mathbf{pc}(s, \mathcal{R}, \lambda) = \{s' \mid \mathcal{R}(s, s') \geq \lambda\}$.

Terms and Substitutions. Given a set of variables $\mathcal{V}$ and a set of fixed arity function symbols $\mathcal{F}$, *terms* over $\mathcal{F}$ and $\mathcal{V}$ are defined as usual, by the grammar $t := x \mid f(t_1, \ldots, t_n)$, where $x \in \mathcal{V}$ and $f \in \mathcal{F}$ is n-ary. The set of terms over $\mathcal{V}$

and $\mathcal{F}$ is denoted by $\mathcal{T}(\mathcal{F}, \mathcal{V})$. We denote variables by x, y, z, arbitrary function symbols by f, g, h, constants by a, b, c, and terms by s, t, r.

Substitutions are mappings from variables to terms, where all but finitely many variables are mapped to themselves. The identity substitution is denoted by Id. We use the usual set notation for substitutions, writing, e.g., a substitution σ as $\{x \mapsto \sigma(x) \mid x \neq \sigma(x)\}$. Substitution application and composition are defined in the standard way. We use the postfix notation for substitution application, e.g., $t\sigma$, and juxtaposition for composition, e.g., $\sigma\vartheta$ means the composition of σ and ϑ (the order matters).

Extended Terms, Extended Substitutions, Name-Neighborhood Mappings. Assume that $\mathcal{N}$ is a countable *set of names*, which are symbols together with associated arity (like function symbols). We use the letters N, M, K for them. It is assumed that $\mathcal{N} \cap \mathcal{F} = \emptyset$ and $\mathcal{N} \cap \mathcal{V} = \emptyset$.

Neighborhood is either a name, or a finite subset of $\mathcal{F}$, where all elements have the same arity. Since in the construction of extended terms below neighborhoods will behave like function symbols, we will use the letters F and G to denote them. $arity(\mathsf{F})$ is defined as the arity of elements of F. The set of all neighborhoods is denoted by Nb.

An *extended term* (or, shortly, an *X-term*) t over $\mathcal{F}$, $\mathcal{N}$, and $\mathcal{V}$ is defined by the grammar:

$$\mathsf{t} := x \mid \mathsf{F}(\mathsf{t}_1, \ldots, \mathsf{t}_n), \text{ where } arity(\mathsf{F}) = n.$$

The set of X-terms is denoted by $\mathcal{T}(\mathcal{F}, \mathcal{N}, \mathcal{V})$. X-terms, in which every neighborhood set is a singleton, are called *singleton X-terms* or, shortly, *SX-terms*. Slightly abusing the notation, we assume that a term (i.e., an element of $\mathcal{T}(\mathcal{F}, \mathcal{V})$) is a special case of an SX-term (as an SX-term without names), identifying a function symbol f with the singleton neighborhood $\{f\}$. We will use this assumption in the rest of the paper.

The notion of *head* is defined as $head(x) = x$ and $head(\mathsf{F}(\mathsf{t}_1, \ldots, \mathsf{t}_n)) = \mathsf{F}$.

The set of variables (resp. names) occurring in an X-term t is denoted by $\mathcal{V}(\mathsf{t})$ (resp. $\mathcal{N}(\mathsf{t})$). Approximate extended equations (X-equations) are pairs of X-terms.

The notion of substitution (and the associated relations and operations) are extended to X-terms straightforwardly. We use the term "*X-substitution*" and denote them by upright Greek letters μ, v, and ξ. When we want to emphasize that we are talking about substitutions for terms, we use the letters σ, ϑ, and φ.

The restriction of an X-substitution μ to a set of variables V is denoted by $\mu|_V := \{x \mapsto x\mu \mid x \in dom(\mu) \cap V\}$.

A *name-neighborhood mapping* $\Phi : \mathcal{N} \longrightarrow \mathsf{Nb} \setminus \mathcal{N}$ is a finite mapping from names to non-name neighborhoods (i.e., finite sets of function symbols of the same arity) such that if $\mathsf{N} \in dom(\Phi)$ (where dom is the domain of mapping), then $arity(\mathsf{N}) = arity(\Phi(\mathsf{N}))$. They are also represented as finite sets, writing Φ as $\{\mathsf{N} \mapsto \Phi(\mathsf{N}) \mid \mathsf{N} \in dom(\Phi)\}$.

A name-neighborhood mapping Φ can *apply* to an X-term t, resulting in anbreak X-term $\Phi(\mathsf{t})$, which is obtained by replacing each name N in t by the neighborhood $\Phi(\mathsf{N})$. The *application of* Φ *to a set of X-equations* P, denoted by $\Phi(P)$, is a set of equations obtained from P by applying Φ to both sides of each equation in P.

Proximity Relations over X-Terms. The proximity relation $\mathcal{R}$ is defined on the set $\mathsf{Nb} \cup \mathcal{V}$ (where neighborhoods are assumed to be nonempty) in such a way that it satisfies the following conditions (in addition to reflexivity and symmetry):

(a) $\mathcal{R}(\mathsf{F}, \mathsf{G}) = 0$ if $arity(\mathsf{F}) \neq arity(\mathsf{G})$;
(b) $\mathcal{R}(\mathsf{F}, \mathsf{G}) = \min\{\mathcal{R}(f, g) \mid f \in \mathsf{F}, g \in \mathsf{G}\}$, if $\mathsf{F} = \{f_1, \ldots, f_n\}$, $\mathsf{G} = \{g_1, \ldots, g_m\}$, and $arity(\mathsf{F}) = arity(\mathsf{G})$;
(c) $\mathcal{R}(\mathsf{N}, \mathsf{F}) = 0$, if $\mathsf{F} \notin \mathcal{N}$.
(d) $\mathcal{R}(\mathsf{N}, \mathsf{M}) = 0$, if $\mathsf{N} \neq \mathsf{M}$;
(e) $\mathcal{R}(x, y) = 0$, if $x \neq y$ for all $x, y \in \mathcal{V}$.
(f) $\mathcal{R}(\mathsf{F}, \mathsf{G})$ is undefined, if $\mathsf{F} = \emptyset$ or $\mathsf{G} = \emptyset$.

We write $\mathsf{F} \approx_{\mathcal{R},\lambda} \mathsf{G}$ if $\mathcal{R}(\mathsf{F}, \mathsf{G}) \geq \lambda$. Note that for $\mathsf{F} = \{f_1, \ldots, f_n\}$ and $\mathsf{G} = \{g_1, \ldots, g_m\}$, $\mathsf{F} \approx_{\mathcal{R},\lambda} \mathsf{G}$ is equivalent to $\mathcal{R}(f, g) \geq \lambda$ for all $f \in \mathsf{F}$ and $g \in \mathsf{G}$. It is easy to see that the obtained relation is again a proximity relation. Furthermore, it can be extended to X-terms (which do not contain the empty neighborhood):

1. $\mathcal{R}(\mathsf{s}, \mathsf{t}) := 0$ if $\mathcal{R}(head(\mathsf{s}), head(\mathsf{t})) = 0$.
2. $\mathcal{R}(\mathsf{s}, \mathsf{t}) := 1$ if $\mathsf{s} = \mathsf{t}$ and $\mathsf{s}, \mathsf{t} \in \mathcal{V}$.
3. $\mathcal{R}(\mathsf{s}, \mathsf{t}) := \mathcal{R}(\mathsf{F}, \mathsf{G}) \wedge \mathcal{R}(\mathsf{s}_1, \mathsf{t}_1) \wedge \cdots \wedge \mathcal{R}(\mathsf{s}_n, \mathsf{t}_n)$, if $\mathsf{s} = \mathsf{F}(\mathsf{s}_1, \ldots, \mathsf{s}_n)$, $\mathsf{t} = \mathsf{G}(\mathsf{t}_1, \ldots, \mathsf{t}_n)$.
4. $\mathcal{R}(\mathsf{s}, \mathsf{t})$ is not defined, if s or t contains the empty neighborhood $\emptyset$.

Two X-terms s and t are $(\mathcal{R}, \lambda)$-*close* to each other, written $\mathsf{s} \simeq_{\mathcal{R},\lambda} \mathsf{t}$, if $\mathcal{R}(\mathsf{s}, \mathsf{t}) \geq \lambda$. We say that s is $(\mathcal{R}, \lambda)$-*more general than* t and write $\mathsf{s} \precsim_{\mathcal{R},\lambda} \mathsf{t}$, if there exists a substitution σ such that $\mathsf{s}\sigma \simeq_{\mathcal{R},\lambda} \mathsf{t}$.

Neighborhood Equations, Unification Problems. We introduce the notions of problems we would like to solve.

Definition 1 (Neighborhood equations). *Given $\mathcal{R}$ and λ, an $(\mathcal{R}, \lambda)$-neighborhood equation is a pair of neighborhoods, written as $\mathsf{F} \approx^?_{\mathcal{R},\lambda} \mathsf{G}$. The question mark indicates that it has to be solved.*

A name-neighborhood mapping Φ is a solution of an $(\mathcal{R}, \lambda)$-neighborhood equation $\mathsf{F} \approx^?_{\mathcal{R},\lambda} \mathsf{G}$ if $\Phi(\mathsf{F}) \simeq_{\mathcal{R},\lambda} \Phi(\mathsf{G})$. The notation implies that $\mathcal{R}(\Phi(\mathsf{F}), \Phi(\mathsf{G}))$ is defined, i.e., neither $\Phi(\mathsf{F})$ nor $\Phi(\mathsf{G})$ contains the empty neighborhood.

An $(\mathcal{R}, \lambda)$-neighborhood constraint is a finite set of $(\mathcal{R}, \lambda)$-neighborhood equations. A name-neighborhood mapping Φ is a solution of an $(\mathcal{R}, \lambda)$-neighborhood constraint C if it is a solution of every $(\mathcal{R}, \lambda)$-neighborhood equation in C.

We shortly write "an $(\mathcal{R}, \lambda)$-solution to C" instead of "a solution to an $(\mathcal{R}, \lambda)$-neighborhood constraint C".

To each X-term t we associate a set of SX-terms $\mathsf{Singl}(\mathsf{t})$ defined as follows:

$\mathsf{Singl}(x) := \{x\},$

$\mathsf{Singl}(\mathsf{N}(\mathsf{t}_1,\ldots,\mathsf{t}_n)) := \{\mathsf{N}(\mathsf{s}_1,\ldots,\mathsf{s}_n) \mid \mathsf{s}_i \in \mathsf{Singl}(\mathsf{t}_i),\ 1 \leq i \leq n\}.$

$\mathsf{Singl}(\mathsf{F}(\mathsf{t}_1,\ldots,\mathsf{t}_n)) := \{f(\mathsf{s}_1,\ldots,\mathsf{s}_n) \mid f \in \mathsf{F},\ \mathsf{s}_i \in \mathsf{Singl}(\mathsf{t}_i),\ 1 \leq i \leq n\}.$

The notation extends to substitutions as well:

$$\mathsf{Singl}(\mu) := \{\vartheta \mid x\vartheta \in \mathsf{Singl}(x\mu) \text{ for all } x \in \mathcal{V}\}.$$

Definition 2 (Approximate X-unification). *Given $\mathcal{R}$ and λ, a finite set P of $(\mathcal{R}, \lambda)$-equations between X-terms is called an $(\mathcal{R}, \lambda)$-X-unification problem. A mapping-substitution pair (Φ, μ) is called an $(\mathcal{R}, \lambda)$-solution of an $(\mathcal{R}, \lambda)$-X-equation $\mathsf{t} \simeq^?_{\mathcal{R},\lambda} \mathsf{s}$, if $\Phi(\mathsf{t}\mu) \simeq_{\mathcal{R},\lambda} \Phi(\mathsf{s}\mu)$. An $(\mathcal{R}, \lambda)$-solution of P is a pair (Φ, μ) which solves each equation in P.*

If (Φ, μ) is an $(\mathcal{R}, \lambda)$-solution of P, then the X-substitution $\Phi(\mu)$ is called an $(\mathcal{R}, \lambda)$-X-unifier of P.

SX-unification problems, SX-solutions and SX-unifiers are defined analogously. For unification between terms, we do not use any prefix, talking about unification problems, solutions, and unifiers.

Instead of writing "a $\cdots$-unifier of an $(\mathcal{R}, \lambda)$-unification problem P", we often shortly say "an $(\mathcal{R}, \lambda)$-$\cdots$-unifier of P".

The notion of more generality for substitutions is defined with the help of syntactic equality: μ is *more general* than v, written $\mu \preceq v$, if there exists ξ such that $\mu\xi = v$. In this case, v is called an *instance* of μ.

Remark 1. Note that we did not use proximity in the definition of this notion. The reason is that in our definition, $\preceq$ is a quasi-order and preserves good properties of unifiers. In particular, if μ is an $(\mathcal{R}, \lambda)$-X-unifier of P, then so is any v for which $\mu \preceq v$ holds.

If we defined this notion as "$\mu \precsim_{\mathcal{R},\lambda} v$ if there exists a substitution ξ such that $x\mu v \simeq_{\mathcal{R},\lambda} x\xi$ for all x", it would not be a quasi-order, because it is not transitive. Therefore, it might happen that μ is an $(\mathcal{R}, \lambda)$-X-unifier of P, but v with $\mu \precsim_{\mathcal{R},\lambda} v$ is not. A simple example is $P = \{x \simeq^?_{\mathcal{R},\lambda} a\}$ and $\mathcal{R}_\lambda = \{(a, b), (b, c)\}$. Then $\mu = \{x \mapsto b\}$ is an $(\mathcal{R}, \lambda)$-unifier of P, but $v = \{x \mapsto c\}$ is not. However, $\mu \precsim_{\mathcal{R},\lambda} v$.

Two substitutions μ and v are called *equigeneral* iff $\mu \preceq v$ and $v \preceq \mu$. In this case we write $\mu \simeq v$. It is an equivalence relation.

Unification Between Terms. Our unification problem will be formulated between terms, and we would like to have a characterization of the set of its unifiers. (Extended terms and substitutions will play a role in the formulating of algorithms, proving their properties, and representing the mentioned unifier set compactly).

Definition 3 (Complete set of unifiers). *Given a proximity relation $\mathcal{R}$, a cut value λ, and an $(\mathcal{R}, \lambda)$-proximity unification problem P, the set of substitutions Σ is a* complete set of $(\mathcal{R}, \lambda)$-unifiers *of P if the following conditions hold:*

Soundness: *Every substitution $\sigma \in \Sigma$ is an $(\mathcal{R}, \lambda)$-unifier of P.*
Completeness: *For any $(\mathcal{R}, \lambda)$-unifier ϑ of P, there exists $\sigma \in \Sigma$ such that $\sigma \preceq \vartheta$.*

Σ is a *minimal complete set of unifiers* of P if it is its complete set of unifiers and, in addition, the following condition holds:

Minimality: *No two elements in Σ are comparable with respect to $\preceq$: For all $\sigma, \vartheta \in \Sigma$, if $\sigma \preceq \vartheta$, then $\sigma = \vartheta$.*

Under this definition, $\{x \simeq_{\mathcal{R},0.5} b\}$ for $\mathcal{R}(a,b) = 0.6$, $\mathcal{R}(b,c) = 0.5$ has a minimal complete set of unifiers $\{\{x \mapsto a\}, \{x \mapsto b\}, \{x \mapsto c\}\}$. Note that the substitutions $\{x \mapsto a\}$ and $\{x \mapsto b\}$ are $\preceq$-incomparable, but $\precsim_{\mathcal{R},\lambda}$-comparable. The same is true for $\{x \mapsto a\}$ and $\{x \mapsto c\}$.

Given an approximate unification problem P, our goal is to obtain a compact representation of its minimal complete set of $(\mathcal{R}, \lambda)$-unifiers. The representation will be constructed as a set of X-unifiers $\mathcal{U}^X_{\mathcal{R},\lambda}(P) = \{\Phi_1(\mu), \ldots, \Phi_n(\mu)\}$. The algorithms below construct this representation.

3   Solving Unification Problems

We start with a high-level view of the process of solving an approximate unification problem $s \simeq^?_{\mathcal{R},\lambda} t$ between terms s and t (we omit $\mathcal{R}$ and λ below):

- First, we treat the input equation as an SX-equation and apply rules of the pre-unification algorithm. Pre-unification works on SX-equations. It either fails (in this case the input terms are not unifiable) or results in a neighborhood constraint C and a substitution μ over $\mathcal{T}(\emptyset, \mathcal{N}, \mathcal{V})$.
- Next, we solve C by the neighborhood constraint solving algorithm. If the process fails, then the input terms are not unifiable. Otherwise, we get a finite set of name-neighborhood mappings $\mathcal{M} = \{\Phi_1, \ldots, \Phi_n\}$. Note that Φ's do not necessarily map names to singleton sets here.
- For each $\Phi_i \in \mathcal{M}$, the pair (Φ_i, μ) solves the original unification problem, i.e., the X-substitution $\Phi_i(\mu)$ is an X-unifier of it.
- From the obtained set $\{\Phi_1(\mu), \ldots, \Phi_n(\mu)\}$ of computed $(\mathcal{R}, \lambda)$-X-unifiers of s and t we can construct a minimal complete set of unifiers $mcsu_{\mathcal{R},\lambda}(s,t)$ of s and t as the set $mcsu_{\mathcal{R},\lambda}(s,t) = \mathsf{Singl}(\Phi(\mu_1)) \cup \cdots \cup \mathsf{Singl}(\Phi(\mu_1))$.

Hence, the algorithm consists of two phases: pre-unification and constraint solving. They are described in separate subsections below.

3.1   Pre-unification Rules

We start with the definition of a technical notion needed later:

Definition 4. *We say that a set of SX-equations* $\{x \simeq^?_{\mathcal{R},\lambda} t\} \uplus P$ *contains an* occurrence cycle *for the variable* x *if* $t \notin V$ *and there exist SX-term-pairs* $(x_0, t_0), (x_1, t_1), \ldots, (x_n, t_n)$ *such that* $x_0 = x$, $t_0 = t$, *for each* $0 \leq i \leq n$ P *contains an equation* $x_i \simeq^?_{\mathcal{R},\lambda} t_i$ *or* $t_i \simeq^?_{\mathcal{R},\lambda} x_i$, *and* $x_{i+1} \in V(t_i)$ *where* $x_{n+1} = x_0$.

Lemma 1. *If a set of SX-equations* P *contains an occurrence cycle for some variable, then it has no* $(\mathcal{R}, \lambda)$-solution for P for any $\mathcal{R}$ and λ.

Proof. The requirement that neighborhoods of different arity are not $(\mathcal{R}, \lambda)$-close to each other guarantees that an SX-term can not be $(\mathcal{R}, \lambda)$-close to its proper subterm. Therefore, equations containing an occurrence cycle can not have an $(\mathcal{R}, \lambda)$-solution. □

In the rules below we will use the *renaming function* $\rho : T(\mathcal{F}, \mathcal{N}, V) \rightarrow T(\mathcal{N}, V)$. Applied to a term, ρ gives its fresh copy, obtained by replacing each occurrence of a symbol from $\mathcal{F} \cup \mathcal{N}$ by a new name and each variable occurrence by a fresh variable. For instance, if the term is $f(N(a, x, x, f(a)))$, where $f, a \in \mathcal{F}$ and $N \in \mathcal{N}$, then $\rho(f(N(a, x, x, f(a))) = N_1(N_2(N_3, x_1, x_2, N_4(N_5)))$, where $N_1, N_2, N_3, N_4, N_5 \in \mathcal{N}$ are new names and x_1, x_2 are new variables.

Given $\mathcal{R}$ and λ, an *equational* $(\mathcal{R}, \lambda)$-*configuration* is a triple $P; C; \mu$, where

- P is a finite set of $(\mathcal{R}, \lambda)$-SX-equations. It is initialized with the unification equation between the original terms;
- C is a $(\mathcal{R}, \lambda)$-neighborhood constraint;
- μ is an X-substitution over $T(\emptyset, \mathcal{N}, V)$, initialized by *Id*. It serves as an accumulator, keeping the pre-unifier computed so far.

The pre-unification algorithm takes given terms s and t, creates the initial configuration $\{s \simeq^?_{\mathcal{R},\lambda} t\}; \emptyset; Id$ and applies the rules given below exhaustively.

The rules are very similar to the syntactic unification algorithm with the difference that here the function symbol clash does not happen unless their arities differ, and variables are not replaced by other variables until the very end. (The notation $\overline{exp_n}$ in the rules below abbreviates the sequence $exp_1, \ldots, exp_n$.)

(Tri) Trivial: $\{x \simeq^?_{\mathcal{R},\lambda} x\} \uplus P; C; \mu \Longrightarrow P; C; \mu.$

(Dec) Decomposition:

$\{F(\overline{s_n}) \simeq^?_{\mathcal{R},\lambda} G(\overline{t_n})\} \uplus P; C; \mu \Longrightarrow \overline{\{s_n \simeq^?_{\mathcal{R},\lambda} t_n\}} \cup P; \{F \approx^?_{\mathcal{R},\lambda} G\} \cup C; \mu,$

where each of F and G is a name or a function symbol treated as a singleton neighborhood.

(VE) Variable Elimination:

$\{x \simeq^?_{\mathcal{R},\lambda} t\} \uplus P; C; \mu \Longrightarrow \{t' \simeq^?_{\mathcal{R},\lambda} t\} \cup P\{x \mapsto t'\}; C; \mu\{x \mapsto t'\},$

where $t \notin V$, there is no occurrence cycle for x in $\{x \simeq^?_{\mathcal{R},\lambda} t\} \uplus P$, and $t' = \rho(t).$

(Ori) Orient: $\{t \simeq^?_{\mathcal{R},\lambda} x\} \uplus P; C; \mu \Longrightarrow \{x \simeq^?_{\mathcal{R},\lambda} t\} \cup P; C; \mu$, if $t \notin \mathcal{V}$.

(Cla) Clash: $F(\overline{s_n}) \simeq^?_{\mathcal{R},\lambda} G(\overline{t_m})\} \uplus P; C; \mu \Longrightarrow \bot$, where $n \neq m$.

(Occ) Occur Check: $\{x \simeq^?_{\mathcal{R},\lambda} t\} \uplus P; C; \mu \Longrightarrow \bot$,

  if there is an occurrence cycle for x in $\{x \simeq^?_{\mathcal{R},\lambda} t\} \uplus P$.

(VO) Variables Only:

$$\{x \simeq^?_{\mathcal{R},\lambda} y, \overline{x_n \simeq^?_{\mathcal{R},\lambda} y_n}\}; C; \mu \Longrightarrow \{\overline{x_n \simeq^?_{\mathcal{R},\lambda} y_n}\}\{x \mapsto y\}; C; \mu\{x \mapsto y\}.$$

Informally, in the (VE) rule, we imitate the structure of t in t' by ρ, replace x by t', and then try to bring t' close to t by solving the equation $t' \simeq^?_{\mathcal{R},\lambda} t$.

Theorem 1 (Termination of pre-unification). *The pre-unification algorithm terminates either with $\bot$ or with a configuration of the form $\emptyset; C; \mu$.*

Proof. The rules (Tri) and (Dec) strictly decrease the size of P. (Ori) does not changes the size, but strictly decreases the number of equations of the form $t \simeq^?_{\mathcal{R},\lambda} x$, where $t \notin \mathcal{V}$. (VO) stands separately, because once it starts applying, no other rule is applicable and (VO) itself is terminating. So are the failure rules.

To see what is decreased by (VE), we need some definitions. First, with each variable occurring in the initial unification problem we associate the set of its copies, which is initialized with the singleton set consisting of the variables themselves. For instance, if the problem contains variables x, y, z, and u, we will have four copy sets: $\{x\}$, $\{y\}$, $\{z\}$, and $\{u\}$. Rules may add new copies to these sets, or remove some copies from them. However, the copy sets themselves are fixed. None of them will be removed, and no new copy sets will be created.

In the process of rule applications, we will maintain a directed acyclic graph, whose vertices are labeled by copy sets, and there is an edge from a vertex V_1 to a vertex V_2 if we have encountered an equation of the form $x \simeq^?_{\mathcal{R},\lambda} t$ such that $x \in V_1$ and t contains a variable $y \in V_2$.

One can notice that the graph is a variable dependency graph. If it contains a cycle, the algorithm stops with failure by the (Occ) rule. From the beginning, the vertices (i.e. the copy sets) are isolated. In the process of rule applications, assume that we reach a configuration that is transformed by the (VE) rule, applied to an equation $x \simeq^?_{\mathcal{R},\lambda} t$, where t contains variables y, z', and z'' (the latter two are copies of z). The rule creates a fresh copy of t, which contains copies of variables: $\rho(y)$, $\rho(z')$, and $\rho(z'')$. They are added to the corresponding copy sets (graph vertices): $\rho(y)$ to the copy set of y, and $\rho(z')$ and $\rho(z'')$ to the copy set of z. Let us call those vertices V_y and V_z. Besides, if there was no edge connecting the vertex V_x (containing the copy set of x) to the vertices V_y and V_z, the edges are created. Finally, x is removed from V_x.

Hence, after each application of the (VE) rule, the copy set decreases in one vertex V (in the example above it is V_x), and stays unchanged in all vertices that are not reachable from V. We say in this case that the graph measure decreases.

This ordering can be seen as a generalization of lexicographic ordering to graphs. It is well-founded. (VE) strictly decreases it, and the other rules have no effect.

Hence, if we take the lexicographic combination of three measures: copy set dags, the size of the set of equations, and the number of equations with non-variable term in the left and variable in the right, each rule except (VO) strictly decrease it. After finitely many steps, either failure will occur, or one reaches the variable-only equations, which are solved in finitely many steps by (VO). Then it stops with the configuration $\emptyset; C; \mu$. $\square$

We say that a mapping-substitution pair (Φ, ν) is a *solution of an equational* $(\mathcal{R}, \lambda)$-*configuration* $P; C; \mu$ if the following conditions hold:

- (Φ, ν) is an $(\mathcal{R}, \lambda)$-solution of P;
- Φ is an $(\mathcal{R}, \lambda)$-solution of C;
- For each $x \in dom(\mu)$, we have $x\nu = x\mu\nu$ (syntactic equality).

Lemma 2. *1. If $P; C; \mu \Longrightarrow \bot$ by (Cla) or (Occ) rules, then $P; C; \mu$ does not have a solution.*
2. Let $P_1; C_1; \mu_1 \Longrightarrow P_2; C_2; \mu_2$ be a step performed by a pre-unification rule (except (Cla) and (Occ)). Then every solution of $P_2; C_2; \mu_2$ is a solution of $P_1; C_1; \mu_1$.

Proof. See [9]. $\square$

Theorem 2 (Soundness of pre-unification). *Let s and t be two terms, such that the pre-unification algorithm gives $\{s \simeq^?_{\mathcal{R}, \lambda} t\}; \emptyset; Id \Longrightarrow^* \emptyset; C; \mu$. Let Φ be an $(\mathcal{R}, \lambda)$-solution of C. Then the X-substitution $\Phi(\mu)$ contains no names and is an $(\mathcal{R}, \lambda)$-X-unifier of $\{s \simeq^?_{\mathcal{R}, \lambda} t\}$.*

Proof. Note that (Φ, μ) is an $(\mathcal{R}, \lambda)$-solution of $\emptyset; C; \mu$, since Φ solves C. From $\{s \simeq^?_{\mathcal{R}, \lambda} t\}; \emptyset; Id \Longrightarrow^* \emptyset; C; \mu$, by induction on the length of the derivation, using Lemma 2, we get that (Φ, μ) is a solution of $\{s \simeq^?_{\mathcal{R}, \lambda} t\}; \emptyset; Id$.

Since s and t do not contain names, Φ has no effect on them: $\Phi(s\mu) = s\Phi(\mu)$ and $\Phi(t\mu) = t\Phi(\mu)$. From these equalities and $\Phi(s\mu) \simeq_{\mathcal{R}, \lambda} \Phi(t\mu)$ we get $s\Phi(\mu) \simeq_{\mathcal{R}, \lambda} t\Phi(\mu)$, which implies that $\Phi(\mu)$ is an $(\mathcal{R}, \lambda)$-X-solution of $\{s \simeq^?_{\mathcal{R}, \lambda} t\}$. By construction of pre-unification derivations, all the names in μ are in the domain of Φ. Hence, $\Phi(\mu)$ contains no names. $\square$

Corollary 1. *Let s and t be two terms, such that the pre-unification algorithm gives $\{s \simeq^?_{\mathcal{R}, \lambda} t\}; \emptyset; Id \Longrightarrow^* \emptyset; C; \mu$. Let Φ be an $(\mathcal{R}, \lambda)$-solution of C. Then every substitution in $\mathsf{Singl}(\Phi(\mu))$ is an $(\mathcal{R}, \lambda)$-unifier of s and t.*

Proof. Direct consequence of Theorem 2 and the definition of Singl. Note that $\mathsf{Singl}(\Phi(\mu))$ in this case is a set of substitutions, not a set of SX-substitutions, because $\Phi(\mu)$ does not contain names. $\square$

For any solution of an approximate unification problem, we can not always compute a solution which is more general than the given one. For instance, for the problem $x \simeq^?_{\mathcal{R},\lambda} y$ we compute $\{x \mapsto y\}$, but the problem might have a solution, e.g., $\{x \mapsto a, y \mapsto b\}$ (when a and b are close to each other). Strictly speaking, $\{x \mapsto y\}$ is not more general than $\{x \mapsto a, y \mapsto b\}$, because there is no substitution σ such that $\{x \mapsto y\}\sigma = \{x \mapsto a, y \mapsto b\}$, but we have the relation $\{x \mapsto a, y \mapsto b\} \in \mathsf{Singl}(\{x \mapsto y\}\{y \mapsto \{a, b\}\}) = \mathsf{Singl}(\{x \mapsto \{a, b\}, y \mapsto \{a, b\}\})$.

The Completeness Theorem below proves a more general statement. It states that for any solution of an approximate unification problem, we can always compute a solution which is more general than a solution close to the given one.

Theorem 3 (Completeness of pre-unification). *Let a substitution ϑ be an $(\mathcal{R}, \lambda)$-unifier of two terms s and t. Then any maximal derivation that starts at $\{s \simeq^?_{\mathcal{R},\lambda} t\}; \emptyset; \mathit{Id}$ must end with an equational configuration $\emptyset; C; \mu$, such that for some $(\mathcal{R}, \lambda)$-solution Φ of C, which maps names to singleton neighborhoods, and some substitution ν such that $\vartheta \simeq_{\mathcal{R},\lambda} \sigma$ for some $\sigma \in \mathsf{Singl}(\nu)$, we have $\Phi(\mu|_{\mathcal{V}(s)\cup\mathcal{V}(t)}) \preceq \nu$.*

Proof. The full proof can be found in [9]. Here we sketch the idea.

Since $\{s \simeq^?_{\mathcal{R},\lambda} t\}$ is solvable, the derivation can not end with $\perp$ by soundness of pre-unification. Since for every equation there is a rule, and the algorithm terminates, the final configuration should have a form $\emptyset; C; \mu$.

Let V be $\mathcal{V}(s) \cup \mathcal{V}(t)$. In the construction of Φ, we need the proposition:

Proposition: Assume $P_1; C_1; \mu_1 \Longrightarrow P_2; C_2; \mu_2$ is a single step rule application in the above mentioned derivation. Let Φ_1 map names occurring in μ_1 to singleton neighborhoods such that equations in $\Phi_1(P_1)$ and in $\Phi_1(C_1)$ remain solvable. Assume that there exists a substitution ν_1 such that $\vartheta \simeq_{\mathcal{R},\lambda} \sigma_1$ for some $\sigma_1 \in \mathsf{Singl}(\nu_1)$ and $\Phi_1(\mu_1|_V) \preceq \nu_1$. Then there exist a substitution ν_2 such that $\vartheta \simeq_{\mathcal{R},\lambda} \sigma_2$ for some $\sigma_2 \in \mathsf{Singl}(\nu_2)$, and a name-neighborhood mapping Φ_2 which maps names occurring in μ_2 to singleton neighborhoods such that equations in $\Phi_2(P_2)$ and in $\Phi_2(C_2)$ remain solvable, and $\Phi_2(\mu_2|_V) \preceq \nu_2$.

In the constructed derivation, for the initial configuration $P_0; C_0; \mu_0 = \{s \simeq^?_{\mathcal{R},\lambda} t\}; \emptyset; \mathit{Id}$ we take $\Phi_0 = \emptyset$. Then $\Phi_0(P_0) = P_0 = \{s \simeq^?_{\mathcal{R},\lambda} t\}$ and $\Phi_0(C_0) = \emptyset$ are solvable, and $\Phi_0(\mu_0|_V) = \mathit{Id}$, $\mathsf{Singl}(\mathit{Id}) = \{\mathit{Id}\}$, and $\mathit{Id} \preceq \vartheta$. By applying the proposition iteratively, we get that for the final configuration $\emptyset; C; \mu$, there exists Φ which maps names to singleton neighborhoods such that $\Phi(C)$ is solvable. By the way how Φ is constructed, we have $dom(\Phi) = \mathcal{N}(\mu)$, but $\mathcal{N}(\mu) = \mathcal{N}(C)$. Hence, $\mathcal{N}(\Phi(C)) = \emptyset$ and its solvability means that it is already solved (trivially solvable). It implies that Φ is a solution of C. Besides, again by an iterative application of the proposition, we show the existence of ν such that $\vartheta \simeq_{\mathcal{R},\lambda} \sigma$ for some $\sigma \in \mathsf{Singl}(\nu)$ and $\Phi(\mu|_V) \preceq \nu$. $\qquad\square$

From Theorems 2 and 3, by definition of Singl we get

Theorem 4. *Given $\mathcal{R}$, λ and two terms s and t, let the pre-unification algorithm produce a derivation $\{s \simeq^?_{\mathcal{R},\lambda} t\}; \emptyset; \mathit{Id} \Longrightarrow^+ \emptyset; C; \mu$. Let $\{\Phi_1, \ldots, \Phi_n\}$ be a complete set of solutions of C, restricted to $\mathcal{N}(C)$. Then the set $\mathsf{Singl}(\Phi_1(\mu)) \cup \cdots \cup \mathsf{Singl}(\Phi_1(\mu))$ is a minimal complete set of unifiers of s and t.*

We should be careful in interpreting Theorem 4. If $\sigma \in mcsu_{\mathcal{R},\lambda}(s,t)$ and ξ is an X-substitution, then $\mathsf{Singl}(\sigma\xi)$ contains at least one $(\mathcal{R}, \lambda)$-unifier of s and t, but it may contain non-unifiers as well. If we restrict ξ to be an SX-substitution, then all elements of $\mathsf{Singl}(\sigma\xi)$ are $(\mathcal{R}, \lambda)$-unifiers of s and t, but SX-substitution instances are too weak to capture all unifiers. See [9, Example 1].

We introduce a neighborhood constraint solving algorithm in the next section. Before that we illustrate the pre-unification rules with a couple of examples:

Example 1. Let $s = p(x, y, x)$ and $t = q(f(a), g(d), y)$. Then the pre-unification algorithm gives $\emptyset; C, \mu$, where $C = \{p \approx^?_{\mathcal{R},\lambda} q, \mathrm{N}_1 \approx^?_{\mathcal{R},\lambda} f, \mathrm{N}_2 \approx^?_{\mathcal{R},\lambda} a, \mathrm{N}_3 \approx^?_{\mathcal{R},\lambda} g, \mathrm{N}_4 \approx^?_{\mathcal{R},\lambda} d, \mathrm{N}_1 \approx^?_{\mathcal{R},\lambda} \mathrm{N}_3, \mathrm{N}_2 \approx^?_{\mathcal{R},\lambda} \mathrm{N}_4\}$ and $\mu = \{x \mapsto \mathrm{N}_1(\mathrm{N}_2), y \mapsto \mathrm{N}_3(\mathrm{N}_4)\}$.

Assume that for the given λ-cut, the proximity relation consists of pairs $\mathcal{R}_\lambda = \{(a, b), (b, c), (c, d), (a, b'), (b', c'), (c', d), (f, g), (p, q)\}$. The obtained constraint can be solved, e.g., by the name-neighborhood mappings $\Phi = [\mathrm{N}_1 \mapsto \{f, g\}, \mathrm{N}_2 \mapsto \{b\}, \mathrm{N}_3 \mapsto \{f, g\}, \mathrm{N}_4 \mapsto \{c\}]$ and $\Phi' = [\mathrm{N}_1 \mapsto \{f, g\}, \mathrm{N}_2 \mapsto \{b'\}, \mathrm{N}_3 \mapsto \{f, g\}, \mathrm{N}_4 \mapsto \{c'\}]$. From them and μ we can get the sets $\Phi(\mu)$ and $\Phi'(\mu)$ of $(\mathcal{R}, \lambda)$-unifiers of s and t.

If we did not have the VO rule and allowed the use of VE rule instead, we might have ended up with the unification problem $\{y \simeq^?_{\mathcal{R},\lambda} f(a), y \simeq^?_{\mathcal{R},\lambda} g(d)\}$, which does not have a solution, because the neighborhoods of a and d do not have a common element. Hence, we would have lost a solution.

Example 2. Let $s = p(x, x)$ and $t = q(f(y, y), f(a, c))$. The pre-unification algorithm stops with $\emptyset; P; \mu$, where $P = \{p \approx^?_{\mathcal{R},\lambda} q, \mathrm{N}_1 \approx^?_{\mathcal{R},\lambda} f, \mathrm{N}_2 \approx^?_{\mathcal{R},\lambda} a, \mathrm{N}_3 \approx^?_{\mathcal{R},\lambda} c, \mathrm{M} \approx^?_{\mathcal{R},\lambda} \mathrm{N}_2, \mathrm{N}_3 \approx^?_{\mathcal{R},\lambda} \mathrm{M}\}$ and $\mu = \{x \mapsto \mathrm{N}_1(\mathrm{N}_2, \mathrm{N}_3), y_1 \mapsto \mathrm{N}_2, y_2 \mapsto \mathrm{N}_3, y \mapsto \mathrm{M}\}$. Let $\mathcal{R}_\lambda = \{(a, a_1), (a_1, b), (b, c_1), (c_1, c), (p, q)\}$. Then C is solved by $\Phi = [\mathrm{N}_1 \mapsto \{f\}, \mathrm{N}_2 \mapsto \{a_1\}, \mathrm{M} \mapsto \{b\}, \mathrm{N}_3 \mapsto \{c_1\}]$ and $\Phi(\mu|_{\mathcal{V}(s) \cup \mathcal{V}(t)})$ contains only one element, an $(\mathcal{R}, \lambda)$-unifier $\sigma = \{x \mapsto f(a_1, c_1), y \mapsto b\}$ of s and t. Indeed, $s\sigma = p(f(a_1, c_1), f(a_1, c_1)) \simeq_{\mathcal{R},\lambda} q(f(b, b), f(a, c)) = t\sigma$.

This example illustrates the necessity of introducing a fresh variable for *each occurrence* of a variable by the renaming function in the VE rule. If we used the same new variable, say y', for both occurrences of y in $f(y, y)$ (instead of using y_1 and y_2 as above), we would get the configuration $\emptyset; \{p \approx^?_{\mathcal{R},\lambda} q, \mathrm{N}_1 \approx^?_{\mathcal{R},\lambda} f, \mathrm{N}_2 \approx^?_{\mathcal{R},\lambda} a, \mathrm{N}_3 \approx^?_{\mathcal{R},\lambda} c, \mathrm{N}_3 \approx^?_{\mathcal{R},\lambda} \mathrm{N}_2\}; \{x \mapsto \mathrm{N}_1(\mathrm{N}_2, \mathrm{N}_2), y' \mapsto \mathrm{N}_2, y \mapsto \mathrm{N}_2\}$. But for the given $\mathcal{R}_\lambda$, the constraint $\{p \approx^?_{\mathcal{R},\lambda} q, \mathrm{N}_1 \approx^?_{\mathcal{R},\lambda} f, \mathrm{N}_2 \approx^?_{\mathcal{R},\lambda} a, \mathrm{N}_3 \approx^?_{\mathcal{R},\lambda} c, \mathrm{N}_3 \approx^?_{\mathcal{R},\lambda} \mathrm{N}_2\}$ does not have a solution (because the neighborhoods of a and c are not close to each other). Hence, we would lose a unifier.

3.2   Rules for Neighborhood Constraints

Let Φ be a *name-neighborhood mapping*. The *combination* of two mappings Φ and Ψ, denoted by $\Phi \odot \Psi$, is defined as

$$\Phi \odot \Psi := \{N \mapsto \Phi(N) \mid N \in dom(\Phi) \setminus dom(\Psi)\} \cup$$
$$\{N \mapsto \Psi(N) \mid N \in dom(\Psi) \setminus dom(\Phi)\} \cup$$
$$\{N \mapsto \Phi(N) \cap \Psi(N) \mid N \in dom(\Psi) \cap dom(\Phi)\}.$$

We call Φ and Ψ *compatible*, if $(\Phi \odot \Psi)(N) \neq \emptyset$ for all $N \in dom(\Phi \odot \Psi)$. Otherwise they are *incompatible*.

A *constraint configuration* is a pair $C; \Phi$, where C is a set of $(\mathcal{R}, \lambda)$-neighborhood constraints to be solved, and Φ is a name-neighborhood mapping (as a set of rules), representing the $(\mathcal{R}, \lambda)$-solution computed so far. We say that Ψ is an *$(\mathcal{R}, \lambda)$-solution of a constraint configuration* $C; \Phi$ if Ψ is an $(\mathcal{R}, \lambda)$-solution to C, and Ψ and Φ are compatible.

The constraint simplification algorithm $\mathcal{CS}$ transforms constraint configurations, exhaustively applying the following rules ($\perp$ indicates failure):

(FFS) Function Symbols: $\{f \approx^?_{\mathcal{R},\lambda} g\} \uplus C; \Phi; \Longrightarrow C; \Phi$, if $\mathcal{R}(f, g) \geq \lambda$.

(NFS) Name vs Function Symbol:

$$\{N \approx^?_{\mathcal{R},\lambda} g\} \uplus C; \Phi \Longrightarrow C; \Phi \odot \{N \mapsto \mathbf{pc}(g, \mathcal{R}, \lambda)\}.$$

(FSN) Function Symbol vs Name: $\{g \approx^?_{\mathcal{R},\lambda} N\} \uplus C; \Phi \Longrightarrow \{N \approx^?_{\mathcal{R},\lambda} g\} \cup C; \Phi.$

(NN1) Name vs Name 1:

$$\{N \approx^?_{\mathcal{R},\lambda} M\} \uplus C; \Phi \Longrightarrow C; \Phi \odot \{N \mapsto \{f\}, M \mapsto \mathbf{pc}(f, \mathcal{R}, \lambda)\},$$

where $N \in dom(\Phi)$, $f \in \Phi(N)$.

(NN2) Name vs Name 2: $\{M \approx^?_{\mathcal{R},\lambda} N\} \uplus C; \Phi \Longrightarrow \{N \approx^?_{\mathcal{R},\lambda} M\} \cup C; \Phi,$

where $M \notin dom(\Phi)$, $N \in dom(\Phi)$.

(Fail1) Failure 1: $\{f \approx^?_{\mathcal{R},\lambda} g\} \uplus C; \Phi \Longrightarrow \perp$, if $\mathcal{R}(f, g) < \lambda$.

(Fail2) Failure 2: $C; \Phi \Longrightarrow \perp$, if there exists $N \in dom(\Phi)$ with $\Phi(N) = \emptyset$.

The NN1 rule causes branching, generating n branches where n is the number of elements in $\Phi(N)$. (Remember that by definition, the proximity class of each symbol is finite.) When the derivation does not fail, the terminal configuration has the form $\{N_1 \approx^?_{\mathcal{R},\lambda} M_1, \ldots, N_n \approx^?_{\mathcal{R},\lambda} M_n\}; \Phi$, where for each $1 \leq i \leq n$, $N_i, M_i \notin dom(\Phi)$. Such a constraint is trivially solvable.

Theorem 5. *The constraint simplification algorithm $\mathcal{CS}$ is terminating.*

Proof. With each configuration $C; \Phi$ we associate a complexity measure, which is a triple of natural numbers (n_1, n_2, n_3): n_1 is the number of symbols occurrences in C, n_2 is the number of equations of the form $g \approx^?_{\mathcal{R},\lambda}$ N in C, and n_3 is the number of equations of the form M $\approx^?_{\mathcal{R},\lambda}$ N in C, where M $\notin dom(\Phi)$ and N $\in dom(\Phi)$. Measures are compared by the lexicographic extension of the ordering $>$ on natural numbers. It is a well-founded ordering. The rules (FFS), (NFS), (NN1) decrease n_1. The rule (FSN) does not change n_1 and decreases n_2. The rule (NN2) does not change n_1 and n_2 and decreases n_3. The failing rules cause termination immediately. Hence, each rule reduces the measure or terminates. It implies the termination of the algorithm. □

In the statements below, we assume $\mathcal{R}$ and λ to be given and the problems are to be solved with respect to them.

Lemma 3. 1. If $C; \Phi \Longrightarrow \bot$ by (Fail1) or (Fail2) rules, then (C, Φ) does not have an $(\mathcal{R}, \lambda)$-solution.
2. Let $C_1; \Phi_1 \Longrightarrow C_2; \Phi_2$ be a step performed by a constraint solving (nonfailing) rule. Then any $(\mathcal{R}, \lambda)$-solution of $C_1; \Phi_2$ is also an $(\mathcal{R}, \lambda)$-solution of $C_1; \Phi_1$.

Proof. 1. For (Fail1), the lemma follows from the definition of $(\mathcal{R}, \lambda)$-solution. For (Fail2), no Ψ is compatible with Φ which maps a name to the empty set.
2. The lemma is straightforward for (FFS), (FSN), and (NN2). To show it for (NFS), we take Ψ, which solves $C; \Phi \odot \{N \mapsto \mathbf{pc}(g, \mathcal{R}, \lambda)\}$. By definition of $\odot$, we get $\Psi(N) \subseteq \mathbf{pc}(g, \mathcal{R}, \lambda)$. But then Ψ is a solution to $\{N \approx^?_{\mathcal{R},\lambda} g\} \uplus C; \Phi$. To show the lemma holds for (NN1), we take a solution Ψ of $C; \Phi \odot \{N \mapsto \{f\}, M \mapsto \mathbf{pc}(f, \mathcal{R}, \lambda)\}$. It implies that $\Psi(N) = \{f\}$ and $\Psi(M) \subseteq \mathbf{pc}(f, \mathcal{R}, \lambda)$. But then we immediately get that Ψ solves $\{N \approx^?_{\mathcal{R},\lambda} M\} \uplus C; \Phi$. □

Theorem 6 (Soundness of $\mathcal{CS}$). *Let C be an $(\mathcal{R}, \lambda)$-neighborhood constraint such that $\mathcal{CS}$ produces a maximal derivation $C; \emptyset \Longrightarrow^* C'; \Phi$. Then Φ is an $(\mathcal{R}, \lambda)$-solution of $C \setminus C'$, and C' is a set of constraints between names which is trivially $(\mathcal{R}, \lambda)$-satisfiable.*

Proof. If a neighborhood equation is not between names, there is a rule in $\mathcal{CS}$ which applies to it. Hence, a maximal derivation can not stop with a C' that contains such an equation. As for neighborhood equations between names, only two rules deal with them: (NN1) and (NN2). But they apply only if at least one of the involved names belongs to the domain of the corresponding mapping. Hence, it can happen that an equation of the form N $\approx^?_{\mathcal{R},\lambda}$ M is never transformed by $\mathcal{CS}$. When the algorithm stops, such equations remain in C' and are trivially solvable. We can remove C' from each configuration in $C; \emptyset \Longrightarrow^* C'; \Phi$ without affecting any step, getting a derivation $C \setminus C'; \emptyset \Longrightarrow^* \emptyset; \Phi$. Obviously, Φ is an $(\mathcal{R}, \lambda)$-solution of $\emptyset; \Phi$. By induction on the length of the derivation and Lemma 3, we get that Φ is an $(\mathcal{R}, \lambda)$-solution of $C \setminus C'; \emptyset$ and, hence, it solves $C \setminus C'$. □

Remark 2. When a neighborhood constraint C is produced by the pre-unification algorithm, then every maximal $\mathcal{CS}$-derivation starting from $C; \emptyset$ ends either in $\bot$ or in the pair of the form $\emptyset; \Phi$. This is due to the fact that the VE rule (which introduces names in pre-unification problems) and the subsequent decomposition steps always produce chains of neighborhood equations of the form $N_1 \approx_{\mathcal{R},\lambda} N_2, N_2 \approx_{\mathcal{R},\lambda} N_3, \ldots, N_n \approx_{\mathcal{R},\lambda} f$, $n \geq 1$, for the introduced N's and for some f.

Theorem 7 (Completeness of $\mathcal{CS}$). *Let C be an $(\mathcal{R}, \lambda)$-neighborhood constraint produced by the pre-unification algorithm, and Φ be one of its solutions. Let $dom(\Phi) = \{N_1, \ldots, N_n\}$. Then for each n-tuple $c_1 \in \Phi(N_1), \ldots, c_n \in \Phi(N_n)$ there exists a $\mathcal{CS}$-derivation $C; \emptyset \Longrightarrow^* \emptyset; \Psi$ with $c_i \in \Psi(N_i)$ for each $1 \leq i \leq n$.*

Proof. We fix $c_1, \ldots, c_n$ such that $c_1 \in \Phi(N_1), \ldots, c_n \in \Phi(N_n)$.

First, note that $dom(\Phi)$ coincides with $\mathcal{N}(C)$. It is implied by the assumption that C is produced by pre-unification, and Remark 2 above.

The desired derivation is constructed recursively, where the important step is to identify a single inference. To see how such a single step is made, we consider a configuration $C_i; \Phi_i$ in this derivation ($i \geq 0$, $C_0 = C$, $\Phi_0 = \emptyset$). We have $dom(\Phi_i) \subseteq dom(\Phi)$. During construction, we will maintain the following two invariants for each $i \geq 0$ (easy to check that they hold for $i = 0$):

(I1) Φ is an $(\mathcal{R}, \lambda)$-solution of (C_i, Φ_i), and
(I2) for all $1 \leq j \leq n$, if $N_j \in dom(\Phi_i)$, then $c_j \in \Phi_i(N_j)$.

We consider the following cases:

- C_i contains an equation of the form $f \approx^?_{\mathcal{R},\lambda} g$. By **(I1)**, $\mathcal{R}(f, g) \geq \lambda$. Then we make the (FFS) step with $f \approx^?_{\mathcal{R},\lambda} g$, obtaining $C_{i+1} = C_i \setminus \{f \approx^?_{\mathcal{R},\lambda} g\}$ and $\Phi_{i+1} = \Phi_i$. Obviously, **(I1)** and **(I2)** hold also for the new configuration.
- Otherwise, assume C_i contains an equation $N_k \approx^?_{\mathcal{R},\lambda} g$, where $1 \leq k \leq n$. Since Φ solves $C; \Phi_i$, we have $\Phi_i(N) \neq \emptyset$ for all $N \in dom(\Phi_i)$ and there is only one choice to make the step: the (NFS) rule. It gives $C_{i+1} = C_i \setminus \{N_k \approx^?_{\mathcal{R},\lambda} g\}$ and $\Phi_{i+1} = \Phi_i \odot \{N_k \mapsto \mathbf{pc}(g, \mathcal{R}, \lambda)\}$. Since Φ solves, in particular, $N_k \approx^?_{\mathcal{R},\lambda} g$, we have $\Phi(N_k) \subseteq \mathbf{pc}(g, \mathcal{R}, \lambda)$ and, hence, $c_k \in \mathbf{pc}(g, \mathcal{R}, \lambda)$. First, assume $N_k \notin dom(\Phi_i)$. Then $\Phi_{i+1}(N_k) = \mathbf{pc}(g, \mathcal{R}, \lambda)$ and both **(I1)** and **(I2)** hold for $i+1$. Now, assume $N_k \in dom(\Phi_i)$. Then $\Phi_{i+1}(N_k) = \Phi_i(N_k) \cap \mathbf{pc}(g, \mathcal{R}, \lambda)$. Besides, **(I2)** implies $c_k \in \Phi_i(N_k)$. Hence, $c_k \in \Phi_{i+1}(N_k)$, which implies that **(I2)** holds for $i + 1$. From $c_k \in \Phi_{i+1}(N_k)$ and $c_k \in \Phi(N_k)$ we get that Φ is compatible with Φ_{i+1}. Moreover, Φ solves C_i, therefore, it solves C_{i+1}. Hence, Φ solves $C_{i+1}; \Phi_{i+1}$ and **(I1)** holds for $i + 1$ as well.
- Otherwise, assume C_i contains an equation of the form $N_k \approx^?_{\mathcal{R},\lambda} N_j$, where $1 \leq k, j \leq n$ and $N_k \in dom(\Phi_i)$. By **(I1)**, we have $N_k, N_j \in dom(\Phi)$, $\Phi(N_k) \cap \Phi(N_j) \neq \emptyset$, and $\Phi(N_k) \cap \Phi_i(N_k) \neq \emptyset$. By **(I2)**, we have $c_k \in \Phi_i(N_k)$. But since $c_k \in \Phi(N_k)$, we have $c_k \in \Phi(N_k) \cap \Phi_i(N_k)$. We make the step with (NN1) rule, choosing the mapping $N_k \mapsto \{c_k\}$. It gives $C_{i+1} = C_i \setminus \{N_k \approx^?_{\mathcal{R},\lambda} N_j\}$ and $\Phi_{i+1} = \Phi_i \odot \{N_k \mapsto \{c_k\}, N_j \mapsto \mathbf{pc}(c_k, \mathcal{R}, \lambda)\}$.
  To see that **(I1)** holds for $i+1$, the only nontrivial thing is to check that Φ and Φ_{i+1} are compatible. For this, $\Phi_{i+1}(N_k) \cap \Phi(N_k) \neq \emptyset$ and $\Phi_{i+1}(N_j) \cap \Phi(N_j) \neq \emptyset$ should be shown.
  Proving $\Phi_{i+1}(N_k) \cap \Phi(N_k) \neq \emptyset$: By construction, $\Phi_{i+1}(N_k) = \{c_k\}$. By assumption, $c_k \in \Phi(N_k)$. Hence, $\Phi_{i+1}(N_k) \cap \Phi(N_k) \neq \emptyset$.
  Proving $\Phi_{i+1}(N_j) \cap \Phi(N_j) \neq \emptyset$: Since Φ solves $N_k \approx^?_{\mathcal{R},\lambda} N_j$ and $c_k \in \Phi(N_k)$, we have $\Phi(N_j) \subseteq \mathbf{pc}(c_k, \mathcal{R}, \lambda)$. If $N_j \notin dom(\Phi_i)$, then $\Phi_{i+1}(N_j) = \mathbf{pc}(c_k, \mathcal{R}, \lambda)$ and $\Phi_{i+1}(N_j) \cap \Phi(N_j) \neq \emptyset$. If $N_j \in dom(\Phi_i)$, then by **(I2)**, $c_j \in \Phi_i(N_j)$.

On the other hand, $c_j \in \Phi(N_j)$ and, therefore, $c_j \in \mathbf{pc}(c_k, \mathcal{R}, \lambda)$. Since $\Phi_{i+1}(N_j) = \Phi_i(N_j) \cap \mathbf{pc}(c_k, \mathcal{R}, \lambda)$, we get $c_j \in \Phi_{i+1}(N_j)$ and, hence, $\Phi_{i+1}(N_j) \cap \Phi(N_j) \neq \emptyset$.

To see that **(I2)** holds is easier. In fact, we have already shown above that $\Phi_{i+1}(N_k) = \{c_k\}$. As for N_j, we have $N_j \in dom(\Phi_{i+1})$ iff $N_j \in dom(\Phi_i)$. In the latter case, we have seen in the proof of **(I1)** that $c_j \in \Phi_{i+1}(N_j)$.

– The other cases will be dealt by the rules (FSN) and (NN2). The invariants for them trivially hold, since these rules do not change the problem.

By **(I1)**, the configurations in our derivation are solvable. Therefore, the failing rules do not apply. Hence, the derivation ends with $\emptyset; \Psi$ for some Ψ. By construction, $dom(\Psi) = \{N_1, \ldots, N_n\}$. By **(I2)**, $c_i \in \Psi(N_i)$ for each $1 \leq i \leq n$. □

Example 3. The pre-unification derivation in Example 1 gives the neighborhood constraint $C = \{p \approx^?_{\mathcal{R},\lambda} q, N_1 \approx^?_{\mathcal{R},\lambda} f, N_2 \approx^?_{\mathcal{R},\lambda} a, N_3 \approx^?_{\mathcal{R},\lambda} g, N_4 \approx^?_{\mathcal{R},\lambda} d, N_1 \approx^?_{\mathcal{R},\lambda} N_3, N_2 \approx^?_{\mathcal{R},\lambda} N_4\}$. For $\mathcal{R}_\lambda = \{(a,b), (b,c), (c,d), (a,b'), (b',c'), (c',d), (f,g), (p,q)\}$, the algorithm $\mathcal{CS}$ gives four solutions:

$$\Phi_1 = \{N_1 \mapsto \{f\}, N_2 \mapsto \{b\}, N_3 \mapsto \{f,g\}, N_4 \mapsto \{c\}\}$$
$$\Phi_2 = \{N_1 \mapsto \{f\}, N_2 \mapsto \{b'\}, N_3 \mapsto \{f,g\}, N_4 \mapsto \{c'\}\}.$$
$$\Phi_3 = \{N_1 \mapsto \{g\}, N_2 \mapsto \{b\}, N_3 \mapsto \{f,g\}, N_4 \mapsto \{c\}\}$$
$$\Phi_4 = \{N_1 \mapsto \{g\}, N_2 \mapsto \{b'\}, N_3 \mapsto \{f,g\}, N_4 \mapsto \{c'\}\}.$$

Referring to the mappings Φ and Φ' and the substitution μ in Example 1, it is easy to observe that $\Phi(\mu) \cup \Phi'(\mu) = \Phi_1(\mu) \cup \Phi_2(\mu) \cup \Phi_3(\mu) \cup \Phi_4(\mu)$.

4   Final Remarks

We described an algorithm that solves unification problems over unrestricted proximity relations. It is terminating, sound, complete, and computes a compact representation of a minimal complete set of unifiers. A next step is to incorporate the computation of unification degree into the procedure and use it to characterize the "best" unifiers. Another future work involves a combination of unranked unification [6] and proximity relations to permit proximal function symbols with possibly different arities, similarly to the analogous extension of similarity-based unification described in [1].

References

1. Aït-Kaci, H., Pasi, G.: Fuzzy unification and generalization of first-order terms over similar signatures. In: Fioravanti, F., Gallagher, J.P. (eds.) LOPSTR 2017. LNCS, vol. 10855, pp. 218–234. Springer, Cham (2018). https://doi.org/10.1007/978-3-319-94460-9_13
2. Dubois, D., Prade, H.: Fuzzy Sets and Systems: Theory and Applications. Mathematics in Science and Engineering, vol. 144. Academic Press, Cambridge (1980)

3. Formato, F., Gerla, G., Sessa, M.I.: Extension of logic programming by similarity. In: Meo, M.C., Ferro, M.V. (eds.) 1999 Joint Conference on Declarative Programming, AGP 1999, L'Aquila, Italy, 6–9 September 1999, pp. 397–410 (1999)
4. Formato, F., Gerla, G., Sessa, M.I.: Similarity-based unification. Fundam. Inform. **41**(4), 393–414 (2000)
5. Julián-Iranzo, P., Rubio-Manzano, C.: Proximity-based unification theory. Fuzzy Sets Syst. **262**, 21–43 (2015)
6. Kutsia, T.: Unification with sequence variables and flexible arity symbols and its extension with pattern-terms. In: Calmet, J., Benhamou, B., Caprotti, O., Henocque, L., Sorge, V. (eds.) AISC/Calculemus -2002. LNCS (LNAI), vol. 2385, pp. 290–304. Springer, Heidelberg (2002). https://doi.org/10.1007/3-540-45470-5_26
7. Kutsia, T., Pau, C.: Proximity-based generalization. In: Ayala Rincón, M., Balbiani, P. (eds.) Proceedings of the 32nd International Workshop on Unification, UNIF 2018 (2018)
8. Kutsia, T., Pau, C.: Computing all maximal clique partitions in a graph. RISC Report 19–04, RISC, Johannes Kepler University Linz (2019)
9. Kutsia, T., Pau, C.: Solving proximity constraints. RISC Report 19–06, RISC, Johannes Kepler University Linz (2019)
10. Rodríguez-Artalejo, M., Romero-Díaz, C.A.: A declarative semantics for CLP with qualification and proximity. TPLP **10**(4–6), 627–642 (2010)
11. Sessa, M.I.: Approximate reasoning by similarity-based SLD resolution. Theor. Comput. Sci. **275**(1–2), 389–426 (2002)

A Certified Functional Nominal C-Unification Algorithm

Mauricio Ayala-Rincón[1(✉)], Maribel Fernández[2(✉)], Gabriel Ferreira Silva[1(✉)], and Daniele Nantes-Sobrinho[1(✉)]

[1] Departments of Computer Science and Mathematics, Universidade de Brasília, Brasília, Brazil
{ayala,dnantes}@unb.br, gabrielfsilva1995@mail.com
[2] Department of Informatics, King's College London, London, UK
maribel.fernandez@kcl.ac.uk

Abstract. The nominal approach allows us to extend first-order syntax and represent smoothly systems with variable bindings, using nominal atoms instead of variables and dealing with renaming through permutations of atoms. Nominal unification is, therefore, the extension of first-order unification modulo α-equivalence by taking into account this nominal setting. In this work, we present a specification of a nominal C-unification algorithm (nominal unification with commutative operators) in PVS and discuss the proofs of soundness and completeness. Additionally, the algorithm has been implemented in Python. In relation to the only known specification of nominal C-unification, there are two novel features in this work: first, the formalization of a functional algorithm that can be directly executed (not just a set of non-deterministic inference rules); second, simpler proofs of termination, soundness and completeness, due to the reduction in the number of parameters of the lexicographic measure, from four parameters to only two.

Keyword: Nominal terms · Nominal C-unification · Verification of functional specifications

1 Introduction

The nominal approach allows us to extend first-order syntax and represent smoothly systems with bindings, which are frequent in computer science and mathematics. However, in order to represent bindings correctly, α-equivalence must be taken into account. For instance, despite their syntactical difference, the formulas $\exists x : x < 0$ and $\exists z : z < 0$ should be considered equivalent. The nominal theory allows us to deal with these bindings in a natural way, using atoms, atom permutations and freshness constraints, instead of using indices as in explicit substitutions *à la de Bruijn* (e.g. [14,19]).

Work supported by FAPDF grant 193001369/2016.

M. Ayala-Rincón—partially funded by CNPq research grant number 307672/2017-4.

G. F. Silva—funded by CNPq scholarship number 139271/2017-1.

© Springer Nature Switzerland AG 2020
M. Gabbrielli (Ed.): LOPSTR 2019, LNCS 12042, pp. 123–138, 2020.
https://doi.org/10.1007/978-3-030-45260-5_8

Unification is an important problem in first-order theories, with applications to logic programming systems, type inference algorithms, theorem provers and so on (e.g. [12]). Since unification is essential for equational reasoning, the development of unification techniques for nominal logic has been an attractive area of research since the invention of the nominal approach.

The problem of nominal unification has been solved by Urban et al. [22], with further research devoted to algorithm improvements (e.g. [10,17]). Extensions of nominal unification have also been studied (e.g [9,16,20]), among them nominal unification modulo equational theories (e.g. [1–3,5]). Here, we consider nominal unification modulo commutative function symbols (nominal C-unification, for short).

Related Work. Nominal unification was first solved by Urban et al. in [22], by proposing a set of transformation rules and showing, using Isabelle/HOL, their correctness and completeness [21]. An alternative specification of nominal unification, as a function that maps (solvable) problems to solutions, was formalised in PVS and proved sound and complete [6]. This work brought two new perspectives to the problem. The first is the specification of a functional algorithm for nominal unification, not a set of inference rules, which made the specification closer to the implementation. The second is the separate treatment of freshness constraints and equational constraints. Both ideas are used in this paper.

Nominal C-unification extends nominal unification to handle commutative function symbols. In previous work, a set of non-deterministic transformation rules to solve nominal C-unification problems, in the style of Urban et al. [21], was shown correct and complete using the Coq proof assistant [2].

Contribution. In this paper, we present the first (to our knowledge) functional nominal C-unification algorithm and formalize its correctness and completeness using the proof assistant PVS. We emphasize the most interesting aspects of its formalization.

Although there is one other specification [2] for nominal C-unification, the approaches taken are different. In [2], a set of rules that gradually transforms the nominal C-unification problem into simpler ones is presented. Here, by contrast, we develop a recursive algorithm, specified and formalized in PVS and implemented in Python, not a set of inference rules. The advantage of this approach is that the algorithm can be executed, while the set of inference rules, specified through inductive definitions cannot, because it is non-deterministic.

As mentioned previously, [6] gave us a nominal unification algorithm and a new insight about the problem: the possibility to handle freshness constraints and equational constraints separately. We adapt a significant portion of the formalization in [6], adding and formalizing the necessary lemmas to obtain a sound and complete algorithm for nominal C-unification and keep the separate treatment of freshness constraints and equational constraints. This insight, along with a trick of separating fixed point equations (see Definition 9) from the unification problem, allowed us to reduce the lexicographic measure found in [2], from 4 parameters to only 2 parameters which made the proofs of termination, soundness and completeness simpler.

Finally, the formalization of soundness and completeness was done in PVS and is available at http://nominal.cic.unb.br. PVS was chosen partly in order to reuse the definitions and lemmas previously used in [6] and partly because its specification language provides great support for the definition (and formalization) of functional recursive algorithms.

Possible Applications. As remarked before, nominal unification is used in logic programming. Therefore, the nominal C-unification algorithm could be used in a logic programming language that uses the nominal setting, such as α-Prolog [12]. Another application is related to matching (see [7,8]). Matching two terms t and s can be seen as unification where one of the terms (suppose t, without loss of generality) is not affected by substitutions [2]. This can be accomplished by adding as an additional parameter to the algorithm a set of variables that are forbidden to be instantiated. Then, matching boils down to unifying, using as this additional parameter the set of variables in t [2]. The C-matching algorithm proposed could then, for instance, be used to extend the nominal rewriting relation introduced in [14] modulo commutativity. Also, nominal C-unification and matching are relevant to implement nominal narrowing introduced in [4] allowing commutative symbols.

Organization. The paper is organized as follows. First, in Sect. 2, we provide the necessary background. The nominal setting is explained and the problem of nominal C-unification is defined. In Sect. 3, we present and explain the pseudocode for the algorithm specified in PVS and implemented in Python. In Sect. 4, we discuss the main aspects of the formalization: the principal lemmas, the hardest cases, how introducing commutativity made the problem more complex and so on. Finally, in Sect. 6, we conclude the paper and offer possible paths of future work. An extended version of this paper is available at http://nominal.cic.unb.br.

2   Background

In this section, we provide the necessary background in nominal theory.

2.1   Nominal Terms, Permutations and Substitutions

In nominal theory, we consider disjoint countable sets of atoms $\mathcal{A} = \{a, b, c, ...\}$ and of variables $\mathcal{X} = \{X, Y, Z, ...\}$. A permutation π is a bijection of the form $\pi : \mathcal{A} \to \mathcal{A}$ such that the domain of π (i.e., the set of atoms that are modified by π) is finite. Permutations are usually represented as a list of swappings, where the swapping $(a\ b)$ exchanges the atoms a and b and fixes the other atoms. Therefore, a permutation is represented as $\pi = (a_1\ b_1) :: ... :: (a_n\ b_n) :: nil.\ \pi^{-1}$, the inverse of this permutation, is computed by simply reversing the list.

Definition 1 (Nominal Terms). *Let Σ be a signature with function symbols and commutative function symbols. The set $\mathcal{T}(\Sigma, \mathcal{A}, \mathcal{X})$ of nominal terms is generated according to the grammar:*

$$s, t \quad ::= \quad \langle\rangle \mid a \mid \pi \cdot X \mid [a]t \mid \langle s, t \rangle \mid f\ t \mid f^C \langle s, t \rangle \qquad (1)$$

where $\langle\rangle$ is the unit, a is an atom term, $\pi \cdot X$ is a moderated variable or suspension (the permutation π is suspended on the variable X), $[a]t$ is an abstraction (a term with the atom a abstracted), $\langle s, t \rangle$ is a pair, $f\ t$ is a function application and $f^C \langle s, t \rangle$ is a commutative function application over a pair.

Remark 1. Pairs can be used to encode tuples with an arbitrary number of arguments. For instance, the tuple (t_1, t_2, t_3) could be constructed as $\langle t_1, \langle t_2, t_3 \rangle \rangle$.

Remark 2. Following [2], we impose that commutative functions receive a pair as their argument. No generality is lost with this restriction and the analysis is simplified.

Definition 2 (Permutation Action). *The permutation action on atoms is defined recursively: $nil \cdot c = c$ and $((a\ b) :: \pi) \cdot c = a$, if $\pi \cdot c = b$; $((a\ b) :: \pi) \cdot c = b$, if $\pi \cdot c = a$; $((a\ b) :: \pi) \cdot c = \pi \cdot c$ otherwise. The action of permutations on terms is defined recursively:*

$$\pi \cdot \langle\rangle = \langle\rangle \qquad\qquad\qquad \pi \cdot (\pi' \cdot X) = (\pi :: \pi') \cdot X$$

$$\pi \cdot [a]t = [\pi \cdot a]\pi \cdot t \qquad\qquad \pi \cdot \langle s, t \rangle = \langle \pi \cdot s, \pi \cdot t \rangle$$

$$\pi \cdot f\ t = f\ \pi \cdot t \qquad\qquad \pi \cdot f^C \langle s, t \rangle = f^C \langle \pi \cdot s, \pi \cdot t \rangle$$

Remark 3. We follow Gabbay's permutative convention, which says that atoms differ in their names. Therefore, if we consider atoms a and b, it is redundant to say $a \neq b$.

Example 1. To illustrate the action of a permutation on a term, consider $\pi = (a\ b) :: (c\ d) :: nil$ and $t = f(a, c)$. Then, the result of the permutation action is $\pi \cdot t = f(b, d)$.

Definition 3 (Nuclear Substitution). *A nuclear substitution is a pair $[X \to t]$, where X is a variable and t is a term. Nuclear substitutions act over terms:*

$$\langle\rangle[X \to t] = \langle\rangle \qquad\qquad\qquad a[X \to t] = a$$

$$([a]s)[X \to t] = [a](s[X \to t]) \qquad \pi \cdot Y[X \to t] = \begin{cases} \pi \cdot Y & \text{if } X \neq Y \\ \pi \cdot t & \text{otherwise} \end{cases}$$

$$\langle s_1, s_2 \rangle[X \to t] = \langle s_1[X \to t], s_2[X \to t] \rangle \qquad (f\ s)[X \to t] = f\ (s[X \to t])$$

$$(f^C \langle s_1, s_2 \rangle)[X \to t] = f^C \langle s_1[X \to t], s_2[X \to t] \rangle$$

Definition 4 (Substitution Action on Terms). *A substitution σ is a list of nuclear substitutions, which are applied consecutively to a term:*

$$s\ id = s, \text{ where } id \text{ is the empty list} \qquad s(\sigma :: [X \to t]) = (s[X \to t])\sigma \qquad (2)$$

Remark 4. The notion of substitution defined here differs from the more traditional view of a substitution as a simultaneous application of nuclear substitutions, although both are correct [6]. In our representation, the nuclear substitution applied first is the furthest from the term, i.e, the last one in the list of nuclear substitutions. The notion here presented is closer to the concept of triangular substitutions [15].

Example 2. Let $\sigma = [X \rightarrow a] :: [Y \rightarrow f(X, b)]$ and $t = [a]Y$. Then, $t\sigma = [a]f(a, b)$.

2.2   Freshness and α-equality

Two valuable notions in nominal theory are freshness and α-equality, which are represented, respectively, by the predicates $\#$ and $\approx_\alpha$.

- $a\#t$ means, intuitively, that if a occurs in t then it does so under an abstractor $[a]$.
- $s \approx_\alpha t$ means, intuitively, that s and t are α-equivalent, i.e, they are equal modulo the renaming of bound atoms.

These concepts are formally defined in Definitions 5 and 6.

Definition 5 (Freshness). *A freshness context ∇ is a set of constraints of the form $a\#X$. An atom a is said to be fresh on t under a context ∇, denoted by $\nabla \vdash a\#t$, if it is possible to build a proof using the rules:*

$$\frac{}{\nabla \vdash a\#\langle\rangle} \ (\#\langle\rangle) \qquad \frac{}{\nabla \vdash a\#b} \ (\#atom) \qquad \frac{(\pi^{-1} \cdot a\#X) \in \nabla}{\nabla \vdash a\#\pi \cdot X} \ (\#X)$$

$$\frac{}{\nabla \vdash a\#[a]t} \ (\#[a]a) \qquad \frac{\nabla \vdash a\#t}{\nabla \vdash a\#[b]t} \ (\#[a]b) \qquad \frac{\nabla \vdash a\#s \quad \nabla \vdash a\#t}{\nabla \vdash a\#\langle s, t\rangle} \ (\#pair)$$

$$\frac{\nabla \vdash a\#t}{\nabla \vdash a\#f\ t} \ (\#app) \qquad \frac{\nabla \vdash a\#s \quad \nabla \vdash a\#t}{\nabla \vdash a\#f^C \ \langle s, t\rangle} \ (\#c\text{-}app)$$

Example 3. Notice that $a\#X \vdash a\#\langle[a]\langle X, a\rangle, [b]h\langle X, b\rangle\rangle$, by application of rules $(\#pair)$, $(\#[a]a)$, $(\#[a]b)$, $(\#app)$, $(\#X)$ and $(\#atom)$.

Definition 6 (α-equality with commutative operators). *Two terms t and s are said to be α-equivalent under the freshness context Δ ($\Delta \vdash t \approx_\alpha s$) if it is possible to build a proof using the rules:*

$$\frac{\Delta \vdash s_0 \approx_\alpha t_i, \quad \Delta \vdash s_1 \approx_\alpha t_{i+1(mod2)}}{\Delta \vdash f^C\langle s_0, s_1\rangle \approx_\alpha f^C\langle t_0, t_1\rangle} \ (\approx_\alpha C) \quad i = 0, 1 \qquad \frac{}{\Delta \vdash a \approx_\alpha a} \ (\approx_\alpha atom)$$

$$\frac{\Delta \vdash s \approx_\alpha t}{\Delta \vdash f\ s \approx_\alpha f\ t} \ (\approx_\alpha app) \qquad \frac{\Delta \vdash s \approx_\alpha t}{\Delta \vdash [a]s \approx_\alpha [a]t} \ (\approx_\alpha [a]a)$$

$$\frac{\Delta \vdash s \approx_\alpha (a\ b) \cdot t, \quad \Delta \vdash a\#t}{\Delta \vdash [a]s \approx_\alpha [b]t} \ (\approx_\alpha [a]b) \qquad \frac{ds(\pi, \pi')\#X \subseteq \Delta}{\Delta \vdash \pi \cdot X \approx_\alpha \pi' \cdot X} \ (\approx_\alpha var)$$

$$\frac{\Delta \vdash s_0 \approx_\alpha t_0, \quad \Delta \vdash s_1 \approx_\alpha t_1}{\Delta \vdash \langle s_0, s_1\rangle \approx_\alpha \langle t_0, t_1\rangle} \ (\approx_\alpha pair) \qquad \frac{}{\Delta \vdash \langle\rangle \approx_\alpha \langle\rangle} \ (\approx_\alpha \langle\rangle)$$

Notation: *We define the difference set between two permutations π and π' as $ds(\pi, \pi') = \{a \in \mathcal{A} | \pi \cdot a \neq \pi' \cdot a\}$. By extension, $ds(\pi, \pi') \# X$ is the set containing every constraint of the form $a \# X$ for $a \in ds(\pi, \pi')$.*

Example 4. Notice that $[a]a \approx_\alpha [b]b$:

$$\frac{\dfrac{\overline{a \approx_\alpha (a\ b) \cdot b}\ (\approx_\alpha atom) \qquad \overline{a \# b}\ (\# atom)}{[a]a \approx_\alpha [b]b}\ (\approx_\alpha [a]b)}{}$$

2.3   Nominal C-Unification

Definition 7 (Unification Problem). *A unification problem is a pair $\langle \nabla, P \rangle$ where ∇ is a freshness context and P is a finite set of equations and freshness constraints of the form $s \approx_? t$ and $a \#_? t$, respectively.*

Remark 5. Consider ∇ and ∇' freshness contexts and σ and σ' substitutions. We need the following notation to define a solution to a unification problem:

- $\nabla' \vdash \nabla \sigma$ denotes that $\nabla' \vdash a \# X \sigma$ holds for each $(a \# X) \in \nabla$.
- $\nabla \vdash \sigma \approx \sigma'$ denotes that $\nabla \vdash X\sigma \approx_\alpha X\sigma'$ for all X in $dom(\sigma) \cup dom(\sigma')$.

Definition 8 (Solution for a Triple or Problem). *Let δ be a substitution. A solution for a triple $\mathcal{P} = \langle \Delta, \delta, P \rangle$ is a pair $\langle \nabla, \sigma \rangle$ that fulfills the following four conditions:*

1. $\nabla \vdash \Delta \sigma$
2. $\nabla \vdash a \#_? t \sigma$, *if* $a \#_? t \in P$
3. $\nabla \vdash s\sigma \approx_\alpha t\sigma$, *if* $s \approx_? t \in P$
4. *There exists λ such that $\nabla \vdash \delta \lambda \approx \sigma$*

Then, a solution for a unification problem $\langle \Delta, P \rangle$ is a solution for the associated triple $\langle \Delta, id, P \rangle$.

Definition 9 (Fixed Point Equation). *An equation of the form $\pi \cdot X \approx_\alpha \pi' \cdot X$ is called a fixed point equation.*

Remark 6. Fixed point equations are not solved in C-unification because they may have an infinite number of independent solutions. Instead, they are carried on, as part of the solution to the unification problem [1].

Remark 7. One of the original features of this work is the separate treatment of fixed point equations from the set of equational and freshness constraints. There is a trivial extension of Definition 8 in order to consider this detachment. Let FP be a set of fixed point equations. $\langle \nabla, \sigma \rangle$ is a solution to the quadruple $\mathcal{P} = \langle \Delta, \delta, P, FP \rangle$ if all conditions of Definition 8 are satisfied and additionally:

- $\nabla \vdash \pi \cdot X\sigma \approx_\alpha \pi' \cdot X\sigma$, if $\pi \cdot X \approx_? \pi' \cdot X \in FP$

Remark 8. The problem of nominal C-unification, as the problem of first-order C-unification, is NP-complete (see [7] and [2]).

3   Specification

We developed a functional nominal C-unification algorithm for unifying the terms t and s. The algorithm is recursive and needs to keep track of the current context, the substitutions made so far, the remaining terms to unify and the current fixed point equations. Therefore, the algorithm receives as input a quadruple $(\Delta, \sigma, PrbLst, FPEqLst)$, where Δ is the context we are working with, σ is a list of the substitutions already done, $PrbLst$ is a list of unification problems which we must still unify (each equational constraint $t \approx_? s$ is represented as a pair (t, s) in Algorithm 1) and $FPEqLst$ is a list of fixed point equations we have already computed.

The first call to the algorithm, in order to unify the terms t and s is simply: $\texttt{UNIFY}(\emptyset, id, [(t, s)], \emptyset)$. The algorithm eventually terminates, returning a list (possibly empty) of solutions, where each solution is of the form $(\Delta, \sigma, FPEqLst)$.

Although extensive, the algorithm is simple. It starts by analysing the list of terms it needs to unify. If $PrbLst$ is an empty list, then it has finished and can return the answer computed so far, which is the list: $[(\Delta, \sigma, FPEqLst)]$. If $PrbLst$ is not empty, then there are terms to unify, and the algorithm starts by trying to unify the terms t and s that are in the head of the list and only after that it goes to the tail of the list. The algorithm is recursive, calling itself on progressively simpler versions of the problem until it finishes.

3.1   Auxiliary Functions

Following the approach of [6], freshness constraints are treated separately from the main function. This has the advantage of making the main function $\texttt{UNIFY}$ smaller, handling only equational constraints. To deal with the freshness constraints, the following auxiliary functions, which come from [6], were used:

- $\texttt{fresh\_subs?}(\sigma, \Delta)$ returns the minimal context (Δ' in Algorithm 1) in which $a \#_? X\sigma$ holds, for every $a \# X$ in the context Δ.
- $\texttt{fresh?}(a, t)$ computes and returns the minimal context (Δ' in Algorithm 1) in which a is fresh for t.

Both functions also return a boolean ($bool1$ in Algorithm 1), indicating if it was possible to find the mentioned context.

3.2   Main Algorithm

The pseudocode of the algorithm is presented in Algorithm 1.

Remark 9. When trying to unify $f^C \langle t_1, t_2 \rangle$ with $f^C \langle s_1, s_2 \rangle$ there are two possible paths to take: try to unify t_1 with s_1 and t_2 with s_2, or try to unify t_1 with s_2 and t_2 with s_1. This means that there are two branches that we must consider, and since each branch can generate a solution, we may have more than one solution. This is the reason why the algorithm here presented gives a list of solutions as output. In nominal unification, by contrast, only one most general unifier is given as solution.

3.3   Examples

A simple example of the algorithm is given in Example 5. In this example, it is possible to see how commutativity introduces branches and how the algorithm calls itself with progressively simpler versions of the problem until it finishes. Example 6 is a slightly more complex example, which uses Example 5.

Algorithm 1 - First Part - Functional Nominal C-Unification

```
 1: procedure UNIFY(Δ, σ, PrbLst, FPEqLst)
 2:     if nil?(PrbLst) then
 3:         return list((Δ, σ, FPEqLst))
 4:     else
 5:         cons((t, s), PrbLst') = PrbLst
 6:         if (s matches π · X) and (X not in t) then
 7:             σ' = {X → π⁻¹ · t}
 8:             σ'' = σ' ∘ σ
 9:             (Δ', bool1) = fresh_subs?(σ', Δ)
10:             Δ'' = Δ ∪ Δ'
11:             PrbLst'' = append((PrbLst')σ', (FPEqLst)σ')
12:             if bool1 then return UNIFY(Δ'', σ'', PrbLst'', nil)
13:             else return nil
14:             end if
15:         else
16:             if t matches a then
17:                 if s matches a then
18:                     return UNIFY(Δ, σ, PrbLst', FPEqLst)
19:                 else
20:                     return nil
21:                 end if
22:             else if t matches π · X then
23:                 if (X not in s) then
24:                                                  ▷ Similar to case above where s is a suspension
25:                 else if (s matches π' · X) then
26:                     FPEqLst' = FPEqLst ∪ { π · X ≈_α π' · X}
27:                     return UNIFY(Δ, σ, PrbLst', FPEqLst')
28:                 else return nil
29:                 end if
30:             else if t matches ⟨⟩ then
31:                 if s matches ⟨⟩ then
32:                     return UNIFY(Δ, σ, PrbLst', FPEqLst)
33:                 else return nil
34:                 end if
35:             else if t matches ⟨t₁, t₂⟩ then
36:                 if s matches ⟨s₁, s₂⟩ then
37:                     PrbLst'' = cons((s₁, t₁), cons((s₂, t₂), PrbLst'))
38:                     return UNIFY(Δ, σ, PrbLst'', FPEqLst)
39:                 else return nil
40:                 end if
```

Example 5. Suppose f is a commutative function symbol. This example shows how the algorithm proceeds in order to unify $f\langle(a\ b) \cdot X, c\rangle$ with $f\langle X, c\rangle$.

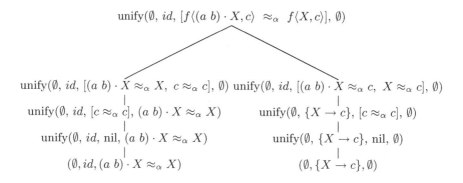

Algorithm 1 - Second Part - Functional Nominal C-Unification

```
41:            else if t matches [a]t₁ then
42:               if s matches [a]s₁ then
43:                  PrbLst'' = cons((t₁, s₁), PrbLst')
44:                  return UNIFY(Δ, σ, PrbLst'', FPEqLst)
45:               else if s matches [b]s₁ then
46:                  (Δ', bool1) = fresh?(a, s₁)
47:                  Δ'' = Δ ∪ Δ'
48:                  PrbLst'' = cons((t₁,  (a b) s₁), PrbLst')
49:                  if bool1 then
50:                     return UNIFY(Δ'', σ, PrbLst'', FPEqLst)
51:                  else return nil
52:                  end if
53:               else return nil
54:               end if
55:            else if t matches f t₁ then                       ▷ f is not commutative
56:               if s matches f s₁ then
57:                  PrbLst'' = cons((t₁, s₁), PrbLst')
58:                  return UNIFY(Δ, σ, PrbLst'', FPEqLst)
59:               else return nil
60:               end if
61:            else                                             ▷ t is of the form fᶜ(t₁, t₂)
62:               if s matches fᶜ(s₁, s₂) then
63:                  PrbLst₁ = cons((s₁, t₁), cons((s₂, t₂), PrbLst'))
64:                  sol₁ = UNIFY(Δ, σ, PrbLst₁, FPEqLst)
65:                  PrbLst₂ = cons((s₁, t₂), cons((s₂, t₁), PrbLst'))
66:                  sol₂ = UNIFY(Δ, σ, PrbLst₂, FPEqLst)
67:                  return APPEND(sol₁, sol₂)
68:               else return nil
69:               end if
70:            end if
71:         end if
72:      end if
73: end procedure
```

Example 6. Suppose f and g are commutative function symbols, and h is a non-commutative function symbol. This example shows how the algorithm would unify $g\langle h\ d, f\langle (a\ b) \cdot X, c\rangle\rangle$ with $g\langle f\langle X, c\rangle, h\ d\rangle$. Because g is commutative, the algorithm explores two branches:

- On the first branch, the algorithm tries to unify $h\ d$ with $f\langle X, c\rangle$ and $f\langle (a\ b) \cdot X, c)$ with $h\ d$. However, since it is impossible to unify $h\ d$ with $f\langle X, c\rangle$ (different function symbols), the algorithm returns an empty list, indicating that no solution is possible for this branch.

– On the second branch, the algorithm tries to unify $h\ d$ with $h\ d$ and $f\langle(a\ b)\cdot X,c\rangle$ with $f\langle X,c\rangle$. First, $h\ d$ unifies with $h\ d$ without any alterations on the context Δ, the substitution σ or the list of fixed point equations $FPEqLst$. Finally, the unification of $f\langle(a\ b)\cdot X,c\rangle$ with $f\langle X,c\rangle$ was shown in Example 5, and gives two solutions, which are also the solutions to this example: $(\emptyset,id,(a\ b)\cdot X\approx_\alpha X)$ and $(\emptyset,\{X\to c\},\emptyset)$.

4 Formalization

4.1 Termination

Termination of the algorithm was proved by proving the type-correctness conditions (TCCs) generated by PVS [18]. In order to do that, a lexicographic measure was defined:

$$lex2(|Vars(PrbLst)\cup Vars(FPEqLst)|, size(PrbLst)) \tag{3}$$

The first component in the lexicographic measure is the cardinality of the set of variables which occur in $PrbLst$ (the list of remaining unification problems) or in $FPEqLst$ (the list of fixed point equations). To compute the variables in a list, we consider the variables in all terms of the list. Finally, the variables in a term are computed recursively, as can be seen in Definition 10.

Definition 10 (Set of Variables). *The set of variables in a term is recursively defined as:*

$$Vars(a) = \emptyset \qquad\qquad Vars(\langle\rangle) = \emptyset$$
$$Vars(\pi\cdot X) = \{X\} \qquad Vars([a]t) = Vars(t)$$
$$Vars(\langle t_0,t_1\rangle) = Vars(t_0)\cup Vars(t_1) \quad Vars(f\ t) = Vars(t)$$
$$Vars(f^C\langle t_0,t_1\rangle) = Vars(t_0)\cup Vars(t_1)$$

The second component in the lexicographic measure is the sum of the size of every unification problem. To calculate the size of the unification problem (t,s), we only calculate the size of the first term t. This was an arbitrary choice, as the measure would still work if we had taken the size of s or even the size of t plus the size of s (in each recursive call, both the size of t and the size of s decrease). Finally, the size of t is computed recursively according to Definition 11.

Definition 11 (Size of Terms). *The size of terms is recursively computed as:*

$$size(a) = 1 \qquad\qquad size(\langle\rangle) = 1$$
$$size(\pi\cdot X) = 1 \qquad size([a]t) = 1 + size(t)$$
$$size(\langle t_0,t_1\rangle) = 1 + size(t_0) + size(t_1) \quad size(f\ t) = 1 + size(t)$$
$$size(f^C\langle t_0,t_1\rangle) = 1 + size(t_0) + size(t_1)$$

The lexicographic measure decreases in each recursive call. The component that decreases depends on the type of the terms t and s that are in the head of the list of problems to unify. If one of them is a variable X, and we are not dealing with a fixed point equation, then the algorithm will instantiate this variable X, and the first component, $|Vars(PrbLst)\cup Vars(FPEqLst)|$, will decrease. In any other case, the second component, $size(PrbLst)$, will decrease.

Remark 10. It was possible to reduce the lexicographic measure used in [2], from 4 parameters to only 2 parameters. The measure adopted in [2] was:

$$|\mathcal{P}| = \langle |Var(P_\approx)|, |P_\approx|, |P_{nfp}|, |P_\#| \rangle \qquad (4)$$

where $P_\approx$ is the set of equation constraints in P, P_{nfp} is the set of non fixed point equations in P and $P_\#$ is the set of freshness constraints in P. Two ideas were used in order to accomplish this reduction. The first was to separate the treatment of freshness constraints from equational constraints, and treat the freshness constraints with the help of the auxiliary functions of Sect. 3.1. This idea comes from [6]. The second one is to separate the fixed point equations from the equational constraints. This way, when a fixed point equation is found in *PrbLst*, it is moved to *FPEqLst*, which makes $size(PrbLst)$ diminish.

4.2 Soundness and Completeness

To state the main theorems that allow us to prove soundness and completeness, we must first define the notion of a *valid* quadruple. A valid quadruple is an invariant of the UNIFY function in Algorithm 1 with useful properties.

Definition 12 (Valid Quadruple). *Let Δ be a freshness context, σ a substitution, P a list of unification problems and FP a list of fixed point equations. $\mathcal{P} = \langle \Delta, \sigma, P, FP \rangle$ is a valid quadruple if the following two conditions hold:*

- *$Vars(im(\sigma)) \cap dom(\sigma) = \emptyset$*   - *$dom(\sigma) \cap (Vars(P) \cup Vars(FP)) = \emptyset$*

where $im(\sigma)$ is the image of σ and $dom(\sigma)$ is the domain of σ.

Remark 11. A valid quadruple has two desirable properties: the substitution is idempotent (condition 1) and applying the substitution to P or FP produces no effect.

Soundness. Corollary 1 states that UNIFY is sound. It follows directly by application of Theorem 1.

Theorem 1 (Main Theorem for Soundness of UNIFY Algorithm). *Suppose $(\Delta_{sol}, \sigma_{sol}, FPEqLst_{sol}) \in$ UNIFY $(\Delta, \sigma, PrbLst, FPEqLst)$, (∇, δ) is a solution to $\langle \Delta_{sol}, \sigma_{sol}, \emptyset, FPEqLst_{sol} \rangle$ and $\langle \Delta, \sigma, PrbLst, FPEqLst \rangle$ is a valid quadruple. Then (∇, δ) is a solution to $\langle \Delta, \sigma, PrbLst, FPEqLst \rangle$.*

Proof. The proof is by induction on the lexicographic measure, according to the form of the terms t and s that are in the head of *PrbLst*, the list of remaining unification problems. The hardest cases are the ones of suspended variables and abstractions (see Remark 14). Below we explain the case of commutative functions.

In the case of commutative function symbols $f\langle t_1, t_2 \rangle$ and $f\langle s_1, s_2 \rangle$, there are no changes in the context or the substitution from one recursive call to the next.

Therefore, it is trivial to check that we remain with a valid quadruple and it is also trivial to check all but the third condition of Definition 8. For the third condition we have either $\nabla \vdash t_1\delta \approx_\alpha s_1\delta$ and $\nabla \vdash t_2\delta \approx_\alpha s_2\delta$ or $\nabla \vdash t_1\delta \approx_\alpha s_2\delta$ and $\nabla \vdash t_2\delta \approx_\alpha s_1\delta$. In any case, we are able to deduce $\nabla \vdash (f\langle t_1, t_2\rangle)\delta \approx_\alpha (f\langle s_1, s_2\rangle)\delta$ by noting that $(f\langle t_1, t_2\rangle)\delta = f\langle t_1\delta, t_2\delta\rangle$, $(f\langle s_1, s_2\rangle)\delta = f\langle s_1\delta, s_2\delta\rangle$ and then using rule $(\approx_\alpha c - app)$ for alpha equivalence of commutative function symbols.

Corollary 1 (Soundness of UNIFY Algorithm). *Suppose (∇, δ) is a solution to $\langle \Delta_{sol}, \sigma_{sol}, \emptyset, FPEqLst_{sol}\rangle$, and $(\Delta_{sol}, \sigma_{sol}, FPEqLst_{sol}) \in$ UNIFY $(\emptyset, id, [(t, s)], \emptyset)$. Then (∇, δ) is a solution to $\langle \emptyset, id, [(t, s)], \emptyset\rangle$.*

Proof. Notice that $\langle \emptyset, id, [(t, s)], \emptyset\rangle$ is a valid quadruple. Then, we apply Theorem 1 and prove the corollary.

Remark 12. An interpretation of Corollary 1 is that if (∇, δ) is a solution to one of the outputs of the algorithm UNIFY, then (∇, δ) is a solution to the original problem.

Completeness. Corollary 2 states that UNIFY is complete. It follows directly by application of Theorem 2.

Theorem 2 (Main Theorem for Completeness of UNIFY). *Suppose (∇, δ) is a solution to $\langle \Delta, \sigma, PrbLst, FPEqLst\rangle$ and that $\langle \Delta, \sigma, PrbLst, FPEqLst\rangle$ is a valid quadruple. Then, there exists a computed output $(\Delta_{sol}, \sigma_{sol}, FPEqLst_{sol}) \in$ UNIFY $(\Delta, \sigma, PrbLst, FPEqLst)$ such that the solution (∇, δ) is also a solution to $\langle \Delta_{sol}, \sigma_{sol}, \emptyset, FPEqLst_{sol}\rangle$.*

Proof. The proof is by induction on the lexicographic measure, according to the form of the terms t and s that are in the head of $PrbLst$, the list of remaining unification problems. The hardest cases are again the ones of suspended variables and abstractions (see Remark 14). Below we explain the case of commutative functions.

In the case of commutative function symbols $f\langle t_1, t_2\rangle$ and $f\langle s_1, s_2\rangle$, there are no changes in the context or the substitution from one recursive call to the next. Therefore, it is trivial to check that we remain with a valid quadruple and it is also trivial to check all but the third condition of Definition 8. For the third condition we have $\nabla \vdash (f\langle t_1, t_2\rangle)\delta \approx_\alpha (f\langle s_1, s_2\rangle)\delta$ and must prove that either $(\nabla \vdash t_1\delta \approx_\alpha s_1\delta$ and $\nabla \vdash t_2\delta \approx_\alpha s_2\delta)$ or $(\nabla \vdash t_1\delta \approx_\alpha s_2\delta$ and $\nabla \vdash t_2\delta \approx_\alpha s_1\delta)$ happens. This again is solved by noting that $(f\langle t_1, t_2\rangle)\delta = f\langle t_1\delta, t_2\delta\rangle$, $(f\langle s_1, s_2\rangle)\delta = f\langle s_1\delta, s_2\delta\rangle$ and then using rule $(\approx_\alpha c - app)$ for alpha equivalence of commutative function symbols.

Corollary 2 (Completeness of UNIFY). *Suppose (∇, δ) is a solution to the input quadruple $\langle \emptyset, id, [(t, s)], \emptyset\rangle$. Then, there exists $(\Delta_{sol}, \sigma_{sol}, FPEqLst_{sol}) \in$ UNIFY $(\emptyset, id, [(t, s)], \emptyset)$ such that (∇, δ) is a solution to $\langle \Delta_{sol}, \sigma_{sol}, \emptyset, FPEqLst_{sol}\rangle$.*

Proof. Notice that $\langle \emptyset, id, [(t, s)], \emptyset \rangle$ is a valid quadruple. Then, we apply Theorem 2 and prove the corollary.

Remark 13. An interpretation of Corollary 2 is that if (∇, δ) is a solution to the initial problem, then (∇, δ) is also a solution to one of the outputs of UNIFY.

5 Interesting Points of Formalization and Implementation

We discuss interesting points of the formalization and implementation here.

Remark 14. To prove correctness and completeness of the algorithm, we work with the terms t and s that are in the head of $PrbLst$. We divide the proof by cases. The most interesting case is when t or s is a suspension $\pi \cdot X$ and X does not occur in the other term (see Algorithm 1).

In this case, the algorithm receives as arguments Δ, σ, $PrbLst$ and $FPEqLst$ and the next recursive call is made with four different parameters: Δ'', σ'', $PrbLst''$ and nil (see Algorithm 1). Therefore, all of the four conditions of the Definition 8 are not trivially satisfied. Moreover, since in the next recursive call we will be working with a new substitution σ'' we must prove that the quadruple we are working with remains valid (this is proved by noting that when a variable X is added to the domain of the substitution, all occurrences of it in $PrbLst$ and in $FPEqLst$ are instantiated, maintaining the validity of the quadruple).

The case of unifying $t = [a]t_1$ with $s = [b]s_1$ is also interesting, since both the context and the list of problems to unify suffer modifications in the recursive call. In all the remaining cases, there are no changes in the context nor in the substitution, making them easier. In these remaining cases, only one condition (the third) of the four in Definition 8 is not trivially satisfied.

Remark 15. Introducing commutative function symbols to the nominal unification algorithm presented in [6] meant we had to:

- Unify terms rooted by commutative function symbols (for instance, $f(t_1, t_2)$ with $f(s_1, s_2)$). First, the algorithm tries to unify t_1 with s_1 and t_2 with s_2, generating a list of solutions sol_1 (see Algorithm 1). Then, the algorithm tries unifying t_1 with s_2 and t_2 with s_1, generating a list of solutions sol_2. The final result is then simply the concatenation of both lists.
- Handle fixed point equations. This was also straightforward. We keep a separate list of fixed point equation ($FPEqLst$), and when the algorithm recognizes a fixed point equation in $PrbLst$ it takes this equation out of $PrbLst$ and puts it on $FPEqLst$.
- Define an appropriate data structure for the problem and the solutions. This was not straightforward. As mentioned before, since commutativity introduced branches, the recursive calls of the algorithm can be seen as a tree (see Example 5). Therefore, initially, an approach using a tree data structure was planned (which would have complicated the analysis). However, since the algorithm simply solves one branch and then the other, we realized all that

was needed was to do two recursive calls (one for each branch) and append the two lists of solutions generated. Therefore, we were able to avoid the tree data structure, working instead with lists, which simplified the specification.

Remark 16. Since PVS does not support automatic extraction of Python code, the translation of the PVS specification for the Python implementation was done manually. The code follows strictly the lines of the specification (Algorithm 1) with small adjustments, such as the inclusion of two parameters in the algorithm implementation, in order to support a verbose mode that prints the tree of recursive calls. This, and the representation of atoms, variables and terms in the implementation is discussed in the extended version. An OCaml implementation of a nominal C-unification algorithm was previously developed [2], but in contrast to the current Python implementation, the OCaml implementation does not correspond in a direct way to the formalized non-deterministic inductive specification [2].

6 Conclusion and Future Work

In this paper, we explained the problem of nominal C-unification and presented a functional algorithm for doing this task. We observed how nominal C-unification has applications on logic programming languages and how the algorithm here presented could be straightforwardly converted to a matching algorithm, which in turn would have applications in nominal rewriting.

Our approach differs from the only other work in nominal C-unification ([2]) in two main points. First, we do not present a set of non-deterministic transformation rules, instead, we opt for a recursive specification, implemented in Python. Second, we follow the approach in [6] and deal with freshness contexts separately. This simplifies the main function and, along with the idea of using a different parameter to represent fixed point equations, allowed us to reduce the lexicographic measure used in [2] from four parameters to only two parameters, thus simplifying the formalizations of termination, soundness and completeness.

We are currently working in running executable code from PVS (using the PVSIO feature that lets you execute verified algorithms inside the PVS environment and provides input and output operators) and comparing this approach with the Python implementation. Further details are discussed in the extended version of the paper.

Finally, a future study would be extending the formalization to handle the more general case of Mal'cev permutative theories, which include n-ary functions with permutative arguments [13]. Other possible path, as indicated in [11], is expanding the algorithm to handle other equational theories such as unification modulo associative and associative-commutative function symbols (A- and AC-unification).

References

1. Ayala-Rincón, M., de Carvalho-Segundo, W., Fernández, M., Nantes-Sobrinho, D.: On solving nominal fixpoint equations. In: Dixon, C., Finger, M. (eds.) FroCoS 2017. LNCS (LNAI), vol. 10483, pp. 209–226. Springer, Cham (2017). https://doi.org/10.1007/978-3-319-66167-4_12
2. Ayala-Rincón, M., de Carvalho-Segundo, W., Fernández, M., Nantes-Sobrinho, D.: Nominal C-unification. In: Fioravanti, F., Gallagher, J.P. (eds.) LOPSTR 2017. LNCS, vol. 10855, pp. 235–251. Springer, Cham (2018). https://doi.org/10.1007/978-3-319-94460-9_14
3. Ayala-Rincón, M., de Carvalho-Segundo, W., Fernández, M., Nantes-Sobrinho, D., Rocha-Oliveira, A.: A formalisation of nominal alpha-equivalence with A, C, and AC function symbols. Theoret. Comput. Sci. **781**, 3–23 (2019)
4. Ayala-Rincón, M., Fernández, M., Nantes-Sobrinho, D.: Nominal narrowing. In: 1st International Conference on Formal Structures for Computation and Deduction (FSCD). LIPIcs, vol. 52, pp. 11:1–11:17 (2016)
5. Ayala-Rincón, M., Fernández, M., Nantes-Sobrinho, D.: Fixed-point constraints for nominal equational unification. In: 3rd International Conference on Formal Structures for Computation and Deduction (FSCD). LIPIcs, vol. 108, pp. 7:1–7:16 (2018)
6. Ayala-Rincón, M., Fernández, M., Rocha-Oliveira, A.: Completeness in PVS of a nominal unification algorithm. Elect. Notes Theor. Comp. Sci. **323**, 57–74 (2016)
7. Baader, F., Nipkow, T.: Term Rewriting and All That. Cambridge University Press, Cambridge (1999)
8. Baader, F., Snyder, W.: Unification theory. In: Handbook of Automated Reasoning (in 2 volumes), pp. 445–532. Elsevier and MIT Press (2001)
9. Baumgartner, A., Kutsia, T., Levy, J., Villaret, M.: Nominal anti-unification. In: 26th International Conference on Rewriting Techniques and Applications (RTA). LIPIcs, vol. 36, pp. 57–73 (2015)
10. Calvès, C., Fernández, M.: A polynomial nominal unification algorithm. Theoret. Comput. Sci. **403**(2–3), 285–306 (2008)
11. de Carvalho Segundo, W.L.R.: Nominal equational problems modulo associativity, commutativity and associativity-commutativity. Ph.D. thesis, Universidade de Brasilia (2019)
12. Cheney, J., Urban, C.: αProlog: a logic programming language with names, binding and α-equivalence. In: Demoen, B., Lifschitz, V. (eds.) ICLP 2004. LNCS, vol. 3132, pp. 269–283. Springer, Heidelberg (2004). https://doi.org/10.1007/978-3-540-27775-0_19
13. Comon, H.: Complete axiomatizations of some quotient term algebras. Theoret. Comput. Sci. **118**(2), 167–191 (1993)
14. Fernández, M., Gabbay, M.: Nominal rewriting. Inf. Comput. **205**(6), 917–965 (2007)
15. Kumar, R., Norrish, M.: (Nominal) unification by recursive descent with triangular substitutions. In: Kaufmann, M., Paulson, L.C. (eds.) ITP 2010. LNCS, vol. 6172, pp. 51–66. Springer, Heidelberg (2010). https://doi.org/10.1007/978-3-642-14052-5_6
16. Levy, J., Villaret, M.: Nominal unification from a higher-order perspective. In: Voronkov, A. (ed.) RTA 2008. LNCS, vol. 5117, pp. 246–260. Springer, Heidelberg (2008). https://doi.org/10.1007/978-3-540-70590-1_17

17. Levy, J., Villaret, M.: An efficient nominal unification algorithm. In: Proceedings of the 21st International Conference on Rewriting Techniques and Applications (RTA). LIPIcs, vol. 6, pp. 209–226 (2010)
18. Owre, S., Shankar, N., Rushby, J.M., Stringer-Calvert, D.W.J.: PVS System Guide - Version 2.4 (2001). http://pvs.csl.sri.com/documentation.shtml
19. Pitts, A.: Nominal Sets: Names and Symmetry in Computer Science. Cambridge University Press, Cambridge (2013)
20. Schmidt-Schauß, M., Kutsia, T., Levy, J., Villaret, M.: Nominal unification of higher order expressions with recursive let. In: Hermenegildo, M.V., Lopez-Garcia, P. (eds.) LOPSTR 2016. LNCS, vol. 10184, pp. 328–344. Springer, Cham (2017). https://doi.org/10.1007/978-3-319-63139-4_19
21. Urban, C.: Nominal techniques in Isabelle/HOL. J. Autom. Reasoning **40**(4), 327–356 (2008)
22. Urban, C., Pitts, A., Gabbay, M.: Nominal unification. Theoret. Comput. Sci. **323**(1–3), 473–497 (2004)

Modeling and Reasoning in Event Calculus Using Goal-Directed Constraint Answer Set Programming

Joaquín Arias[1,2](✉) [iD], Zhuo Chen[3] [iD], Manuel Carro[1,2] [iD], and Gopal Gupta[3] [iD]

[1] IMDEA Software Institute, Madrid, Spain
{joaquin.arias,manuel.carro}@imdea.org
[2] Universidad Politécnica de Madrid, Madrid, Spain
manuel.carro@upm.es
[3] University of Texas at Dallas, Richardson, USA
{zhuo.chen,gupta}@utdallas.edu

Abstract. Automated commonsense reasoning is essential for building human-like AI systems featuring, for example, explainable AI. Event Calculus (EC) is a family of formalisms that model commonsense reasoning with a sound, logical basis. Previous attempts to mechanize reasoning using EC faced difficulties in the treatment of the continuous change in dense domains (e.g., time and other physical quantities), constraints among variables, default negation, and the uniform application of different inference methods, among others. We propose the use of s(CASP), a query-driven, top-down execution model for Predicate Answer Set Programming with Constraints, to model and reason using EC. We show how EC scenarios can be naturally and directly encoded in s(CASP) and how its expressiveness makes it possible to perform deductive and abductive reasoning tasks in domains featuring, for example, constraints involving both dense time and dense fluents.

Keywords: ASP · Goal-directed · Event Calculus · Constraints

1 Introduction

The ability to model continuous characteristics of the world is essential for Commonsense Reasoning (**CR**) in many domains that require dealing with continuous change: time, the height of a falling object, the gas level of a car, the water level in a sink, etc.

Event Calculus (**EC**) is a formalism based on many-sorted predicate logic [13,23] that can represent continuous change and capture the commonsense law of inertia, whose modeling is a pervasive problem in CR. In EC, time-dependent properties and events are seen as objects and reasoning is performed on the truth values of properties and the occurrences of events at a point in time.

Work partially supported by EIT Digital, MINECO project TIN2015-67522-C3-1-R (TRACES), Comunidad de Madrid project S2018/TCS-4339 BLOQUES-CM co-funded by EIE Funds of the European Union, and US NSF Grant IIS 1718945.

M. Gabbrielli (Ed.): LOPSTR 2019, LNCS 12042, pp. 139–155, 2020.
https://doi.org/10.1007/978-3-030-45260-5_9

Answer Set Programming (**ASP**) is a logic programming paradigm that was initially proposed to realize non-monotonic reasoning [17]. ASP has also been used to model the Event Calculus [15,16]. Classical implementations of ASP are limited to variables ranging over discrete and bound domains and use mechanisms such as *grounding* and SAT solving to find out models (called *answer sets*) of ASP programs. However, non-monotonic reasoning often needs variables ranging over dense domains (e.g., those involving time or physical quantities) to faithfully represent the properties of these domains.

This paper presents an approach to modeling Event Calculus using s(CASP) [1] as the underlying reasoning infrastructure. The s(CASP) system is an implementation of Constraint Answer Set Programming over first-order predicates which combines ASP and constraints. It features predicates, constraints among non-ground variables, uninterpreted functions, and, most importantly, a top-down, query-driven execution strategy. These features make it possible to return answers with non-ground variables (possibly including constraints among them) and to compute partial models by returning only the fragment of a stable model that is necessary to answer a given query. Thanks to its interface with constraint solvers, sound non-monotonic reasoning with constraints is possible.

This approach achieves more conciseness and expressiveness than other related approaches because dense domains can be faithfully modeled as continuous quantities, while in other proposals such domains [15,20] had to be discretized, therefore losing precision or even soundness. Additionally, in our approach the amalgamation of ASP and constraints and its realization in s(CASP) is considerably more natural: under s(CASP), answer set programs are executed in a goal-directed manner so constraints encountered along the way are collected and solved dynamically as execution proceeds—this is very similar to the way in which Prolog has been extended with constraints. The implementation of other ASP systems featuring constraints is considerably more complex.

2   Related Work

Previous work translated *discrete* EC into ASP [15,16] by reformulating the EC models as first-order stable models and translating the (almost universal) formulas of EC into a logic program that preserves stable models. Given a finite domain, EC2ASP (and its evolution, F2LP) compile (discrete) Event Calculus formulas into ASP programs [15,16]. This translation scheme relies on two facts: second order circumscription and first order stable model semantics coincide on canonical formulas, and almost-universal formulas can be transformed into a logic program while preserving the stable models. As a result, computing models of Event Calculus descriptions can be done by computing the stable models of an appropriately generated program.

Clearly, approaches featuring discrete domains cannot faithfully handle continuous quantities such as time. In addition, because of their reliance on SAT solvers to find the stable models, they can only handle *safe* programs. In contrast, the s(CASP) system, because of its direct support for predicates with arbitrary terms, constructive negation, and the novel *forall mechanism* [1,18], program safety is not a requirement. Thus, s(CASP) can model Event Calculus axioms much more directly and elegantly.

The approaches mentioned above assume discrete quantities and do not support reasoning about continuous time or change. As long as SAT-based ASP systems are used to model Event Calculus, continuous fluents cannot be straightforwardly expressed since they require unbounded, dense domains for the variables. The work closest to incorporating continuous time makes use of SMT solvers. In this approach, constraints are incorporated into ASP and the grounded theory is executed using an SMT solver [14]. However, this approach has not been directly applied to modeling the Event Calculus. The closest tool chain is ASPMT2SMT [3] that uses *gringo* to partially ground the ASPMT theories and generate constraints that are processed by *Z3*. However, regular, discrete ASP variables are at the heart of the model, and these are grounded and used to generate the constraints. Therefore, if these discrete variables approximate continuous variables in the model, the constraints generated will only approximate the conditions of the original problem and therefore their solutions will also be an approximation (or a subset) of the solutions for the real problem. In other words, the initial discretization done for the ASP variables will be propagated via the generated constraints to the final solutions that will, in the best case, be a discretized version of the actual solutions. As an example, if time is discretized, the solutions to the model will suffer from this discretization.

Other ASP-based approaches to deal with planning in continuous domains include, for example, action languages [10] which were developed to model the elements of natural language that are used to describe the effects of actions, and PDDL+ [6], which was developed to allow reasoning with continuous time-dependent effects. Action languages have been implemented using answer set programming [8] and there have been extensions of action languages to accommodate time: for example, the action language C+ has been extended to accommodate continuous time [14]. PPDL+ models temporal behavior in terms of the initiation and termination of processes, which in turn act upon the numeric components of states. Processes are initiated and terminated instantaneously by actions or exogenous events. Continuous changes are made by concurrent processes. In PDDL+, reasoning is monotonic and thus the degree of elaboration tolerance is low. There are implementations of PDDL+ using constraint answer set programming (CASP) [2] though these have not been applied to modeling the Event Calculus and requires the use of discrete variables to model some quantities, e.g., time.

EC can be written as a (Horn-clause) logic program, but it cannot be executed directly by Prolog [25], as it lacks some necessary features, such as constructive negation, deduction of negative literals, and (to some extent) detection of infinite failure [21]. A common approach is to write a metainterpreter specific to the EC variant at hand. This can be as complex as writing a (specialized) theorem prover or, more often, a specialized interpreter whose correctness is difficult to ascertain (see the code at [4]). Therefore, some Prolog implementations of EC do not completely formalize the calculus or implement a reduced version. In our case, we leverage on the capabilities of s(CASP) to provide constructive, sound negation, negative rule heads, and loop detection [1].

3 Background

Answer Set Programming is a logic programming and modelling language that evaluates normal logic programs under the stable model semantics [9]. s(ASP) [18] is a top-down, goal-driven ASP system that can evaluate ASP programs with function symbols (*functors*) **without** *grounding* them either before or during execution. Grounding is a procedure that substitutes program variables with the possible values from their domain. For most classical ASP solvers, grounding is a necessary pre-processing phase. Grounding, however, requires program variables to be restricted to take values in a finite domain. As a result, ASP solvers cannot be used to model continuous time or change.

3.1 s(CASP)

s(CASP) [1] extends s(ASP) similarly to how CLP extends Prolog. s(CASP) adds constraints to s(ASP); these constraints are kept and used both during execution and in the answer sets. Constraints have historically proved to be effective in improving both expressiveness and efficiency in logic programming, as constraints can succinctly express properties of a solution and reduce the search space. As a result, s(CASP) is more expressive and faster than s(ASP), while retaining the capability of executing non-ground predicate answer set programs. An s(CASP) program is a set of clauses of the following form:

$$a \text{ :- } c_a, \text{ } b_1, \text{ } \ldots, \text{ } b_m, \text{ not } b_{m+1}, \text{ } \ldots, \text{ not } b_n.$$

where a and $b_1, \ldots, b_n$ are atoms and **not** corresponds to *default* negation. The difference w.r.t. an ASP program is c_a, a simple constraint or a conjunction of constraints.

In s(CASP), and unlike Prolog's negation as failure, **not** $p(X)$ can return bindings for X on success. This is possible thanks to the use of constructive negation [18] and coinduction [11]. This highlights two differences w.r.t. Prolog: first, s(CASP) resolves negated atoms **not** b_i against *dual rules* of the program [1,18], which makes it possible for a non-ground call **not** $p(X)$ to return the bindings for X for which the positive call $p(X)$ would have failed, therefore supporting constructive negation. Second, the dual program is **not** interpreted under SLD semantics in order to handle the different kinds of loops that can appear in s(CASP) [1,18].

The execution of an s(CASP) program starts with a *query* of the form ?- c_q, $l_1, \ldots, l_m$, where l_i are (negated) literals and c_q is a conjunction of constraint(s). The answers to the query are partial stable models where each partial model is a subset of a stable model [9] including only the literals necessary to support the query (see [1] for details). Additionally, for each partial stable model s(CASP) returns on backtracking the justification tree and the bindings

Predicate	Meaning
$InitiallyN(f)$	fluent f is false at time 0
$InitiallyP(f)$	fluent f is true at time 0
$Happens(e, t)$	event e occurs at time t
$Initiates(e, f, t)$	if e happens at time t, f is true and not released from the commonsense law of inertia after t
$Terminates(e, f, t)$	if e occurs at time t, f is false and not released from the commonsense law of inertia after t
$Releases(e, f, t)$	if e occurs at time t, f is released from the commonsense law of inertia after t
$Trajectory(f_1, t_1, f_2, t_2)$	if f_1 is initiated by an event that occurs at t_1, then f_2 is true at t_2
$StoppedIn(t_1, f, t_2)$	f is stopped between t_1 and t_2
$StartedIn(t_1, f, t_2)$	f is started between t_1 and t_2
$HoldsAt(f, t)$	fluent f is true at time t

Fig. 1. Basic event calculus (BEC) predicates (e = event, f, f_1, f_2 = fluents, t, t_1, t_2 = timepoints)

for the free variables of the query that correspond to the most general unifier (*mgu*) of a successful top-down derivation consistent with this stable model.

3.2   Event Calculus

EC is a formalism for reasoning about events and change [23], of which there are several axiomatizations. There are three basic, mutually related, concepts in EC: *events*, *fluents*, and *time points* (see Fig. 1). An event is an action or incident that may occur in the world: for instance, a person dropping a glass is an event. A fluent is a time-varying property of the world, such as the altitude of a glass. A time point is an instant in time. Events may happen at a time point; fluents have a truth value at any time point or over an interval, and their truth values are subject to change upon the occurrence of an event. In addition, fluents may have (continuous) quantities associated with them when they are true. For example, the event of dropping a glass initiates the fluent that captures that the glass is falling, and perhaps its height above the ground, and the event of holding a glass terminates the fluent that the glass is falling. An EC description consists of a universal theory and a domain narrative. The universal theory is a conjunction of EC axioms and the domain narrative consists of the causal laws of the domain and the known events and fluent properties.

Circumscription [19] is applied to EC domain narratives to minimize the extension of predicates and has two effects: the only events that happen are those defined and the only effects of events are those defined.

The original EC (OEC) was introduced by Kowalski and Sergot in 1986 [13]. OEC has sorts for event occurrences, fluents, and time periods. In this paper

BEC1. $StoppedIn(t_1, f, t_2)$ $\equiv$
$\quad\quad \exists e, t \;(\; Happens(e, t) \wedge t_1 < t < t_2 \wedge (\; Terminates(e, f, t) \vee Releases(e, f, t)\;)\;)$

BEC2. $StartedIn(t_1, f, t_2)$ $\equiv$
$\quad\quad \exists e, t \;(\; Happens(e, t) \wedge t_1 < t < t_2 \wedge (\; Initiates(e, f, t) \vee Releases(e, f, t)\;)\;)$

BEC3. $HoldsAt(f_2, t_2)$ $\leftarrow$
$\quad Happens(e, t_1) \wedge Initiates(e, f_1, t_1) \wedge Trajectory(f_1, t_1, f_2, t_2) \wedge \neg StoppedIn(t_1, f_1, t_2)$

BEC4. $HoldsAt(f, t)$ $\leftarrow$ $\hspace{3cm} InitiallyP(f) \wedge \neg StoppedIn(0, f, t)$

BEC5. $\neg HoldsAt(f, t)$ $\leftarrow$ $\hspace{2.8cm} InitiallyN(f) \wedge \neg StartedIn(0, f, t)$

BEC6. $HoldsAt(f, t_2)$ $\leftarrow$
$\quad\quad Happens(e, t_1) \wedge Initiates(e, f, t_1) \wedge t_1 < t_2 \wedge \neg StoppedIn(t_1, f, t_2)$

BEC7. $\neg HoldsAt(f, t_2)$ $\leftarrow$
$\quad\quad Happens(e, t_1) \wedge Terminates(e, f, t_1) \wedge t_1 < t_2 \wedge \neg StartedIn(t_1, f, t_2)$

Fig. 2. Formalization of BEC axioms [23].

we use the Basic Event Calculus (BEC) formulated by Shanahan [21]. Figure 2 summarizes the seven BEC axioms. An explanation of these axioms follows:

- **Axiom BEC1.** A fluent f is stopped between time points t_1 and t_2 iff it is terminated or released by some event e that occurs after t_1 and before t_2.
- **Axiom BEC2.** A fluent f is started between time points t_1 and t_2 iff it is initiated or released by some event e that occurs after t_1 and before t_2.
- **Axiom BEC3.** A fluent f_2 is true at time t_2 if a fluent f_1 initiated at t_1 does not finish before t_2 and it makes fluent f_2 be true.[1]
- **Axiom BEC4.** A fluent f is true at time t if it is true at time 0 and is not stopped on or before t.
- **Axiom BEC5.** A fluent f is false at time t if it is false at time 0 and it is not started on or before t.
- **Axiom BEC6.** A fluent f is true at time t_2 if it is initiated at some earlier time t_1 and it is not stopped before t_2.
- **Axiom BEC7.** A fluent f is false at time t_2 if it is terminated at some earlier time t_1 and it is not started on or before t_2.

4   From Event Calculus to s(CASP)

4.1   Modeling BEC with s(CASP)

Two key factors contribute to s(CASP)'s ability to model Event Calculus: the preservation of non-ground variables during the execution and the integration with constraint solvers.

---

[1] For implementation convenience, and without loss of expressiveness, we assume that argument t_2 in $Trajectory(f_1, t_1, f_2, t_2)$ is not a time difference w.r.t. t_1, but an absolute time after t_1.

```
1   %% BEC1                              25   %% BEC4
2   stoppedIn(T1,F,T2) :-               26   holdsAt(F,T) :-
3       T1 #< T, T #< T2,               27       0 #< T,
4       terminates(E,F,T),             28       initiallyP(F),
5       happens(E,T).                   29       not stoppedIn(0,F,T).
6   stoppedIn(T1,F,T2) :-               30   %% BEC5
7       T1 #< T, T #< T2,               31   -holdsAt(F,T) :-
8       releases(E,F,T),               32       0 #< T,
9       happens(E,T).                   33       initiallyN(F),
10  %% BEC2                              34       not startedIn(0,F,T).
11  startedIn(T1,F,T2) :-               35   %% BEC6
12      T1 #< T, T #< T2,               36   holdsAt(F,T) :-
13      initiates(E,F,T),              37       T1 #< T,
14      happens(E,T).                   38       initiates(E,F,T1),
15  startedIn(T1,F,T2) :-               39       happens(E,T1),
16      T1 #< T, T #< T2,               40       not stoppedIn(T1,F,T).
17      releases(E,F,T),               41   %% BEC7
18      happens(E,T).                   42   -holdsAt(F,T) :-
19  %% BEC3                              43       T1 #< T,
20  holdsAt(F2,T2) :-                   44       terminates(E,F,T1),
21      initiates(E,F1,T1),            45       happens(E,T1),
22      happens(E,T1),                 46       not startedIn(T1,F,T).
23      trajectory(F1,T1,F2,T2),       47   %% Consistency
24      not stoppedIn(T1,F1,T2).       48   :- -holdsAt(F,T), holdsAt(F,T).
```

Fig. 3. Basic Event Calculus (BCE) modeled in s(CASP)

Treatment of Variables in s(CASP): Thanks to the usage of non-ground variables, s(CASP) is able to directly model Event Calculus axioms that would otherwise require "unsafe" rules. In classical ASP, a rule is safe when every variable that appears in its head or in a negated literal in its body also appears in a positive literal in the body of the rule, and it is unsafe otherwise. Safety guarantees that every variable can be grounded. For example, BEC4 is unsafe since parameter t, which appears in the head, does not appear in a positive literal in the body (i.e., it only appears in $\neg StoppedIn(0, f, t)$). A SAT-based ASP solver such as *clingo* [7] will not be able to directly process unsafe rules like this. However, the top-down execution strategy of s(CASP) makes it possible to keep logical variables both during execution and in answer sets and therefore free (logical) variables can be handled in heads and in negated literals.

Integration with Constraint Solvers: The s(CASP) system has a generic interface to enable plugging in constraint solvers. s(CASP) currently uses Holzbaur's CLP(Q) linear constraints solver [12], that supports the constraints $<, >, =, \neq, \leq, \geq$. As we saw, the definitions and axioms of BEC require inequality comparisons over time points, and the ability of s(CASP) to make use of constraint solvers makes it ideal to model continuous time in EC.

4.2   Translating the BEC Axioms into s(CASP)

Our translation of the BEC axioms into s(CASP) is similar to that of the systems EC2ASP and F2LP [15,16], but we differ in some key aspects that improve performance and are relevant for expressiveness: *the treatment of rules with negated heads, the possibility of generating unsafe rules,* and *the use of constraints over rationals.* We describe below, with the help of a running example, the translation that turns logic statements (as found in BEC) into an s(CASP) program. The code corresponding to the translations of the axioms of BEC in Fig. 2 can be found in Fig. 3. s(CASP) code follows the syntactical conventions of logic programming: constants (including function names) and predicate symbols start with a lowercase letter and variables start with an uppercase letter. In addition, logic constraints are written as constraints in s(CASP), (e.g., #<) to make it clear that they do not correspond to Prolog's arithmetic comparisons:

- **Atoms and Constants:** Their names are preserved. *Uniqueness of Names* [24] is assumed by default (and enforced) in logic programming.
- **Constraints:** Predicates that represent constraints (e.g., on time) are directly translated to their counterparts in s(CASP). E.g., $t_1 < t_2$ becomes T1 #< T2, which is handled by CLP(Q), one of the available constraint solvers. The translation (and s(CASP) itself) is parametric on the constraint domain.
- **Definitions:** The axiomatization of BEC uses definitions of the form $D(x) \equiv \exists y B(x, y)$, where $B(x, y)$ is a conjunction of (negated) atoms, disjunctions of atoms, and constraints (e.g., BEC1). The use of definitions makes it easier to build conceptual blocks out of basic predicates. However, for performance reasons we treat them as if they were written as $\forall x(D(x) \leftarrow \exists y B(x, y))$, following [15]. Intuitively, if we ignore the truth value of D in the (partial) models that s(CASP) generates, the models returned using implication and/or equivalence are the same, and the literal D can be ignored because if were expanded where it is used, it would have disappeared. Additionally, s(CASP) internally performs Clark's completion [5] to the s(CASP) program, and therefore, we can assume that s(CASP) rules expresses all possible ways in which heads can be true.
- **Rules with Positive Heads:** A rule (e.g., BEC6)

$$\forall x(H(x) \leftarrow \exists y(A(y) \wedge \neg B(x, y) \wedge x < y))$$

where $x < y$ is a constraint, is translated into

```
1  h(X) :- X #< Y, a(Y), not b(X,Y).
```

s(CASP) performs left-to-right evaluation, and since constraint solvers are deterministic, constraining variables as soon as possible helps reduce the size of the search tree.

- **Rules with Negated Heads:** BEC rules 5 and 7 infer negated heads $\neg HoldsAt(f, t)$ while rules 4 and 6 infer positive heads $HoldsAt(f, t)$, i.e., they follow, respectively, the scheme

$$\forall x(H(x) \leftarrow \exists y A(x, y)) \quad \wedge \quad \forall x(\neg H(x) \leftarrow \exists y B(x, y))$$

The standard approach to translate rules with negated heads is to convert them into global constraints [16]:

```
1   :- b(X,Y), h(X).
```

Our approach is to define instead a rule for the literal -h(X) that captures the explicit evidence that h(X) is false:

```
1   -h(X) :- b(X,Y).
```

which makes it possible to call -h(X) in a top-down execution. This construct was termed *classical* negation in [18] and behaves as a regular predicate, except that the s(CASP) compiler, to ensure that -h(X) and h(X) cannot be simultaneously true, automatically adds the global constraint :- -h(X),h(X). Therefore, s(CASP) can detect an inconsistency (and will return an empty model) if both $HoldsAt(f,t)$ and $\neg HoldsAt(f,t)$ can be simultaneously derived from an BEC narrative. Since circumscription is not applied to the EC theory, not being able to derive $HoldsAt(f,t)$ does not immediately determine that its negation is true. We will see how this is connected with the translation of the narrative.

– **Rules with Disjunctive Bodies:** A rule (e.g., BEC1)

$$\forall x[H(x) \leftarrow \exists y(\ (A(x,y) \vee B(x,y)) \wedge C(x,y)\ )]$$

is translated into two separate clauses:

```
1   h(X) :- a(X,Y), c(X,Y).
2   h(X) :- b(X,Y), c(X,Y).
```

4.3   Translation of the Narrative

The definition of a given scenario (its *narrative* part) states the basic actions and effects using the predicates in Fig. 1. EC assumes circumscription of the predicates defined in the *narrative*: the events (resp., effects) known to occur are the only events (resp., effects) that occur. Note that this is automatic in s(CASP), since it produces the Clark's completion of s(CASP) programs when generating the dual program. In addition, global constraints can restrict the admissible states of the system.

Every basic BEC predicate $P(x)$ (where P can stand for an event occurrence, an effect of an event on a fluent, etc.) is translated into an s(CASP) rule $P(x) \leftarrow \gamma$, where γ states **all** the cases where $P(x)$ is true. In many cases, these are *facts*, but in other cases γ captures the conditions for $P(x)$ to hold.

Let us consider example 14 in [23], which reasons about turning a light switch on and off. Figure 4 shows the encoding of this example under s(CASP).

– **Events:** The description below (translated in lines 1–3 of Fig. 4):

$$Happens(e,t) \equiv (e = TurnOn \wedge (t = 2 \vee t = 6)) \vee$$
$$(e = TurnOff \wedge t = 4)$$

states that the $TurnOn$ event will happen at time $t = 2$ and $t = 6$, and that $TurnOff$ will happen at $t = 4$.

```
1  happens(turn_on, 2).              7  trajectory(on, T1, red, T2) :-
2  happens(turn_off, 4).             8      T1 #< T2, T2 #< T1 + 1.
3  happens(turn_on, 6).              9  trajectory(on, T1, green, T2) :-
4                                   10      T2 #>= T1 + 1.
5  initiates(turn_on, on, T).       11  releases(turn_on, red, T).
6  terminates(turn_off, on, T).     12  releases(turn_on, green, T).
```

Fig. 4. Narrative of the light scenario modeled in s(CASP)

- **Event effects:** When the event *TurnOn* happens, the light is put in *on* status; similarly, when the event *TurnOff* happens, the *on* status of the light is terminated. In both cases, this can happen at any time t (lines 5 and 6 in Fig. 4)
- **Release from Inertia:** When turned on, the light emits red light within the first second, and then green light is emitted. *Trajectory* expresses how this change depends on the time elapsed since an event occurrence. The *Trajectory* formula has the shape $P(x) \leftarrow \gamma$, as we need to state the (time) conditions for the fluent to become activated (see lines 7–10 in Fig. 4). *Releases* states that the color of the light is released from the commonsense law of inertia. After a fluent is released, its truth value is not determined by BEC and it can change. Thus, there may be models in which the fluent is true, and models in which the fluent may be false. Releasing a fluent (see lines 11 and 12 in Fig. 4) frees it up so that other axioms in the domain description can be used to determine its truth value, thus allowing us to represent continuous change of the fluent.
- **State Constraints:** State constraints usually contain $HoldsAt(f,t)$ or $\neg HoldsAt(f,t)$ and represent restrictions on the models. In our running example, a light cannot be red and green at the same time: $\forall t.\neg(HoldsAt(Red,t) \land HoldsAt(Green,t))$. This is translated as `:- holdsAt(red,T),holdsAt(green,T)` Adding this constraint to the program in Fig. 4 does not change its models. However, if we change line 8 stating that the light is red for 2 s (i.e., `T2 #< T1+2`), the state constraint is violated and therefore there are no valid models.
- **A Note on using** $\neg HoldsAt(f,t)$ **in** γ: The basic BEC predicates may depend on what the BEC theory can deduce, e.g., γ may depend on $HoldsAt(f,t)$ or $\neg HoldsAt(f,t)$ (see Fig. 5). $HoldsAt(f,t)$ can be invoked directly, but $\neg HoldsAt(f,t)$ ought to be called using classical negation, e.g., `-holdsAt(F,T)`. The reason is that since BEC does not apply circumscription to its axioms, we can deduce only the truth (or falsehood) of a predicate when we have direct evidence of either of them—i.e., what the positive (`holdsAt(F,T)`) and negative (`-holdsAt(F,T)`) heads provide.

4.4   Continuous Change: A Complete Encoding

We consider now an example from [24]: a water tap fills a vessel, whose water level is subject to continuous change. When the level reaches the bucket rim, it

```
1   #include bec_theory.                15   releases(tapOn,level(0),T):-
2                                        16       happens(tapOn,T).
3   max_level(10):- not max_level(16).  17
4   max_level(16):- not max_level(10).  18   trajectory(filling,T1,level(X2),T2):-
5                                        19       T1 #< T2, X2 #= X + T2-T1,
6   initiallyP(level(0)).                20       max_level(Max), X2 #=< Max,
7   happens(overflow,T).                 21       holdsAt(level(X),T1).
8   happens(tapOn,5).                    22   trajectory(filling,T1,level(overflow),T2):-
9                                        23       T1 #< T2, X2 #= X + T2-T1,
10  initiates(tapOn,filling,T).          24       max_level(Max), X2 #> Max,
11  terminates(tapOff,filling,T).        25       holdsAt(level(X),T1).
12  initiates(overflow,spilling,T):-     26   trajectory(spilling,T1,leak(X),T2):-
13      max_level(Max),                  27       holdsAt(filling, T2),
14      holdsAt(level(Max), T).          28       T1 #< T2, X #= T2-T1.
```

Fig. 5. Encoding of an Event Calculus narrative with continuous change

starts spilling. We will present the main ideas behind its encoding (Fig. 5) and will show some queries we can ask about its state and behavior.

- **Continuous Change:** The fluent $Level(x)$ represents that the water is at level x in the vessel. The first $Trajectory$ formula (lines 18–21) determines the time-dependent value of the $Level(x)$ fluent,[2] which is active as long as the $Filling$ fluent is true and the rim of the vessel is not reached. Additionally, the second $Trajectory$ formula (lines 22–25) allows us to capture the fact that the water reached the rim of the vessel and overflowed.
- **Triggered Fluent:** The fluent $Spilling$ is triggered (lines 12–14) when the water level reaches the rim of the vessel. As a consequence, the $Trajectory$ formula in lines 26–28 starts the fluent $Leak(x)$ and captures the amount of water leaked while the fluent $Spilling$ holds.
- **Different Worlds:** The clauses in lines 3–4 force the vessel capacity to be either 10 or 16, i.e., they create two possible worlds/models: {max_level(10), not max_level(16), ...} and {max_level(16), not max_level(10), ...}. The same mechanism can be used to state whether an event happens or not. For this, a keyword #abducible is provided as a shortcut in s(CASP). We will use it in the *Abduction* subsection later on.

5   Examples and Evaluation

The benchmarks used in this section are available as part of the s(CASP) distribution at https://gitlab.software.imdea.org/ciao-lang/sCASP/. They were run on a MacOS 10.14.3 laptop with an Intel Core i5 at 2 GHz.

---

[2] For simplicity the amount of water filled/leaked correspond directly to how long the water has been pouring in/spilling from the vessel.

Deduction: Deduction determines whether a state of the world is possible given a theory (in our case, BEC) and an initial narrative. We can perform deduction in BEC for the previous examples through queries to the corresponding s(CASP) program. For the lights scenario (Fig. 4):

> ?- holdsAt(on,3) succeeds: it deduces that the light is on at time 3.
> ?- -holdsAt(on,5) succeeds: the light is not on at time 5.
> ?- holdsAt(F,3) is true in one stable model containing holdsAt(green,3) and holdsAt(on,3), meaning that at time 3, the light is on and green.

In the water level scenario (Fig. 5) we can make queries involving time and the water level:

> ?- holdsAt(level(H),15/2) is true when H=5/2.
> ?- holdsAt(level(5/2),T) is true when T=15/2.

Note that, as explained with more detail in the *Evaluation* subsection below, s(CASP) can operate and answer correctly queries involving rationals without having to modify the original program to introduce domains for the relevant variables or to *scale* the constants to convert rationals into integers.

Abduction: Abductive reasoning tries to determine a sequence of events/actions that reaches a final state. In the case of ASP, actions are naturally captured as the set of atoms that are true in a model which includes the initial and final states and are consistent with BEC. For the water scenario, (Fig. 5), let us assume we want to reach water level 14 at time 19. The query ?- holdsAt(level(14),19) will return a single model with a vessel size of 16 and the rest of the atoms in the model capturing what must (not) happen to reach this state.

More interesting abductive tasks can be performed: adding the line #abducible happens(tapOff,U) to the program, we specify that it is possible (but not necessary) for the tap to close at some time U. As we mentioned in Sect. 4.4, this directive is translated into code that creates different worlds/models. The query ?- holdsAt(spilling,T) determines if the water may overspill and under which conditions. s(CASP) returns two models:

– One containing T>15, holdsAt(spilling,T), happens(tapOn,5), 5<U<15, not happens(TapOff,U), max_level(10) meaning that the water will spill at T=15 if the vessel has a capacity of 10, the tap is open at T=5, and it is **not** closed between times 5 and 15.
– Another similar model, with the water spilling at T=21 in a vessel with capacity of 16 and where the tap was not closed before U=21.

Note that s(CASP) determined the truth value of *Happens* and, more importantly, performed constraint solving to infer the time ranges during which some events ought (and ought not) to take place, represented by the negated atoms in the models inferred by constructive negation. Since all relevant atoms have a time parameter, they actually represent a *timed plan*. Due to the expressiveness of constraints, this plan contains information on time points when events

Table 1. Run time (ms) comparison for the light scenario.

Queries	s(CASP)	F2LP+clingo
?-holdsAt(red,6.9).	216	**73**
?-holdsAt(red,6.99).	**217**	8,798
?-holdsAt(red,6.999).	**213**	>5 min.

must (not) happen and also on time *windows* (sometimes in relation with other events) during which events must (not) take place. Note that it would be impossible to (finitely) represent this interval with ground atoms, as it corresponds to an infinite number of points.

Evaluation: Comparing directly our implementation of BEC in s(CASP) with implementations in other systems is not easy: most previous systems implemented *discrete* Event Calculus (DEC) and they do not support continuous quantities. One of them is F2LP [15], an ASP-based system that according to [16] outperforms *DEC reasoner* [22], reported by [16] as the more efficient SAT-based implementation. F2LP is a tool that executes DEC by turning first order formulas under the stable model semantics into a logic program w.o. constraints that is evaluated using an ASP solver.

We compared the light scenario in Fig. 4 running under s(CASP) with the F2LP translation under *clingo 5.1.1*, the current version of the state-of-the-art ASP system. Since the directive #domain is no longer available in *clingo*, we had to adapt the translation of F2LP adding timestep(1..10) and timestep/1 to make the clauses safe (Appendix A). While under s(CASP) we can reason about time points in an unbounded continuous domain, the previous encoding of F2LP will make time belong to the integers from 1 to 10. Therefore, since the light is red for $t > 2, t < 3$ and for $t > 6, t < 7$, there are no integer time points from 1 to 10 when the emitted light is red. I.e., for the query ?- holdsAt(red,T) the execution under *clingo* fails and the execution under s(CASP) returns the constraint T #> 2, T #<3 and T #> 6, T #<7.

In order to find at what time point the light red is on under *clingo*, we had to modify the program generated by F2LP to refine the timestep domain with timestep(1..10*P):- precision(P), where the new predicate precision(P) makes it possible to have a finer grain for the possible values of timestep by increasing the value of P. E.g, for P = 10 it is possible to check if the light is red at time $t = 6.9$ by querying ?- holdsAt(red,69), for P=100 it is possible to check for $t = 6.99$ by querying ?- holdsAt(red,699), and so on. This modification (Appendix B) obfuscates the resulting encoding (and for more complex narratives it would be harder or even infeasible) and also impact negatively its performance. Table 1 shows that additional precision in the F2LP encoding (to handle each of the queries) increases the execution run-time of *clingo* by orders of magnitude. On the other hand, s(CASP) does not have to adapt its encoding/queries and its performance does not change.

6   Conclusions

We showed how Event Calculus can be modeled in s(CASP), a goal-directed implementation of constraint answer set programming with predicates, with much fewer limitations than other approaches. s(CASP) can capture the notion of continuous time (and, in general, fluents) in Event Calculus thanks to its grounding-free top-down evaluation strategy. It can also represent complex models and answer queries in a flexible manner thanks to the use of constraints.

The main contribution of the paper is to show how Event Calculus can be directly modeled using s(CASP), an ASP system that seamlessly supports constraints. The modeling of Event Calculus using s(CASP) is more elegant and faithful to the original axioms compared to other approaches such as F2LP, where time has to be discretized. While other approaches such as ASPMT do support continuous domains, their reliance on SMT solvers makes their implementation really complex as associations among variables are lost during grounding. The use of s(CASP) brings other advantages: for example, the justification for the answers to a query is obtained for free, since in a query-driven system, the justification is merely the trace of the proof. Likewise, explanations for observations via abduction are also generated for free, thanks to the goal-directed, top-down execution of s(CASP).

To the best of the authors' knowledge, our approach is the only one that faithfully models continuous-time Event Calculus under the stable model semantics. All other approaches discretize time and thus do not model EC in a sound manner. Our approach supports both deduction and abduction with little or no additional effort.

The work reported in this paper can be seen as the first serious application of s(CASP) [1]. It illustrates the advantages that goal-directed ASP systems have over grounding and SAT solver-based ones for certain applications. Our future work includes applying the s(CASP) system to solving planning problems where a generated plan must obey real-time constraints.

A   F2LP Encoding of the *Light* Scenario

The next figure shows the F2LP [15] program for the light scenario described in Sect. 5 using *discrete* Event Calculus. Since the directive #domain is not available in *clingo 5.1.1* [7], we had to adapt the translation of F2LP adding timestep(1..10) and timestep/1 to make the clauses safe.

```
1   timestep(0..10).
2
3   % If a light is turned on, it will be on:
4   initiates(turn_on,on,T) :- timestep(T).
5
6   % If a light is turned on, whether it is red or green will be released
7   % from the commonsense law of inertia:
8   releases(turn_on,red,T) :- timestep(T).
```

```
9    releases(turn_on,green,T) :- timestep(T).
10
11   % If a light is turned off, it will not be on
12   terminates(turn_off,on,T) :- timestep(T).
13
14   % After a light is turned on, it will emit red for up to 1 second
15   % and green after at least 1 second
16   trajectory(on, T1, red, T2) :-
17                      timestep(T1), timestep(T2),
18                      T1 < T2, T2 < T1 + 1.
19   trajectory(on, T1, green, T2) :-
20                      timestep(T1), timestep(T2),
21                      T2 >= T1 + 1.
22
23   initiallyN(on).
24
25   %% Actions
26   happens(turn_on,2).
27   happens(turn_off,4).
28   happens(turn_on,6).
29
30   %% Query
31   :- not query.
32   query :- holdsAt(red,_).
```

B   Adapted F2LP Translation of the *Light* Scenario with Increased Precision

The next figure shows an F2LP [15] program for the light scenario described in Sect. 5, where the new predicate precision/1 makes it possible to have a finer grain for the possible values of timestep by increasing the value of P.

```
1    timestep(0..10*P) :- precision(P).
2
3    % If a light is turned on, it will be on:
4    initiates(turn_on,on,T) :- timestep(T).
5
6    % If a light is turned on, whether it is red or green will be released
7    % from the commonsense law of inertia:
8    releases(turn_on,red,T) :- timestep(T).
9    releases(turn_on,green,T) :- timestep(T).
10
11   % If a light is turned off, it will not be on
12   terminates(turn_off,on,T) :- timestep(T).
13
14   % After a light is turned on, it will emit red for up to 1 second
15   % and green after at least 1 second
16   trajectory(on, T1, red, T2) :-
17                      timestep(T1), timestep(T2), precision(P),
18                      T1 < T2, T2 < T1 + (1*P).
19   trajectory(on, T1, green, T2) :-
```

```
20                         timestep(T1), timestep(T2), precision(P),
21                         T2 >= T1 + (1*P).
22
23  initiallyN(on).
24
25  %% Actions
26  happens(turn_on,2*P) :- precision(P).
27  happens(turn_off,4*P) :- precision(P).
28  happens(turn_on,6*P) :- precision(P).
29
30  %% Query
31  :- not query.
32
33  precision(10).
34  query :- holdsAt(red,69).
```

References

1. Arias, J., Carro, M., Salazar, E., Marple, K., Gupta, G.: Constraint answer set programming without grounding. Theory Pract. Logic Program. **18**(3–4), 337–354 (2018)

2. Balduccini, M., Magazzeni, D., Maratea, M.: PDDL+ planning via constraint answer set programming. In: 9th Workshop on Answer Set Programming and Other Computing Paradigms, October 2016

3. Bartholomew, M., Lee, J.: System ASPMT2SMT: computing ASPMT theories by SMT solvers. In: Fermé, E., Leite, J. (eds.) JELIA 2014. LNCS (LNAI), vol. 8761, pp. 529–542. Springer, Cham (2014). https://doi.org/10.1007/978-3-319-11558-0_37

4. Chittaro, L., Montanari, A.: Efficient temporal reasoning in the cached event calculus. Comput. Intell. **12**, 359–382 (1996)

5. Clark, K.L.: Negation as failure. In: Gallaire, H., Minker, J. (eds.) Logic and Data Bases, pp. 293–322. Springer, Boston (1978). https://doi.org/10.1007/978-1-4684-3384-5_11

6. Fox, M., Long, D.: PDDL+: modeling continuous time dependent effects. In: Proceedings of the 3rd International NASA Workshop on Planning and Scheduling for Space, vol. 4, p. 34 (2002)

7. Gebser, M., Kaminski, R., Kaufmann, B., Schaub, T.: Clingo = ASP + control: preliminary report. arXiv preprint arXiv:1405.3694 (2014)

8. Gelfond, M., Kahl, Y.: Knowledge Representation, Reasoning, and the Design of Intelligent Agents: The Answer-Set Programming Approach. Cambridge University Press, Cambridge (2014)

9. Gelfond, M., Lifschitz, V.: The stable model semantics for logic programming. In: 5th International Conference on Logic Programming, pp. 1070–1080 (1988)

10. Gelfond, M., Lifschitz, V.: Representing action and change by logic programs. J. Logic Program. **17**(2–4), 301–321 (1993)

11. Gupta, G., Bansal, A., Min, R., Simon, L., Mallya, A.: Coinductive logic programming and its applications. In: Dahl, V., Niemelä, I. (eds.) ICLP 2007. LNCS, vol. 4670, pp. 27–44. Springer, Heidelberg (2007). https://doi.org/10.1007/978-3-540-74610-2_4

12. Holzbaur, C.: OFAI CLP(Q, R) manual, edition 1.3.3. Technical report TR-95-09, Austrian Research Institute for Artificial Intelligence, Vienna (1995)
13. Kowalski, R., Sergot, M.: A logic-based calculus of events. In: Schmidt, J.W., Thanos, C. (eds.) Foundations of Knowledge Base Management. Topics in Information Systems, pp. 23–55. Springer, Heidelberg (1989). https://doi.org/10.1007/978-3-642-83397-7_2
14. Lee, J., Meng, Y.: Answer set programming modulo theories and reasoning about continuous changes. IJCAI **2013**, 990–996 (2013)
15. Lee, J., Palla, R.: F2LP: Computing Answer Sets of First Order Formulas (2009). http://reasoning.eas.asu.edu/f2lp/. Accessed on Feb 2020
16. Lee, J., Palla, R.: Reformulating the situation calculus and the event calculus in the general theory of stable models and in answer set programming. J. Artif. Intell. Res. **43**, 571–620 (2012)
17. Lifschitz, V.: What is answer set programming? In: 23rd National Conference on Artificial Intelligence, vol. 3, pp. 1594–1597. AAAI Press (2008)
18. Marple, K., Salazar, E., Gupta, G.: Computing stable models of normal logic programs without grounding. CoRR eprint arXiv:1709.00501 (2017)
19. McCarthy, J.: Circumscription - a form of non-monotonic reasoning. Artif. Intell. **13**(1–2), 27–39 (1980)
20. Mellarkod, V.S., Gelfond, M., Zhang, Y.: Integrating answer set programming and constraint logic programming. Ann. Math. Artif. Intell. **53**(1–4), 251–287 (2008)
21. Mueller, E.T.: Chapter 17: Event calculus. In: Handbook of Knowledge Representation, Foundations of AI, vol. 3, pp. 671–708. Elsevier (2008)
22. Mueller, E.T.: Discrete event calculus reasoner documentation. Software documentation, IBM Thomas J. Watson Research Center (2008). http://decreasoner.sourceforge.net/. Accessed Feb 2020
23. Mueller, E.T.: Commonsense Reasoning: An Event Calculus Based Approach. Morgan Kaufmann, Burlington (2014)
24. Shanahan, M.: The event calculus explained. In: Wooldridge, M.J., Veloso, M. (eds.) Artificial Intelligence Today. LNCS (LNAI), vol. 1600, pp. 409–430. Springer, Heidelberg (1999). https://doi.org/10.1007/3-540-48317-9_17
25. Shanahan, M.: An abductive event calculus planner. J. Logic Program. **44**(1–3), 207–240 (2000)

Debugging and Verification

An Integrated Approach to Assertion-Based Random Testing in Prolog

Ignacio Casso[1](✉)[iD], José F. Morales[1][iD], Pedro López-García[1,3][iD], and Manuel V. Hermenegildo[1,2][iD]

[1] IMDEA Software Institute, Madrid, Spain
{ignacio.decasso,josef.morales,pedro.lopez,manuel.hermenegildo}@imdea.org
[2] ETSI Informática, Universidad Politécnica de Madrid (UPM), Madrid, Spain
[3] Spanish Council for Scientific Research (CSIC), Madrid, Spain

Abstract. We present an approach for assertion-based random testing of Prolog programs that is tightly integrated within an overall assertion-based program development scheme. Our starting point is the Ciao model, a framework that unifies unit testing and run-time verification, as well as static verification and static debugging, using a common assertion language. Properties which cannot be verified statically are checked dynamically. In this context, the idea of generating random test values from assertion preconditions emerges naturally since these preconditions are conjunctions of literals, and the corresponding predicates can in principle be used as generators. Our tool generates valid inputs from the properties that appear in the assertions shared with other parts of the model, and the run time-check instrumentation of the Ciao framework is used to perform a wide variety of checks. This integration also facilitates the combination with static analysis. The generation process is based on running standard predicates under non-standard (random) search rules. Generation can be fully automatic but can also be guided or defined specifically by the user. We propose methods for supporting (C)LP-specific properties, including combinations of shape-based (regular) types and variable sharing and instantiation, and we also provide some ideas for shrinking for these properties. We also provide a case study applying the tool to the verification and checking of the code of some of the abstract domains used by the Ciao system.

1 Introduction and Motivation

Code validation is a vital task in any software development cycle. Traditionally, two of the main approaches used to this end are *verification* and *testing*. The former uses formal methods to prove automatically or interactively some specification of the code, while the latter mainly consists in executing the code for concrete inputs or test cases and checking that the program input-output relations (and behaviour, in general) are the expected ones.

Research partially funded by MINECO TIN2015-67522-C3-1-R *TRACES* project, and the Madrid P2018/TCS-4339 *BLOQUES-CM* program. We are also grateful to the anonymous reviewers for their useful comments.

© Springer Nature Switzerland AG 2020
M. Gabbrielli (Ed.): LOPSTR 2019, LNCS 12042, pp. 159–176, 2020.
https://doi.org/10.1007/978-3-030-45260-5_10

The Ciao language [11] introduced a novel development workflow [12,13,21] that integrates the two approaches above. In this model, program assertions are fully integrated in the language, and serve both as specifications for static analysis and as run-time check generators, unifying run-time verification and unit testing with static verification and static debugging. This model represents an alternative approach for writing safe programs without relying on full static typing, which is specially useful for dynamic languages like Prolog, and can be considered an antecedent of the popular *gradual-* and *hybrid-typing* approaches [5,22,24].

The Ciao Model: For our purposes, assertions in the Ciao model can be seen as a shorthand for defining instrumentation to be added to programs, in order to check dynamically preconditions and postconditions, including conditional postconditions, properties at arbitrary program points, and certain computational (non-functional) properties. The run-time semantics implemented by the translation of the assertion language ensures that execution paths that violate the assertions are captured during execution, thus detecting errors. Optionally, (abstract interpretation-based [4]) compile-time analysis is used to detect assertion violations, or to prove (parts of) assertions true, verifying the program or reducing run-time checking overhead. As an example, consider the following Ciao code (with the standard definition of quick-sort):

```
1  :- pred qs(Xs,Ys) : (list(Xs), var(Ys)) => (list(Ys), sorted(Ys)) + not_fails.
2
3  :- prop list/1.
4  list([]).
5  list([_|T]) :- list(T).
6
7  :- prop sorted/1.
8  ...
```

The assertion has a *calls* field (the conjunction after ':'), a *success* field (the conjunction after '=>'), and a computational properties field (after '+'), where all these fields are optional. It states that a valid calling mode for qs/2 is to invoke it with its first argument instantiated to a list, and that it will then return a list in Ys, that this list will be sorted, and that the predicate will not fail. Properties such as list/1 or sorted/1 are normal predicates, but which meet certain conditions (e.g., termination) [13] and are marked as such via prop/1 declarations. Other properties like var/1 or not_fails are builtins.

Compile-time analysis with a types/*shapes* domain can easily detect that, if the predicate is called as stated in the assertion, the list(Ys) check on success will always succeed, and that the predicate itself will also succeed. If this predicate appears within a larger program, analysis can also typically infer whether or not qs/2 is called with a list and a free variable. However, perhaps, e.g., sorted(Ys) cannot be checked statically (this is in fact often possible, but let us assume that, e.g., a suitable abstract domain is not at hand). The assertion would then be simplified to:

```
:- pred qs(Xs,Ys) => sorted(Ys).
```

At run time, `sorted(Ys)` will be called within the assertion checking-harness, right after calls to `qs/2`. This harness ensures that the variable bindings (or constraints) and the whole checking process are kept isolated from the normal execution of the program (this can be seen conceptually as including a Prolog `copy_term`, or calling within a double negation, `\+\+`, executing in a separate process, etc.).

Testing vs. Run-Time Checking: The checking of `sorted/1` in the example above will occur in principle during execution of the program, i.e., in *deployment*. However, in many cases it is not desirable to wait until then to detect errors. This is the case for example if errors can be catastrophic or perhaps if there is interest in testing, perhaps for debugging purposes, more general properties that have not been formally proved and whose main statements are not directly part of the program (and thus, will never be executed), such as, e.g.:

```
1  :- pred revrev(X) : list(X) + not_fails.
2  revrev(X) :- reverse(X,Y),reverse(Y,X).
```

This implies performing a *testing* process prior to deployment. The Ciao model includes a mechanism, integrated with the assertion language, that allows defining *test assertions*, which will run (parts of) the program for a given input and check the corresponding output, as well as *driving* the run-time checks independently of concrete application data [16]. For example, if the following (unit) tests are added to `qs/2`:

```
1  :- test qs(Xs,Ys) : (Xs = []) => (Ys = []).
2  :- test qs(Xs,Ys) : (Xs = [3,2,4,1]) => (Ys = [1,2,3,4]).
```

`qs/2` will be *run* with, e.g., `[3,2,4,1]` as input in `Xs`, and the output generated in `Ys` will be checked to be instantiated to `[1,2,3,4]`. This is done by extracting the *test drivers* [16]:

```
1  :- texec qs([],_).
2  :- texec qs([3,2,4,1],_).
```

and the rest of the work (checking the assertion fields) is done by the standard assertion run-time checking machinery. In our case, this includes checking at run time the simplified assertion "`:- pred qs(Xs,Ys) => sorted(Ys).`", so that the output in `Ys` will be checked by calling the implementation of `sorted/1`. This overall process is depicted in Fig. 1 and will be discussed further in Sect. 2.

Towards Automatic Generation: Hand-written test cases such as those above are quite useful in practice, but they are also tedious to write and even when they are present they may not cover some interesting cases. An aspect that is specific to (Constraint-)Logic Programming (CLP) and is quite relevant in this context is that predicates in general (and properties in particular) can be used as both checkers and generators. For example, calling `list(X)` from the revrev/1 example above with X uninstantiated generates lazily, through back-tracking, an infinite set of lists, Xs = []; Xs = [_]; Xs = [_,_,_] ..., which can be used to catch cases in which an error in the coding of reverse/2 makes revrev/1 fail. This leads naturally to the idea of generating systematically and automatically test cases by running in generation mode (i.e., "backwards") the properties in the calls fields of assertions.

While this idea of using properties as test case generators has always been present in the descriptions of the Ciao model [12,21], it has not really been exploited significantly to date. Our purpose in this paper is to fill this gap. We report on the development of LPtest, an implementation of random testing [8] with a more natural connection with Prolog semantics, as well as with the Ciao framework. Due to this connection and the use of assertions, this *assertion-based testing* allows supporting complex properties like combinations of shape-based (regular) types, variable sharing, and instantiation, and also non-functional properties.

Our contributions can be summarized as follows:

- We have developed an approach and a tool for assertion-based random test generation for Prolog and related languages. It has a number of character-istics in common with property-based testing from functional languages, as exemplified by QuickCheck [3], but provides the assertions and properties required in order to cover (C)LP features such as logical variables and non-ground data structures or non-determinism, with related properties such as modes, variables sharing, non-failure, determinacy and number of solutions, etc. In this, LPtest is most similar to PrologTest [1], but we argue that our framework is more general and we support richer properties.
- Our approach offers a number of advantages that stem directly from framing it within the Ciao model. This includes the integration with compile-time checking (static analysis) and the combination with the run-time checking framework, etc. using a single assertion language. This for example greatly simplifies error reporting and diagnosis, which can all be inherited from these parts of the framework. It can also be combined with other test-case genera-tion schemes. To the extent of our knowledge, this has only been attempted partially by PropEr [20]. Also, since Erlang is in many ways closer to a func-tional language, PropEr does not support Prolog-relevant properties and it is not integrated with static analysis. In comparison to PrologTest, we provide combination with static analysis, through an integrated assertion language, whereas the assertions of PrologTest are specific to the tool, and we also support a larger set of properties.
- In our approach the automatic generation of inputs is performed by run-ning in generation mode the properties (predicates) in those preconditions, taking advantage of the specialized SLD *search rules* of the language (e.g., breadth first, iterative deepening, and, in particular, random search) or imple-mentations specialized for such generation. In particular, we perform auto-matic generation of instances of Prolog regular types, instantiation modes, sharing relations among variables and grounding, arithmetic constraints, etc.

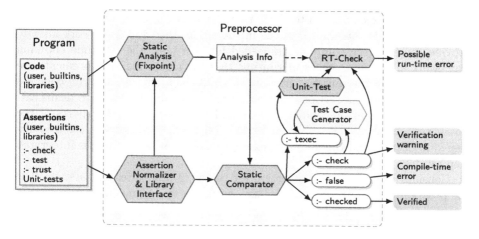

Fig. 1. The Ciao assertion framework (CiaoPP's verification/testing architecture). (Color figure online)

To the extent of our knowledge all previous tools only supported generation for types, while we also consider the latter.

– We have enhanced assertion and property-based test generation by combining it with static analysis and abstract domains. To the extent of our knowledge previous work had at most discarded properties that could be proved statically (which in LPtest comes free from the overall setting, as mentioned before), but not used static analysis information to guide or improve the testing process.

– We have implemented automatic shrinking for our tool, and in particular we have developed an automatic shrinking algorithm for Prolog regular types.

The rest of this paper is organized as follows. In Sect. 2 we review our approach to assertion-based testing in the context of Prolog and Ciao. In Sect. 3 we introduce our test input generation schema. In Sect. 4, we show how assertion-based testing can be combined with and enhanced by static analysis. Sect. 5 is dedicated to shrinking of test cases in LPtest. In Sect. 6 we show some preliminary results of a case study in which our tool is applied to checking some of the domain operations in the static analyses of CiaoPP (the Ciao "preprocessor"). Finally, we review the related work in Sect. 7 and provide our conclusions in Sect. 8.

2   Using LPtest Within the Ciao Model

As mentioned before, the goal of LPtest is to integrate random testing of assertions within Ciao's assertion-based verification and debugging framework (Fig. 1). Given an assertion for a predicate, we want to generate goals for that predicate satisfying the assertion precondition (i.e., valid call patterns for the predicate) and execute them to check that the assertion holds for those cases or find errors. As also mentioned in the introduction, the Ciao framework already provides most of the components needed for this task: the run-time checking framework allows us to check at runtime that the assertions for a predicate are not violated, and the unit-test framework allows us to specify and run concrete goals to check those assertions. We only need to be able to generate terms satisfying the assertion preconditions and feed them into the other parts of the framework (the new yellow box in Fig. 1). This generation of test cases is discussed in Sect. 3, and the following example shows how everything is integrated step by step.

Consider again a similar assertion for the qs/2 predicate, and assume that the program has a bug and *fails* for lists with repeated elements:

```
1  :- module(qs,[qs/2],[assertions, nativeprops]).
2  ...
3  :- pred qs(Xs,Ys) : (list(Xs,int), var(Ys))
4                => (list(Ys,int), sorted(Ys)) + not_fails.
5  ...
6  partition([],_,[],[]).
7  partition([X|Xs],Pv,[X|L],R) :- X < Pv, !, partition(Xs,Pv,L,R). % should be =<
8  partition([X|Xs],Pv,L,[X|R]) :- X > Pv, partition(Xs,Pv,L,R).
```

Following Fig. 1, the assertions of the qs module are verified statically [13]. As a result, parts of each assertion may be proved true or false (in which case no testing is needed for them), and, if any other parts are left after this process, run-time checking and/or testing is performed for them. CiaoPP generates a new source file which includes the original assertions marked with *status* checked, false, or, for the ones that remain for run-time checking, check. LPtest starts by reporting a simple adaptation of CiaoPP's output. E.g., for our example, LPtest will output:

```
1  Testing assertion:
2  :- pred qs(Xs,Ys) : (list(Xs,int), var(Ys))
3                => (list(Ys,int), sorted(Ys)) + not_fails.
4
5  Assertion was partially verified statically:
6    :- checked pred qs(Xs,Ys) (list(Xs,int), var(Ys)) => list(Ys,int).
7  Left to check::
8    :- check   pred qs(Xs,Ys) => sorted(Ys) + not_fails.
```

LPtest will then try to test dynamically the remaining assertion. For that, it will first collect the Ciao properties that the test case must fulfill (i.e., those in the precondition of the assertion, which is taken from the *original* assertion, which is also output by CiaoPP), and generate a number of *test case drivers* (texec's) satisfying those properties. Those test cases will be pipelined to the *unit-test framework*, which, relying on the standard run-time checking instrumentation, will manage their execution, capture any error reported during run-time checking, and return them to LPtest, which will output:

```
1  Assertion
2     :- check    pred qs(Xs,Ys) => sorted(Ys) + not_fails.
3  proven false for test case:
4     :- texec qs([5,9,-3,8,9,-6,2],_).
5  because:
6     call to qs(Xs,Ys) fails for
7     Xs = [5, 9,-3,8,9,-6,2]
```

Finally, LPtest will try to shrink the test cases, enumerating test cases that are progressively smaller and repeating the steps above in a loop to find the smallest test case which violates the assertion. LPtest will output:

```
1  Test case shrinked to:
2     :- texec qs([0,0],_).
```

The testing algorithm for a module can thus be summarized as follows:

1. (CiaoPP) Use *static analysis* to check the assertions. Remove proved assertions, simplify partially proved assertions.
2. (LPtest) For each assertion, *generate N test cases* from the properties in the precondition, following the guidelines in Sect. 3. For each test case, go to **3**. Then go to **4**.
3. (RTcheck) Use the unit-test framework to execute the test case and capture any run-time checking error (i.e., assertion violation).
4. (LPtest) Collect all failed test cases from RTcheck. For each of them, go to **5** to shrink them, and then report them (using RTcheck).
5. (LPtest) Generate a simpler test case not generated yet.
   - If not possible, finalize and return current test case as shrinked test case. If possible, go to **3** to run the test.
     * If the new test case fails, go to **5** with the new test case.
     * If it succeeds, repeat this step.

The use of the Ciao static verification and run-time checking framework in this (pseudo-)algorithm, together with the rich set of native properties in Ciao, allows us to specify and check a wide range of properties for our programs. We provide a few examples of the expressive power of the approach:

(Conditional) Postconditions. We can write postconditions using the *success* (=>) field of the assertions. Those postconditions can range from user-defined predicates to properties native to CiaoPP, for which there are built-in checkers in the run-time checking framework. These properties include types, which can be partially instantiated, i.e., contain variables, and additional features particular to logic programming such as modes and sharing between variables. As an example, one can test with LPtest the following assertions, where covered(X,Y) means that all variables occurring in X also occur in Y:

```
1 :- pred rev(Xs,Ys) : list(Xs) => list(Ys).
2 :- pred sort(Xs,Ys) : list(Xs,int) => (list(Ys,int), sorted(Ys)).
3 :- pred numbervars(Term,N,M) => ground(Term).
4 :- pred varset(Term,Xs) => (list(Xs,var), covered(Term,Xs)).
```

For this kind of properties, LPtest tries to ensure that at least some of the test cases do not succeed trivially (by the predicate just failing), and warns otherwise.

Computational Properties. LPtest can also be used to check properties regarding the computation of a predicate. These properties are typically native and talk about features that range from determinism and multiplicity of solutions to resource usage (cost). They can be checked with LPtest, as long as the run-time checking framework supports it (e.g., some properties, like termination, are not decidable). Examples of this would be:

```
1 :- pred rev(X,Y) : list(X) + (not_fails, is_det, no_choicepoints).
2 :- pred append(X,Y,Z) : list(X) => cost(steps,ub,length(X)).
```

Rich Generation. The properties supported for generation include not only types, but also modes and sharing between variables, and arithmetic constraints, as well as a restricted set of user-defined properties. As an example, LPtest can test the following assertion:

```
1 :- prop sorted_int_list(X).
2
3 sorted_int_list([]).
4 sorted_int_list([N]) :- int(N).
5 sorted_int_list([N,M|Ms]) :- N =< M, sorted_int_list([M|Ms]).
6
7 :- pred insert_ord(X,Xs,XsWithX)
8      : (int(X), sorted_int_list(X))
9    => sorted_int_list(XsWithX).
```

3   Test Case Generation

The previous section illustrated specially the parts that LPtest inherits from the Ciao framework, but a crucial step was skipped: the generation of test cases from the *calls* field of the assertions, i.e., the generation of Prolog terms satisfying a conjunction of Ciao properties. This was obviously one of the main challenges we faced when designing and implementing LPtest. In order for the tool to be integrated naturally within the Ciao verification and debugging framework, this generation had to be as automatic as possible. However, full automation is not always possible in the presence of arbitrary properties potentially using the whole Prolog language (e.g., cuts, dynamic predicates, etc.). The solution we arrived at is to support fully automatic and efficient generation for reasonable subsets of the Prolog language, and provide means for the user to guide the generation in more complex scenarios.

Pure Prolog. The simplest and essential subset of Prolog is pure Prolog. In pure Prolog every predicate, and, in particular, every **Ciao** property, is itself a generator: if it succeeds with some terms as arguments, those terms will be (possibly instances of) answers to the predicate when called with free variables as arguments. The problem is that the classic depth-first search strategy used in Prolog resolution, with which those answers will be computed, is not well suited for test-case generation. One of **Ciao**'s features comes here to the rescue. **Ciao** has a concept of *packages*, syntactic and/or semantic extensions to the language that can be loaded module-locally. This mechanism is used to implement language extensions such as functional syntax, constraints, higher order, etc., and, in particular *alternative search rules*. These include for example (several versions of) breadth first, iterative deepening, Andorra-style execution, etc. These rules can be activated on a per-module basis. For example, the predicates in a module that starts with the following header:

```
1  :- module( myprops, _, [bf]).
```

(which loads the **bf** package) will run in breadth-first mode. While breadth-first is useful mostly for teaching, other alternative search rules are quite useful in practice. Motivated by the **LPtest** context, i.e., with the idea of running properties in generation mode, we have developed also a *randomized alternative search strategy* package, **rnd**, which can be described by the following simplified meta-interpreter:

```
1  solve_goal(G) :- random_clause(G,Body), solve_body(Body).
2
3  random_clause(Head,Body) :-
4      findall(cl(Head,B),meta_clause(Head,B),ClauseList),
5      once(shuffle(ClauseList,ShuffleList)),
6      member(cl(Head,Body),ShuffleList). % Body=[] for facts
7
8  solve_body([]).
9  solve_body([G|Gs]) :- solve_goal(G), solve_body(Gs).
```

The actual algorithm used for generation is of course more involved. Among other details, it only does backtracking on failure (on success it starts all over again to produce the next answer, without repeating traces), and it has a growth control mechanism to avoid getting stuck in traces that lead to non-terminating generations.

Using this search strategy, a set of terms satisfying a conjunction of pure Prolog properties can be generated just by running all those properties sequentially with unbounded variables. This is implemented using different versions of each property (generation, run-time check) which are generated automatically from the declarative definition of the property using instrumentation. In particular, this simplest subset of the language allows us to deal directly with regular types (e.g., `list/1`).

Mode, Sharing, and Arithmetic Constraints. We extend the subset of the language for which generation is supported with arithmetic (e.g., `int/1`, `flt/1`,

</2), mode-related extralogical predicates and properties (e.g., free/1, gnd/1), and sharing-related native properties (e.g., mshare/1, which describes the sharing –aliasing– relations of a set of variables using *sharing sets* [15], and indep/2, that states that two variable do not share). When a goal or a property of this kind appears during generation, the variables occurring in it are constrained using a constraints domain. The domain ensures that those constraints are satisfiable during all steps of generation, failing and backtracking otherwise. There is a last step in generation in which all free variables are randomly further intantiated in a way that those constraints are satisfied.

This can be seen conceptually as choosing first a trace at random for each property and collecting constraints in the trace, and then randomly sampling (enumerating) the constrains. However, since the constraints introduced by unification are terms, it is equivalent to solving a predicate with the random search strategy and treating each builtin or native property as a constraint. In practice, we support more builtins for generation in properties (e.g., ==/2 just unifies two variables, we have shape constraints that handle =../2, and support negation to some extent), but the approach has only been tested significantly for the subset of Prolog presented so far.

In the last phase of constraints (random sampling), unconstrained free variables can be further instantiated with some probability, using random shape and sharing constraints, chosen among native properties and properties defined by the users on modules that are loaded at the time. This way, random terms are still generated for an assertion without precondition, or the generated term for list(X) is not always a list of free variables. This is also the technique used to further instantiate a free variable constrained as *ground* but for which no shape information is available.

Generation for Other Properties. For the remaining properties which use Prolog features not covered so far (e.g., dynamic predicates), there is a last step in the generation algorithm in which they are simply checked for the terms generated so far. User-defined generators are encouraged for assertions with preconditions that are complex enough to reach this step. There is a limit to how many times generation can reach this step and fail, to avoid getting stuck in an inefficient or non-terminating generate-and-check loop. To recognize these properties without inspecting the code (left as future work), users are trusted to mark the properties suitable for generation, and only the native properties discussed and the regular types are considered suitable by default.

4   Integration with Static Analysis

The use of a unified assertion framework for testing and analysis allows us to enhance LPtest random testing by combining it with static analysis.

First of all, as illustrated in Sect. 2 and Fig. 1, CiaoPP first performs a series of static analyses through which some of the assertions may be verified statically, possibly partially. Thus, only some parts of some assertions may need to be checked in the testing phase [13].

Beyond this, and perhaps more interestingly in our context, statically inferred information can also help while testing the remaining assertions. In particular, it is used to generate more relevant test cases in the generation phase. Consider for example the following assertion:

```
:- pred qs(Xs,Ys) => sorted(Ys).
```

Without the usual precondition, LPtest would have to generate arbitrary terms to test the assertion, most of which would not be relevant test cases since the predicate would fail for them, and therefore the assertion would be satisfied trivially. However, static analysis typically infers the output type for this predicate:

```
:- pred qs(Xs,_) => list(Xs,int).
```

I.e., analysis infers that on success Xs must be a list, and so on call it must be *compatible* with a list if it is to succeed (inputs that generate failure are also interesting of course, but not to check properties that should hold on *success*). Therefore the assertion can also be checked as follows:

```
:- pred qs(Xs,_) : compat(Xs,list(int)) => sorted_int_list(Xs).
```

where compat(Xs,list(int)) means that Xs is either a list of integers or can be further instantiated to one. Now we would only generate relevant inputs (generation for compat/2 is implemented by randomly uninstantiating a term), and LPtest is able to prove the assertion false. The same can be done for modes and sharing to some extent: variables that are inferred to be free on success must also be free on call, and variables inferred to be independent must be independent on call too. Also, when a predicate is not exported, the *calls* assertions inferred for it can be used for generation. In general, the idea here is to perform some backwards analysis. However, this can also be done without explicit backwards analysis by treating testing and (forward) static analysis independently and one after the other, which makes the integration conceptually simple and easy to implement.

A Finer-Grain Integration. We now propose a finer-grained integration of assertion-based testing and analysis, which still treats analysis as a black box, although not as an independent step. So far our approach has been to try to check an assertion with static analysis, and if this fails we perform random testing. However, the analysis often fails to prove the assertion because its precondition (i.e., the entry abstract substitution to the analysis) is too general, but it can prove it for refinements of that entry, i.e., refinements of the precondition. In that case, all test cases satisfying that refined precondition are guaranteed to succeed, and therefore useless in practice. We propose to work with different refined versions of an assertion, by adding further, exhaustive constraints in a native domain to the precondition, and performing testing only on the versions which the analysis cannot verify statically, thus pruning the test case input space. For example, for an assertion of a predicate of arity one, without mode properties, a set of assertions equivalent to the original one would result by generating three different assertions with the same success but preconditions ground(X), var(X), and (nonground(X), nonvar(X)). The idea is to generalize this to arbitrary, maybe infinite abstract domains, for which a given abstract value is not so easily partitioned as in the example above. Alternatively, the test exploration can be limited to subsets of the domain, since in any case the testing process cannot achieve completeness in general. The core of an algorithm for this domain partition would be the following: to test an assertion for a given entry $A \in D_\alpha$, the assertion is proved by the analysis or tested recursively for a set of abstract values $S \subseteq \{B | B \in D_\alpha, B \sqsubseteq A\}$ lower than that entry, and random test cases are generated in the "space" between the entry and those lower values $\gamma(A) \setminus \bigcup \gamma(B)$, where γ is the concretization function in the domain. For this it is only necessary to provide a suitable sampling function in the domain, and a rich generation algorithm for that domain. But note that, e.g., for the *sharing-freeness* domain, we already have the latter: we already have generation for mode and sharing constraints, and a transformation scheme between abstract values and mode/sharing properties. Note also that all this can still be done while treating the static analysis as a black box, and that if the enumeration of abstract values is fine-grained enough, this algorithm also ensures coverage of the test input space during generation.

5   Shrinking

One flaw of random testing is that often the failed test cases reported are unnecessary complex, and thus not very useful for debugging. Many property-based tools introduce shrinking to solve this problem: after one counter-example is found, they try to reduce it to a simpler counter-example that still fails the test in the same way. LPtest supports shrinking too, both user-guided and automatic. We present the latter.

The shrinking algorithm mirrors that of generation, and in fact reuses most of the generation framework. It can be seen as a new generation with further constraints: bounds on the shape and size of the generated goal. The traces followed to generate the new term from a property must be "subtraces" of the ones followed to generate the original one. The random sampling of the constraints for the new terms must be "simpler" than for the original ones. The final step in which the remaining properties are checked is kept.

We present the algorithm for the first step. Generation for the shrinked value follows the path that leads to the to-be-shrinked value, but at any moment it can non-deterministically stop following that trace and generate a new subterm using size parameter 0. Applying this method to shrink lists of Peano numbers is equivalent to the following predicate, where the first argument is the term to be shrinked and the second a free variable to be the shrinked value on success:

```
1   shrink_peano_list([X|Xs],[Y|Ys]) :-
2     shrink_peano_number(X,Y),
3     shrink_peano_list(Xs,Ys).
4   shrink_peano_list(_,Ys) :-
5     gen_peano_list(0,Ys). % X=[]
6
7   shrink_peano_number(s(X),s(Y)) :-
8     shrink_peano_number(X,Y).
9   shrink_peano_number(_,Y) :-
10    gen_peano_number(0,Y). % Y=0.
```

This method can shrink the list `[s(0),0,s(s(s(0)))]` to `[s(0),0]` or `[s(0),0,s(s(0))]`, but never to `[s(0),s(s(s(0)))]`. To solve that, we allow the trace of the to-be-shrinked term to advance non-deterministically at any moment to an equivalent point, so that the trace of the generated term does not have to follow it completely in parallel. It would be as if the following clauses were added to the the previous predicate (the one which sketches the actual workings of the method during meta-interpretation):

```
1   shrink_peano_list([_|Xs],Ys) :-
2     shrink_peano_list(Xs,Ys).
3
4   shrink_peano_number(s(X),Y) :-
5     shrink_peano_number(X,Y).
```

With this method, `[s(0),s(s(s(0)))]` would now be a valid shrinked value.

This is implemented building shrinking versions of the properties, similarly to the examples presented, and running them in generation mode. However, since we want shrinking to be an enumeration of simpler values, and not random, the search strategy used is the usual depth-first strategy and not the randomized one presented in Sect. 3. The usual sampling of constraints is used too, instead of the random one.

The number of potential shrinked values grows exponentially with the size of the traces. To mitigate this problem, `LPtest` commits to a shrinked value once it checks that it violates the assertion too, and continues to shrink that value, but never starts from another one on backtracking. Also, the enumeration of shrinked values returns first the values closer to the original term, i.e., if X is returned before Y, then shrinking Y could never produce X. Therefore we never repeat a shrinked value[1] in our greedy search for the simplest counterexample.

6   A Case Study

In order to better illustrate our ideas, we present now a case study which consists in testing the correctness of the implementation of some of `CiaoPP`'s abstract domains. In particular, we focus herein on the *sharing-freeness* domain [19] and

---

[1] Actually, we do not repeat subtraces, but two different subtraces can represent the same value (e.g., there are two ways to obtain s(0) from s(s(0))).

the correctness of its structure as a lattice and its handling of builtins. Tested predicates include leq/2, which checks if an abstract value is below another in the lattice, lub/3 and glb/3, which compute the *least upper bound* and *greatest lower bound* of two abstract values, builtin_success/3, which computes the *success substitution of a builtin* from a *call substitution*, and abstract/2, which computes the abstraction for a list of substitutions.

Generation. Testing these predicates required generating random values for abstract values and builtins. The latter is simple: a simple declaration of the property builtin(F,A), which simply enumerates the builtins together with their arity, is itself a generator, and using the generation scheme proposed in Sect. 3 it becomes a random generator, while it can still be used as a checker in the run-time checking framework. The same happens for a simple declarative definition of the property shfr(ShFr,Vs), which checks that ShFr is a valid *sharing-freeness* value for a list of variables Vs. This is however not that trivial and proves that our generation scheme works and is useful in practice, since that property is not a regular type, and among others it includes sharing constraints between free variables. These two properties allowed us to test assertions like the following:

```
1  :- pred leq_reflexive(X) : shfr(X,_) + not_fails.
2  leq_reflexive(X) :- leq(X,X).
3
4  :- pred lub(X,Y,Z) : (shfr(X,Vs), shfr(Y,Vs)) => (leq(X,Z), leq(Y,Z)).
5
6  :- pred builtin_sucess(Func,Ar,Call,Succ)
7       : (builtin(Func,Ar), length(Vs,A), shfr(Call,Vs))
8       + (not_fails, is_det, not_further_inst([Call]))}
```

To check some assertions we needed to generate related pairs of abstract values. That is encoded in the precondition as a final literal leq(ShFr1,ShFr2), as in the next assertion:

```
1  :- pred builtins_monotonic(F, A, X, Y)
2       : (builtin(F,A), length(Vs,A), shfr(X,Vs), shfr(Y,Vs), leq(X,Y))
3       + not_fails.
4
5  builtins_monotonic(F,A,X,Y) :-
6       builtin_success(F,A,X,X2), builtin_success(F,A,Y,Y2), leq(X2,Y2).
```

In our framework the generation is performed by producing first the two values independently, and checking the literal. This became inefficient, so we decided to write our own generator for this particular case. Finally, we tested the generation for arbitrary terms with the following assertion, which checks that the abstract value resulting from executing a builtin and abstracting the arguments on success is lower than the one resulting of abstracting the arguments on call and calling builtin_success/3:

```
1  :- pred builtin_soundness(Blt, Args)
2       : (builtin(Blt), Blt=F/A, length(Args,A), list(Args, term))
3       + not_fails.
4
5  builtin_soundess(Blt,Args) :- ...
```

Analysis. Many properties used in our assertions were user-defined, complex, and not native to CiaoPP, so there were many cases in which the analysis could not abstract them precisely. However, the analysis did manage to simplify or prove some of the remaining ones, particularly regular types and those dealing with determinism (+ is_det) and efficiency (no_choicepoints). Additionally, we successfully did the experiment of not defining the regular type builtin/2, and letting the analysis infer it on its own and use it for generation. We also tested by hand the finer integration between testing and analysis proposed in Sect. 4: some assertions involving builtins could not be proven for the general case, but this could be done for some of the simpler builtins, and thus testing could be avoided for those particular cases.

Bugs Found. We did not find any bugs in the implementations for different domains of the lattice operations leq/2, lub/2, and glb/2. This was not surprising: they are relatively simple and commonly used in CiaoPP. However, we found several bugs in builtin_success/2 (part of the description of the "transfer function" for some language built-ins) in some domains. Some of them were minor and thus had never been found or reported before: some builtin handlers left unnecessary choicepoints, or failed for the abstract value ⊥ (with which they are never called in CiaoPP). Others were more serious: we found bugs for less commonly-used builtins, and even two larger bugs for the builtins =/2 and ==/2. The handler failed for the literal X=X and for literals like f(X)==g(Y), both of which do not normally appear in realistic programs and thus were not detected before.

7   Related Work

Random testing has been used for a long time in Software Engineering [8]. As mentioned before, the idea of using properties and assertions as test case generators was proposed in the context of the Ciao model [12,21] for logic programs, although it had not really been exploited significantly until this work. QuickCheck [3] provided the first full implementation of a property-based random test generation system. It was first developed for Haskell and functional programming languages in general and then extended to other languages, and has seen significant practical use [14]. It uses a domain-specific language of testable specifications and generates test data based on Haskell types. ErlangQuickCheck and PropEr [20] are closely related systems for Erlang, where types are dynamically checked and the value generation is guided by means of functions, using quantified types defined by these generating functions. We use a number of ideas from `QuickCheck` and the related systems, such as applying shrinking to reduce the test cases. However, `LPtest` is based on the ideas of the (earlier) `Ciao` model and we do not propose a new assertion language, but rather use and extend that of the `Ciao` system. This allows supporting Prolog-relevant properties, which deal with non-ground data, logical variables, variable sharing, etc., while `QuickCheck` is limited to ground data. Also, while `QuickCheck` offers quite flexible control of the random generation, we argue that using random search strategies over predicates defining properties is an interesting and more natural approach for Prolog.

The closest related work is `PrologTest` [1], which adapts `QuickCheck` and random property-based testing to the Prolog context. We share many objectives with `PrologTest` but we argue that our framework is more general, with richer properties (e.g., variable sharing), and is combined with static analysis. Also, as in `QuickCheck`, `PrologTest` uses a specific assertion language, while, as mentioned before, we share the `Ciao` assertions with the other parts of the `Ciao` system. `PrologTest` also uses Prolog predicates as random *generators*. This can also be done in `LPtest`, but we also propose an approach which we argue is more elegant, based on separating the code of the generator from the random generation strategy, using the facilities present in the `Ciao` system for running code under different SLD *search rules*, such as breadth first, iterative deepening, or randomized search.

Other directly related systems are `EasyCheck` [2] and `CurryCheck` [9] for the `Curry` language. In these systems test cases are generated from the (strong) types present in the language, as in `QuickCheck`. However, they also deal with determinism and modes. To the extent of our knowledge test case minimization has not been implemented in these systems.

There has also been work on generating test cases using CLP and partial evaluation techniques, both for Prolog and imperative languages (see, e.g., [6,7] and its references). This work differs from (and is complementary to) ours in that the test cases are generated via a symbolic execution of the program, with the traditional aims of path coverage, etc., rather than from assertions and with the objective of randomized testing.

Other related work includes *fuzz testing* [18], where "nonsensical" (i.e., fully random) inputs are passed to programs to trigger program crashes, and grammar-based testing, where inputs generation is based on a grammatical definition of inputs (similar to generating with regular types) [10]. Schrijvers proposed `Tor` [23] as a mechanism for supporting the execution of predicates using alternative search rules, similar in spirit to `Ciao`'s implementation of search-strategies via packages. Midtgaard and Moller [17] have also applied property-based testing to checking the correctness of static analysis implementations.

8   Conclusions and Future Work

We have presented an approach and a tool, `LPtest`, for assertion-based random testing of Prolog programs that is integrated with the `Ciao` assertion model.

In this context, the idea of generating random test values from assertion preconditions emerges naturally since preconditions are conjunctions of literals, and the corresponding predicates can conceptually be used as generators. LPtest generates valid inputs from the properties that appear in the assertions shared with other parts of the model. We have shown how this generation process can be based on running the property predicates under non-standard (random) search rules and how the run time-check instrumentation of the Ciao framework can be used to perform a wide variety of checks. We have proposed methods for supporting (C)LP-specific properties, including combinations of shape-based (regular) types and variable sharing and instantiation. We have also proposed some integrations of the test generation system with static analysis and provided a number of ideas for shrinking in our context. Finally, we have shown some results on the applicability of the approach and tool to the verification and checking of the implementations of some of Ciao's abstract domains. The tool has already proven itself quite useful in finding bugs in production-level code.

References

1. Amaral, C., Florido, M., Santos Costa, V.: PrologCheck – property-based testing in prolog. In: Codish, M., Sumii, E. (eds.) FLOPS 2014. LNCS, vol. 8475, pp. 1–17. Springer, Cham (2014). https://doi.org/10.1007/978-3-319-07151-0_1
2. Christiansen, J., Fischer, S.: EasyCheck — test data for free. In: Garrigue, J., Hermenegildo, M.V. (eds.) FLOPS 2008. LNCS, vol. 4989, pp. 322–336. Springer, Heidelberg (2008). https://doi.org/10.1007/978-3-540-78969-7_23
3. Claessen, K., Hughes, J.: QuickCheck: a lightweight tool for random testing of Haskell programs. In: Fifth ACM SIGPLAN International Conference on Functional Programming, ICFP 2000, pp. 268–279. ACM (2000)
4. Cousot, P., Cousot, R.: Abstract interpretation: a unified lattice model for static analysis of programs by construction or approximation of fixpoints. In: Proceedings of POPL 1977, pp. 238–252. ACM Press (1977)
5. Flanagan, C.: Hybrid type checking. In: 33rd ACM SIGPLAN-SIGACT Symposium on Principles of Programming Languages, POPL 2006, pp. 245–256, January 2006
6. Gómez-Zamalloa, M., Albert, E., Puebla, G.: On the generation of test data for prolog by partial evaluation. In: Proceedings of WLPE 2008, pp. 26–43 (2008)
7. Gómez-Zamalloa, M., Albert, E., Puebla, G.: Test case generation for object-oriented imperative languages in CLP. Theor. Pract. Logic Prog. 10(4–6), 659–674 (2010). ICLP 2010 Special Issue
8. Hamlet, D.: Random testing. In: Marciniak, J. (ed.) Encyclopedia of Software Engineering, pp. 970–978. Wiley, New York (1994)
9. Hanus, M.: CurryCheck: checking properties of curry programs. In: Hermenegildo, M.V., Lopez-Garcia, P. (eds.) LOPSTR 2016. LNCS, vol. 10184, pp. 222–239. Springer, Cham (2017). https://doi.org/10.1007/978-3-319-63139-4_13
10. Hennessy, M., Power, J.F.: An analysis of rule coverage as a criterion in generating minimal test suites for grammar-based software. In: 20th IEEE/ACM International Conference on Automated Software Engineering (ASE 2005), pp. 104–113, November 2005

11. Hermenegildo, M.V., et al.: An overview of ciao and its design philosophy. TPLP **12**(1–2), 219–252 (2012). http://arxiv.org/abs/1102.5497
12. Hermenegildo, M.V., Puebla, G., Bueno, F.: Using global analysis, partial specifications, and an extensible assertion language for program validation and debugging. In: Apt, K.R., Marek, V.W., Truszczynski, M., Warren, D.S. (eds.) The Logic Programming Paradigm: A 25-Year Perspective, pp. 161–192. Springer, Heidelberg (1999). https://doi.org/10.1007/978-3-642-60085-2_7
13. Hermenegildo, M.V., Puebla, G., Bueno, F., Lopez-Garcia, P.: Integrated program debugging, verification, and optimization using abstract interpretation (and the Ciao system preprocessor). Sci. Comput. Program. **58**(1–2), 115–140 (2005). https://doi.org/10.1016/j.scico.2005.02.006
14. Hughes, J.: QuickCheck testing for fun and profit. In: Hanus, M. (ed.) PADL 2007. LNCS, vol. 4354, pp. 1–32. Springer, Heidelberg (2006). https://doi.org/10.1007/978-3-540-69611-7_1
15. Jacobs, D., Langen, A.: Accurate and efficient approximation of variable aliasing in logic programs. In: North American Conference on Logic Programming (1989)
16. Mera, E., Lopez-García, P., Hermenegildo, M.: Integrating software testing and run-time checking in an assertion verification framework. In: Hill, P.M., Warren, D.S. (eds.) ICLP 2009. LNCS, vol. 5649, pp. 281–295. Springer, Heidelberg (2009). https://doi.org/10.1007/978-3-642-02846-5_25
17. Midtgaard, J., Møller, A.: QuickChecking static analysis properties. Softw. Test. Verif. Reliab. **27**(6) (2017). https://doi.org/10.1002/stvr.1640
18. Miller, B.P., Fredriksen, L., So, B.: An empirical study of the reliability of UNIX utilities. Commun. ACM **33**(12), 32–44 (1990). https://doi.org/10.1145/96267.96279
19. Muthukumar, K., Hermenegildo, M.: Combined determination of sharing and freeness of program variables through abstract interpretation. In: ICLP 1991, pp. 49–63. MIT Press (June 1991)
20. Papadakis, M., Sagonas, K.: A PropEr integration of types and function specifications with property-based testing. In: 10th ACM SIGPLAN Workshop On Erlang, pp. 39–50, September 2011
21. Puebla, G., Bueno, F., Hermenegildo, M.: Combined static and dynamic assertion-based debugging of constraint logic programs. In: Bossi, A. (ed.) LOPSTR 1999. LNCS, vol. 1817, pp. 273–292. Springer, Heidelberg (2000). https://doi.org/10.1007/10720327_16
22. Rastogi, A., Swamy, N., Fournet, C., Bierman, G., Vekris, P.: Safe & efficient gradual typing for typescript. In: 42nd POPL, pp. 167–180. ACM, January 2015
23. Schrijvers, T., Demoen, B., Triska, M., Desouter, B.: Tor: modular search with hookable disjunction. Sci. Comput. Program. **84**, 101–120 (2014)
24. Siek, J.G., Taha, W.: Gradual typing for functional languages. In: Scheme and Functional Programming Workshop, pp. 81–92 (2006)

Trace Analysis Using an Event-Driven Interval Temporal Logic

María-del-Mar Gallardo and Laura Panizo[✉]

Departamento de Lenguajes y Ciencias de la Computación, Universidad de Málaga,
Andalucía Tech, Campus de Teatinos s/n, 29071 Málaga, Spain
{gallardo,laurapanizo}@lcc.uma.es

Abstract. Nowadays, many critical systems can be characterized as hybrid ones, combining continuous and discrete behaviours that are closely related. Changes in the continuous dynamics are usually fired by internal or external discrete events. Due to their inherent complexity, it is a crucial but not trivial task to ensure that these systems satisfy some desirable properties. An approach to analyze them consists of the combination of model-based testing and run-time verification techniques. In this paper, we present an interval logic to specify properties of event-driven hybrid systems and an automatic transformation of the logic formulae into networks of finite-state machines. Currently, we use PROMELA/SPIN to implement the network of finite-state machines, and analyze non-functional properties of mobile applications. We use the TRIANGLE testbed, which implements a controllable network environment for testing, to obtain the application traces and monitor network parameters.

1 Introduction

In the last years, the improvement of sensor technology has led to the development of different software systems that monitor some physical magnitudes to control many everyday tasks. Water resource management systems [8], or aeronautics [9] are some examples of this type of systems. As it is well known, hybrid systems are composed of the so-called discrete and continuous components, which are strongly interrelated. Usually, the role of the discrete part is to control the continuous one, modifying its behaviour when necessary according to some system conditions. The continuous component may follow complex dynamics, which are usually represented by differential equations. The verification of critical properties on these systems is crucial since they may carry out critical tasks that affect the health of people or with a great economic impact. In the literature, hybrid automata constitute the best known mechanism to model hybrid systems. For example, tools like UPPAAL [2] focus on the verification by

This work has been supported by the Spanish Ministry of Science, Innovation and Universities project RTI2018-099777-B-I00 and the European Union's Horizon 2020 research and innovation programme under grant agreement No. 777517 (EuWireless).

© Springer Nature Switzerland AG 2020
M. Gabbrielli (Ed.): LOPSTR 2019, LNCS 12042, pp. 177–192, 2020.
https://doi.org/10.1007/978-3-030-45260-5_11

model checking of some hybrid automata subclasses (timed automata). However, not all hybrid systems can be easily represented as hybrid automata, not only because of their complex dynamics but also because of their interaction with an unpredictable environment. For this reason, in the last decades, other computational hybrid models have appeared such as *extended hybrid systems* [4] in which the hybrid systems are parameterized to incorporate the influence of the environment, or sampled-data control systems [12] in which the continuous and discrete components alternate their execution using a fixed time duration.

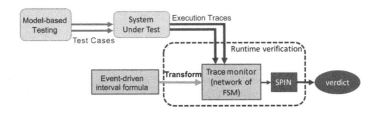

Fig. 1. Approach for testing event-driven hybrid systems

In a previous work [6], we proposed a framework to test event-driven hybrid systems using a combination of model-based testing (to automatically generate test cases) and runtime verification (to check the traces obtained against the desirable properties). The framework, shown in Fig. 1, was implemented in the context of the TRIANGLE project to analyze non-functional properties on traces produced by the execution of mobile applications. In this work, we implemented an ad-hoc trace monitoring system that was able to analyze some non-functional properties of interest.

In this paper, we concentrate on the trace analysis using runtime verification. In particular, we propose an event-driven linear temporal logic (eLTL) that allows us to extend the set of non-functional properties that can be specified and analyzed in the framework described above. The motivation for the definition of the new logic is twofold. On the one hand, we need a logic in which properties on monitored magnitudes are evaluated on time intervals determined by internal or external events that have occurred during the execution trace. For instance, in the context of mobile applications (apps), in a video streaming app, the video resolution can vary depending on network parameters (e.g. radio technology, signal strength, etc.). The exact moment when the video starts playing is a priori unknown, but during video playback, determined, for instance, by events vstart and vstop, different network and device parameters must be monitored to determine the suitable video resolution. On the other hand, we also need a logic whose formulae can be transformed into monitors that act as listeners of the trace events to dynamically evaluate the specified property. Thus, the contributions of the paper are both the definition of the event-driven linear time logic eLTL and the transformation of the logic formulae into finite-state machines (FSM) that act as observers of the execution traces. A preliminary version of the logic was presented in a Spanish workshop [7]. With respect to this former paper, the current version has been extended with a more formal presentation of the logic, and with the implementation section which is completely new.

The paper is organized as follows. Section 2 summarizes some work related to interval logics. Section 3 presents the syntax and semantics of the event-driven interval logic. We also show its expressiveness with some examples and briefly compare eLTL and LTL. Section 4 describes the transformation of each eLTL formula into a network of FSM and proves the correctness of the transformation. Finally, Sect. 5 gives the conclusions and future work. Appendices contain the proof of all the results presented in the paper, along with the current PROMELA implementation of the network of FSM which allows us to check the satisfaction of eLTL formulae on traces using SPIN [11].

2   Related Work

In Linear Temporal Logic (LTL) is not easy to express requirements to be held in a bounded future. Thus, the extension of LTL with *intervals* seems a natural idea to easily express these other type of properties. This is the approach followed in [20], where the authors use events to determine the intervals on which formulae must be evaluated, although they do not deal with real-time. The temporal logic FIL is also defined with similar purposes but the formulae are written using a graphical representation. Real-time FIL [19] is an extension of FIL that incorporates a new predicate $len(d_1, d_2]$ that bounds the length of the intervals on which properties have to be evaluated. In other context, the duration calculus [3] (DC) was defined to verify real-time systems. In DC system states have a *duration* in each time interval that can be measured taking into account the presence of the state in the interval. DC includes modalities (temporal operators) able to express relations between intervals and states, which constitute the basis of the logic.

The Metric Interval Logic (MITL) [1] is a real-time temporal logic that extends LTL by using modal operators of the form $\Box_I$, $\Diamond_I$ where I is an open/-close, bounded/unbounded interval of $\mathbb{R}$. $\text{MITL}_{[a,b]}$ [13] is a bounded version of MITL with all temporal modalities restricted to bounded intervals of the form $[a, b]$. $\text{MITL}_{[a,b]}$ formulae can be translated into deterministic timed automata. More recently, $\text{MITL}_{[a,b]}$ was extended to Signal Temporal Logic STL [14] including numerical predicates that allow analogue and mixed-signal properties to be specified. Lately, the MITL logic has been extended to xSTL [16] by adding *timed regular expressions* to express behaviour patterns to be met by signals.

Finally, the differential dynamic logic (dL) [18] is a specification language to describe safety and liveness properties of hybrid systems. In dL, formulae are of the form $[\alpha]\phi$ or $\langle\alpha\rangle\phi$ meaning that the behaviour of hybrid system α always (eventually) is inside the region defined by ϕ.

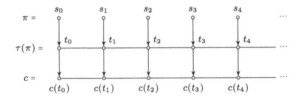

Fig. 2. Synchronization of trace π and continuous variable c using $\tau(\pi)$

3   Event-Driven Systems and Logic eLTL

In this section, we introduce a general model of event-driven hybrid systems, which is characterized by containing continuous variables whose values can be monitored. From a very abstract perspective, the behaviour of such a system may be given by a transition system $P = \langle \Sigma, \longmapsto, L, s_0 \rangle$ where Σ is a non-enumerable set of observable states, L is a finite set of labels, $\longmapsto \subseteq \Sigma \times L \times \Sigma$ is the transition relation, and $s_0 \in \Sigma$ is the initial state. Transitions labels represent the external/internal system events or system instructions that make the system evolve. In addition, we assume that $\iota \in L$ is an special label that represents the time passing between two successive states during which no event or instruction is executed. Thus, transitions may take place when an event arrives, when a system discrete instruction is carried out, or when a continuous transition occur in which the only change in the state is the passing of time.

We denote with $\mathcal{O}_f(P)$ the set of execution traces of finite length determined by P. The elements of $\mathcal{O}_f(P)$ are traces of the form $\pi = s_0 \overset{l_0}{\longmapsto} s_1 \overset{l_1}{\longmapsto} \cdots \overset{l_{n-2}}{\longmapsto} s_{n-1}$ where each $l_i \in L$ is the event/instruction/ι that fired the transition. The length of a trace $\pi = s_0 \overset{l_0}{\longmapsto} s_1 \overset{l_1}{\longmapsto} \cdots \overset{l_{n-2}}{\longmapsto} s_{n-1}$ is the number of its states n. Given a trace π of length n, we define the set $\mathcal{O}bs(\pi)$ of observable states of π; that is, $\mathcal{O}bs(\pi) = \{s_0, \cdots, s_{n-1}\}$. It is worth noting that although event-driven hybrid systems have continuous variables, we assume that their values are only visible at observable states. In addition, we assume that the time instant in which each state occurs is given by function $\tau : \Sigma \longrightarrow \mathbb{R}^{\geq 0}$ which relates each state s with the moment it happens $\tau(s) \in \mathbb{R}^{\geq 0}$.

In the following, given a trace π of length n and $t \in \{\tau(s_0), \cdots \tau(s_{n-1})\}$, we denote with $\langle \pi, t \rangle$ the observable state s_i of the trace at time instant t. In addition, we use function $\sigma : \{\tau(s_0), \cdots \tau(s_{n-1})\} \rightarrow \mathcal{O}bs(\pi)$ as the inverse function of τ, i.e., $\forall 0 \geq i < n.\tau(\sigma(t_i)) = t_i$ and $\sigma(\tau(s_i)) = s_i$.

Each continuous variable c of the system is a function $c : \mathbb{R}^{\geq 0} \longrightarrow \mathbb{R}$ that gives the value of c, $c(t)$, at each time instant t. Figure 2 shows the relation between the states in a trace, the time instants where they occur and the corresponding values of continuous variable c at these instants. By abuse of notation, in the figure and in the rest of the section, we use $\tau(\pi)$ to denote set $\{\tau(s_0), \cdots \tau(s_{n-1})\}$.

We have decided to define the behaviour of event-driven hybrid systems by means of the simple notion of transition systems on purpose. The definition is highly general in the sense that it is able to capture the behaviour of hybrid event-driven systems described by hybrid automata or other formalisms. Transitions correspond to changes of the system variables producing *observable states* in the traces that can be the result of the system that accepts an event or executes an instruction, or the result of an internal evolution ι where time passing is the only change in the trace. Anyway, the number of observable states in each trace is finite. In practice, in our current implementation, the time instants and the value of continuous variables in traces is recorded in log files, although other time models could also be managed by the logic presented below.

3.1   Syntax and Semantics of eLTL

We consider two types of state formulae to be analyzed on states of Σ. On the one hand, we have those that can be evaluated on single states as used in propositional linear temporal logic LTL, for instance. On the other hand, we assume that events of L are also state formulae that can be checked on states. Thus, let $\mathcal{F}$ be the set of all state formulae to be evaluated on elements of Σ. As usual, we suppose that state formulae may be constructed by combining state formulae and Boolean operators. Relation $\vdash \subseteq \Sigma \times \mathcal{F}$ associates each state with the state formulae it satisfies, that is, given $s \in \Sigma$, and $p \in \mathcal{F}$, $s \vdash p$ iff the state s satisfies the state formula p. In the following, given $\pi \in \mathcal{O}_f(P)$, $t_i \in \tau(\pi)$ and $p \in \mathcal{F}$, we write $\langle \pi, t_i \rangle \vdash p$ iff $\sigma(t_i) \vdash p$. When $l_i \in L$ is an event occurred at state s_i that evolves to s_{i+1} in trace $\pi = s_0 \xmapsto{l_0} s_1 \xmapsto{l_1} \cdots \xmapsto{l_{n-2}} s_{n-1}$, we assume that state s_{i+1} records the fact that l_i has just occurred and, in consequence, we have that $s_{i+1} \vdash l_i$, or equivalently, $\langle \pi, t_{i+1} \rangle \vdash l_i$. Other logics such as HML [10] or ACTL [5] focus on actions versus state formulae. We have decided to keep them at the same level to allow the use of both in the logic.

In order to analyze the behaviour of continuous variables, it is useful to observe them not only in a given time instant, but also during *time intervals* to know, for example, whether their values hold inside some expected limits or whether they never exceed a given threshold. To this end, we use *intervals of states* (inside the traces) to determine the periods of time during which continuous variables should be observed. Our proposal is inspired in the interval calculus introduced by [3], where the domain of interval logic is the set of time intervals $\mathbb{I}$ defined as $\{[t_1, t_2] | t_1, t_2 \in \mathbb{R}^{\geq 0}, t_1 \leq t_2\}$. Considering this, we define the so-called *interval formulae* as functions of the type $\phi : \mathbb{I} \to \{true, false\}$ to represent the formulae that describe the expected behaviour of continuous variables on time intervals. For instance, assume that $c : \mathbb{R}^{\geq 0} \to \mathbb{R}$ is a continuous variable of our system. Given a constant $K \in \mathbb{R}^{\geq 0}$, function $\phi_c : \mathbb{I} \to \{true, false\}$ given as $\phi_c([t_1, t_2]) = |c(t_2) - c(t_1)| < K$ defines an interval formula that is *true* on an interval $[t_1, t_2]$ iff the absolute value of difference between c in the interval endpoints t_1 and t_2 is less than K. Let us denote with Φ the set of interval formulae. We assume that Φ contains the special interval formula $True : \mathbb{I} \to \{true, false\}$ that returns *true* for all positive real intervals, that is, $\forall I \in \mathbb{I}. True(I) = true$.

In the following, given two state formulae $p, q \in \mathcal{F}$, we use expressions of the form $[p, q]$, that we call *event intervals*, to delimit intervals of states in traces.

Intuitively, given a trace $\pi = s_0 \xrightarrow{l_0} s_1 \xrightarrow{l_1} \cdots \xrightarrow{l_{n-2}} s_{n-1}$, $[p, q]$ represents time intervals $[t_i, t_j]$ with $t_i, t_j \in \tau(\pi)$ such that $\langle \pi, t_i \rangle \vdash p$ and $\langle \pi, t_j \rangle \vdash q$; that is, $s_i \vdash p$ and $s_j \vdash q$. We also consider simple state formulae p to denote states in π satisfying p. Now, we formally define relation $\Vdash$ that relates event intervals with intervals of states in traces.

Definition 1. *Given a trace $\pi \in \mathcal{O}_f(P)$, two state formulae $p, q \in \mathcal{F}$ and two time instants $t_p, t_q \in \tau(\pi)$ such as $t_p < t_q$, we say that the time interval $[t_p, t_q]$ satisfies the event interval $[p, q]$, and we denote it as $\pi \downarrow [t_p, t_q] \Vdash [p, q]$, iff the following four conditions hold: (1) $\langle \pi, t_p \rangle \vdash p$; (2) $\forall t_j \in (t_p, t_q) \cap \tau(\pi), \langle \pi, t_j \rangle \nvdash q$; (3) $\langle \pi, t_q \rangle \vdash q$; and (4) there exists no interval $[t'_p, t_q] \neq [t_p, t_q]$, verifying conditions 1–3 of this definition, such that $[t_p, t_q] \subset [t'_p, t_q]$.*

That is, $\pi \downarrow [t_p, t_q] \Vdash [p, q]$ iff $\sigma(t_p) = s_p$ satisfies p and $\sigma(t_q) = s_q$ is the first state following s_p that satisfies q. In addition, the fourth condition ensures that the interval of states from s_p until s_q is maximal in the sense that it is not possible to find a larger interval ending at s_q satisfying the previous conditions. This notion of maximality guarantees that the evaluation of interval formulae starts at the state when event p first occurs, although it could continue being true in some following states. In the previous definition, the time instants t_p and t_q must be different elements of $\tau(\pi)$, that is, $[t_p, t_q]$ cannot be a point.

Example 1. The following trace (π) tries to clarify Definition 1. Given $p, q \in \mathcal{F}$, and assuming that $\tau(s_i) = t_i$ for all states, we have that $\pi \downarrow [t_p, t_q] \Vdash [p, q]$, but $\pi \downarrow [t_r, t_q] \nVdash [p, q]$, since condition (4) does not hold.

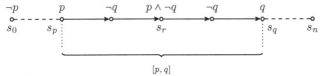

Definition 2 [eLTL formulae]. *Given $p, q \in \mathcal{F}$, and $\phi \in \Phi$, the formulae of eLTL logic are recursively constructed as follows:*

$$\psi ::= \phi \mid \neg\psi \mid \psi_1 \vee \psi_2 \mid \psi_1 \mathcal{U}_{[p,q]} \psi_2 \mid \psi_1 \mathcal{U}_p \psi_2$$

The rest of the temporal operators are accordingly defined as:
$$\Diamond_{[p,q]}\psi \equiv True\; \mathcal{U}_{[p,q]}\psi, \quad \Box_{[p,q]}\psi \equiv \neg(\Diamond_{[p,q]} \neg \psi),$$
$$\Diamond_p\psi \equiv True\; \mathcal{U}_p\psi, \quad \Box_p\psi \equiv \neg(\Diamond_p \neg \psi)$$

The following definition gives the semantics of eLTL formulae given above. Given a trace $\pi \in \mathcal{O}_f(P)$, and $t_i, t_f \in \tau(\pi)$ with $t_i \leq t_f$, we use $\langle \pi, t_i, t_f \rangle$ to represent the subtrace of π from state $s_i = \sigma(t_i)$ to state $s_f = \sigma(t_f)$.

Definition 3 (Semantics of eLTL formulae). *Given $p, q \in \mathcal{F}$, $\phi \in \Phi$, and the eLTL formulae ψ, ψ_1, ψ_2, the satisfaction relation $\models$ is defined as follows:*

$$\langle \pi, t_i, t_f \rangle \models \phi \qquad \textit{iff} \quad \phi([t_i, t_f]) \tag{3.1}$$

$$\langle \pi, t_i, t_f \rangle \models \neg\psi \qquad \textit{iff} \quad \langle \pi, t_i, t_f \rangle \neq \models \psi \tag{3.2}$$

$$\langle \pi, t_i, t_f \rangle \models \psi_1 \vee \psi_2 \qquad \textit{iff} \quad \langle \pi, t_i, t_f \rangle \models \psi_1 \textit{ or } \langle \pi, t_i, t_f \rangle \models \psi_2 \tag{3.3}$$

$$\langle \pi, t_i, t_f \rangle \models \psi_1 \mathcal{U}_{[p,q]} \psi_2 \qquad \textit{iff} \quad \exists I = [t_p, t_q] \subseteq [t_i, t_f] \textit{ such that } \pi \downarrow [t_p, t_q] \tag{3.4}$$
$$[p, q] \, and \, \langle \pi, t_i, t_p \rangle \models \psi_1, \langle \pi, t_p, t_q \rangle \models \psi_2$$

$$\langle \pi, t_i, t_f \rangle \models \psi_1 \mathcal{U}_p \psi_2 \qquad \textit{iff} \quad \exists t_p. \; t_i \leq t_p \leq t_f \textit{ and } \langle \pi, t_i, t_p \rangle \models \psi_1, \langle \pi, t_p, t_p \rangle \models \psi_2 \tag{3.5}$$

The semantics given by $\models$ is similar to that of LTL, except that $\models$ manages interval formulae instead of state formulae. For instance, case 3.1 states that the subtrace $\langle \pi, t_i, t_f \rangle$ of π satisfies an interval formula ϕ iff $\phi([t_i, t_f])$ holds. Case 3.4 establishes that $\mathcal{U}_{[p,q]}$ holds on the subtrace $\langle \pi, t_i, t_f \rangle$ iff there exists an interval $[t_p, t_q] \subset [t_i, t_f]$ such that ψ_1 and ψ_2 hold on $[t_i, t_p]$ and $[t_p, t_q]$, respectively. Case 3.5 is similar except for the interval in which ψ_2 has to be true is $[t_p, t_p]$, which represents the time instant t_p.

Proposition 1. *The semantics of operators $\square_{[p,q]}, \diamondsuit_{[p,q]}, \square_p$ and $\diamondsuit_p$, given in Definition 2, is the following:*

$$\langle \pi, t_i, t_f \rangle \models \diamondsuit_{[p,q]} \psi \quad \textit{iff} \quad \exists I = [t_p, t_q] \subseteq [t_i, t_f], \textit{ such that } \pi \downarrow [t_p, t_q] \Vdash [p, q] \tag{3.6}$$
$$and \, \langle \pi, t_p, t_q \rangle \models \psi$$

$$\langle \pi, t_i, t_f \rangle \models \square_{[p,q]} \psi \quad \textit{iff} \quad \forall I = [t_p, t_q] \subseteq [t_i, t_f], \textit{ if } \pi \downarrow [t_p, t_q] \Vdash [p, q] \textit{ then} \tag{3.7}$$
$$\langle \pi, t_p, t_q \rangle \models \psi$$

$$\langle \pi, t_i, t_f \rangle \models \diamondsuit_p \psi \quad \textit{iff} \quad \exists t_p \in [t_i, t_f] \textit{ such that } \langle \pi, t_p \rangle \vdash p \tag{3.8}$$
$$and \, \langle \pi, t_p, t_p \rangle \models \psi$$

$$\langle \pi, t_i, t_f \rangle \models \square_p \psi \quad \textit{iff} \quad \forall t_p \in [t_i, t_f] \textit{ if } \langle \pi, t_p \rangle \vdash p \textit{ then } \langle \pi, t_p, t_p \rangle \models \psi \tag{3.9}$$

3.2   Examples

We now give some examples to show the use of the logic. In [6,17], we proposed a model-based testing approach to test mobile applications (apps) under different network scenarios. We automatically generated app user flows, that is, different interactions of the user with the app, using model-based testing techniques.

Then, we executed these app user flows in the TRIANGLE testbed, which provides a controlled mobile network environment, to obtain measurements and execution traces in order to evaluate the performance of the apps.

In this section, we make use of eLTL to describe desirable properties regarding to the values of continuous variables of the ExoPlayer app, a video streaming mobile app that implements different adaptive video streaming protocols. Using the current implementation of the eLTL operators, and with the execution traces provided by the evaluation presented in [17], we can determine if the execution traces of ExoPlayer satisfy the properties. The execution traces of the app contain the following events: the start of video playback (*stt*), the load of the first complete picture (*fp*), the end of the video playback (*stp*), and the changes in the video resolution (*low*, *high*). In addition, the TRIANGLE testbed measures every second (approximately) the amount and rate of transmitted and received data, as well as different parameters of the network (e.g. signal strength and signal quality) and the device (e.g. RAM, CPU and radio technology).

Property 1: We can write the property *"during video playback, the first picture must be loaded at least once in all network conditions"* which may be specified using the formula $\Box_{[stt,stp]} \Diamond_{fp}$ *True*. The following trace satisfies this property, where the expressions over each state represent the state formulae it holds.

$$
\begin{array}{cccccccc}
\neg stt & stt & \neg stp \wedge fp & \neg stp & stp & stt & \neg stp \wedge fp & stp \\
s_0 & s_{stt} & s_{fp} & & s_{stp} & s'_{stt} & s'_{fp} & s'_{stp} \quad s_{n-1}
\end{array}
$$

Property 2: We can also specify the property *"during video playback, if the video resolution is high, the average received data rate is greater than 5 Mbps, and if the video resolution is low the average data rate is below 1Mbps."* The video resolution is high in the time interval between h and l events. Similarly, the video resolution is low between the events l and h. The eLTL formula is

$$\Box_{[stt,stp]}(\Box_{[high,low]}\phi_1 \wedge \Box_{[low,high]}\phi_2)$$

where ϕ_1 and ϕ_2 are defined as: $\phi_1([t_i, t_f]) = RxRate(t_i, t_f) \geq 5\,\text{Mbps}$ and $\phi_2([t_i, t_f]) = RxRate(t_i, t_f) \leq 1\,\text{Mbps}$.

This formula uses function $RxRate(t_i, t_f)$ that accesses to the file of the trace and workouts the average in the corresponding time interval. In the current implementation on SPIN, it is calculated using PROMELA embedded C code.

Property 3: The eLTL formula for property *"during video playback, if the video resolution changes from High to Low, the peak signal strength (rssi) is less than -45 dBm"* can be written as:

$$\Box_{[stt,stp]}(\Box_{[high,low]}\phi), \quad where \quad \phi([t_i, t_f]) = \begin{cases} true & if \ \exists t \in [t_i, t_f], \\ & maxRSSI(t) \leq -45\,dBm \\ false & otherwise \end{cases}$$

Using this formula with different thresholds for the peak rssi, we can determine whether the adaptive protocols take into consideration the signal strength in the terminal to make a decision and change the video resolution.

Other Examples. In the health field, eLTL can also be useful. For instance, patients with type 1 diabetics should be monitored to assure that their glucose levels are always inside safe limits. Related to this problem, we could describe different properties of interest. Given the interval formula $\psi_K([t_1, t_2]) = t_2 - t_1 \geq K$ with $K \in \mathbb{R}$, and events *sleep, awake, run, end, break, endBreak, drink* and *over* 70 that denote when the patient goes to sleep, awakes, starts running, stops running, drinks and his/her glucose level is over 70 mg/l:

– Property *"while sleeping, the glucose level is never below* 70 mg/l*"* can be expressed as $\square_{[sleep, awake]} \square_{true}$ *over* 70. Observe that in this property *over* 70 acts as a simple interval formulae that holds on each state inside [*sleep, awake*] iff the glucose level is over 70.
– Property *"if the patient is running more than* 60 min*, he/she has to make a stop of more than* 5 min *to drink"* can be written as

$$\square_{[run, end]}(\psi_{60} \rightarrow (\Diamond_{[break, endBreak]}(\psi_5 \wedge \Diamond_{drink} True)))$$

3.3   Comparison with LTL

In this section, we briefly compare the expressiveness of logics LTL and eLTL. One important difference between both logics is that LTL is evaluated on infinite traces while, on the contrary, eLTL deals with finite traces. This makes some LTL properties hard to specify in eLTL. In addition, eLTL is thought to analyze extra-functional properties on traces, that is, properties that refer to the behaviour of certain magnitudes in subtraces (as in the examples presented above), which cannot easily be expressed in LTL. The context where eLTL formulae are checked is determined by the event intervals $[p, q]$ associated to the modal operators. However, this context is implicit in LTL since formulae are evaluated on the whole infinite trace. In conclusion, we can say that although both logic have similarities, they are different regarding expressiveness. The following table shows some usual patterns of LTL formulae with its corresponding eLTL versions. The inverse transformation is not so easy. For instance, eLTL formula $\square_{[a,b]} \Diamond_p True$, which forces that p occurs between each pair of a and b events, is hard to write in LTL. In the table, we use interval formulae ϕ_p ($p \in \mathcal{F}$) defined as $\phi_p([t_i, t_f]) = \sigma(t_i) \vdash p$. In addition, $a, b, q \in \mathcal{F}$ are events used to delimit finite subtraces.

LTL	eLTL	Comments
$\Diamond p$	$\Diamond_p True$	In both cases, p has to be *true* eventually, but in eLTL, p must be *true* inside of the finite trace.
$\Box p$	$\Box_{true}\phi_p$	in both cases, p has to be always *true*, but in eLTL It is limited to the states of the finite trace.
$\Box\Diamond p$	$\Box_{[a,b]}\Diamond_p\ True$	In LTL, p has to be *true* infinitely often. In eLTL, p has to Occur always inside the subtraces determined by $[a,b]$.
$\Diamond\Box p$	$\Diamond_{[a,b]}\Box_{true}\ \phi_p$	The LTL formula says that p has to be always *true* from some unspecified state. The eLTL says the same, but limited by the extreme states of the finite trace $[a,b]$.
$p\,\mathcal{U}q$	$(\Box_{true}\phi_p)\mathcal{U}_q\ True$	In this case, the LTL formula is clearly easier to write, since eLTL is thought to evaluate magnitudes on subtraces.
$(\Diamond p)\mathcal{U}q$	$(\Diamond_p\ True)\mathcal{U}_q\ True$	the LTL formula could be *true* even if p occur after p in the trace. However, in the eLTL version, p has to occur *before* p.

4 Implementation

In this section, we describe the translation of eLTL formulae into a network of state machines $\mathcal{M}$ that check the satisfiability of the property on execution traces. As described in Sect. 3, formulae are evaluated against time bounded traces π that execute in time intervals of the form $[t_i, t_f]$. Formulae can include nested temporal operators whose evaluation can be restricted to subintervals. The implementation described below assumes that traces are analyzed *offline*, i.e., given a particular trace, for each state, we have stored the time instant when it occurred and the set of state formulae of $\mathcal{F}$ which it satisfies. In consequence, we can use the trace to build a simple state machine $\mathcal{T}$ that runs concurrently with the network of machines $\mathcal{M}$. $\mathcal{T}$ sends to $\mathcal{M}$ events to start and finalize the analysis, and also the events included in the formula which are of interest for the correct execution of the network.

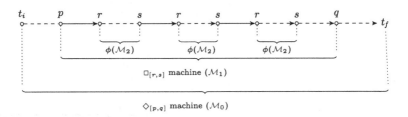

Fig. 3. Example of a network of state machines

We use an example to intuitively explain how the network of machines $\mathcal{M}$ is constructed. Assume we want to evaluate $\langle\pi, t_i, t_f\rangle \vDash \Diamond_{[p,q]}\Box_{[r,s]}\ \phi$. The outer operator $\Diamond_{[p,q]}$ must find the different time intervals $[t_p, t_q] \subseteq [t_i, t_f]$, delimited by events p and q, to check if there exists at least one satisfying the sub-formula $\Box_{[r,s]}\phi$. Similarly, given one of the time intervals $[t_p, t_q]$, the inner operator $\Box_{[r,s]}$

has to find all time intervals $[t_r, t_s] \subseteq [t_p, t_q]$, determined by events r and s, to check whether ϕ holds in all of them.

The network $\mathcal{M}$ is composed of the parallel composition of *finite-state machines*, each one monitoring a different sub-formula. The network is hierarchized, that is, each state machine communicates through channels with the trace $\mathcal{T}$ being analysed and with the state machine of the formula in which it is nested. The state machine of the outer eLTL temporal operator starts and ends the evaluation, reporting the analysis result to $\mathcal{T}$. Each state machine has a unique identifier id which allows it to access the different input/output channels. Thus, channel cm[id] is a synchronous channel through which the state machine id is started and stopped. Channel rd[id] is used by machine id to send the result of its evaluation. Finally, ev[id] is an asynchronous channel through which each state machine receives from $\mathcal{T}$ the events in which it is interested along with the time instant they have occurred ([t_e,e]).

Figure 3 gives an intuition about how the network of state machines of the example is constructed. The network of the example is composed by three state machines $\mathcal{M}_0 \| \mathcal{M}_1 \| \mathcal{M}_2$. $\mathcal{M}_0$ is the highest level state machine that monitors operator $\Diamond_{[p,q]}$. Thus, it should receive from $\mathcal{T}$ events p and q each time they occur in the trace. Similarly, $\mathcal{M}_1$ monitors $\Box_{[r,s]}$, and it should be informed when events r or s occur. Finally, $\mathcal{M}_2$ is devoted to checking ϕ. It is worth noting that all machines are initially active, although they are blocked until the reception of the start message STT. Machine $\mathcal{A}_0$ is started when $\mathcal{T}$ begins its execution. Each machine id receives the start and stop messages STT and STP though channel cm[id]. Events arrive to machine id via channel ev[id] and it returns the result of its evaluation (*true* or *false*) using channel rd[id]. In the example, when $\mathcal{M}_0$ receives event p, it sends a STT message to the nested machine $\mathcal{M}_1$. Similarly, when $\mathcal{M}_1$ receives event r, it sends message STT to $\mathcal{M}_2$. Each time $\mathcal{M}_1$ receives event s sends STP to $\mathcal{M}_2$. When $\mathcal{M}_2$ receives STP, it ends its execution, evaluates the interval formula and sends the result through channel rd[2]. Similarly, when $\mathcal{M}_0$ receives event q via channel ev[0], it sends STP to $\mathcal{M}_1$. When a machine receives STP, it *tries* to finish its execution immediately. But, before stopping, it has to process all the events stored in its ev channel since they could have occurred before the STP were sent. To know this, each message contains a timestamp with the time instant when the event took place. This is needed since events and STP are sent via different channels. Thus, it is possible for a machine to read STP before reading a previous event in the trace.

Finite-State Machine Templates. We now show finite-state machines *templates* that implement eLTL operators. In these machines, id refers to the state machine being implemented, and c1, c2 are, respectively, the identifiers of the state machines of the first and the second nested operators, if they exist. All machines described below follow the same pattern. First, each machine starts after receiving message STT, and initiates its sub-machines, if necessary. Then, it continues processing the input events in which it is interested. These events are directly sent from the instrumented trace $\mathcal{T}$ that is being monitored. When the

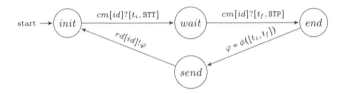

Fig. 4. State machine of an interval formulae

machine receives STP, it returns the result of its evaluation via channel rd. To simplify the diagrams, we have used sometimes guarded transitions of the form $G|Action$. When guard G is a message reception via a synchronous channel, it is executable iff it is possible to read the message and, as a side effect, the message is extracted from the channel. Due to lack of space, we have not included operator $\mathcal{U}_p$ since its machine is a simplified version of that of $\mathcal{U}_{[p,q]}$.

Interval formula (ϕ): Figure 4 shows the state machine for an interval formula ϕ without eLTL operators. An interval formula is evaluated on a time interval $[t_i, t_f]$ that is communicated to the process via the channel cm[id] with messages [t_i,STT] and [t_f,STP]. After detecting the interval end, the state machine evaluates the expression $\phi([t_i, t_f])$ and sends the result to the parent machine through rd[id].

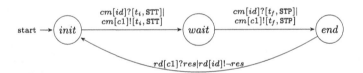

Fig. 5. State machine of the *not* operator

Negation ($\neg\psi$): Figure 5 shows the negation operator. The state machine synchronizes with the machine of its nested formula (ψ) as soon as it receives the STT and STP commands. Observe that, in this case, to simplify the diagram, we have used guarded transitions. When the nested machine finishes, the machine negates the result and returns it through the rd channel.

Or ($\psi_1 \vee \psi_2$): Figure 6 shows the state machine of the *or* operator. This machine checks if any of the two sub-formulae ψ_1 and ψ_2 holds on the same interval $[t_i, t_f]$ over which the *or* operator is being evaluated. Similarly to the NOT machine, this machine waits the successive reception of the STT and STP messages and resends them to the machines of its sub-formulae to start and stop them.

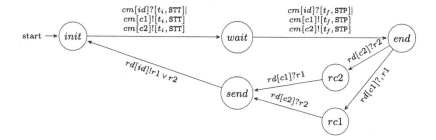

Fig. 6. State machine for *or* operator

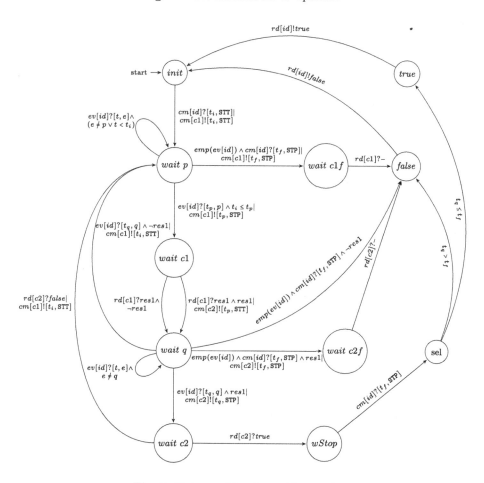

Fig. 7. State machine for *until* operator

Until ($\psi_1 U_{[p,q]}\psi_2$): Figure 7 shows the state machine template of the *until* operator. As can be observed, it is much more complex than the previous templates. Assuming that the whole formula is evaluated on interval $[t_i, t_f]$, the first subformula ψ_1 must be true on an interval $[t_i, t_p]$ (t_p being a time instant when event p has occurred), and the second one ψ_2 must be true on the time interval $[t_p, t_q]$ (t_q being the time instant when event q has first occurred after p). The machine id starts accepting the message STT from its parent and, then, it resends the message to the state machine of ψ_1. In state wait p, the machine is waiting for the p event to occur or for the STP message to arrive. If p arrives at a correct time instant (after t_i), the machine sends STP to machine c1 and waits for its result in state wait c1. If ψ_1 is not valid in the interval $[t_i, t_p]$, machine id records *false* in variable res1 and waits in state wait q the following event q, then it transits to wait p and restarts machine c1. This is because machine id has found that formula does not hold on a time interval determined by the occurrence of p and q and, in consequence, it starts searching for the following interval given by $[p, q]$ in the trace. Otherwise, if ψ_1 holds on $[t_i, t_p]$, machine id sends STT to machine c2 and waits for its result in state wait c2. In this state, machine id behaves in a similar way as in state wait p. If c2 returns *false*, it restarts again machine c1 and goes back to state wait p to search for the following time interval determined by events p and q. Conversely, if c2 returns *true*, machine id waits for message STP to send its result. Note that it only sends *true* if event q has occurred before the end of the interval t_f. Otherwise, the machine returns *false*, since ψ_2 could not be evaluated in time. Observe that in states wait p and wait q, message STP is only accepted when the event channel is empty (emp(ev[id])). This is to prioritize reading events p and q before STP and simplify the implementation.

Theorem 1. *Let f be an eLTL formula, and $\mathcal{M}_{id}$ the network of state machines implementing f, then given a finite trace $\langle \pi, t_i, t_f \rangle$, $\langle \pi, t_i, t_f \rangle \vDash f$ if and only if $\mathcal{M}_{id}$ finishes its execution by sending true via channel rd[id] (rd[id] ! true).*

5   Conclusions

In this paper, we have presented an event-driven interval logic (eLTL) suitable for describing properties in terms of time intervals determined by trace events. We have transformed each eLTL formula into network of finite state machines to evaluate it using runtime verification procedures, and have proved the correctness of the transformation. We have constructed a prototype implementation of these machines in PROMELA to be executed on SPIN.

Our final goal is to apply the approach to analyze execution traces of real systems against extra-functional properties, such as evaluating the performance of mobile apps in different network scenarios [17]. Currently, the transformation from eLTL formula into PROMELA code, and the transformation of the traces are manually done, although the automatic transformation will be carried out in the near future. We also plan to use the approach in other domains such as the

EuWireless project [15]. This project is designing an architecture to dynamically create network slices to run experiments. In this context, it is of great importance to monitor the different network slices and the underlying infrastructure to ensure safety (e.g. isolation of slices) and extra-functional properties related to performance and quality of service.

References

1. Alur, R., Feder, T., Henzinger, T.A.: The benefits of relaxing punctuality. J. ACM **43**(1), 116–146 (1996)
2. Behrmann, G., David, A., Larsen, K.G.: A Tutorial on UPPAAL. In: Bernardo, M., Corradini, F. (eds.) SFM-RT 2004. LNCS, vol. 3185, pp. 200–236. Springer, Heidelberg (2004). https://doi.org/10.1007/978-3-540-30080-9_7
3. Chaochen, Z., Hansen, M.R.: Duration Calculus - A Formal Approach to Real-Time Systems. Monographs in TCS. EATCS Series. Springer, Heidelberg (2004). https://doi.org/10.1007/978-3-662-06784-0
4. Dang, T., Nahhal, T.: Coverage-guided test generation for continuous and hybrid systems. Form. Methods Syst. Des. **34**(2), 183–213 (2009)
5. De Nicola, R., Vaandrager, F.: Action versus state based logics for transition systems. In: Guessarian, I. (ed.) LITP 1990. LNCS, vol. 469, pp. 407–419. Springer, Heidelberg (1990). https://doi.org/10.1007/3-540-53479-2_17
6. Espada, A.R., Gallardo, M.M., Salmeron, A., Panizo, L., Merino, P.: A formal approach to automatically analyze extra-functional properties in mobile applications. Soft. Test. Verif. Rel. (2019). https://doi.org/10.1002/stvr.1699
7. Gallardo, M.M., Panizo, L.: An event-driven interval temporal logic for hybrid systems. In: Actas de las XVIII Jornadas de Programación y Lenguajes (PROLE 2018). (Work in progress)
8. Gallardo, M.M., Merino, P., Panizo, L., Linares, A.: A practical use of model checking for synthesis: generating a dam controller for flood management. Softw. Pract. Experience **41**(11), 1329–1347 (2011)
9. Goodloe, A.E., Muñoz, C., Kirchner, F., Correnson, L.: Verification of Numerical Programs: From Real Numbers to Floating Point Numbers. In: Brat, G., Rungta, N., Venet, A. (eds.) NFM 2013. LNCS, vol. 7871, pp. 441–446. Springer, Heidelberg (2013). https://doi.org/10.1007/978-3-642-38088-4_31
10. Hennessy, M., Milner, R.: On observing nondeterminism and concurrency. In: de Bakker, J., van Leeuwen, J. (eds.) ICALP 1980. LNCS, vol. 85, pp. 299–309. Springer, Heidelberg (1980). https://doi.org/10.1007/3-540-10003-2_79
11. Holzmann, G.: The model checker SPIN. IEEE Trans. Software Eng. **23**(5), 279–295 (1997)
12. Lerda, F., Kapinski, J., Maka, H., Clarke, E.M., Krogh, B.H.: Model checking in-the-loop: finding counterexamples by systematic simulation. In: 2008 American Control Conference, pp. 2734–2740 (2008)
13. Maler, O., Nickovic, D., Pnueli, A.: Real Time Temporal Logic: Past, Present, Future. In: Pettersson, P., Yi, W. (eds.) FORMATS 2005. LNCS, vol. 3829, pp. 2–16. Springer, Heidelberg (2005). https://doi.org/10.1007/11603009_2
14. Maler, O., Ničković, D.: Monitoring properties of analog and mixed-signal circuits. STTT **15**(3), 247–268 (2013)
15. Merino, P., Panizo, L., Díaz, A., et al.: EuWireless: design of a pan-European mobile network operator for research. In: European Conference on Networks and Communications (EuCNC2018), pp. 392–393 (2018)

16. Ničković, D., Lebeltel, O., Maler, O., Ferrère, T., Ulus, D.: AMT 2.0: qualitative and quantitative trace analysis with extended signal temporal logic. In: 24th International Conference of TACAS, pp. 303–319 (2018)
17. Panizo, L., Díaz-Zayas, A., García, B.: Model-based testing of apps in real network scenarios. STTT, 1–10 (2019)
18. Platzer, A.: A temporal dynamic logic for verifying hybrid system invariants. In: Artemov, S.N., Nerode, A. (eds.) LFCS 2007. LNCS, vol. 4514, pp. 457–471. Springer, Heidelberg (2007). https://doi.org/10.1007/978-3-540-72734-7_32
19. Ramakrishna, Y., Melliar-Smith, P., Moser, L., Dillon, L., Kutty, G.: Interval logics and their decision procedures: Part ii: a real-time interval logic. Theoret. Comput. Sci. **170**(1), 1–46 (1996)
20. Schwartz, R.L., Melliar-Smith, P.M., Vogt, F.H.: An interval logic for higher-level temporal reasoning. In: Proceedings of the 2nd Annual ACM Symposium on Principles of Distributed Computing. PODC 1983, pp. 173–186 (1983)

The Prolog Debugger and Declarative Programming

Włodzimierz Drabent[1,2]([⊠]) [iD]

[1] Institute of Computer Science, Polish Academy of Sciences, Warsaw, Poland
drabent@ipipan.waw.pl
[2] IDA, Linköping University, Linköping, Sweden

Abstract. Logic programming is a declarative programming paradigm. Programming language Prolog makes logic programming possible, at least to a substantial extent. However the Prolog debugger works solely in terms of the operational semantics. So it is incompatible with declarative programming. This report discusses this issue and tries to find how the debugger may be used from the declarative point of view. The results are rather not encouraging. Also, the box model of Byrd, used by the debugger, is explained in terms of SLD-resolution.

Keywords: Declarative diagnosis/Algorithmic debugging · Prolog · Declarative programming · Program correctness · Program completeness

1 Introduction

The idea of logic programming is that a program is a set of logic formulae, and a computation means producing logical consequences of the program. So it is a *declarative* programming paradigm. The program is not a description of any computation, it may be rather seen as a description of a problem to solve. Answers of a given program (the *logic*) may be computed under various strategies (the *control*), the results depend solely on the former. This semantics of programs, based on logic, is called *declarative semantics*.

Programming language Prolog is a main implementation of logic programming. Its core, which may be called "pure Prolog", is an implementation of SLD-resolution under a fixed control. (SLD-resolution with Prolog selection rule is called LD-resolution.) For a given program P and query Q, Prolog computes logical consequences of P which are instances of Q. If the computation is finite then, roughly speaking, all such consequences are computed[1].

On the other hand, Prolog may be viewed without any reference to logic, as a programming language with a specific control flow, the terms as the data, and

---

[1] See e.g. [1] for details. We omit the issue of unification without occur-check; it may lead to incorrect answers (i.e. not being logical consequences of the program). Technically, by an answer of a program we mean the result of applying a (correct or computed) answer substitution to a query.

© Springer Nature Switzerland AG 2020
M. Gabbrielli (Ed.): LOPSTR 2019, LNCS 12042, pp. 193–208, 2020.
https://doi.org/10.1007/978-3-030-45260-5_12

a certain kind of term matching as the main primitive operation. Such a view is even necessary when we deal with non logical features of full Prolog, like the built-ins dealing with input/output. Of course such *operational view* loses all the advantages of declarative programming.

In the author's opinion, Prolog makes declarative programming possible in practice. A Prolog program treated as a set of logical clauses is a logic program. The logic determines the answers of the program. At a lower level, the programmer can influence the control. This can be done by setting the order of program clauses and the order of premises within a clause (and by some additional Prolog constructs). Changing the control keeps the logic intact, and thus the program's answers are unchanged; the logic is separated from the control [9]. What is changed is the way they are computed, for instance the computation may be made more efficient. In particular, an infinite computation may be changed into a finite one.

In some cases, programs need to contain some non-logical fragments, for instance for input-output. But the practice shows that Prolog makes possible building programs which are to a substantial extent declarative; in other words, a substantial part of such program is a logic program. Numerous examples are given in the textbooks, for instance [14]. For a more formal discussion of this issue see [6].

It should be noted that the operational, low-level approach to Prolog programming is often overused. In such programs it is not the declarative semantics that matters. A typical example is the red cut [14] – a programming technique which is based on pruning the search space; the program has undesired logical consequences, which are however not computed due to the pruning. Understanding such program substantially depends on its operational semantics. And understanding the operational semantics is usually more difficult than that of the declarative semantics. In particular, examples of programs with the red cut are known, for which certain choices of the initial query lead to unexpected results [14, p. 202–203], [3, Chapter 4]. In seems that some Prolog textbooks over-use such style of programming (like [2,3], at least in their earlier editions).

Debugging Tools of Prolog. We begin with a terminological comment. Often the term "debugging" is related to locating errors in programs. However its meaning is wider; it also includes correcting errors. So a better term for locating errors is *diagnosis*. However this text still does not reject the first usage, as it is quite common.

Despite Prolog has been designed mainly as an implementation of logic programming, its debugging tools work solely in terms of the operational semantics. So all the advantages of declarative programming are lost when it comes to locating errors in a program. The Prolog debugger is basically a tracing tool. It communicates with the programmer only in terms of the operational semantics. She (the programmer) must abandon the convenient high abstraction level of the declarative semantics and think about her program in operational terms.

Declarative Diagnosis. In principle, it is well known how to locate errors in logic programs declaratively, i.e. abstracting from the operational semantics (see e.g. [4, Section 7] and the references therein). The approach is called *declarative diagnosis* (and was introduced under a name *algorithmic debugging* by Shapiro [13]). Two kinds of errors of the declarative semantics of a program are dealt with: *incorrectness* – producing results which are wrong according to the specification, and *incompleteness* – not producing results which are required by the specification. We learn about an error by encountering a *symptom* – a wrong or missing answer obtained at program testing. Given a symptom, an incorrectness (respectively incompleteness) diagnosis algorithm semi-automatically locates an error in the program, asking the user some queries about the specification.

Unfortunately, declarative diagnosis was not adapted in practice. No tools for it are included in current Prolog systems.

Intended Model Problem. A possibly main reason for lack of acceptance of declarative diagnosis was discussed in [4, Section 7]. Namely, declarative diagnosis requires that the programmer exactly knows the relations to be defined by the program. Formally this means that the programmer knows the least Herbrand model of the intended program. (In other words, the least Herbrand model is the specification.) This requirement turns out to be unrealistic. For instance, in an insertion sort program we do not know how inserting an element into an unsorted list should be performed. This can be done in any way, as the algorithm inserts elements only into sorted lists. Moreover, this can be done differently in various versions of the program. See [6] for a more realistic example[2]. Let us call this difficulty *intended model problem.*

Usually the programmer knows the intended least Herbrand model of her program only approximately. She has an *approximate specification*: she knows a certain superset S_{corr} and a certain subset S_{compl} of the intended model. The superset tells what may be computed, and the subset – what must be computed. Let us call the former, S_{corr}, the *specification for correctness* and the latter, S_{compl}, the *specification for completeness.* Thus the program should be correct with respect to the former specification and complete with respect to the latter: $S_{compl} \subseteq M_P \subseteq S_{corr}$ (where M_P is the least Herbrand model of the program). In our example, it is irrelevant how an element is inserted into an unsorted list; thus the specification for correctness would include all such possible insertions (and the specification for completeness would include none).

Now it is obvious that when diagnosing incorrectness the programmer should use the specification for correctness instead of the intended model, and the specification for completeness should be used when diagnosing incompleteness [4]. The author believes that this approach can make declarative diagnosis useful in practice.

---

[2] In the main example of [6], the semantics of a particular predicate differs at various steps of program development.

Intended model problem was possibly first noticed by Pereira [12]. He introduced the notion of *inadmissible* atomic queries. A formal definition is not given[3]. We may suppose that ground inadmissible atoms are those from $S_{corr} \setminus S_{compl}$. Generally, this notion is not declarative; an inadmissible atom seems to be one that should not appear as a selected atom in an LD-tree of the program.

Naish [11] proposed a 3-valued diagnosis scheme. The third value, *inadmissible*, is related to the search space of a diagnosis algorithm, and to its queries. The form of queries depends on the particular algorithm, e.g. it may be an atom together with its computed answers. So the third value is not (directly) related to the declarative semantics of programs. It turns out that applying the scheme to incorrectness diagnosis ([11, Section 5.1]) boils down to standard diagnosis w.r.t. S_{corr}, and applying it to incompleteness diagnosis ([11, Section 5.2]) – to the standard diagnosis w.r.t. S_{compl} (where S_{compl} is the set of correct atoms, and S_{corr} is the set of correct or inadmissible ones). So introducing the 3-valued scheme seems unnecessary (at least for incorrectness and incompleteness diagnosis).

This Paper. The role of this paper is to find if, how, and to which extent the Prolog debugger can be used as a tool for declarative logic programming. We focus on the debugger of SICStus Prolog. We omit its advanced debugging features, which are sophisticated, but seem not easy to learn and not known by most of programmers.

The paper is organized as follows. The next section deals with the Prolog debugger and the information it can provide. Section 3 discusses applying the debugger for diagnosing incorrectness and incompleteness. The last section contains conclusions.

2   Prolog Debugger

In this section we present the Prolog debugger and try to find out how to use it to obtain the information necessary from the point of view of declarative programming. First we relate the computation model used by the debugger to the standard operational semantics (LD-resolution). We also formalize the information needed for incorrectness and incompleteness diagnoses. For incorrectness diagnosis, given an atomic answer A we need to know which clause $H \leftarrow B_1, \ldots, B_n$ have been used to obtain the answer A (A is an instance of H), and which top-level atomic answers (instances of $B_1, \ldots, B_n$) have been involved. For incompleteness diagnosis, the related information is which answers have been computed for each selected instance of each body atom B_i of each clause $H \leftarrow B_1, \ldots, B_n$ resolved with a given atomic query A. In Sect. 2.2 we describe the messages of the debugger. Section 2.3 investigates how to extract from the debugger's output the information of interest.

---

[3] "a goal is admissible if it complies with the intended use of the procedure for it – i.e. it has the correct argument types – irrespective of whether the goal succeeds or not" (p. 6 of the extended version of [12]).

2.1   Byrd Box Model and LD-Resolution

The debugger refers to the operational semantics of Prolog in terms of a "Byrd box model". Roughly speaking, the model assigns four ports to each atom selected in LD-resolution. From a programmer's point of view such atom can be called a procedure call. The model is usually easily understood by programmers. However it will be useful to relate it here to LD-resolution, and to introduce some additional notions. In this paper, we often skip "LD-" and by "derivation" we mean "LD-derivation" (unless stated otherwise).

Structuring LD-derivations. Let us consider a (finite or infinite) LD-derivation D with queries $Q_0, Q_1, Q_2 \ldots$, the input clauses $C_1, C_2, \ldots$, and the mgu's $\theta_1, \theta_2, \ldots$. By a **procedure call** of D we mean the atom selected in a query of D. Following [5,7], we describe a fragment of D which may be viewed as the evaluation of a given procedure call A.

Definition 1. Consider a query $Q_{k-1} = A, B_1, \ldots, B_m$ $(m \geq 0)$ in a derivation D as above. If D contains a query $Q_l = (B_1, \ldots, B_m)\theta_k \cdots \theta_l$, $k \leq l$, then the call A (of Q_{k-1}) **succeeds** in D.

In such case, by the **subderivation** for A (of Q_{k-1} in D) we mean the fragment of D consisting of the queries Q_i where $k - 1 \leq i \leq l$, and for $k - 1 \leq i < l$ each Q_i contains more than m atoms[4]. We call such subderivation **successful**. The (computed) **answer** for A (of Q_{k-1} in D) is $A\theta_k \cdots \theta_l$.

If A (of Q_{k-1}) does not succeed in D then the **subderivation** for A (of Q_{k-1} in D) is the fragment of D consisting of the queries Q_i where $k - 1 \leq i$.

By a *subderivation* (respectively an *answer*) for A of Q in an LD-tree $\mathcal{T}$ we mean a subderivation (answer) for A of Q in a branch D of $\mathcal{T}$.

Now we structure a subderivation D for an atom A by distinguishing in D top-level procedure calls. Assume A is resolved with a clause $H \leftarrow A_1, \ldots, A_n$ in the first step of D. If then an instance of A_i becomes a procedure call, we call it a top-level call. More precisely:

Definition 2. Consider a subderivation D for A, with first two queries $Q_{k-1} = A, Q'$ and $Q_k = (A_1, \ldots, A_n, Q')\theta_k$, where $n > 0$. So $A_1, \ldots, A_n$ is the body of the clause used in the first step of the subderivation. Let $|Q_k|$ be the length of Q_k (the number of atoms in Q_k).

Consider an index j, $1 \leq j \leq n$. If there exists in D a query of the length $|Q_k| + 1 - j$ and $Q_{i_j} = (A_j, \ldots, A_n, Q')\theta_k \cdots \theta_{i_j}$ is the first such query then we say that $A_j\theta_k \cdots \theta_{i_j}$ (of Q_{i_j}) is a **top-level call** of D, and the subderivation D' for $A_j\theta_k \cdots \theta_{i_j}$ (of Q_{i_j}) in D is a **top-level subderivation** of D.

A top-level call of a subderivation D for A will be also called a top-level call for A.

---

[4] Thus each such Q_i is of the form $A_1, \ldots, A_{m_i}, (B_1, \ldots, B_m)\theta_k \cdots \theta_i$ where $m_i > 0$. This implies that the least $l > k$ is taken such that Q_l is of the form $(B_1, \ldots, B_m)\theta_k \cdots \theta_l$.

Notice that if A is resolved with a unary clause ($n = 0$, and D consists of two queries) then D has no top-level subderivations. Also, if a top-level subderivation D' of D is successful then the last query of D' is the first query of the next subderivation, or it is the last query of D.

We are ready to describe what information to obtain from the debugger in order to facilitate incorrectness and incompleteness diagnosis. First we describe which top-level answers correspond to an answer for A; we may say that they have been used to obtain the answer for A.

Definition 3. If subderivation D for A as in Definition 2 is successful then it has n top-level subderivations, for atoms $A_j \theta_k \cdots \theta_{i_j}$ ($j = 1, \ldots, n$). Their answers in D are, respectively, $A'_j = A_j \theta_k \cdots \theta_{i_{j+1}}$ (where i_{n+1} is the index of the last query $Q_{i_{n+1}} = Q' \theta_k \cdots \theta_{i_{n+1}}$ of D). In such case, by the **top-level success trace** for A (in D) we mean the sequence $A'_1, \ldots, A'_n$ of the answers.

Top-level success traces will be employed in incorrectness diagnosis. For diagnosing incompleteness, we need to collect all the answers for each top-level call.

Definition 4. Consider an LD-tree $\mathcal{T}$ with a node Q. Let A be the first atom of Q. By the *top-level search trace* (or simply **top-level trace**) for A (of Q in $\mathcal{T}$) we mean the set of pairs

$$
\left\{ (B, \{B_1, \ldots, B_k\}) \;\middle|\; \begin{array}{l} B \text{ is the first atom of a node } Q' \text{ of } \mathcal{T}, \\ Q' \text{ occurs in a subderivation } D' \text{ for } A \text{ of } Q \text{ in } \mathcal{T}, \\ B \text{ is a top-level call of } D', \\ B_1, \ldots, B_k \text{ are the answers for } B \text{ of } Q' \text{ in } \mathcal{T} \end{array} \right\}.
$$

2.2   Debugger Output

For the purposes of this paper, this section should provide a sufficient description of the debugger. We focus on the debugger of SICStus. For an introduction and further information about the Prolog debugger see e.g. the textbook [3] or the manual http://sicstus.sics.se/.

Prolog computation can be seen as traversal of an LD-tree. The Prolog debugger reports the current state of the traversal by displaying one-line items; such an item contains a single atom augmented by other information. A procedure call A is reported as an item

$$n \quad d \; \texttt{Call:} \; A$$

and a corresponding answer $A' = A\theta_k \cdots \theta_i$ as

$$n \quad d \; \texttt{Exit:} \; A'$$

Here n, d are, respectively, the unique invocation number and the current depth of the invocation; we skip the details. What is important is that, given an Exit item, the invocation number uniquely determines the corresponding Call item.

Note that a node in an LD-tree may be visited many times, and usually more than one item correspond to a single visit. For instance, to the last node Q_l of a successful subderivation for A (say that from Definition 1) there correspond, at least, an Exit item with atom $A\theta_k \cdots \theta_l$ and a Call item with atom $B_1\theta_k \cdots \theta_l$ (provided $m > 0$). Note that such a node is often the last query of more than one successful subderivations (cf. Definition 2). In such case other Exit items correspond to Q_l. They are displayed in the order which may be described as leaving nested procedure calls. More formally, the order of displaying the Exit items is that of the increasing lengths of the corresponding successful subderivations. (The displayed invocation depths of these items are decreasing consecutive natural numbers.)

An Exit item is preceded by ? when backtrack-points exist between the corresponding Call and the given Exit. Thus more answers are possible for (the atom of) this Call.

At backtracking the debugger displays Redo items of the form

$$n \quad d \; \texttt{Redo:} \; A'$$

Such item corresponds to an Exit item with the same numbers n, d and atom A'. Both items correspond to the same node of the LD-tree. The Redo item appears, speaking informally, when the answer A' is abandoned, and the computation of a new answer for the same query begins. SICStus usually does not display a Redo item when the corresponding Exit item was not preceded by ?.

A Fail item

$$n \quad d \; \texttt{Fail:} \; A$$

is displayed when no (further) answer is obtained for A. This means that a node with A selected is being left (and will not be visited anymore). The numbers and the atom in a Fail item are the same as those in the corresponding Call item. Both the Call and Fail items correspond to the same node of the LD-tree.

We described the output of the debugger of SICStus. Commands of the debugger will be described when necessary. The debuggers of most Prolog systems are similar. However important differences happen. For instance the debugger of SWI-Prolog (http://swi-prolog.org/) does not display the invocation numbers. This may make difficult e.g. finding the Call item corresponding to a given Exit item. On the other hand, the debuggers or Ciao (http://ciao-lang.org/) and Yap (https://github.com/vscosta/yap-6.3) seem to display such numbers.

2.3 Obtaining Top-Level Traces

We are ready to describe how to obtain top-level traces using the Prolog debugger. We first deal with the search trace.

Algorithm 1 (All answers). Assume that we are at a Call port; the debugger displays

$$n \quad d \; \texttt{Call:} \; B$$

We show how to obtain all the answers for B. Do repetitively the following.

1. Type **s** to skip the details of processing the query B and to go to the corresponding **Exit** or **Fail** port.

2. If the obtained port is n d `Exit:` B' then B' is a computed answer for B. Type **jr** (to jump to the `Redo` port; n d `Redo:` B' is displayed). Repeat (step 1) to compute further answers
If the obtained port is a `Fail` then all the answers have been obtained. To come back to the initial `Call` port, type **r**.

An alternative to using this algorithm is to simply run Prolog on query B (e.g. using the "break" option of the debugger).

Algorithm 2 (Top-level trace). Assume that we are at a Call port

$$n \quad d \; \texttt{Call:} \; A$$

We show a way of obtaining the top-level search trace for A. Repetitively do the following.

1. If an item

$$n \quad d \; \texttt{Call:} \; A \qquad \text{or} \qquad n \quad d \; \texttt{Redo:} \; A'$$

is displayed then type ⟨enter⟩ to make one step of computation.[5]
2. If

$$n \quad d \; \texttt{Fail:} \; A$$

is displayed then the search is completed. The trace has been obtained.
3. If

$$n \quad d \; \texttt{Exit:} \; A'$$

is displayed then type **jr** (to jump to the `Redo` port of A, in order to continue the search).
4. If

$$n_i \quad d{+}1 \; \texttt{Call:} \; B_i$$

is displayed then employ Algorithm 1 to obtain the answers for B_i. Query B_i together with the answers is an element of the top-level trace for A.
Now we are again at the same `Call:` B_i item. Type **s** to arrive at the first answer for B_i, (or to a `Fail` if there is none).
5. If

$$n_i \quad d{+}1 \; \texttt{Exit:} \; B'_i \qquad \text{or} \qquad n_i \quad d{+}1 \; \texttt{Fail:} \; B_i$$

is displayed then type ⟨enter⟩, to make a single step.[6]

---

[5] In the case of `Call` there are three possibilities. If the result is an item n_1 $d{+}1$ `Call:` B_1 then B_1 is an instance of the first atom of the body of the clause used in the resolution step. Obtaining n d `Exit:` A' means that a unary clause was used and A succeeded immediately. Obtaining n d `Fail:` A means that A failed immediately, as it was not unifiable with any clause head.
In the case of `Redo:` A', we deal with backtracking after having obtained an answer A' for A. Then there is a fourth possibility: obtaining a `Redo:` B'_j item, where B'_j is an answer obtained for (an instance of) an atom B_j from the body of the clause used to obtain the answer A'.

[6] After an `Exit`, this leads to a `Call:` B_{i+1} item, or to an `Exit:` A' item; the latter when B_i is (an instance of) the last atom of the used clause. After a `Fail`, this leads (in a simple case) to a `Redo:` B_{i-1}.
Here B_{i-1}, B_i, B_{i+1} are instances of three consecutive atoms of the used clause.

6. If
$$n_i \quad d+1 \ \texttt{Redo:} \ B_i'$$
is displayed then type **s** to arrive at the next answer for B_i (or to a `Fail` if there is none).

The algorithm outputs the same answers (`Exit` items) twice (by Algorithm 1 and after an **s** at steps 4 and 6). So all the details of the trace are displayed even if we do not invoke Algorithm 1. But obtaining the top-level trace from such output seems too tedious; we need to group each query with its answers (e.g. by sorting by the invocation numbers), and remove unnecessary items. This can be done by a shell command `cut -b 2- | sort -nk 1 | egrep 'Call:|Exit:'`.

Algorithm 3 (Top-level success trace). Assume that we obtained an Exit item containing an answer A'. The item corresponds to the last query of a successful subderivation D for an atom A. In order to extract from the debugger output the top-level success trace for A in D, we need that the debugger has displayed the Call and Exit items containing the top-level calls of D and the corresponding answers. If this is not the case then, at the n d `Exit:` A' item, type **r** to arrive to the corresponding Call item, n d `Call:` A. Then perform Algorithm 2 until arriving again to the `Exit:` A' item (all the invocations of Algorithm 1 may be skipped).

To select a top-level success trace from the printed debugger items, do repetitively the following. The trace will be constructed backwards. Initially the current item is n d `Exit:` A'. Repetitively do the following:

The current item is

$$n \quad d \ \texttt{Exit:} \ A' \qquad \text{or} \qquad n_j \quad d+1 \ \texttt{Call:} \ B_j$$

Consider the preceding item. If the immediately preceding item is

$$n_{j'} \quad d+1 \ \texttt{Exit:} \ B_{j'}'$$

then $B_{j'}'$ is obtained as an element of the success trace. Find the corresponding

$$n_{j'} \quad d+1 \ \texttt{Call:} \ B_{j'}$$

item, and make it the current item.
Otherwise, the preceding item is

$$n \quad d \ \texttt{Call:} \ A \qquad \text{or} \qquad n \quad d \ \texttt{Redo:} \ A''$$

and all the elements of the top-level success trace for A have been found.

The construction of a top-level success trace can be made more efficient, by re-starting the computation with A' as the initial query. Then the search space to obtain a success of A' (and the corresponding top-level success trace) may be substantially smaller than that for original atomic query from the Call item.

3   Diagnosis

This section first discusses diagnosis of incorrectness, and then that of incompleteness. In each case we first present the diagnosis itself, and then discuss how it may be performed employing the Prolog debugger.

3.1   Diagnosing Incorrectness

A *symptom* of incorrectness is an incorrect answer of the program. More formally, consider a program P and an Herbrand interpretation S_{corr}, which is our specification for correctness. A symptom is an answer Q such that $S_{corr} \not\models Q$, where S_{corr} is the specification for correctness. (In other words, Q has a ground instance $Q\theta$ such that $Q \notin S_{corr}$.) When testing finds such a symptom, the role of diagnosis is to find the error, this means the reason of incorrectness. An error is a clause of the program which out of correct (w.r.t. S_{corr}) premises produces an incorrect conclusion. More precisely:

Definition 5. Given a definite program P and a specification S_{corr} (for correctness), an **incorrectness error** is an instance

$$H \leftarrow B_1, \ldots, B_n \qquad (n \geq 0)$$

of a clause of P such that $S_{corr} \models B_i$ for all $i = 1, \ldots, n$, but $S_{corr} \not\models H$.

An *incorrect clause* is a clause C having an instance $C\theta$ which is an incorrectness error.

In other words, C is an incorrect clause iff $S_{corr} \not\models C$. In what follows, by a *correct atom* we consider an atom A such that $S_{corr} \models A$ (where S_{corr} is the considered specification for correctness).

Note that we cannot formally establish which part of the clause is erroneous. Easy examples can be constructed showing that an incorrect clause C can be corrected in various ways; and each atom of C remains unchanged in some corrected version of C [4, Section 7.1].

The incorrectness diagnosis algorithm is based on the notion of a proof tree, called also implication tree.

Definition 6. Let P be a definite program and Q an atomic query. A **proof tree** for P and Q is a finite tree in which the nodes are atoms, the root is Q and

if $B_1, \ldots, B_n$ are the children of a node B then $B \leftarrow B_1, \ldots, B_n$ is an instance of a clause of P $(n \geq 0)$.

Note that the leaves of a proof tree are instances of unary clauses of P.

Now diagnosing incorrectness is rather obvious. If an atom Q is a symptom then there exists a proof tree for P, Q. The tree must contain an incorrectness error (otherwise the root of the tree is correct, i.e. $S_{corr} \models Q$). A natural way of searching for the error, in other words an incorrectness diagnosis algorithm, is as follows: Begin from the root and, recursively, check the children $B_1, \ldots, B_n$

of the current node whether they are correct (formally, whether $S_{corr} \models B_i$). If all of them are correct, the error is found; it is $B \leftarrow B_1, \ldots, B_n$ (where B the parent of $B_1, \ldots, B_n$). Otherwise take an incorrect child B_i, and continue the search taking B_i as the current node.

Obviously, such search locates a single error. So correcting the error does not guarantee correctness of the program.[7]

3.2 Prolog Debugger and Incorrectness

Now we try to find out to which extent the algorithm described above can be mimicked by the standard Prolog debugger. Unfortunately, the debugger does not provide a way to construct a proof tree for a given answer. We can however employ top-level success traces to perform a search similar to that done by the incorrectness diagnosing algorithm described in Sect. 3.1.

A Strategy for Incorrectness Errors. Here we describe how to locate incorrectness errors using the Prolog debugger.

Algorithm 4. Assume that while tracing the program we found out an incorrect answer A' (for a query A). So we are at an Exit item containing A'. Type **r** to arrive to the corresponding Call item n d `Call: A`. Do repetitively the following:

1. Construct the top-level success trace $B'_1, \ldots, B'_m$ for the subderivation D (for an atom A, where A' is the answer for A in D), as described in Algorithm 3.
2. Check whether the atoms of the trace are correct (formally, whether $S_{corr} \models B'_i$). If all of them are, then the search ends.
   Otherwise take an item n_i $d{+}1$ `Exit: ` B'_i, in which B'_i is incorrect, and find the corresponding Call item n_i $d{+}1$ `Call: B`. Now repeat the search, with A, A' replaced by, respectively, B, B'_i, by typing a command **jc** n_i, or by starting new tracing from query B (in some cases **jc** n_i does not lead to the expected Call item).

The last obtained top-level success trace $B'_1, \ldots, B'_m$ points out the incorrect clause (Definition 5) of the program. The clause is $C = H \leftarrow B_1, \ldots, B_m$ such that the obtained answers are instances of the body atoms of C: each B'_i is an instance of B_j, for $j = 1, \ldots, m$. The head H of C is unifiable with the last call B for which the top-level success trace was built.

Obviously, the algorithm can be improved by checking the correctness of each element B'_i of the trace as soon as it is located. (So the success trace needs to be constructed only until an incorrect element is found.)

The approach of Algorithm 4 is rather tedious. A more natural way to locate incorrectness errors is as follows.

---

[7] This does not even guarantee that the symptom we began with would disappear – there may be some other errors involved.

Algorithm 5

1. Assume, as above, that an incorrect answer A' was found. Begin as in Algorithm 4: arrive to the `Call`: A that resulted in the incorrect answer, and start constructing a top-level search trace.
2. For each obtained item n_i $d+1$ `Exit`: B' check if B' is correct.
3. If B' is an incorrect answer, then restart the search from B'.
4. If no incorrect answer has appeared until arriving to the incorrect answer A' then the error is found. It is the last clause C whose head was unified with A in the computation. (Formally, an instance of C is an incorrectness error.) The clause may be identified, as previously, by extracting the top-level success trace (for the subderivation that produced A').

Comments. In Algorithms 4 and 5, it is often not necessary to know the (whole) top-level success trace to identify the incorrect clause in the program. In many cases, knowing the last one or two answers of the trace is sufficient. For instance, let n' d' `Call`: B be the last call for which top-level trace was inspected. The last item displayed by the debugger is n' d' `Exit`: B' (where B' is incorrect). Assume that the previous item is n_j $d'+1$ `Exit`: B'_j. Then the top-level trace of interest is not empty, B'_j is its last atom and is an instance of the last body atom of an erroneous clause. If the program has only one such clause, then finding the rest of the top-level success trace is unnecessary.

The error located by the second approach (Algorithm 5) may be not the one that caused the initial incorrect answer A'. This is because the search may go into a branch of the LD-tree distinct from the branch in which A' is produced. Anyway, an actual error has been discovered in the program. This outcome is useful, as each error in the program should be corrected.

Note that the approach is complete, in the sense that the error(s) responsible for A' can be found. This is due to the nondeterministic search performed by the algorithm. The error(s) will be located under some choice of incorrect answers in the top-level search traces.

The search may be made more efficient if, instead of tracing the original computation, we re-start it with an incorrect answer as a query. The corresponding modification (of both algorithms) is as follows. Whenever an incorrect answer B' is identified, instead of continuing the search for the corresponding call B, one interrupts the debugger session and begins a new one by starting Prolog with query B'. The query will succeed with B' (i.e. itself) as an answer, but the size of the trace may be substantially smaller (and is never greater). Moreover, any incorrect instance of B' may be used instead of B'.

The Prolog debugger does not facilitate searching for the reason of incorrectness. Finding a top-level success trace is tedious and not obvious. In particular, there seems to be no way of skipping the backtracking that precedes obtaining the wrong answer. The abilities of the debugger make Algorithm 5 preferable; this approach in a more straightforward way uses what is offered by the debugger.

Looking for the reason of an incorrect answer is a basic task. It is strange that such a task is not conveniently facilitated by the available debugging tools.

3.3 Diagnosing Incompleteness

A specification for completeness is, as already stated, an Herbrand interpretation which is the set of all required ground answers of the program. A symptom of incompleteness is lack of some answers of the program. More formally, given a program P and a specification S_{compl}, by an incompleteness symptom we may consider a ground atom A such that $S_{compl} \models A$ but $P \not\models A$. As a symptom is to be obtained out of an actual computation, we additionally require that the LD-tree for A is finite. We will consider a more general notion of a symptom:

Definition 7. Consider a definite program P and a specification S_{compl} (for completeness). Let A be an atomic query for which an LD-tree is finite and let $A\theta_1, \ldots, A\theta_n$ be the computed answers for A from the tree. If there exists an instance $A\sigma \in S_{compl}$ such that $A\sigma$ is not an instance of any $A\theta_i$ $(i = 1, \ldots, n)$ then $A, A\theta_1, \ldots, A\theta_n$ is an **incompleteness symptom** (for P w.r.t. S_{compl}).

We will often skip the sequence of answers, and say that A alone is the symptom. The definition can be generalized to non-atomic queries in an obvious way.

Definition 8. Let P be a definite program, and S_{compl} a specification. A ground atom A is **covered** by a clause C w.r.t. S_{compl} if there exists a ground instance $A \leftarrow B_1, \ldots, B_n$ of C $(n \geq 0)$ such that all the atoms $B_1, \ldots, B_n$ are in S_{compl}.

A is *covered by the program* P (w.r.t. S_{compl}) if A is covered by some clause $C \in P$.

Informally, A is covered by P if it can be produced by a rule from P out of some atoms from the specification.

If there exists an incompleteness symptom for P w.r.t. S_{compl} then there exists an atom $p(t) \in S_{compl}$ uncovered by P w.r.t. S_{compl} [4,13]. Such an atom locates the error in P. This is because no rule of P can produce $p(t)$ out of atoms required to be produced. This shows that the procedure p (the set of clauses beginning with p) is the reason of the incompleteness and has to be modified, to make the program complete. Note that similarly to the incorrectness case, we cannot locate the error more precisely. Various clauses may be modified to make $p(t)$ covered, or a new clause may be added. An extreme case is adding to P a fact $p(t)$.

Incompleteness diagnosis means looking for an uncovered atom, or – more generally – for an atom with an instance which is uncovered: Such atom localizes the procedure of the program which is responsible for incompleteness.

Definition 9. Let P be a definite program, and S_{compl} a specification. An **incompleteness error** (for P w.r.t. S_{compl}) is an atom that has an instance which is not covered (by P w.r.t. S_{compl}).

Name "incompleteness error" may seem unnatural, but we find it convenient.

A class of incompleteness diagnosis algorithms employs the following idea. Start with an atomic query A (which is a symptom) and construct a top level trace for it. Inspect the trace, whether it contains a symptom B. If so then invoke the search recursively with B. Otherwise A is an incompleteness error; we located in the program the procedure that is responsible for the incompleteness. Such approach (see e.g. [8, 12]) is sometimes called *Pereira-style* incompleteness diagnosis [10].

3.4 Prolog Debugger and Incompleteness

We show how Pereira-style diagnosis may be done using the Prolog debugger.

Algorithm 6 (Incompleteness diagnosis). Begin with a symptom A. Obtain the top-level search trace for A. In the trace, check if the atom B from a Call item together with the answers $B_1, \ldots, B_n$ from the corresponding Exit items is an incompleteness symptom. If yes, invoke the same search starting from B. If the answer is no for all Call items of the trace, the search is ended as we located A as an incompleteness error.

Comments. Standard comments about incompleteness diagnosis apply here. To decrease the search space, it is useful to start the diagnosis from a ground instance $A\theta \notin S_{compl}$ of the symptom A (instead of A itself). The same for each symptom B found during the search – re-start the computation and the diagnosis from an appropriate instance of B.

Often an incorrectness error coincides with an incompleteness error – a wrong answer is produced instead of a correct one. The programmer learns about this when facing an incorrect answer B_i (appearing in a top-level trace). A standard advice in such case [8, 10] is to switch to incorrectness diagnosis. This is because incorrectness diagnosis is simpler, and it locates an error down to a program clause (not to a whole procedure, as incompleteness diagnosis does). The gain of such switch is less obvious in our case, since the effort needed for incorrectness diagnosis (Algorithm 5) may be not smaller than that for incompleteness (Algorithm 6).

4 Conclusions

Prolog makes declarative logic programming possible – programs may be written and reasoned about in terms of their declarative semantics, to a substantial extent abstracting from the operational semantics. This advantage is lost when it comes to locating errors in programs, as the Prolog debugger works solely in terms of the operational semantics. We may say that logic programming would not deserve to be called a declarative programming paradigm if debugging had to be based on the operational semantics.

This paper is an attempt to study if and how the Prolog debugger can be used for declarative programming. It presents how the debugger can be used to perform incorrectness and incompleteness diagnosis[8]. Examples, missing here, are available at http://arxiv.org/abs/2003.01422/. The debugger used is that of SICStus; the presented approach may be difficult to apply with the debugger of SWI-Prolog, as the latter does not display unique invocation numbers (needed in incorrectness diagnosis, Algorithms 3 and 4).

The results are rather disappointing. Declarative diagnosis based on the Prolog debugger is tedious and unnatural. Rather obvious information (like the proof tree leading to a given answer, or a top-level success trace) is impossible or difficult to obtain. Possibly, this drawback is a substantial obstacle for employing declarative logic programming in practice.

This drawback particularly concerns incorrectness diagnosis. Additionally, debugging of incorrectness seems more important than that of incompleteness. This is because incompleteness is often caused by producing incorrect answers instead of correct ones. Also, incorrectness diagnosis is more precise, as it locates a smaller erroneous fragment of the program than incompleteness diagnosis does. Hence the first step towards making Prolog debugging declarative is to implement a tool supporting incorrectness diagnosis. Experiments show that it is sufficient to provide a tool for convenient browsing of a proof tree (which provides an abstraction of the part of computation responsible for the considered incorrect answer).

The Introduction contains a discussion about how to avoid the "intended model problem", which is possibly the main reason why declarative diagnosis of logic programs was abandoned. The author believes that the proposed solution [4] can make declarative diagnosis useful in practice. What is missing are tools.

References

1. Apt, K.R.: From Logic Programming to Prolog. International Series in Computer Science, Prentice-Hall (1997)
2. Bratko, I.: Prolog Programming for Artificial Intelligence, 4th edn. Addison-Wesley, New York (2012)
3. Clocksin, W., Mellish, C.: Programming in Prolog: Using the ISO Standard, 5th edn. Springer, Heidelberg (2003). https://doi.org/10.1007/978-3-642-55481-0
4. Drabent, W.: Correctness and completeness of logic programs. ACM Trans. Comput. Log. **17**(3), 18:1–18:32 (2016). https://doi.org/10.1145/2898434
5. Drabent, W.: Proving completeness of logic programs with the cut. Formal Aspects Comput. **29**(1), 155–172 (2017). https://doi.org/10.1007/s00165-016-0392-0
6. Drabent, W.: Logic + control: on program construction and verification. Theory Pract. Logic Program. **18**(1), 1–29 (2018). https://doi.org/10.1017/S1471068417000047

---

[8] We may informally present the underlying idea of this paper in a different way: To understand what the Prolog debugger can tell us about the declarative semantics of the program, we need to be able to obtain the following information. 1. For a given atomic answer A, what are the top-level answers that have lead to A? (This is formalized as top-level success trace.) 2. For a given atomic query Q, and for each top-level atomic query B in the computation for Q, what are all the answers for B?

7. Drabent, W., Małuszyński, J.: Inductive assertion method for logic programs. Theor. Comput. Sci. **59**, 133–155 (1988). https://doi.org/10.1016/0304-3975(88)90099-0
8. Drabent, W., Nadjm-Tehrani, S., Małuszyński, J.: Algorithmic debugging with assertions. In: Abramson, H., Rogers, M.H. (eds.) Meta-Programming in Logic Programming, pp. 501–522. The MIT Press, Cambridge (1989)
9. Kowalski, R.A.: Algorithm = logic + control. Commun. ACM **22**(7), 424–436 (1979). https://doi.org/10.1145/359131.359136
10. Naish, L.: Declarative diagnosis of missing answers. New Generation Comput. **10**(3), 255–286 (1992). https://doi.org/10.1007/BF03037939
11. Naish, L.: A three-valued declarative debugging scheme. In: 23rd Australasian Computer Science Conference (ACSC 2000), pp. 166–173. IEEE Computer Society (2000). https://doi.org/10.1109/ACSC.2000.824398
12. Pereira, L.M.: Rational debugging in logic programming. In: Shapiro, E. (ed.) ICLP 1986. LNCS, vol. 225, pp. 203–210. Springer, Heidelberg (1986). https://doi.org/10.1007/3-540-16492-8_76. Extended version at https://userweb.fct.unl.pt/~lmp/
13. Shapiro, E.: Algorithmic Program Debugging. The MIT Press, Cambridge (1983)
14. Sterling, L., Shapiro, E.: The Art of Prolog, 2nd edn. The MIT Press, Cambridge (1994)

Program Transformation

A Port Graph Rewriting Approach to Relational Database Modelling

Maribel Fernández[1], Bruno Pinaud[2], and János Varga[1(✉)]

[1] Department of Informatics, King's College London,
Bush House, London WC2B 4BG, UK
janos.varga@kcl.ac.uk
[2] LaBRI, Université de Bordeaux,
351 Cours de la Libération, 33405 Talence Cedex, France

Abstract. We present new algorithms to compute the Syntactic Closure and the Minimal Cover of a set of functional dependencies, using strategic port graph rewriting. We specify a Visual Domain Specific Language to model relational database schemata as port graphs, including an extension to port graph rewriting rules. Using these rules we implement strategies to compute a syntactic closure, analyse it and find minimal covers, essential for schema normalisation. The graph program provides a visual description of the computation steps coupled with analysis features not available in other approaches. We show soundness and completeness of the computed closure, and implement it in PORGY.

Keywords: Relational databases · Database design · Port graph · Graph transformation · Functional dependency · Minimal cover

1 Introduction

Relational database design includes conceptual and logical modelling, as well as physical modelling. The theory behind these steps is well-understood (it is part of the syllabus of many databases courses [16]), and highlights the advantages of developing normalised database designs. Yet, database professionals often consider normalisation too cumbersome and do not apply normalisation theory, due to the lack of adequate tools to support logical modelling [6].

Formal, graph-based approaches to database design have used labelled graphs or hypergraphs [1,5,7]. We advocate a new approach to database modelling using *attributed port graphs*, which are graphs where edges are connected to nodes at specific points, called ports. Attributes of nodes, edges and ports are used to represent properties of the system modelled. Port graphs were introduced to model biochemical systems [2] and were later used in various domains [14].

Port graphs are a good data structure to store and to visualise relational schema: ports provide additional visual information about the design. We propose to represent relational attributes and functional dependencies as nodes, and use edges to link attributes and dependencies; ports indicate the role of the attribute in the dependency. This representation has advantages when

© Springer Nature Switzerland AG 2020
M. Gabbrielli (Ed.): LOPSTR 2019, LNCS 12042, pp. 211–227, 2020.
https://doi.org/10.1007/978-3-030-45260-5_13

computing properties of the schema, such as syntactic closure of the set of dependencies, a crucial step in schema normalisation. We specify an algorithm to compute closures using *port graph rewriting rules* controlled by strategies. Our system has been implemented in PORGY [3] – a visual, interactive modelling tool. PORGY provides a graphical interface to specify an initial model, port graph rewriting rules and strategies. It displays the set of rewrite derivations (a *derivation tree*) and includes features such as cycle detection, to facilitate debugging.

Summarising, our main contributions are:

1. a Visual Domain Specific Language (VDSL) specifically tailored to model relational database schemata (Sect. 3);
2. a new visual representation of Armstrong's axioms to infer functional dependencies, using the port graph VDSL mentioned above (Sect. 4.1);
3. a sound and complete strategic graph program to compute the syntactic closure of a set of functional dependencies, with examples (Sects. 4.2, 4.3);
4. an implementation[1] in PORGY, together with a set of techniques to query the relational database design, using PORGY's derivation tree and graphical interface to analyse properties of the model: in particular, we show how to solve *the membership problem* (Sect. 4.4);
5. a strategy and a set of transformation rules to simplify sets of dependencies, as required to compute a minimal cover (Sect. 5).

Related Work. Hypergraphs are used for relational database design in [7,13]. Using directed graphs candidate keys of a relation are computed in polynomial time [24]. A special family of labelled graphs, FD-graphs, were introduced in [5] to obtain closures of functional dependencies. In terms of graph transformations for database modelling we highlight two works. Hypergraph rewriting was used for the representation of functional dependencies [7] and Triple Graph Grammars were used to optimise a database schema [17].

Our contribution and main difference with respect to these works is the design of a domain-specific visual language with emphasis on interactive modelling, including strategies to control the application of rules, and the use of the derivation tree as part of the visualisation framework, giving the modeller access to all the sequences of transformation steps, to facilitate the analysis of the system. Port graphs were used to compute transitive closures in [27]. Here we compute the full Armstrong closure (not just transitive closure), and show how to use the derivation tree to analyse closures and answer queries about the database model, such as whether a given functional dependency is in the closure of a set of dependencies (the membership problem), and compute minimal covers.

PORGY's strategy language is strongly inspired by PROGRES [25], GP [23] and by strategy languages developed for term rewriting [11,19]. None of the available graph rewriting tools permits users to visualise the derivation tree, as in PORGY, where users can interactively visualise alternative derivations, follow the development of specific redexes, etc. When computing the closure of

---

[1] github.com/janos-varga/Porgy.

a set of dependencies, the derivation tree permits to see how each dependency is generated, offering a direct visualisation of the inference steps according to Armstrong's axioms.

2   Background

2.1   Relational Databases

We assume familiarity with the theory of logical design of relational databases, in particular, the definitions of: *relation schema, attribute, candidate key* and *functional dependency* (FD) [22]. We refer to a single attribute with a letter from the beginning of the alphabet $A, B, \ldots$ and to attribute sets with letters from the end of the alphabet W, X, Y, Z. Let $\mathcal{R}(\mathcal{A}) = \{R_1, \ldots, R_k\}$ be a set of relation schemata over a set $\mathcal{A}$ of attributes. Let $\mathcal{FD} = \{\Sigma_1, \ldots, \Sigma_k\}$ be the respective sets of functional dependencies and $\mathcal{CK} = \{C_1, \ldots, C_k\}$ be the respective sets of candidate keys. A relational database schema is a tuple $\mathcal{DB} = (\mathcal{R}(\mathcal{A}), \mathcal{FD}, \mathcal{CK})$.

The *syntactic closure* Σ^+ of a set Σ of FDs is the set of all FDs that can be inferred from Σ using Armstrong's Axioms [4,9], or equivalently, using the sound and complete subset consisting of Reflexivity, Transitivity and Augmentation [9].

(A1) Reflexivity: **if** $Y \subseteq X$ **then** $X \to Y$.
(A2) Augmentation: **if** $Z \subseteq W$ and $X \to Y$ **then** $XW \to YZ$.
(A3) Transitivity: **if** $X \to Y$ and $Y \to Z$ **then** $X \to Z$.

Syntactic closures are used to compute minimal covers of sets of FDs [21]. The *minimal cover* Σ_{min} of Σ is a set of dependencies that fully represent Σ and:

1. all the FDs in Σ_{min} have singleton right-hand sides;
2. Σ_{min} is left-reduced: if one attribute is removed from any left-hand side then Σ can no longer be inferred from Σ_{min};
3. Σ_{min} is nonredundant: if any FD is removed from Σ_{min} then Σ can no longer be inferred from it.

Our goal is to provide visual algorithms to compute syntactic closures and minimal covers. This work assumes that (a) FDs have singleton right sides and (b) there are no cyclical dependencies. Assumption (a) is standard in the relational database literature, without loss of generality, under Armstrong's Decomposition rule. The problem of finding cyclical dependencies reduces to kernel search in a directed graph, which is NP-complete.

2.2   Port Graph Rewriting and PORGY

We recall the notion of attributed port graph rewriting (see [14] for more details).

Definition 1 (Attributed port graph). *An* attributed port graph $G = (V, P, E, D)_{\mathcal{F}}$ *is a tuple* (V, P, E, D) *of pairwise disjoint sets where:*

  – *V is a finite set of nodes; $n, n_1, \ldots$ range over nodes;*

– P is a finite set of ports; $p, p_1, \ldots$ range over ports;
– E is a finite set of edges between ports; $e, e_1, \ldots$ range over edges; two ports may be connected by more than one edge;
– D is a set of records, which are sets of pairs attribute-value (values can include variables);

and a set $\mathcal{F}$ of functions Connect, Attach and $\mathcal{L}abel$ such that:

– for each edge $e \in E$, Connect(e) is the pair (p_1, p_2) of ports connected by e;
– for each port $p \in P$, Attach(p) is the node n to which the port belongs;
– $\mathcal{L}abel : V \cup P \cup E \mapsto D$ is a labelling function that returns a record for each element in $V \cup P \cup E$.

A *port graph rewrite rule* is itself a port graph $L \Rightarrow_C R$ consisting of two sub-graphs L and R, called *left-hand side* and *right-hand side*, respectively, together with an *arrow* node that links them. Each rule is characterised by its arrow node, which has a unique name (the rule's label), an optional attribute *Where* defining a Boolean condition C that restricts the rule's matching, and ports to control the rewiring operations when rewriting steps are computed. Each port in the arrow node has an attribute *Type*. A port of type *bridge* must have edges connecting it to L and to R (one edge to L and one or more to R): it thus connects a port from L to ports in R. A port of type *blackhole* must have edges connecting it only to L (one edge or more). The ports and edges associated with the arrow node specify a mapping between ports in the left and right-hand sides of the rule, following the Single-PushOut approach [20].

For examples of rewrite rules, we refer the reader to Sect. 4. It is possible to specify a rule condition requiring that a particular edge does NOT exist in the graph to be rewritten. In PORGY such conditions are graphically represented as a double line grey edge with an X, which is called an anti-edge [15].

A *redex* $g(L)$ is found in G if there is a total port graph morphism g from L to G such that if the arrow node has an attribute *Where* with value C, then $g(C)$ is true in G (g is a *matching morphism*). C is of the form *saturated*(p_1) $\wedge \ldots \wedge$ *saturated*(p_n) $\wedge B$, and *saturated*($g(p_i)$) holds if there are no edges between $g(p_i)$ and ports outside $g(L)$ in G – this ensures that no edges will be left dangling in rewriting steps. B is a Boolean expression such that all its variables occur in L.

Let G be a port graph. A *rewrite step* $G \Rightarrow H$ via the rule $L \Rightarrow_C R$ is obtained by replacing in G a redex $g(L)$ by $g(R)$, and connecting $g(R)$ to the rest of the graph as indicated by the arrow-node edges in the rule: Any edges arriving to a port in g(L) connected by a bridge arrow port to R are transferred to the corresponding ports in $g(R)$; edges connecting to ports in $g(L)$ that are connected to a blackhole port in the arrow node are deleted.

A sequence of rewriting steps is called a *derivation*. A *derivation tree* is a collection of rewriting derivations with a common root.

In PORGY [14] rules are displayed as graphs, and edges that run between ports of L, R and the arrow node are coloured red to distinguish them from normal edges. PORGY also provides a visual representation of the rewriting derivations, which can be used to analyse the rewriting system. PORGY's *strategy language* allows us to control the way derivations are generated. We can specify the rule to be used in a rewriting step and also the position where the rule should (or should not) be applied. Formally, the rewriting engine works with *graph programs*.

Definition 2 (Graph Program). *A graph program consists of a* located port graph, *a set of port graph rewriting rules, and a strategy expression. A* located port graph *is a port graph with two distinguished subgraphs: a* position *subgraph and a* banned *subgraph, denoted* G_Q^P. *Rewrite rules can only be applied to G if they match a subgraph which superposes P and does not superpose Q.*

We briefly describe below the strategy constructs that we use in our programs (see [14] for more details). The keywords `crtGraph`, `crtPos`, `crtBan` denote, respectively, the current graph being rewritten and its Position and Banned subgraphs. For example, the strategy expression `setPos(crtGraph)` sets the position graph as the full current graph. If T is a rule, then the strategy `one(T)` randomly selects one possible redex for rule T in the current graph G, which should superpose the position subgraph P and not overlap the banned subgraph Q. This strategy fails if the rule cannot be applied. Constants id and fail denote success and failure, respectively. `while(S)[(n)]do(S')` executes strategy S' (not exceeding n iterations if the optional parameter n is specified) while S succeeds. `repeat(S)[max n]` repeatedly executes a strategy S, not exceeding n times. It can never fail (when S fails, it returns id).

3   Port Graphs for Database Modelling

We present a visual domain specific language (VDSL) for logical design of relational databases. It includes a class of attributed port graphs to represent objects of a relational database, and a language to specify rewrite rules and strategies for those graphs. We also define Database Port Graphs, to represent a relational database schema $\mathcal{DB} = (\mathcal{R}(\mathcal{A}), \mathcal{FD}, \mathcal{CK})$ (see Sect. 2.1).

3.1   A Visual Domain Specific Language for Database Modelling

The visual building blocks of the language correspond to those of relational databases. Port graph nodes will have an attribute DbType whose value indicates the role of the node. To avoid confusion, we will use Upper Case for relational database concepts (e.g., Attribute) and lower case for port graph concepts (e.g., attributed port graph).

We note here that an Attribute can occur in multiple relations. To this end, we can define a conceptual attribute node. Then we can define an attribute occurrence node to distinguish between appearances in different Relations. In this work, from now on, we only use occurrences and we call them Attribute.

Definition 3 (Relational Database Port Graph VDSL, RDPG-VDSL). *A* Relational Database Port Graph VDSL *consists of attributed port graphs* $G_{RDB} = (V, P, E, D)_{\mathcal{F}}$, *such that*

- V *includes the following pairwise disjoint sets of nodes (as well as application specific nodes): V_R: relation nodes (DbType = REL); V_A: attribute nodes (DbType = ATTR); V_{FD}: functional dependency nodes (DbType = FD); V_{CK}: candidate key nodes (DbType = CK).*
- P *includes the following pairwise disjoint sets of ports: P_{ATT}: contained attribute ports pATT; P_{REL}: parent relation ports pREL; P_{DA}: dependency attribute ports pFD; P_{FD}: functional dependency ports pFDLHS and pFDRHS; P_{CK}: relation candidate key ports pCK; P_{KEY}: (candidate) key attribute ports pKEY.*
- *and the functions Attach and Connect are such that:*
  - *if $p \in P_{ATT}$, $Attach(p) \in \{V_R \cup V_{CK}\}$;*
  - *if $p \in P_{REL}$, $Attach(p) \in \{V_A \cup V_{CK}\}$;*
  - *if $p \in P_{DA}$, $Attach(p) \in V_A$;*
  - *if $p \in P_{FD}$, $Attach(p) \in V_{FD}$; each node in V_{FD} has two ports, pFDLHS and pFDRHS;*
  - *if $p \in P_{CK}$, $Attach(p) \in V_R$;*
  - *if $p \in P_{KEY}$, $Attach(p) \in V_A$.*

  Connect includes the following pairs of ports (and associated edges):
  - Functional Dependency: (pFD, pFDLHS) and (pFDRHS, pFD), *where pFD $\in P_{DA}$ and pFDLHS, pFDRHS $\in P_{FD}$. Given a dependency φ : $X \rightarrow A$ the pFD port of every attribute node corresponding to X will be connected to the pFDLHS port of the dependency node corresponding to φ and the pFDRHS port of the FD node representing φ will be connected to the pFD port of the attribute node representing A.*
  - Attribute in relation: (pATT, pREL), *where pATT $\in P_A$ and pREL $\in P_{REL}$. Given a relation R_i and its attribute A, the pATT port of the node representing R_i will be connected to the pREL port of the node representing A.*
  - Attribute in candidate key: (pATT, pKEY), *where pATT $\in P_A$ and pKEY $\in P_{CK}$. Given a candidate key CK_i and every attribute $A_j \in CK_i$, the pKEY port of the node corresponding to A_j will be connected to the pATT port of the node corresponding to CK_i.*
  - Candidate Key of Relation: (pREL, pCK), *where pREL $\in P_{REL}$ and pCK $\in P_{CK}$. Given a relation R_i and its candidate key CK_j, the pCK port of the node representing R_i will be connected to the pREL port of the node representing CK_j.*

As a particular case of the above defined class, we now define the Database Port Graph (DBPG) that represents $\mathcal{DB} = (\mathcal{R}(\mathcal{A}), \mathcal{FD}, \mathcal{CK})$. Most importantly, we constrain that one Relation is represented by only one relation node, each Attribute occurrence is represented by one attribute node and each FD occurrence by one FD node. This design decision is based on the separation of concerns principle and will be required for the addition of Foreign Keys in future work.

Definition 4 (Database Port Graph, DBPG). *A Database Port Graph is an RDPG such that the following constraints are satisfied:*

- V_R: one node **DbType** = REL *per Relation schema in* $\mathcal{R}$;
- V_A: one node **DbType** = ATTR *per Attribute occurrence in any of the* R_i;
- V_{FD}: one node **DbType** = FD *per Functional Dependency occurrence in* $\mathcal{FD}$;
- V_{CK}: one node **DbType** = CK *per Candidate Key in* $\mathcal{CK}$.

The Functional Dependency Port Graph (FDPG) [27] is a particular case of DBPG, with single occurrences of Attribute and FD nodes only ($V_R = V_{CK} = \emptyset$).

3.2   Variadic Rewriting Rules

To deal with functional dependencies of various arities, previous works used multiple rules [27] or internal data structures (e.g. compound node in [5]). Here, we present an extension to the port graph rewriting rule language, called variadic rewriting rules (VRRs), inspired by Variadic Interaction Nets [18]. A variadic rule represents a family of rules that differ only in the number of times a subgraph is repeated. First, we propose a container structure that clearly identifies in a port graph the subgraph that will be repeated.

Definition 5 (Pattern Container). *A pattern container is a subgraph within a port graph such that if an edge links two ports that belong to the container, the edge also belongs to the container.*

A pattern container has two attributes: a name, *and a* multiplicity *that specifies the maximum number of times the encapsulated pattern will be repeated.*

Edges that connect a port in a pattern container and a port in the outside graph are called variadic edges. *Variadic edges also have an attribute* multiplicity *to control the number of repetitions.*

Definition 6 (Variadic Port Graph Rewrite Rule, VRR). *A variadic port graph rewrite rule, denoted* $L \Rightarrow^V R$, *is a port graph rewrite rule with at least one pattern container on the LHS. Multiple pattern containers must not overlap. Pattern container names must be unique on the LHS.*

Given a VRR, we obtain its family of rules by running the Expansion algorithm defined below.

Definition 7 (Variadic Pattern Expansion). *For each pattern container, we generate i copies, where i is the value of the* multiplicity *attribute, as follows:*

1. *Synchronised Expansion:*
   If a pattern container is present on both sides of a VRR (i.e. their names are identical), then the pattern is expanded in an iterative way on both sides of the rule until i number of copies of the encapsulated subgraph are generated. If variables are used in attributes then a different variable should be used in each copy. The expansion iterator works pairwise; that is, not all combinations of expansions are generated on LHS and RHS, but only the same number of repetitions on the two sides.
2. *LHS-only Expansion:*
   If the pattern container is defined on LHS only, the expansion happens on LHS only, in the same iterative way.

If multiple patterns are defined, they are expanded independently, i.e. all combinations are generated, by nested iteration. Generally, the order in which the combinations are generated, does not matter.

A variadic edge is expanded based on the value j of its multiplicity attribute. If it equals the multiplicity i of the container it belongs to, then it is fully expanded, i.e. it is created in all i instances of the container. A partially expanded variadic edge ($j < i$) is only created in the first $1 \ldots j$ instances. In other words, in the nth iteration of the expansion of the pattern container the variadic edge belongs to, if $n < j$ then n copies are created; otherwise j copies are created.

In PORGY, which does not have a mechanism to define variadic rules, Definition 7 can be implemented as a macro expansion. The pattern container is visually represented by an enclosing rectangle (a metanode): attributes *name* and i are displayed at the top of the rectangle; and, on the LHS, also a + sign in its upper-right corner as shown in Fig. 1. Fully expanded variadic edges are also marked with a + sign over them and partially expanded variadic edges have the attribute value j displayed over them. In this example, because the pattern appears in both sides, the expansion will generate a rule version with one node Y, another with 2 and another with 3; we show in Fig. 2 the version corresponding to 3. If the node Y has an attribute a whose value is an expression containing variables, for example x, then each copy of the node Y will have attribute a with values x_1, x_2, x_3.

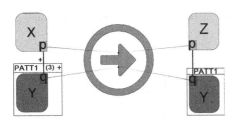
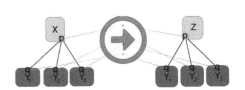

Fig. 1. VRR example (Color figure online)

Fig. 2. VRR example expanded, $i = 3$ (Color figure online)

4   Computing the Syntactic Closure of Σ

Given an FDPG representing set of functional dependencies Σ, we compute its syntactic closure by applying the rules Reflexivity, Augmentation and Transitivity, defined below, controlled by Strategy 1: Syntactic Closure. From now on, we colour-code nodes, as a visual aid. Attribute nodes are green, FD nodes are purple and ports are dark blue. We use other colours for highlighting purposes.

4.1   Rewriting Rules

In the rules below, $x, y, \ldots$ represent name variables for attribute nodes, and $f1, f2, \ldots$ are name variables for FD nodes.

Augmentation. The Augmentation rule (see Fig. 3) finds every attribute node y not connected to the FDLHS port of $f1$, regardless of what other attributes are connected there already. All non-connected attribute nodes are found by using the anti-edge feature [26] of PORGY. An anti-edge is represented by a grey double line with an X on top. The matching algorithm deems the candidate sub-graph isomorphic if no edge is found between the two ports connected by the anti-edge.

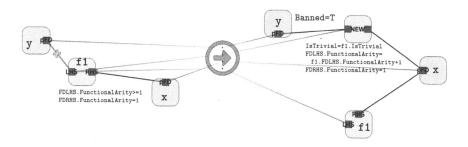

Fig. 3. Augmentation rule. (Color figure online)

The rule creates a new FD node and assigns all pre-existing attributes and y to the left side of $f1$. The original $f1$ dependency node is kept and y is banned to avoid augmenting $f1$ again with y. We use bridge ports (red edges) to keep and copy the already existing edges into the FDLHS ports of $f1$ and *NEW*. If $f1$ was trivial then the new dependency will also be marked trivial. The rule also increases the *FunctionalArity* counter by 1 indicating that a new attribute is connected to the FDLHS port.

Reflexivity. The Reflexivity rule (Fig. 4) applies to a node representing the attribute x and generates a trivial dependency $x \rightarrow x$. Then the attribute node x is banned so the rule cannot apply again on the same attribute.

The red edges in the arrow node indicate that when applying the rule, any edges connected to the pFD port of x in the left-hand side should be transferred to the corresponding pFD port of x in the right-hand side.

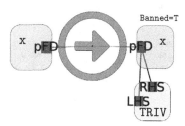

Fig. 4. Reflexivity rule. (Color figure online)

Transitivity. A family of Transitivity rules was described in [27] to detect transitive functional dependency chains $f_1 : X \rightarrow Y$ and $f_2 : Y \rightarrow A$. Instead, here we provide a compact representation of the transitivity axiom in the form of a variadic rule, shown in Fig. 5. This rule subsumes the family of Transitivity rules used in previous work.

As mentioned in Sect. 3.2, $|Y| = k \geq 1$ means that f_1 turns into a set of dependencies $f_1^1 \ldots f_1^k$. The connections between the pFD ports of X attribute nodes and the pFDLHS ports of $f_1^1 \ldots f_1^k$ nodes have to be preserved as well as copied onto the pFDLHS port of the newly created FD node (called NEW in Fig. 5). We achieve this without needing to include the attribute nodes representing X in the rule, thanks to the bridge ports of the arrow node and the connecting red edges, as explained in Definition 6. Then, to cover all cases, we define a VRR pattern over f_1 and Y, with $i = 1 \ldots k$. By definition the bridge ports, red edges and the normal edges into $y_1.\text{pFD}, \ldots, y_k.\text{pFD}$ will be repeated during the expansion.

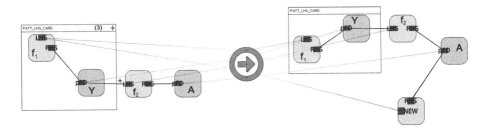

Fig. 5. Variadic Transitivity rule. (Color figure online)

We show an example expansion of the Transitivity VRR to Transitivity-3, i.e. with 3 repetitions, in Fig. 6.

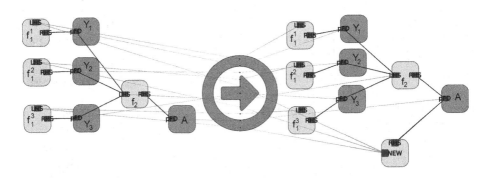

Fig. 6. An example expansion: Transitivity-3 rule. (Color figure online)

FD nodes are labelled by records containing an attribute UID that uniquely identifies the Functional Dependency, except for trivial dependencies that are all given UID = 1. Nodes representing non-trivial FDs are given a prime number as UID. This offers extra, domain-specific backtracking functionality for dependencies, as explained below.

Note that the Reflexivity, Augmentation and Transitivity rules never remove the matching subgraph. Therefore, these rules could run for ever. To prevent this, we use conditional rules and focusing constructs in Sect. 4.2 to define the Syntactic Closure strategy. To ensure that the iteration of the Transitivity rule terminates when no new transitive dependencies can be inferred, we use the UID attribute of FD nodes. When the Transitivity rule creates a transitive dependency node, it multiplies the UIDs of the contributing FDs and assigns the result as UID of the new FD node. We forbid the application of the rule if a node already exists with that UID (using NotNode() in the rule condition).

4.2   Syntactic Closure Strategy

The Strategy 1: Syntactic Closure applies first the Reflexivity rule as much as possible in the current graph. Each application bans an Attribute node, which ensures termination since matching is not allowed on banned nodes.

Strategy 1: Syntactic Closure

```
1  //———— Reflexivity ————
2  setPos(all(crtGraph));
3  repeat(one(Reflexivity));
4  //———— Augmentation ————
5  setPos(all(crtGraph));
6  setBan(all([emptySet]));
7  while(match(AugIterOn))do(
8     one(AugIterOn);
9     repeat(one(Augmentation));
10    one(AugIterOff);
11    setBan(all([emptySet]))
12 );
13 update("GenerateNextPrime"{result : UID});
14 //———— Transitivity ————
15 while(match(IterOn))do(
16    one(IterOn);
17    repeat(one(Transitivity); #Augmentation#);
18    update("GenerateNextPrime"{result : UID});
19    one(IterOff)
20 );
21 repeat(one(ResetVisitedFlags));
22 //———— Cleanup ————
23 repeat(one(Cleanup));
24 repeat(one(CleanupTriv))
```

In lines 5–6, we set the Position subgraph to be the whole graph and the Banned subgraph to empty. Then, while there is at least one FD node the Augmentation rule hasn't *visited* and *iterated*, one(*AugIterOn*) sets *AugIter* and *AugVisit* flags to true on a randomly selected FD node. The Augmentation rule will be applied on this FD node and all attribute nodes that are not connected to the FDLHS port of said FD node. Every attribute node used by this rule is banned to prevent re-application. Once all possible applications are processed,

AugIter flag is set to false and the Banned subgraph to empty. The iteration proceeds to the next, not yet visited, FD node. All new FD nodes, created by the Augmentation rule, are assigned a unique UID using the `update()` construct to call the function, `GenerateNextPrime()`, using PORGY's Python API.

Next, we compute transitive dependencies (lines 15–21), calling the Augmentation strategy (lines 5–12) after each application of the Transitivity variadic rewriting rule in line 17.

Since the rewrite rules may generate functional dependencies that already exist in the graph (despite the condition in the Transitivity rule), we add CleanUp variadic rules to remove duplicates (line 23).

4.3   Example of Application

Our strategy computed the syntactic closure of $\Sigma = \{AB \rightarrow C, ABC \rightarrow D\}$; the resulting FDPG can be seen in Fig. 7.

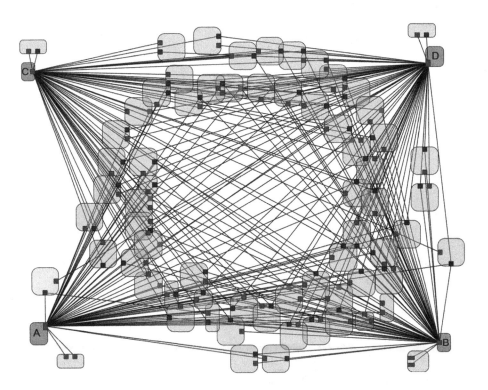

Fig. 7. Syntactic closure of $\Sigma = \{AB \rightarrow C, ABC \rightarrow D\}$. (Color figure online)

Attributes A, B, C and D and their trivial dependencies can be seen in the four corners of the graph. As an example, we highlighted two FD nodes. The first one, in orange on the right hand side of the image, represents the dependency

$ABD \rightarrow C$ which was created by augmenting $AB \rightarrow C$ with D. The second one represents $AB \rightarrow D$. This FD, shown on the left side of Fig. 7 in yellow, was found by the Transitivity rule, matching on dependencies $A \rightarrow A, B \rightarrow B, AB \rightarrow C$ and $ABC \rightarrow D$.

4.4 Visual Analysis of the Closure

We now turn our attention to usual questions about Σ^+. For example, using the derivation tree in PORGY, it is possible to track how and when a particular dependency was generated: If we alter the colour of any FD node in a leaf node of the derivation tree, PORGY will back-propagate this change up the tree. This way, we can identify the exact step where the FD was created, and by zooming on the edges of the derivation tree we can see which of Armstrong's axioms generated the dependency.

Strategy 2: Membership Problem

```
 1 setPos(all(
 2 property(crtGraph, port,DbType == "FDLHS" && FunctionalArity == 3)
 3 ∩ ngb(property(crtGraph, node,DbType == "ATTR"
 4       && viewLabel == "A"), edge,DbType == "L")
 5 ∩ ngb(property(crtGraph, node,DbType == "ATTR"
 6       && viewLabel == "B"), edge,DbType == "L")
 7 ∩ ngb(property(crtGraph, node,DbType == "ATTR"
 8       && viewLabel == "D"), edge,DbType == "L")
 9 ∩ ngb(property(crtGraph, node,DbType == "ATTR"
10       && viewLabel == "C"), edge, DbType == "R") ) ); //end setPos
11 (isEmpty(crtPos))orelse(repeat(one(Highlight)))
```

Another important question in database design is the *Membership Problem* [8]: given a set of FDs Σ, and an FD, φ, determine if $\varphi \in \Sigma^+$. Two groups of algorithms were developed to solve the membership problem: 1. generate a syntactic closure and check if $\varphi : X \rightarrow A$ is in it, or 2. compute the closure of X, X^+ and check if A is in it. Following the first approach, we can solve the problem by running a strategy to find and highlight the FD node that represents φ in the syntactic closure, if it exists, and fail if $\varphi \notin \Sigma^+$. For example, Strategy 2 was used to find the dependency $ABD \rightarrow C$, highlighted in Fig. 7 (due to space constraints, we refer the reader to [14] for explanations of the constructs used). Following the second approach, we can simply use Strategy 1 but focusing on the set X of attributes. We only need to replace the expression setPos(all(crtGraph)) in Strategy 1 with one that describes X, then the rewriting steps will apply on the attribute set in question. For example, if $X = B$, we write setPos(all(property(crtGraph, node, DbType=="ATTR" && viewLabel=="B"))).

4.5   Correctness

The strategic program $Cl = [\mathcal{F}, closure]$ consisting of an initial port graph $\mathcal{F}$ representing a set of functional dependencies Σ, and the syntactic closure strategy defined in Strategy 1, correctly computes the syntactic closure Σ^+.

Proposition 1 (Termination). *For any initial FDPG $\mathcal{F}$, the strategic program $Cl = [\mathcal{F}, closure]$ terminates.*

To prove the correctness of our program, we first show that the three rules Reflexivity, Augmentation and Transitivity are sound and complete, that is, given Σ, we can compute Σ^+ by applying these three rules exhaustively.

Proposition 2 (Soundness and Completeness of the Rules). *The Reflexivity, Augmentation and Transitivity rules stated below are sound and complete:*

1. *Reflexivity: for any attribute A, $A \rightarrow A$.*
2. *Augmentation: If $X \rightarrow A$ then $XY \rightarrow A$ for any attribute A and sets X, Y of attributes.*
3. *Transitivity: If $X \rightarrow A_i$ $(1 \leq i \leq n)$ and $A_1, \ldots, A_n \rightarrow B$ then $X \rightarrow B$.*

Since the Reflexivity, Augmentation and Transitivity port graph rewriting rules implement the rules stated in Proposition 2, to prove that Cl is sound and complete it suffices to show that any sequence of applications of these three rules can be transformed into a sequence in the order defined by the closure strategy.

Definition 8 (Canonical Form). *A sequence of applications of Reflexivity, Augmentation and Transitivity is in canonical form if it consists of applications of Reflexivity, followed by Augmentation, followed by Transitivity and Augmentation: $(Reflexivity)^*(Augmentation)^*(Transitivity; Augmentation^*)^*$*

Proposition 3 (Soundness and Completeness of Strategy 1). *Canonical sequences are sound and complete.*

5   Finding a Minimal Cover

To generate a Minimal Cover (see Sect. 2 for the definition) we have to ensure that there are no extraneous attributes on FD left sides and there are no redundant FDs (we already have singleton right sides). Standard algorithms check this by running the Membership algorithm on an altered Σ: remove $X \rightarrow A$ and replace it with $X \setminus B \rightarrow A$. If this still yields the same Σ^+ then B is extraneous in X. Instead, since we have Σ^+ at hand, it suffices to check if there exists $Z \subset X \rightarrow A$, for all proper subsets Z. We use a variadic rewriting rule (Sect. 3.2) to specify a family of rules for every possible subset pair (n, k), where $n = |X|$ and $k = |Z|$. Since $Z \subset X$, we make use of the partially expanded variadic edge feature by restricting one variadic edge to only k expansions. We show the variadic rule (parameterised already with $n = 3, k = 2$) in Fig. 8.

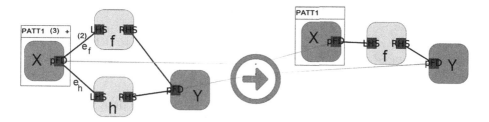

Fig. 8. Extraneous variadic rule. (Color figure online)

Next, we have to remove redundant FDs. A functional dependency $\varphi : X \to A$ is redundant, if $(\Sigma \setminus \varphi)^+ = \Sigma^+$ [21]. Previously published algorithms detected this by running a Membership check on $(\Sigma \setminus \varphi)$ to see if it yields φ. We note that in an FDPG representing $(\Sigma \setminus \varphi)^+$ there is an FDPG-Path from X to A. This path exists as an FD node created by the Syntactic Closure strategy, and if a dependency can be inferred in multiple ways, it is present multiple times. Since $|X| \geq 1$, we use a VRR to detect and remove the redundant FD nodes. We present the rule and an expansion in Figs. 9 and 10.

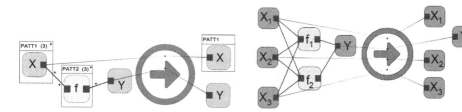

Fig. 9. Nonredundancy VRR. (Color figure online)

Fig. 10. Nonredundancy rule, $i_1 = 3$, $i_2 = 2$. (Color figure online)

Using the Extraneous and Nonredundancy rules, Strategy 3 computes a Minimal Cover under the assumption that there are no FD-cycles. We reuse the Syntactic Closure strategy, but without the Clean Up rules. The Nonredundancy rule gets rid of duplicates. Lastly, we remove trivial dependencies (FD nodes where UID = 1), as they are not in the minimal cover.

Strategy 3: Minimal Cover

---

1 #Syntactic Closure without Cleanup#
2 setPos(all($crtGraph$)); setBan(all([$emptySet$]));
3 repeat(one($Extraneous$)); repeat(one($Nonredundancy$));
4 repeat(one($RemoveTrivial$));

---

6   Conclusion and Future Work

We introduced variadic rewriting rules and used these rules to define strategies that compute and analyse the syntactic closure of a set of Functional Dependencies. These strategies are terminating, sound and complete. We have also defined additional rules and a strategy to compute Minimal Covers.

A minimal cover is the input of algorithms to find candidate keys [24] and of Bernstein's 3NF Synthesis Algorithm [10]. The strategies that find these will make use of the already defined CK and Relation nodes. Furthermore, 3NF Relations will require the introduction of the notion of Foreign Key.

References

1. Abrial, J.: Data semantics. In: Klimbie, J.W., Koffeman, K.L. (eds.) Proceeding of the IFIP Working Conference Data Base Management, Cargèse, Corsica, France, 1–5 April 1974, pp. 1–60. North-Holland (1974)
2. Andrei, O.: Rewriting calculus for graphs: applications to biology and autonomous systems. Ph.D. thesis, Institut National Polytechnique de Lorraine, Nancy, France, November 2008
3. Andrei, O., Fernández, M., Kirchner, H., Melançon, G., Namet, O., Pinaud, B.: Porgy: strategy-driven interactive transformation of graphs. In: Echahed, R. (ed.) TERMGRAPH. EPTCS, vol. 48, pp. 54–68 (2011)
4. Armstrong, W.W.: Dependency structures of data base relationships. In: Proceedings of IFIP Congress, Information processing, vol. 74, pp. 580–583, North-Holland, Amsterdam (1974)
5. Ausiello, G., D'Atri, A., Saccà, D.: Graph algorithms for functional dependency manipulation. J. ACM **30**(4), 752–766 (1983). https://doi.org/10.1145/2157. 322404
6. Badia, A., Lemire, D.: A call to arms: revisiting database design. SIGMOD Rec. **40**(3), 61–69 (2011). https://doi.org/10.1145/2070736.2070750
7. Batini, C., D'Atri, A.: Rewriting systems as a tool for relational data base design. In: Claus, V., Ehrig, H., Rozenberg, G. (eds.) Graph Grammars 1978. LNCS, vol. 73, pp. 139–154. Springer, Heidelberg (1979). https://doi.org/10.1007/BFb0025717
8. Beeri, C., Bernstein, P.A.: Computational problems related to the design of normal form relational schemas. ACM Trans. Database Syst. **4**(1), 30–59 (1979)
9. Beeri, C., Fagin, R., Howard, J.H.: A complete axiomatization for functional and multivalued dependencies in database relations. In: Smith, D.C.P. (ed.) SIGMOD Conference, pp. 47–61. ACM (1977)
10. Bernstein, P.A.: Synthesizing third normal form relations from functional dependencies. ACM Trans. Database Syst. **1**(4), 277–298 (1976)
11. Borovanský, P., Kirchner, C., Kirchner, H., Moreau, P., Ringeissen, C.: An overview of ELAN. Electr. Notes Theor. Comput. Sci. **15**, 55–70 (1998). https://doi.org/10. 1016/S1571-0661(05)82552-6
12. Ehrig, H., Engels, G., Kreowski, H., Rozenberg, G. (eds.): Handbook of Graph Grammars and Computing by Graph Transformation: Applications, Languages and Tools, vol. 2. World Scientific, River Edge (1999)
13. Embley, D.W., Mok, W.Y.: Mapping conceptual models to database schemas. In: Embley, D.W., Thalheim, B. (eds.) Handbook of Conceptual Modeling, vol. XIX, pp. 123–164. Springer, Heidelberg (2011). https://doi.org/10.1007/978-3-642-15865-0_5

14. Fernández, M., Kirchner, H., Pinaud, B.: Strategic Port Graph Rewriting: an Inter-active Modelling Framework. Math. Struct. Comput. Sci. 1–48 (2018). https://doi.org/10.1017/S0960129518000270. https://hal.inria.fr/hal-01251871
15. Fernández, M., Kirchner, H., Pinaud, B., Vallet, J.: Labelled graph strategic rewriting for social networks. J. Log. Algebr. Meth. Program. **96**, 12–40 (2018). https://doi.org/10.1016/j.jlamp.2017.12.005
16. Garcia-Molina, H., Ullman, J.D., Widom, J.: Database Systems - The Complete Book, 2nd edn. Pearson Education, Harlow (2014)
17. Jahnke, J.H., Zündorf, A.: Applying graph transformations to database re-engineering. In: Ehrig et al., vol. 12, pp. 267–286 (1999)
18. Jiresch, E.: Extending the interaction nets calculus by generic rules. In: Alves, S., Mackie, I. (eds.) Proceedings 2nd International Workshop on Linearity, LIN-EARITY 2012, Tallinn, Estonia, 1 April 2012. EPTCS, vol. 101, pp. 12–24 (2012). https://doi.org/10.4204/EPTCS.101.2
19. Kalleberg, K.T.: Stratego: a programming language for program manipulation. ACM Crossroads **12**(3), 4 (2006). https://doi.org/10.1145/1144366.1144370
20. Löwe, M.: Algebraic approach to single-pushout graph transformation. Theor. Comput. Sci. **109**(1 and 2), 181–224 (1993). https://doi.org/10.1016/0304-3975(93)90068-5
21. Maier, D.: Minimum covers in relational database model. J. ACM **27**(4), 664–674 (1980). https://doi.org/10.1145/322217.322223
22. Maier, D.: The Theory of Relational Databases. Computer Science Press, Rockville (1983)
23. Plump, D.: The design of GP 2. In: Escobar, S. (ed.) Proceedings 10th International Workshop on Reduction Strategies in Rewriting and Programming, WRS 2011, Novi Sad, Serbia, 29 May 2011. EPTCS, vol. 82, pp. 1–16 (2011). https://doi.org/10.4204/EPTCS.82.1
24. Saiedian, H., Spencer, T.: An efficient algorithm to compute the candidate keys of a relational database schema. Comput. J. **39**(2), 124–132 (1996). https://doi.org/10.1093/comjnl/39.2.124
25. Schürr, A., Winter, A.J., Zündorf, A.: The PROGRES approach: language and environment. In: Ehrig et al., vol. 12, pp. 551–603 (1999)
26. Vallet, J.: Where social networks, graph rewriting and visualisation meet: application to network generation and information diffusion. Ph.D. thesis, University of Bordeaux, France (2017). https://tel.archives-ouvertes.fr/tel-01691037
27. Varga, J.: Finding the transitive closure of functional dependencies using strategic port graph rewriting. In: Fernández, M., Mackie, I. (eds.) Proceedings Tenth International Workshop on Computing with Terms and Graphs, Oxford, UK, 7th July 2018. Electronic Proceedings in Theoretical Computer Science, vol. 288, pp. 50–62. Open Publishing Association (2019). https://doi.org/10.4204/EPTCS.288.5

Generalization-Driven Semantic Clone Detection in CLP

Wim Vanhoof[ID] and Gonzague Yernaux[✉][ID]

Faculty of Computer Science, Namur Digital Institute University of Namur,
Namur, Belgium
{wim.vanhoof,gonzague.yernaux}@unamur.be

Abstract. In this work we provide an algorithm capable of searching for semantic clones in CLP program code. Two code fragments are considered semantically cloned (at least to some extent) when they can both be transformed into a single code fragment thus representing the functionality that is shared between the fragments. While the framework of what constitutes such semantic clones has been established before, it is parametrized by a set of admissible program transformations and no algorithm exists that effectively performs the search with a concrete set of allowed transformations. In this work we use the well-known unfolding and slicing transformations to establish such an algorithm, and we show how the generalization of CLP goals can be a driving factor both for controlling the search process (i.e. keeping it finite) as for guiding the search (i.e. choosing what transformation(s) to apply at what moment).

1 Introduction and Motivation

Clone detection refers to the process of finding source code fragments that exhibit a sufficiently similar computational behavior, independent of them being textually equal or not. Such fragments are often called *clones*. While there is no standard definition of what constitutes a clone [16], in the literature one often distinguishes between four different classes, or types, of clones. The simplest class, sometimes called type-1 clones, refers to code fragments that differ only in layout and whitespace, whereas type-2 and type-3 clones allow for more (syntactical) variation such as renamed identifiers and statements and/or expressions that are different or lacking in one of the fragments. Type-4 clones on the other hand refer to fragments that are *semantically* equivalent, even if the respective source code fragments are quite different and seemingly unrelated [16]. This type of clones, also known as *semantic clones*, is arguably the most interesting albeit the most difficult type to find by automatic analysis.

While detecting semantic clones is an undecidable problem in general, it has applications in different domains such as program comprehension [6,15,18], plagiarism detection [24] and malware detection [23]. When approximated by program analysis, the resulting knowledge can also be used to drive advanced program transformations such as removal of redundant functionality from source

© Springer Nature Switzerland AG 2020
M. Gabbrielli (Ed.): LOPSTR 2019, LNCS 12042, pp. 228–242, 2020.
https://doi.org/10.1007/978-3-030-45260-5_14

code [14] and the automatic detection of a suitable parallelization strategy for a given code fragment [10,12]. Unsurprisingly, most current clone detection techniques are based on somehow comparing the syntactical structure of two code fragments and, consequently, are limited to detecting type-3 clones at best. Examples include the abstract syntax-tree based approaches for Erlang [9] and Haskell [2], as well as our own work [4] in the context of logic programming. Some approaches try to capture the essence of the algorithm at hand such as [1], where algorithms are converted into a system of recurrence equations or [20,21] where programs are abstracted by means of software metrics and program schemas.

In previous work, we have devised a framework for detecting semantic clones in logic programming [3]. The basic idea in that work is that two predicates are considered semantic clones if they can each be transformed – by a sequence of semantics-preserving program transformations – into a single common predicate definition. This is in line with other approaches towards semantic clone detection [16] where fragments are often considered implementing the same functionality if one can be transformed in the other. This framework was generalized to handle CLP in [11], which is of particular interest since CLP (or constrained Horn clauses in general) has been recognized before as a suitable abstraction to represent algorithmic logic [5]. As such, the framework for detecting semantic clones is lifted to a framework for characterizing *algorithmic equivalence* between the code fragments that were translated into CLP. However, in neither of these works an attempt was made to formulate *how* the search for a suitable series of program transformations could be performed or controlled. The question is far from trivial, given the literally enormous search space involved and the fact that the set of admissible transformations isn't known, being one of the framework's parameters. The use of CLP as the representation language for the input programs nevertheless allows us to restrict our attention to a limited number of powerful transformations such as slicing and unfolding, whereas more traditional approaches [12] usually consider a wide variety of more low-level transformations as they are working on the program's source code (such as renaming variables, loop unrolling, array manipulations, etc.). In this work, we present an algorithm capable of controlling the search for semantic clones when only the usual unfolding and slicing transformations are allowed. When concretized, it thus represents a workable decision procedure to test whether two given CLP fragments are (at least partially) algorithmically equivalent.

2   Semantic Clones: Setting the Stage

While in practice CLP is typically used over a concrete domain, we will in this work make abstraction of the concrete domain over which the constraints are expressed. A program P is defined as a set of constraint Horn clause definitions where each clause definition is of the form $p(V_1, \ldots, V_n) \leftarrow G$ with $p(V_1, \ldots, V_n)$ an atom called the head of the clause, and G a goal called the body of the clause. When necessary, we will decompose the body G in a set of domain constraints $\{C\}$ and a set of atoms $\{B\}$. For simplicity we suppose that all arguments in the head are variables (represented, as usual, by uppercase letters) and that all clauses defining a predicate have the same head (i.e. use the same variables to represent the arguments). A goal is a set of atoms and/or constraints. When we say "a predicate p", it will be clear from the context whether we mean the symbol p or the set of clauses defining p. When the arity of the predicate is relevant, we will use p/n to represent the fact that the predicate p has n arguments.

As usual substitutions, being mappings from variables to terms, will be denoted by Greek letters. The application of a substitution θ to a term t will be represented by $t\theta$ and the composition of substitutions θ and σ will be denoted $\theta\sigma$. A renaming is a substitution mapping variables to variables. We say that terms t_1 and t_2 are variants, denoted $t_1 \approx t_2$ iff they are equal modulo a bijective renaming.

While different semantics have been defined for CLP programs, for the remainder of this paper we can stick to the basic non-ground declarative semantics [7]. However, since the CLP predicates we wish to relate may originate from different sources, they potentially have a different number of arguments and, even if the predicates basically compute the same results, they may use different argument positions for storing what may essentially be the same values. The following definition captures what it means for two such predicates to compute the same result. It states that both predicates must have a subsequence of their argument positions (both sequences having the same size but containing possibly different argument positions and not necessarily in the same order) such that when the predicates are invoked with the corresponding arguments initialized with the same terms, then each predicate computes the same result. This means that for each pair of corresponding argument positions, the terms represented by these arguments must be the same (modulo a variable renaming) both at the moment the predicates are invoked (condition 1 in the definition) and at the moment the predicates return (condition 2 in the definition). As for notation, given a sequence R, we denote by R_i the i'th element of R.

Definition 1. *Given CLP programs P_1 and P_2, let p_s/n_s and p_q/n_q denote predicates in, respectively, P_1 and P_2 and let R and R' denote sequences of argument positions from respectively $\{1,\dots n_s\}$ and $\{1,\dots n_q\}$ such that $|R| = |R'| = n$. We say that (p_s, R) computes in P_1 a subset of (p_q, R') in P_2 if and only if for each call of the form $p_s(V_0,\dots,V_{n_s})\theta$ with computed answer substitution θ', there also exists a call $p_q(V_0,\dots,V_{n_q})\sigma$ with computed answer substitution σ' such that the following holds for all $k \in 1\dots n$:*

1. $(V_{R_k})\theta \approx (V_{R'_k})\sigma$
2. $(V_{R_k})\theta\theta' \approx (V_{R'_k})\sigma\sigma'$

Moreover, we say that (p_s, R) computes the same in P_1 as does (p_q, R') in P_2, denoted by $[\![p_s]\!]_R^{P_1} = [\![p_q]\!]_{R'}^{P_2}$ if and only if (p_s, R) computes a subset of (p_q, R') and vice versa in their respective programs.

The above definition allows us to characterize predicates as computing the same results, even if these predicates only *partially* exhibit the same behavior.

Indeed, what matters is that they compute the same values when restricted to the arguments in R, respectively R'. The values computed by arguments *not* comprised in either R or R' are not concerned and may be different. When the programs are clear from the context, we will drop the superscript notation and simply write $[\![p_s]\!]_R = [\![p_q]\!]_{R'}$

Example 1. Consider the predicate $p/3$ computing in its third argument the product of its first two arguments

$$p(A, B, P) \leftarrow B = 1, P = A$$
$$p(A, B, P) \leftarrow B' = B - 1, p(A, B', P'), P = P' + A$$

and $sp/4$ computing in its third and four arguments the sum, respectively, the product of its first two arguments:

$$sp(A, B, S, P) \leftarrow A = 1, S = B + 1, P = B.$$
$$sp(A, B, S, P) \leftarrow A' = A - 1, sp(A', B, S', P'), S = S' + 1, P = P' + B.$$

Note how both predicates share the functionality of computing the product of their first two arguments (although the role of A and B is switched). Therefore, we have that $[\![sp]\!]_{\langle 1,2,4 \rangle} = [\![p]\!]_{\langle 2,1,3 \rangle}$.

In order to further define our notion of semantic clones, we first need to introduce the following notions. First, we define the notion of an $\mathcal{R}_\alpha$-transformation sequence as follows, based on [13].

Definition 2. *Let P be a CLP program and $\mathcal{R}$ be a set of CLP program transformations. Then a $\mathcal{R}$-transformation sequence of P is a finite sequence of CLP programs, denoted $\langle P_0, P_1, \ldots, P_n \rangle$, where $P_0 = P$ and $\forall i \ (0 < i \le n) : P_i$ is obtained by the application of a transformation in $\mathcal{R}$ on P_{i-1}.*

Given CLP programs P and Q, we will often use $P \leadsto_{\mathcal{R}}^* Q$ to represent the fact that there exists an $\mathcal{R}$-transformation sequence $\langle P_0, P_1, \ldots, P_n \rangle$ with $P_0 = P$ and $P_n = Q$. We are only interested in transformation sequences that preserve the semantics of the original predicate, at least partially, i.e. with respect to a given sequence of argument positions.

Definition 3. *Let p and p' be predicates, and R and R' sequences of argument positions. A $\mathcal{R}$-transformation sequence $\langle P_0, P_1, \ldots, P_n \rangle$ correctly transforms (p, R) into (p', R') if and only if (p, R) computes the same result in P_0 as (p', R') in P_n.*

An example of transformation that could be part of the set $\mathcal{R}$ is the well-known *slicing* transformation, defined as an operation removing the constraints and/or atoms that concern a given argument of the predicate on which it is applied (based on [19]):

Definition 4. *Given the definition of a predicate p/n in a program P with head $p(X_1, \ldots, X_n)$. Then slicing the argument $X_i \in \{X_1, \ldots, X_n\}$ of p/n consists in removing from each clause of p/n all the constraints, atoms and arguments having a (direct or indirect) impact on X_i.*

The slicing operation, when part of $\mathcal{R}$, allows to transform a predicate into a lighter version where some of its arguments have been disregarded.

Example 2. Reconsider the definitions from Example 1 as well as a set of candidate transformations $\mathcal{R}$ containing at least the slicing transformation. It is not hard to see that there exists an $\mathcal{R}$-transformation sequence that correctly transforms $(sp, \langle 1, 2, 4 \rangle)$ into $(p, \langle 2, 1, 3 \rangle)$. Indeed, it suffices to remove the third argument (S) from sp and slice away the literals that manipulate S to obtain

$$sp(A, B, P) \leftarrow A = 1, P = B.$$
$$sp(A, B, P) \leftarrow A' = A - 1, sp(A', B, P'), P = P' + B.$$

which is, basically, a variant of p where the role of the first and second argument has been switched.

Definition 3 essentially defines what we will see as a correct transformation sequence: one that preserves the computation performed by a predicate of interest, at least with respect to a subset of its arguments. Note that the definition is parametrized with respect to the set $\mathcal{R}$ of allowed transformations. Also note that the definition is quite liberal, in the sense that it allows predicates to be renamed, arguments (and thus computations) to be left out of the equation, and arguments to be permuted. We are now in a position to define what we mean for the predicates to be semantic clones, at least with respect to a subset of their computations. The definition is loosely based on the notion of a semantic clone pair [3].

Definition 5. *Let p and q be predicates defined in, respectively the programs P and Q, and let R and S be sequences of argument positions. Then we define (p, R) and (q, S) $\mathcal{R}$-clones in P and Q if and only if there exists a program $\mathcal{T}$, predicate t and sequence of argument positions T such that $P \leadsto_{\mathcal{R}}^* \mathcal{T}$ correctly transforms (p, R) into (t, T) and $Q \leadsto_{\mathcal{R}}^* \mathcal{T}$ correctly transforms (q, S) into (t, T).*

Example 3. Reconsider the definitions from Example 1. If we permute, in the definition of p, the first and second arguments we obtain a predicate, say p', defined as follows:

$$p'(B, A, P) \leftarrow B = 1, P = A$$
$$p'(B, A, P) \leftarrow B' = B - 1, p'(B', A, P'), P = P' + A$$

which is a variant of the predicate in which sp was transformed using the transformation sequence from Example 2. Hence $(sp, \langle 1, 2, 4 \rangle)$ and $(p, \langle 2, 1, 3 \rangle)$ can be considered a clone pair since each can be correctly transformed into $(p', \langle 1, 2, 3 \rangle)$.

Our approach towards defining semantic clones is somewhat different from other transformation-based approaches in the sense that we consider (parts of) programs to be semantic clones if each of them can be transformed into a third, common, program while preserving the semantics (with respect to a subset of argument positions). As such, the third program captures the essence of the computations performed by the two given programs. Essentialy this corresponds to defining a *family* of semantic clones, depending on the instanciation of the set of allowable transformations $\mathcal{R}$.

In the following we study a first concrete incarnation of this framework for semantic code clones detection. We therefore define $\mathcal{R}_\alpha$ as the set composed only of slicing and unfolding. The unfolding transformation [13] allows to replace a call to a predicate with the body (or bodies) of the predicate in question as defined in the program, thereby unrolling (i.e. *unfolding*) the atom under scrutiny. Formally ([11]):

Definition 6. *Given a program P, let c be a clause $H \leftarrow \{C\}, \{B\}$ in P, B_s one of the atoms in $\{B\}$, and*
$$H_1 \leftarrow \{C_1\}, \{L_1\}$$
$$\vdots$$
$$H_n \leftarrow \{C_n\}, \{L_n\}$$
the (renamed apart) set of clauses in P such that $C \wedge C_i \wedge (B_s = H_i)$ is satisfiable for all $1 \leq i \leq n$. Then unfolding the atom B_s in the clause c consists in replacing c by the set of clauses $\{H \leftarrow \{C \wedge C_i \wedge (B_s = H_i)\}, \{B_i'| 1 \leq i \leq n\}\}$ where B_i' represents the conjunction obtained by replacing, in B, the atom B_s by the conjunction L_i.

Example 4. Let us consider the following predicates

$$p(X, Y, Z) \leftarrow X > Z, f(Y).$$
$$f(A) \qquad \leftarrow A < 5.$$

Unfolding the atom $f(Y)$ in the first predicate transforms its clause into:

$$p(X, Y, Z) \leftarrow X > Z, Y < 5.$$

In this clause, as the first and third arguments of $p/3$ are dependent on each other, slicing X away results in the following predicate (the same holds if it is Z that is sliced away):
$$p(Y) \leftarrow Y < 5.$$

As suggested above, our framework instanciated with the set $\mathcal{R}_\alpha$ defines a class of clones, namely the pairs of predicates that can be reduced to a third, common predicate through the application of only slicing and unfolding operations (modulo renaming). Although this class of clones is in essence restricted by $\mathcal{R}_\alpha$, it still constitutes a representative categorization, slicing and unfolding having proven to be powerful tools for transforming (constraint) logic programs.

3   Generalization-Driven Clone Detection Process

Searching whether two predicates $p \in P_0$ and $q \in Q_0$ are considered cloned necessitates thus to construct two transformation sequences, one for each program in the hope to arrive at a common program $\mathcal{T}$. Two problems present themselves: (1) even when limiting the allowed transformations to slicing and unfolding, there might be a considerable number of ways in which a partial transformation sequence $\langle P_0, \ldots, P_{k-1} \rangle$ can be extended into $\langle P_0, \ldots, P_k \rangle$. And (2), since we don't know the target program $\mathcal{T}$ in advance, it is hard to steer the search process. To tackle these problems, we first organize the constructed transformation sequences into a tree structure composed of the successive transformed programs, where each node is labeled by the argument positions that are preserved by the sequence of transformations thus far:

Definition 7. *Given a program P_0 along with a predicate $p/n \in P_0$, a $\mathcal{R}_\alpha$-transformation tree (sometimes abbreviated to $\mathcal{R}_\alpha$-tree) for p in P_0 is a tree in which each node has the form (P, R, R') where P is a program and R and R' are sequences over $\{1, \ldots, n\}$. The root of the tree is $(P_0, \langle 1, \ldots, n \rangle, \langle 1, \ldots, n \rangle)$ and for each node (P, R, R') it holds that $P_0 \leadsto_{\mathcal{R}_\alpha}^* P_k$ correctly transforms (p, R) into (p, R'). For a $\mathcal{R}_\alpha$-transformation tree τ we use $leafs(\tau)$ to represent the leaves of the tree.*

In other words, a $\mathcal{R}_\alpha$-transformation tree can be constructed by repeatedly extending one of its leaves by transforming the program contained in the leaf using one of the program transformations from $\mathcal{R}_\alpha$.

Next, we introduce the concept of abstraction that allows both to keep the tree finite and to guide the choice of the successive transformations to apply. We assume given a quasi-order $\preceq$ defined on goals such that for goals G and G', $G \preceq G'$ denotes that G is more general than G'. We furthermore assume an abstraction operator based on $\preceq$.

Definition 8. *Given a quasi-order $\preceq$ on goals, an abstraction operator $\mathcal{A}$ allows to compute a generalization of two goals. Given goals G_1, G_2 then $\mathcal{A}(G_1, G_2)$ represents a goal G such that $G \preceq G_1$ and $G \preceq G_2$.*

While different incarnations of such a quasi-order can be defined, one typical definition could be the following: $G \preceq G'$ if and only if there exists a substitution θ such that $G\theta \subseteq G'$. This is a straightforward adaption of the well-known "more general than" relation defined on atoms and (ordered) conjunctions (e.g. ([17]) and the one we use in this work. Given an abstraction operator on goals, it is possible to define the generalization of clauses and predicates as illustrated by the following example.

Example 5. Consider the predicate $s/3$ computing in its third argument the sum of its first two arguments.

$$s(A, B, S) \leftarrow B = 0, S = A$$
$$s(A, B, S) \leftarrow B' = B - 1, s(A, B', P'), S = S' + 1$$

Then it is not hard to see that

$$s'(A, B, S, N, I) \leftarrow B = N, S = A$$
$$s'(A, B, S, N, I) \leftarrow B' = B - 1, s'(A, B', S', N, I), S = S' + I$$

can be considered a generalization of the $s/3$ predicate defined in the present example and the $p/3$ predicate defined in Example 1. Indeed, it can be obtained by pairwise considering the predicates' clauses, constructing a new (generalized) clause by generalizing the respective body goals using the abstraction operator, introducing (a subset of) the new variables as arguments and carefully renaming these arguments so that all clauses share the same head.

In previous work, we have showed that computing these generalizations – in particular the most specific, or most precise, generalization – is not a straightforward problem, and have proposed an algorithm for computing a generalization that approximates the most specific generalization of two sets of atoms in polynomially bounded time [22]. In this work we take such an abstraction algorithm for granted (formalized by our abstraction operator $\mathcal{A}$) and we study how such an abstraction operator can be used for steering the search for $\mathcal{R}_\alpha$-clone pairs. First we introduce the notion of a size measure, represented by $|.|$, being a function that defines the size of a syntactic construction (be it a goal, clause, or predicate definition). The size measure is such that:

- for any syntactical constructs a and b that are variants of each other, then $|a| = |b|$;
- for any syntactical constructs a and b, if a is more general than b ($a \preceq b$), then $|a| \leq |b|$.

Such a size measure can be used to define a distance between two predicate definitions as in the following definition.

Definition 9. *Given an abstraction operator $\mathcal{A}$ and a size measure $|.|$ measuring the size of a predicate definition, then we define the* distance *between predicates p and q as follows:*

$$\delta(p, q) = 1 - \frac{2 \times |\mathcal{A}(p, q)|}{|p| + |q|}$$

Since, by definition, $|\mathcal{A}(p, q)| \leq |p|$ and $|\mathcal{A}(p, q)| \leq |q|$, we have that $\delta(p, q)$ is a value between 0 and 1. If the generalization $\mathcal{A}(p, q)$ is empty (meaning there is no pair of atoms that can be generalized by a single atom in the generalization), the distance will be 1. On the other hand, the distance will be zero if the predicates are variants of each other. Now, given programs P_0 and Q_0 and predicates $p/n \in P_0$ and $q/m \in Q_0$, we can use this distance to steer a process that transforms p and q so that the distance between the (transformed) predicates becomes smaller. If, at some point, the distance becomes zero, we can conclude that the predicates are $\mathcal{R}_\alpha$-cloned, at least with respect to a subset of their arguments. The process is depicted in Algorithm 1. The main loop of the algorithm will extend the transformation trees τ_1 for p in P_0 and τ_2 for q in Q_0 and is repeated as long as at least one pair of leafs from the respective trees gets closer than the minimum distance obtained between leaves at the previous iteration. In other words, the process is repeated as long as some progress is achieved in making the predicate definitions closer through the application of transformations on the versions of p and q contained in the tree leaves. Since the distances are bounded by zero, the algorithm is necessarily terminating.

The idea of the algorithm is thus to select at each iteration the most promising candidates for extension, which are the couples of leaves for which the definitions of p and q are the closest in distance. For readability we use the notation $closest\_leaves(\tau_1, \tau_2, n)$ to denote the n pairs $((P_i, R_i, R'_i), (Q_j, S_j, S'_j))$ in $leafs(\tau_1) \times leafs(\tau_2)$ for which the corresponding definitions of $p \in P_i$ and $q \in Q_j$ are closest in distance. Slightly abusing notation, to refer to this distance we will use $\delta((P_i, R_i, R'_i), (Q_j, S_j, S'_j))$.

The algorithm will extend each of those selected pairs by applying a judicious transformation to pairwise corresponding clauses in the predicates. However, the predicates can be composed of several clauses and we yet have to determine which of those should be considered to be pairwise corresponding clauses. Once again, we will tackle this problem by computing the pairs of clauses for which the distance δ is minimal. For two nodes (P_i, R_i, R'_i) and (Q_j, S_j, S'_j) we denote the K closest independent pairs of clauses of p and q in the respective programs P_i and Q_j by $closest\_clauses((P_i, R_i, R'_i), (Q_j, S_j, S'_j), K)$. Each of these pairs of clauses will be transformed in either P_i, Q_j or both, giving rise to a new child node of (P_i, R_i, R'_i), respectively (Q_j, S_j, S'_j), or both. When unfolding is applied, the argument sequences R_i and R'_i (resp. S_j and S'_j) will stay untouched, while slicing might rearrange the sequences, resulting in R'_i (resp. S'_j) denoting the new positions of the unsliced arguments in the target programs.

The trees constructed by the algorithm are correct $\mathcal{R}_\alpha$-trees in the sense of Definition 7.

Proposition 1. *Given predicates and programs $p/n \in P_0$ and $q/m \in Q_0$. Let (τ_1, τ_2) be transformation trees created by Algorithm 1. Then for each node (P, R, R') in τ_1 it holds that $P_0 \leadsto^*_{\mathcal{R}_\alpha} P$ correctly transforms (p, R) into (p, R') and for each node (Q, S, S') in τ_2 it holds that $Q_0 \leadsto^*_{\mathcal{R}_\alpha} Q$ correctly transforms (q, S) into (q, S').*

Proof. We prove the result for τ_1 by induction; the proof is analogous for τ_2. Note that the root of τ_1, namely $(P_0, \langle 1, \ldots, n \rangle, \langle 1, \ldots, n \rangle)$ trivially satisfies the condition in the proposition with the empty $\mathcal{R}_\alpha$-transformation sequence. Now let (P, R, R') be a non-root node in τ_1 with parent node (P_i, R_i, R'_i), such that $P_0 \leadsto^*_{\mathcal{R}_\alpha} P_i$ correctly transforms (p, R_i) into (p, R'_i). The node (P, R, R') has either been obtained with the application of unfolding or by slicing on p in (P_i, R_i, R'_i). Unfolding being known to be a sound transformation in the most general and usual sense, all the computations of p are strictly preserved after having unfolded an atom in one of its clauses. Therefore in the case of unfolding, the child node has the same argument sequences as its parent, i.e. $R = R_i$ and $R' = R'_i$. As for the slicing of an argument, it has by definition no incidence on the remaining (untouched) arguments. In that case the algorithm sets R to the subsequence of R_i denoting the arguments that are left unsliced, and R' to their new positions in the resulting predicate. It follows that the sequences of arguments that are preserved after the application of the transformations are correctly identified in the successive nodes, hence the result.

Algorithm 1. Construction of $\mathcal{R}_\alpha$-transformation trees τ_1 and τ_2

$\tau_1 \leftarrow (P_0, \langle 1, \ldots, n \rangle, \langle 1, \ldots, n \rangle)$
$\tau_2 \leftarrow (Q_0, \langle 1, \ldots, m \rangle, \langle 1, \ldots, m \rangle)$
$\delta_1 \leftarrow 2$
while $\delta(closest\_leaves(\tau_1, \tau_2, 1)) > 0$ and $\delta(closest\_leaves(\tau_1, \tau_2, 1)) < \delta_1$ **do**
    $\delta_1 \leftarrow \delta(closest\_leaves(\tau_1, \tau_2, 1))$
    for all $((P_i, R_i, R_i'), (Q_j, S_j, S_j'))$ in $closest\_leaves(N)$ **do**
        EXTEND$((P_i, R_i, R_i'), (Q_j, S_j, S_j'))$
    end for
end while

function EXTEND$((P_i, R_i, R_i'), (Q_j, S_j, S_j'))$
    for all $(H_p \leftarrow G_p, H_q \leftarrow G_q)$ in $closest\_clauses((P_i, R_i, R_i'), (Q_j, S_j, S_j'), K)$ **do**
        $G \leftarrow \mathcal{A}(G_p, G_q)$ such that $G_p = G\theta_p \cup \Delta_p$ and $G_q = G\theta_q \cup \Delta_q$
        if $\Delta_p = \emptyset$ **then**
            apply slicing on q in such a way that literals from Δ_q are eliminated
        else if $\Delta_q = \emptyset$ **then**
            apply slicing on p in such a way that literals from Δ_p are eliminated
        else if unfolding atoms in Δ_p gives rise to variants of constraints in Δ_q **then**
            apply unfolding on these atoms
        else if unfolding atoms in Δ_q gives rise to variants of constraints in Δ_p **then**
            apply unfolding on these atoms
        else
            apply slicing on p and/or q in such a way that literals from Δ_p and/or Δ_q
are eliminated
        end if
        if p has been transformed **then**
            Create (P, R, R') as a child of (P_i, R_i, R_i') where P is a variation of P_i with
the transformed version of p replacing p, and where in case of unfolding, $R = R_i$ and
$R' = R_i'$ and in case of slicing, R denotes the arguments that are left unsliced, and
R' denotes their new positions in the transformed version of p.
        end if
        if q has been transformed **then**
            Create (Q, S, S') as a child of (Q_j, S_j, S_j') similarly
        end if
    end for
end function

Note that the process is parametrized by N and K. If $N = 1$ the process continues by transforming in each step *the* most promising couple of leaves. While this might be efficient, it is in no way guaranteed that the search finds the "right" transformation sequences as it can be stuck in a local optimum. Using a larger value for N is a rudimentary way of eliminating this problem. The parameter K on the other hand allows to explore the transformation of different pairs of clauses (at least when $K > 1$) in order to extend a single leaf.

While the main loop of Algorithm 1 details how the search is controlled (it specifies how to guarantee termination while extending the N *most promising* pairs of leafs in each round), the EXTEND procedure specifies how to choose which of slicing or unfolding to apply to a couple of clauses in two nodes (P_i, R_i, R'_i) and (Q_j, S_j, S'_j). In order to steer this selection, we search for the program transformation that, again, lowers the distance between the current definitions of predicates p and q as they are defined in P_i and Q_j respectively. For this, once more information from the generalization process can be used to guide the selection. Indeed, the generalization G represents the part that is common to p and q while Δ_p and Δ_q represent the parts specific to the current definition of p, respectively q. Information from these structures can be exploited in order to select the most promising transformation to apply on one of the predicates (i.e. the transformation that will bring the two predicates' definitions closer). Such a strategy is outlined in the EXTEND operation. The two first conditions check whether the generalization $\mathcal{A}(p, q)$ is of maximal size. In that case, the only meaningful way in which the search can continue is by slicing parts of the non-empty delta. If neither Δ_p nor Δ_q are empty, the search should focus on making Δ_p and Δ_q more similar, in order to enlarge the common part G shared by both clauses (with the use of unfolding) or, less preferably, render both Δ_p and Δ_q smaller (by slicing). Although the EXTEND function relies on the analysis of pairs of corresponding clauses, its application effectively modifies the definition of the considered predicate as a whole, yielding new nodes containing the modified programs and the corresponding argument positions.

Corollary 1. *Let P_0 and Q_0 be programs, $p \in P_0$ and $q \in Q_0$ predicates, τ_1 and τ_2 the transformation trees created by Algorithm 1. Let closest_leaves$(\tau_1, \tau_2, 1) = \{((P, R, R'), (Q, S, S'))\}$. If $\delta((P, R, R'), (Q, S, S')) = 0$, then (p, R) and (q, S) are $\mathcal{R}_\alpha$-clones in P_0 and Q_0.*

Proof. If the distance between the two nodes is zero, the code of p in P and q in Q is equivalent at least with respect to the argument sequences R and S. Because of Proposition 1 we have that $P_0 \leadsto^*_{\mathcal{R}_\alpha} P$ correctly transforms (p, R) into (p, R') and $Q_0 \leadsto^*_{\mathcal{R}_\alpha} Q$ correctly transforms (q, S) into (q, S'). Now, $p \in P$ and $q \in Q$ is essentially the same predicate (modulo renaming and reordering of the arguments) and so they can be considered $\mathcal{R}_\alpha$-clones in the sense of Definition 5.

Given the limited search space explored by Algorithm 1, it is trivial to see that the process is *incomplete*, in the sense that there exist $\mathcal{R}_\alpha$-clones that are *not* detected by the process.

We conclude this section with the following (simplified) example serving as an illustration for the ideas driving the process described above.

Example 6. Let us consider the following predicates defined in some program P_0:

$$max(X, Y, Z, M) \leftarrow X \geq Y, m(X, Z, M).$$
$$max(X, Y, Z, M) \leftarrow Y > X, m(Y, Z, M).$$
$$m(A, B, M) \quad\quad \leftarrow A \geq B, M = A.$$
$$m(A, B, M) \quad\quad \leftarrow B > A, M = B.$$

as well as the following predicates defined in some program Q_0:

$$minmax(U, V, W, Min, Max) \leftarrow U \geq V, U \geq W, Max = U, min(V, W, Min).$$
$$minmax(U, V, W, Min, Max) \leftarrow U \geq V, W > U, Max = W, min(U, V, Min).$$
$$minmax(U, V, W, Min, Max) \leftarrow V > U, V \geq W, Max = V, min(U, W, Min).$$
$$minmax(U, V, W, Min, Max) \leftarrow V > U, W \geq V, Max = W, min(U, V, Min).$$
$$min(A, B, M) \qquad\qquad\qquad \leftarrow A > B, M = B.$$
$$min(A, B, M) \qquad\qquad\qquad \leftarrow B \geq A, M = A.$$

Suspicious that $max/4$ in P_0 and $minmax/5$ in Q_0 might exhibit some common functionality, let us apply Algorithm 1 to the two predicates. First, we need to compute $\mathcal{A}(max, minmax)$, which yields (a variant of) the following predicate:

$$g(G_1, G_2, G_3, G_4, G_5) \leftarrow X \geq Y.$$
$$g(G_1, G_2, G_3, G_4, G_5) \leftarrow Y > X.$$

Obviously for each clause from max, Δ_{max} (the differences between pairwise clauses from max and g) is not empty, as the clauses from g harbor less information than the corresponding clauses from max. The same holds for Δ_{minmax}. We will thus try to apply unfolding on one of the input predicates in the hope of bringing the predicate definitions closer to each other. It is easy to see that unfolding the calls to $min/3$ in $minmax$ would not lead to the generalization being any larger; on the other hand, unfolding the calls to $m/3$ in max is an adequate way to enlarge the common parts of both predicates. Indeed, after unfolding all the calls to $m/3$, the predicate max becomes defined as the following:

$$max(X, Y, Z, M) \leftarrow X \geq Y, X \geq Z, M = X.$$
$$max(X, Y, Z, M) \leftarrow X \geq Y, Z > X, M = Z.$$
$$max(X, Y, Z, M) \leftarrow Y > X, Y \geq Z, M = Y.$$
$$max(X, Y, Z, M) \leftarrow Y > X, Z > Y, M = Z.$$

Now computing the most specific generalization of this new version of the max predicate and the unchanged $minmax$ predicate yields (a variant of) the following:

$$g(G_1, G_2, G_3, G_4, G_5) \leftarrow G_1 \geq G_2, G_1 \geq G_3, G_5 = G_1.$$
$$g(G_1, G_2, G_3, G_4, G_5) \leftarrow G_1 \geq G_2, G_3 > G_1, G_5 = G_3.$$
$$g(G_1, G_2, G_3, G_4, G_5) \leftarrow G_2 > G_1, G_2 \geq G_3, G_5 = G_2.$$
$$g(G_1, G_2, G_3, G_4, G_5) \leftarrow G_2 > G_1, G_3 > G_2, G_5 = G_3.$$

which is easily identified as a variant of max (with one variable, namely G_4, having no correspondence with a variable of max).

Therefore by computing the differences between g and our input predicates we get empty Δ_{max} values while the corresponding Δ_{minmax} values contain the calls to $min/3$. In this situation the EXTEND procedure prescribes to use slicing on those parts of $minmax$ that are part of the Δ_{minmax} sets (including the Min variable only used in the call to $min/3$). This yields a new version of $minmax$:

$$minmax(U, V, W, Max) \leftarrow U \geq V, U \geq W, Max = U$$
$$minmax(U, V, W, Max) \leftarrow U \geq V, W > U, Max = W.$$
$$minmax(U, V, W, Max) \leftarrow V > U, V \geq W, Max = V.$$
$$minmax(U, V, W, Max) \leftarrow V > U, W \geq V, Max = W.$$

This time, the most specific generalization of max and $minmax$ is of maximal size as it is a variant of both predicates. In this setting we have achieved a distance of 0 between the predicates and their common generalization g, thus exiting the loop of Algorithm 1 with the conclusion that $(max, \langle 1, 2, 3, 4 \rangle)$ and $(minmax, \langle 1, 2, 3, 5 \rangle)$ are $\mathcal{R}_\alpha$-clones in P_0 and Q_0 (at least modulo renaming).

4   Conclusions and Future Work

While the theoretical framework of semantic clones in logic programming has been established before, this work is – to the best of our knowledge – the first attempt in devising a practical algorithm capable of *searching* for a series of unfolding and slicing transformations that reduce two given CLP fragments to a single code fragment representing the functionality that is common to the two fragments; as such proving that the fragments are (at least to some extent) semantic clones. Slicing and unfolding are powerful transformations; yet the set $\mathcal{R}_\alpha$ constitutes a somewhat restricted incarnation of the general set of allowable transformations $\mathcal{R}$ defined as a parameter in the framework from [11]. Of course, this limitation narrows down the degree of clone detection that can be achieved. Working out a way to generalize our search procedure, e.g. by incorporating other candidate transformations in the process, is a topic of ongoing and future research. Transformations such as arguments reordering and folding [13] for instance constitute a first natural extension of our set $\mathcal{R}_\alpha$, the consequences of which yet have to be explored. In particular, studying transformations that are specific to certain domains, such as numeric constraints normalization, is also an open field for future research.

The search algorithm that we propose is essentially comprised of two control levels: one level that controls the termination of the process and a second one that considers what transformation to apply next. In that respect, it is not unlike control techniques used in partial deduction [8] where a *global* control level is used to ensure termination of the process and a *local* control is concerned by constructing a suitable SLD tree for an atom or a conjunction of atoms.

A key ingredient in our approach is a generalization operator that allows to generalize two goals and that can, additionally, be used to compute a distance between these goals. Generalization (or anti-unification) is a simple and well-known syntactical process, at least as far as single atoms or (ordered) conjunctions are concerned. It becomes more complicated when, as is the case in our setting, sets of atoms and/or constraints need to be considered. We have for this reason recently devised an approximation algorithm for computing most specific generalizations of sets of literals [22], and aim to incorporate this further into the algorithm developed above. Another topic of future work is to include higher-order anti-unification capabilities in the algorithm, which is currently restricted to first-order generalizations only.

Acknowledgements. We thank anonymous reviewers and the participants of LOP-STR 2019 for their constructive input and remarks.

References

1. Alias, C., Barthou, D.: Algorithm recognition based on demand-driven data-flow analysis. In: Proceedings of the 10th Working Conference on Reverse Engineering (WCRE), pp. 296–305 (2003). https://doi.org/10.1109/WCRE.2003.1287260
2. Brown, C., Thompson, S.: Clone detection and elimination for Haskell. In: Proceedings of the 2010 SIGPLAN Workshop on Partial Evaluation and Program Manipulation (PEPM 2010), pp. 111–120. ACM (2010). https://doi.org/10.1145/1706356.1706378
3. Dandois, C., Vanhoof, W.: Semantic code clones in logic programs. In: Albert, E. (ed.) LOPSTR 2012. LNCS, vol. 7844, pp. 35–50. Springer, Heidelberg (2013). https://doi.org/10.1007/978-3-642-38197-3_4
4. Dandois, C., Vanhoof, W.: Clones in logic programs and how to detect them. In: Vidal, G. (ed.) LOPSTR 2011. LNCS, vol. 7225, pp. 90–105. Springer, Heidelberg (2012). https://doi.org/10.1007/978-3-642-32211-2_7
5. Gange, G., Navas, J.A., Schachte, P., Søndergaard, H., Stuckey, P.J.: Horn clauses as an intermediate representation for program analysis and transformation. TPLP **15**(4–5), 526–542 (2015). https://doi.org/10.1017/S1471068415000204
6. Green, C., Luckham, D., Balzer, R., Cheatham, T., Rich, C.: Report on a knowledge-based software assistant. Technical report, Kestrel Institute (1983). https://doi.org/10.5555/31870.31893
7. Jaffar, J., Maher, M.J., Marriott, K., Stuckey, P.J.: The semantics of constraint logic programs. J. Logic Program. **37**(1–3), 1–46 (1998). https://doi.org/10.1016/S0743-1066(98)10002-X
8. Leuschel, M., Bruynooghe, M.: Logic program specialisation through partial deduction: control issues. Theory Pract. Logic Program. **2**(4–5), 461–515 (2002). https://doi.org/10.1017/S147106840200145X
9. Li, H., Thompson, S.: Clone detection and removal for Erlang/OTP within a refactoring environment. In: Proceedings of the 2009 SIGPLAN Workshop on Partial Evaluation and Program Manipulation (PEPM 2009), pp. 169–178. ACM (2009). https://doi.org/10.1145/1480945.1480971
10. Martino, B.D., Iannello, G.: PAP recognizer: a tool for automatic recognition of parallelizable patterns. In: 4th International Workshop on Program Comprehension (WPC), p. 164 (1996). https://doi.org/10.1109/WPC.1996.501131
11. Mesnard, F., Payet, E., Vanhoof, W.: Towards a framework for algorithm recognition in binary code. In: Proceedings of the 18th International Symposium on Principles and Practice of Declarative Programming, pp. 202–213. PPDP 2016, ACM, New York (2016). https://doi.org/10.1145/2967973.2968600
12. Metzger, R., Wen, Z.: Automatic Algorithm Recognition and Replacement. MIT Press, Cambridge (2000)
13. Pettorossi, A., Proietti, M.: Transformation of logic programs. In: Gabbay, D.M., Hogger, C.J., Robinson, J.A. (eds.) Handbook of Logic in Artificial Intelligence and Logic Programming, vol. 5, pp. 697–787. Oxford University Press, Oxford (1998)
14. Rattan, D., Bhatia, R.K., Singh, M.: Software clone detection: a systematic review. Inf. Softw. Technol. **55**(7), 1165–1199 (2013). https://doi.org/10.1016/j.infsof.2013.01.008

15. Rich, C., Shrobe, H.E., Waters, R.C.: Overview of the programmer's apprentice. In: Proceedings of the Sixth International Joint Conference on Artificial Intelligence (IJCAI), pp. 827–828 (1979). https://doi.org/10.5555/1623050.1623101

16. Roy, C.K., Cordy, J.R., Koschke, R.: Comparison and evaluation of code clone detection techniques and tools: a qualitative approach. Sci. Comput. Program. **74**(7), 470–495 (2009). https://doi.org/10.1016/j.scico.2009.02.007

17. Sørensen, M.H., Glück, R.: An algorithm of generalization in positive supercompilation. In: Logic Programming, Proceedings of the 1995 International Symposium, Portland, Oregon, USA, 4–7 December 1995, pp. 465–479 (1995). https://doi.org/10.7551/mitpress/4301.003.0048

18. Storey, M.D.: Theories, methods and tools in program comprehension: past, present and future. In: 13th International Workshop on Program Comprehension (IWPC), pp. 181–191 (2005). https://doi.org/10.1007/s11219-006-9216-4

19. Szilágyi, G., Gyimóthy, T., Małuszyński, J.: Static and dynamic slicing of constraint logic programs. Autom. Softw. Eng. **9**(1), 41–65 (2002). https://doi.org/10.1023/A:1013280119003

20. Taherkhani, A.: Using decision tree classifiers in source code analysis to recognize algorithms: an experiment with sorting algorithms. Comput. J. **54**(11), 1845–1860 (2011). https://doi.org/10.1093/comjnl/bxr025

21. Taherkhani, A., Malmi, L.: Beacon- and schema-based method for recognizing algorithms from students' source code. J. Educ. Data Min. **5**(2), 69–101 (2013). https://doi.org/10.5281/zenodo.3554635

22. Yernaux, G., Vanhoof, W.: Anti-unification in constraint logic programming. Theory Pract. Logic Program. **19**(5–6), 773–789 (2019). https://doi.org/10.1017/S1471068419000188

23. Zhang, F., Huang, H., Zhu, S., Wu, D., Liu, P.: Viewdroid: towards obfuscation-resilient mobile application repackaging detection. In: Proceedings of the 2014 ACM Conference on Security and Privacy in Wireless and Mobile Networks, WiSec 2014, pp. 25–36. ACM (2014). https://doi.org/10.1145/2627393.2627395

24. Zhang, F., Jhi, Y.C., Wu, D., Liu, P., Zhu, S.: A first step towards algorithm plagiarism detection. In: Proceedings of the 2012 International Symposium on Software Testing and Analysis, ISSTA 2012, pp. 111–121. ACM (2012). https://doi.org/10.1145/2338965.2336767

Semi-inversion of Conditional Constructor Term Rewriting Systems

Maja Hanne Kirkeby[1]($\boxtimes$) and Robert Glück[2]

[1] Roskilde University, Roskilde, Denmark
kirkebym@acm.org
[2] DIKU, University of Copenhagen, Copenhagen, Denmark
glueck@acm.org

Abstract. Inversion is an important and useful program transformation and has been studied in various programming language paradigms. Semi-inversion is more general than just swapping the input and output of a program; instead, parts of the input and output can be freely swapped. In this paper, we present a polyvariant semi-inversion algorithm for conditional constructor term rewriting systems. These systems can model logic and functional languages, which have the advantage that semi-inversion, as well as partial and full inversion, can be studied across different programming paradigms. The semi-inverter makes use of local inversion and a simple but effective heuristic and is proven to be correct. A Prolog implementation is applied to several problems, including inversion of a simple encrypter and of a program inverter for a reversible language.

Keywords: Program transformation · Program inversion · Conditional term rewriting systems · Logic and functional programs

1 Introduction

Programs that are inverse to each other are widely used, such as encoding and decoding of data. The transformation of an encoder into a decoder, or vice versa, is called full inversion. *Semi-inversion*, the most general type of program inversion, transforms one relation into a new relation that takes a subset of the original input and output as the new input. For example, the transformation of a symmetric encrypter into a decrypter cannot be achieved by conventional full inversion because both programs take the same key as input.

In this paper, we present a polyvariant semi-inversion algorithm for an oriented *conditional constructor term rewriting system* (CCS) [22]. The algorithm makes use of local inversion and a simple but effective heuristic and is proven to be correct. A Prolog implementation is applied to several transformation problems, including the inversion of a simple symmetric encrypter. As a special transformation challenge, a program inverter for a reversible imperative language was inverted into a copy of itself modulo variable renaming.

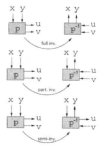

© Springer Nature Switzerland AG 2020
M. Gabbrielli (Ed.): LOPSTR 2019, LNCS 12042, pp. 243–259, 2020.
https://doi.org/10.1007/978-3-030-45260-5_15

We distinguish between three forms of program inversion: *Full inversion* turns a program p into a new program p^{-1}, where the original inputs and outputs are exchanged. If p is injective, then p^{-1} implements a function. *Partial inversion* yields a program p^{-1} that inputs the original output (u, v) and some of the original input (x) and then returns the remaining input (y). *Semi-inversion* yields a program p^{-1} that, given some of the original input (x) and some of the original output (v), returns the remaining input (y) and output (u). The programs p and p^{-1} may implement functions or more general relations. Full inversion is a subproblem of partial inversion, which is a subproblem of semi-inversion:

$$\text{full inversion} \subseteq \text{partial inversion} \subseteq \text{semi-inversion.}$$

Dijkstra was the first to study the full inversion of programs in a guarded command language [6]. Subsequently, some program inversion algorithms were developed for different forms of inversion and for different programming languages. Of those, only Nishida et al. [19] and Almendros-Jiménez et al. [2] have considered term rewriting systems, where the latter constrained the systems such that terms have a unique normal form, i.e., the systems express functional input-output relations. Mogensen [14,15], who developed the first semi-inversion algorithm, did so for a deterministic guarded equational language, i.e., with functional input-output relations. Methods for inversion have been studied in the context of functional languages [7–11]. The motivation for using *program inversion* instead of *inverse interpretation*, such as [1,13], is similar to the motivation for using translation instead of interpretation.

The main advantage of oriented conditional constructor term rewriting systems is that they can model both *logic* and *functional* languages [5], and, hence, *functional logical* languages [12]. When modeling logic languages, an efficient evaluation requires narrowing (unification) [5,12], which typically has a larger search space than standard rewriting (matching). By requiring that the rewrite rules be not only left-orthogonal but also right-orthogonal and non-deleting, we can also model *reversible* languages [23]. This enables us to focus on the essence of semi-inversion without considering language-specific details. The semantics of *functions* and *relations* can be expressed and efficiently calculated in the same formalism (*cf.*, Ex. 2). The idea to use CCSs to investigate semi-inversion for different language paradigms was inspired by the partial inverter developed by Nishida et al. [19].

The new semi-inverter relates to some of the mentioned inversion algorithms:

	Functions	Relations
Full inversion	Glück and Kawabe [8]	Nishida et al. [17,20]
Partial inversion	Almendros-Jiménez et al. [2]	Nishida et al. [19]
Semi-inversion	Mogensen [14]	*This algorithm*

This paper provides (1) a polyvariant semi-inversion algorithm for CCSs that uses local inversion and is proven correct; (2) a simple but effective heuristic to avoid narrowing and to minimize the search space; and (3) an experimental evaluation by applying the Prolog implementation to a simple encryption algorithm, a physical discrete-event simulation, and a program inverter for a reversible language.

Overview: After an brief overview of the semi-inverter (Sect. 2), we formally define conditional term rewriting systems and semi-inversion (Sect. 3). Then, we present our algorithm (Sect. 4) and report on the experimental results (Sect. 5).[1]

2 The Semi-inversion Algorithm—An Overview

This section gives an informal overview of semi-inversion and illustrates the semi-inversion algorithm with a short, familiar example. Both semi-inversion and the algorithm will be formalized and defined in the following sections.

We let semi-inversion cover *rewritings* of the form

$$f(s_1, \ldots, s_n) \ \to_{\mathcal{R}}^* \ \langle t_1, \ldots, t_m \rangle,$$

where f is an n-ary *function symbol* with co-arity m defined in the conditional term rewriting system $\mathcal{R}$; *input and output terms* $s_1, \ldots, s_n$ and $t_1, \ldots, t_m$ are ground constructor terms; and $\langle \ldots \rangle$ is a special m-ary constructor containing the m output terms. The transformation of f into a semi-inverse $\underline{f}$ is w.r.t. indices of known input and output terms. If we assume that the first a input and b output terms are the known arguments, then the semi-inverse $\underline{f}_{\{1,\ldots,a\}\{1,\ldots,b\}}$ takes the form

$$\underline{f}_{\{1,\ldots,a\}\{1,\ldots,b\}}(s_1, \ldots, s_a, t_1, \ldots, t_b) \ \to_{\underline{\mathcal{R}}}^* \ \langle s_{a+1}, \ldots, s_n, t_{b+1}, \ldots, t_m \rangle.$$

The *input-output index sets* $\{1, \ldots, a\}$ and $\{1, \ldots, b\}$ label the new function symbol $\underline{f}$ and serve to distinguish different semi-inverses of the same f. The semi-inversion algorithm locally inverts each rule needed for the rewriting sequence in the *semi-inverted rewriting system* $\underline{\mathcal{R}}$ such that the known parameters specified by the two index sets occur on the left-hand side and all others occur on the right-hand side of the semi-inverted rules of f. Semi-inversion is *polyvariant* because $\underline{\mathcal{R}}$ may include several different semi-inversions of the rules defining f in $\mathcal{R}$, while, in contrast, full inversion is *monovariant*, as it requires only one variant per f.

Example 1. Take as an example the multiplication $x \cdot y = z$ of two unary numbers x and y defined by adding y x times (s1–s4, Fig. 1), which is similar to the unconditional system (r1–r4, Fig. 1) suggested by [19]. Inversion of multiplication mul is w.r.t. the second input y and the first (and only) output z. That is, input-output index sets $I = \{2\}$ and $O = \{1\}$ yield the rewrite rules for division $z/y = x$ and, as a subtask, partially inverts addition $x + y = z$ into subtraction $z - x = y$ (t1–t4, as shown in Fig. 1). Multiplication mul(x,y) and addition add(x,y) are inverted into division $\underline{\text{mul}}_{\{2\}\{1\}}$(y,z) and subtraction $\underline{\text{add}}_{\{1\}\{1\}}$(x,z) and are replaced by the forms div(z,y) and sub(z,x) for readability. Some of

---

[1] The extended abstract of a talk, Nordic Workshop on Programming Theory, Univ. of Bergen, Dept. of Informatics, Report 403, 2012, is partially used in Sects. 1 and 5.

the inverted rules have a conditional part (the conjunction to the right of $\Leftarrow$), which must be satisfied to apply a rule and may bind variables, *e.g.*, y, in rule t4.

The algorithm is illustrated in Fig. 2 by the stepwise inversion of rule s2. First, all function symbols are labeled with index sets, starting with the given index sets on the left-hand side and then repeatedly (from left to right) labeling the function symbols in the conditions with indices of the known arguments (Step 1). Variable w is known after add is rewritten, so the rightmost mul is labeled $\text{mul}_{\{2\}\{1\}}$. Finally, *local inversion* brings all known parts to the left-hand side according to the index sets (Step 2), *e.g.*, $\text{mul}_{\{2\}\{1\}}(\text{s}(\text{x}),\text{y}) \to \langle\text{z}\rangle$ into $\underline{\text{mul}}_{\{2\}\{1\}}(\text{y},\text{z}) \to \langle\text{s}(\text{x})\rangle$.

We note that in Fig. 1, division by zero, div(z,0), is undefined (due to infinite rewriting by repeatedly subtracting 0 from z). Division of zero, div(0,y), where $\text{y} > 0$, correctly defines zero as a result. Both rules t1 and t2 match, but only rule t1 can be applied. The pre-processing and post-processing that transform between unconditional and flat conditional constructor systems are standard techniques and not discussed here; see, *e.g.*, [19, 21, 22].

Unconditional rules:
r1: $\text{mul}(0,\text{y}) \to 0$ r2: $\text{mul}(\text{s}(\text{x}),\text{y}) \to \text{add}(\text{y},\text{mul}(\text{x},\text{y}))$
r3: $\text{add}(0,\text{y}) \to \text{y}$ r4: $\text{add}(\text{s}(\text{x}),\text{y}) \to \text{s}(\text{add}(\text{x},\text{y}))$

Flat rules:
s1: $\text{mul}(0,\text{y}) \to \langle 0 \rangle$ s2: $\text{mul}(\text{s}(\text{x}),\text{y}) \to \langle\text{z}\rangle \Leftarrow \text{add}(\text{y},\text{w}) \to \langle\text{z}\rangle \wedge \text{mul}(\text{x},\text{y}) \to \langle\text{w}\rangle$
s3: $\text{add}(0,\text{y}) \to \langle\text{y}\rangle$ s4: $\text{add}(\text{s}(\text{x}),\text{y}) \to \langle\text{s}(\text{z})\rangle \Leftarrow \text{add}(\text{x},\text{y}) \to \langle\text{z}\rangle$

Inverted rules (after renaming):
t1: $\text{div}(0,\text{y}) \to \langle 0 \rangle$ t2: $\text{div}(\text{z},\text{y}) \to \langle\text{s}(\text{x})\rangle \Leftarrow \text{sub}(\text{z},\text{y}) \to \langle\text{w}\rangle \wedge \text{div}(\text{w},\text{y}) \to \langle\text{x}\rangle$
t3: $\text{sub}(\text{y},0) \to \langle\text{y}\rangle$ t4: $\text{sub}(\text{s}(\text{z}),\text{s}(\text{x})) \to \langle\text{y}\rangle \Leftarrow \text{sub}(\text{z},\text{x}) \to \langle\text{y}\rangle$

Fig. 1. Partial inversion of multiplication into division.

Label all function symbols (index set propagation):
Step 1 $\left\{ \begin{array}{l} \text{mul}(\text{s}(\text{x}),\text{y}) \to \langle\text{z}\rangle \quad \Leftarrow \text{add}(\text{y},\text{w}) \to \langle\text{z}\rangle \quad \wedge \text{mul}(\text{x},\text{y}) \to \langle\text{w}\rangle \\ \text{mul}_{\{2\}\{1\}}(\text{s}(\text{x}),\text{y}) \to \langle\text{z}\rangle \Leftarrow \text{add}_{\{1\}\{1\}}(\text{y},\text{w}) \to \langle\text{z}\rangle \wedge \text{mul}_{\{2\}\{1\}}(\text{x},\text{y}) \to \langle\text{w}\rangle \end{array} \right.$

Local inversion:
Step 2 $\left\{ \begin{array}{l} \text{mul}_{\{2\}\{1\}}(\text{s}(\text{x}),\text{y}) \to \langle\text{z}\rangle \Leftarrow \text{add}_{\{1\}\{1\}}(\text{y},\text{w}) \to \langle\text{z}\rangle \wedge \text{mul}_{\{2\}\{1\}}(\text{x},\text{y}) \to \langle\text{w}\rangle \\ \underline{\text{mul}}_{\{2\}\{1\}}(\text{y},\text{z}) \to \langle\text{s}(\text{x})\rangle \Leftarrow \underline{\text{add}}_{\{1\}\{1\}}(\text{y},\text{z}) \to \langle\text{w}\rangle \wedge \underline{\text{mul}}_{\{2\}\{1\}}(\text{y},\text{w}) \to \langle\text{x}\rangle \end{array} \right.$

Fig. 2. Stepwise inversion of rule s2 in Fig. 1 w.r.t. the input-output index sets {2} {1}.

---

3   Conditional Constructor Systems and Semi-inversion

First, we recall the basic concepts of conditional term rewriting systems following the terminology of Ohlebusch [22] and their ground constructor-based relation [20]. Then, we define what we call conditional constructor term rewriting systems (CCSs) and describe how they model a series of language paradigms. We also describe the properties for when they can be evaluated efficiently, which relates to the design goals for our semi-inverter. Finally, we define semi-inversion of such systems and give the first insights into the nature of semi-inversion.

3.1 Preliminaries for Conditional Term Rewriting

We assume a countable set of variables $\mathcal{V}$. A finite signature $\mathcal{F}$ is assumed to be partitioned into two disjoint sets: a set of *defined function* symbols $\mathcal{D}$, each $f \in \mathcal{D}$ with an arity n and a co-arity m, written $f/n/m$, and a set of constructor symbols $\mathcal{C}$, each $a \in \mathcal{C}$ with an arity n. We denote the set of all terms over $\mathcal{F}$ and $\mathcal{V}$ by $T(\mathcal{F}, \mathcal{V})$. A term s is a *ground* term if it has no variables, a *constructor* term if it contains no function symbols, and a *ground constructor* term if it is both a ground term and a constructor term. Every subterm s of a term t has at least a position p, and we denote this subterm by $t|_p = s$, with the root symbol denoted $root(t)$. Furthermore, we let $t[s']_p$ denote a new term where the subterm at position p in t is replaced by a new (sub)term s'. A *substitution* σ is a mapping from variables to terms, a *ground substitution* is a mapping from variables to ground terms, and a *constructor substitution* is a mapping from variables to constructor terms.

A *conditional rewrite rule* is of the form $l \to r \Leftarrow c$, where the left-hand side l is a non-variable and $root(l) \in \mathcal{D}$, the right-hand side r is a term, and the *conditions* c are a (perhaps empty) conjunction of conditions $l_1 \to r_1 \wedge \ldots \wedge l_k \to r_k$.

A *conditional term rewriting system* $\mathcal{R}$ over a signature $\mathcal{F}$, abbreviated *CTRS*, is a finite set of conditional rewrite rules $l_0 \to r_0 \Leftarrow l_1 \to r_1 \wedge \ldots \wedge l_k \to r_k$ over all terms in $T(\mathcal{F}, \mathcal{V})$ such that the defined functions $\mathcal{D} = \{root(l) \mid l \to r \Leftarrow c \in \mathcal{R}\}$ and constructors $\mathcal{C} = \mathcal{F} \setminus \mathcal{D}$. The conditions are interpreted as reachability, defining a so-called oriented CTRS, e.g., [22].

A *ground constructor-based rewrite relation* $\to_{\mathcal{R}}$ associated with a CTRS over $\mathcal{F}$ $\to_{\mathcal{R}}$ is the smallest binary relation for a pair of ground terms $s, t \in T(\mathcal{F}, \emptyset)$, where there is a position p, a ground constructor substitution σ and a rewrite rule $l \to r \Leftarrow c$ such that $s|_p = l\sigma$, $s[r\sigma]_p = t$ and, for each condition $(l_i \to r_i) \in c$, $l_i\sigma \to_{\mathcal{R}}^* r_i\sigma$.

3.2 Conditional Constructor Systems

In this study, we focus on a subclass of CTRSs we call *conditional constructor term rewriting systems*. These systems are both input to and output from the semi-inversion algorithm. They are also referred to as pure constructor CTRSs in the literature [16] and are a subset of 4-CTRSs [22]. They can model first-order functional programs, logic programs, and functional logic programs [5] and are suitable for observing and discussing common problems arising from inversion without considering different language specifications.

The purpose of these systems is to describe relations f from n ground constructor terms to m ground constructor terms, that is,

$$f(s_1, \ldots, s_n) \ \to_{\mathcal{R}}^* \ \langle t_1, \ldots, t_m \rangle.$$

We assume that the signature includes special constructors $\langle \rangle / m$ intended to contain the m output and function symbols of the form $\mathtt{mul}/2/1$ and $\mathtt{mul}_{\{2\}\{1\}}/2/1$.

Definition 1 (CCS).   *A conditional constructor term rewriting system $\mathcal{R}$, abbreviated CCS, is a CTRS over $\mathcal{F} = \mathcal{C} \uplus \mathcal{D}$ if each rule in $\mathcal{R}$ is of the form*

$$l_0 \to r_0 \Leftarrow l_1 \to r_1 \wedge \ldots \wedge l_k \to r_k,$$

where each $l_i \to r_i$ $(0 \le i \le k)$ is of the form $f^i(p_1^i, \ldots, p_{n_i}^i) \to \langle q_1^i, \ldots, q_{m_i}^i \rangle$ such that $f^i/n_i/m_i \in \mathcal{D}$, $\langle \rangle / m_i \in \mathcal{C}$, and p_j^i and $q_{j'}^i$ are constructor terms.

We shall only consider the associated ground constructor-based rewrite relation [20] described in Sect. 3.1. The reductions $f(s_1, \ldots, s_n) \to_{\mathcal{R}}^* \langle t_1, \ldots, t_m \rangle$, where all s_i and t_j are ground constructor terms, specified by a CCS, can only be 1-step reductions, that is, $f(s_1, \ldots, s_n) \to_{\mathcal{R}} \langle t_1, \ldots, t_m \rangle$. The left- and right-hand side of the rules are not unifiable, prohibiting 0-step reductions; there is one function symbol in the initial term, and each rule-application removes exactly one function symbol, prohibiting reductions with more than one step. This also simplifies the correctness proof of the semi-inversion algorithm, which can be proven by induction over the depth of the rewrite steps [22, Def. 7.1.4].

The next example defines a rewrite relation by overlapping rules.

Example 2. This CCS defines a one-to-many rewrite relation $\mathtt{perm}/1/1$ between a list and all its permutations, *e.g.*, $\mathtt{perm}([1|[2|[]]]) \to \langle [1|[2|[]]] \rangle$ and $\mathtt{perm}([1|[2|[]]]) \to \langle [2|[1|[]]] \rangle$. It has two defined function symbols $\mathtt{perm}/1/1$ and $\mathtt{del}/1/2$ and a set of constructors, including two list constructors, $[]/0$ and $[\cdot|\cdot]/2$, and two special output constructors, $\langle \cdot \rangle / 1$ and $\langle \cdot, \cdot \rangle / 2$. The defined function symbol $\mathtt{perm}$ depends on $\mathtt{del}$, which removes an arbitrary element from a list and returns the removed element and the remaining list. The nondeterministic relation is caused by the overlapping rules $\mathtt{r3}$ and $\mathtt{r4}$.

$\quad\quad$ $\mathtt{r1}$: $\mathtt{perm}([]) \to \langle [] \rangle$
$\quad\quad$ $\mathtt{r2}$: $\mathtt{perm}(x) \to \langle [y|z] \rangle \Leftarrow \mathtt{del}(x) \to \langle y,u \rangle \wedge \mathtt{perm}(u) \to \langle z \rangle$
$\quad\quad$ $\mathtt{r3}$: $\mathtt{del}([x|y]) \to \langle x,y \rangle$
$\quad\quad$ $\mathtt{r4}$: $\mathtt{del}([x|y]) \to \langle z, [x|u] \rangle \Leftarrow \mathtt{del}(y) \to \langle z,u \rangle$

A CCS can be nondeterministic by overlapping rules, as in Example 2, and by what we call *extra variables*[2], i.e., variables occurring on the right-hand side r of a rule but neither in its left-hand l side nor in its conditions c, i.e., $Var(r) \setminus (Var(l) \cup Var(c))$. In case a system has no extra variables, we call it *extra-variable free*, abbreviated *EV-free*. EV-free CCSs are a subset of 3-CTRSs [22], and pcDCTRSs [18] are a subset of EV-free CCSs.

---

[2] In this case, we follow the terminology of [19] —these are not to be confused with "extra variables" as defined by Ohlebusch [22], i.e., $(Var(r) \cup Var(c)) \setminus Var(l)$.

The extra variables cause infinite branching in the ground constructor-based rewrite relation; for example, a rule $f() \rightarrow \langle x \rangle$ represents an infinite ground constructor-based rewrite relation $\{f() \rightarrow_{\mathcal{R}} \langle a \rangle, f() \rightarrow_{\mathcal{R}} \langle b \rangle, \ldots\}$. Intuitively, these variables can be interpreted as *logic variables* subsuming all possible ground constructor terms. Extra variables require efficient implementations that do not naively produce the entire ground constructor-based rewrite relation. *Narrowing* is a well-established rewriting method, where matching is replaced by unification; see, e.g., [5] for further details, [3,12] for a survey, and [19] for the use in partial inversion.

3.3   Semi-inverse

The reader has already seen an example of semi-inversion in Sect. 2. Next, we define semi-inversion formally and illustrate it with examples of the algorithm.

Definition 2 (semi-inverse). *Let $\mathcal{R}$ and $\underline{\mathcal{R}}$ be CCSs over $\mathcal{F} = \mathcal{C} \uplus \mathcal{D}$ and $\underline{\mathcal{F}} = \underline{\mathcal{C}} \uplus \underline{\mathcal{D}}$, respectively, with $f/n/m \in \mathcal{D}$ and $\underline{f}_{IO}/\underline{n}/\underline{m} \in \underline{\mathcal{D}}$, where $I = \{i_1, \ldots, i_a\}$ and $O = \{o_1, \ldots, o_b\}$ are index sets such that $\underline{n} = a + b$ and $\underline{m} = m + n - \underline{n}$. Then, $\underline{\mathcal{R}}$ is a semi-inverse of $\mathcal{R}$ w.r.t. f, I, and O if for all ground constructor terms $s_1, \ldots, s_n, t_1, \ldots, t_m \in T(\mathcal{C} \setminus \{\langle \rangle\}, \emptyset)$,*

$$f(s_1, \ldots, s_n) \rightarrow_{\mathcal{R}} \langle t_1, \ldots, t_m \rangle \quad \Leftrightarrow$$
$$\underline{f}_{IO}(s_{i_1}, \ldots, s_{i_a}, t_{o_1}, \ldots, t_{o_b}) \rightarrow_{\underline{\mathcal{R}}} \langle s_{i_{a+1}}, \ldots, s_{i_n}, t_{o_{b+1}}, \ldots, t_{o_m} \rangle$$

where divisions $\{i_1, \ldots, i_a\} \uplus \{i_{a+1}, \ldots, i_n\} = \{1, \ldots, n\}$ and $\{o_1, \ldots, o_b\} \uplus \{o_{b+1}, \ldots, o_m\} = \{1, \ldots, m\}$. We assume that the name and the parameters of $\underline{f}_{IO}$ are ordered according to $<$-order on the indices.

The reason the semi-inversion algorithm produces a CCS and not an EV-free CCS lies in the nature of full-inversion, i.e., the most specific inversion problem, as demonstrated by the next example.

Example 3. Full inversion of the EV-free CCS $\mathtt{fst}(x,y) \rightarrow \langle x \rangle$ unavoidably creates a CCS with extra variables, namely, $\underline{\mathtt{fst}}_{\emptyset,\{1\}}(x) \rightarrow \langle x,y \rangle$.

Sometimes the semi-inverted system and its original system define the same rewrite relation but are defined differently, as in the following examples.

Example 4 (Ex. 2, continued). The semi-inverse of $\mathtt{perm}$ w.r.t. index sets $I = \emptyset$ and $O = \{1\}$, i.e., a full inversion, is a CCS that defines the same permutation relation by different rules. Here, $\underline{\mathtt{del}}_{\emptyset,\{1,2\}}$ inserts an element randomly into a list, whereas the original $\mathtt{del}$ removes an arbitrary element from the list.

$\underline{\mathtt{r1}}$: $\underline{\mathtt{perm}}_{\emptyset,\{1\}}([]) \rightarrow \langle[]\rangle$

$\underline{\mathtt{r2}}$: $\underline{\mathtt{perm}}_{\emptyset,\{1\}}([y|z]) \rightarrow \langle x \rangle \Leftarrow \underline{\mathtt{perm}}_{\emptyset,\{1\}}(z) \rightarrow \langle u \rangle \wedge \underline{\mathtt{del}}_{\emptyset,\{1,2\}}(y,u) \rightarrow \langle x \rangle$

$\underline{\mathtt{r3}}$: $\underline{\mathtt{del}}_{\emptyset,\{1,2\}}(x,y) \rightarrow \langle[x|y]\rangle$

$\underline{\mathtt{r4}}$: $\underline{\mathtt{del}}_{\emptyset,\{1,2\}}(z,[x|u]) \rightarrow \langle[x|y]\rangle \Leftarrow \underline{\mathtt{del}}_{\emptyset,\{1,2\}}(z,u) \rightarrow \langle y \rangle$

3.4   Modeling Programming Languages and Evaluation Strategies

EV-free CCSs are suitable for modeling logic languages such as Prolog, as seen in the next example, where predicates are modeled by function symbols with co-arity 0. In general, logic programs require narrowing, as we shall see below.

Example 5. The classic predicate append can be modeled by the two rules
app([],y,y) $\rightarrow$ $\langle\rangle$ and app([h|t],y,[h|z]) $\rightarrow$ $\langle\rangle$ $\Leftarrow$ app(t,y,z) $\rightarrow$ $\langle\rangle$.

The evaluation order of the conditions, i.e., the *strategy*, does not affect the correctness of a rewriting, but the conditions and their order may require narrowing. Instead of describing when there exists an evaluation order, which would only require the faster term rewriting, it is standard to fix the order to be from left to right and to define for which systems there is an order that would only require term rewriting. We follow [16] and define these properties for CCSs, and not only EV-free CCSs as in [22]. For a rule $l \rightarrow r \Leftarrow l_1 \rightarrow r_1 \wedge \ldots \wedge l_k \rightarrow r_k$, a variable x in a condition l_i, i.e., $x \in \mathcal{V}ar(l_i)$, is *known* if $x \in \mathcal{V}ar(l, r_1, \ldots, r_{i-1})$, and *unknown* otherwise. The rule is *left-to-right deterministic*[3] if all variables on the left-hand sides of the conditions are known, i.e., $\mathcal{V}ar(l_i) \subseteq \mathcal{V}ar(l, r_1, \ldots, r_{i-1})$, and a CCS is *left-to-right deterministic* if all its rules are left-to-right deterministic.

A left-to-right deterministic and EV-free CCS does *not* require narrowing, and it is desirable for a semi-inverter to produce such systems [22, Sect. 7.2.5]. In addition, these systems provide a good basis for modeling functional programs [5]. However, other requirements include *orthogonal* rules, i.e., non-overlapping rules and left-linearity. These requirements will not be a part of our design focus for the semi-inversion algorithm, but we will comment on where to check for such paradigm-specific properties in the algorithm in Sect. 4.

Moreover, an EV-free CCS can model reversible languages by ensuring right-orthogonality and non-deletion. Nishida et al. [18] performed a reversibilization of a possibly irreversible pcDCTRS[4] by labeling each right-hand side of a rule with a unique constructor, i.e., right-orthogonality, and recording all deleted values in a trace, i.e., non-deletion. Thus, their resulting pcDCTRSs are reversible.

4   The Semi-inversion Algorithm

The polyvariant semi-inverter is presented in a modular way, including the local inversion and a heuristic to improve the semi-inversion by reordering the conditions. The algorithm semi-inverts a CCS w.r.t. a given function symbol and a pair of input-output index sets into a new CCS. It terminates and yields correct semi-inverse systems, as shown at the end of this section.

---

[3] Left-to-right determinism is referred to as "determinism" in term rewriting literature, but we make a rather clear distinction between this property, deterministic computations, and deterministic input-output relations, i.e., functions.

[4] Equivalent to left-to-right deterministic EV-free CCSs with orthogonal rules.

The semi-inverter labels all function symbols with two index sets, I and O, that contain the indices of the known terms of the left-hand and right-hand sides of a rule, respectively, and locally inverts every rule after reordering the conditions such that all known variables given by the index sets occur on the left-hand side and the rest occur on the right-hand side of the new rule. The control of rule generation, the heuristic and indices O extend the partial inverter [19].

4.1   Control of Rule Generation

The recursive semi-inversion algorithm (Fig. 3) controls the local inversion (Fig. 4) of the conditional rewrite rules. Given a rewrite system $\mathcal{R}$, an initial function symbol f and the initial input-output index sets I and O, the algorithm produces the semi-inverse rewrite system $\underline{\mathcal{R}}_{f_{IO}}$. It keeps track of the function symbols that have been semi-inverted (in set Done) and those that are pending semi-inversions (in set Pend) to address circular dependencies between rules.

A pending task $(f, I, O) \in$ Pend is selected, and each of the rules defining f in $\mathcal{R}$ is semi-inverted, which may lead to new semi-inversion tasks. The auxiliary procedure getdep collects all function symbols and their input-output index sets on which the conditions of a set of inverted rules depend. This procedure helps determine new reachable tasks after semi-inverting the rules. Using reachability for semi-inversion reduces the risk of exponentially increasing the size of $\underline{\mathcal{R}}_{f_{IO}}$; semi-inversion is *polyvariant inversion* of $\mathcal{R}$ in that it may produce several semi-inversions of the same function symbol, namely, one for each input-output index set. Eventually, all reachable semi-inverses are generated then no pending task exist and the algorithm returns the self-contained semi-inverted system $\underline{\mathcal{R}}_{f_{IO}}$.

At this point, as an add-on, the type of the new rewrite system can be syntactically checked. For example, if none of the semi-inverted rules contains an extra variable, then the system is marked as EV-free, and if all function symbols in the CSS are defined by orthogonal rules, then this system corresponds to a first-order

```
seminv(Pend, Done) =
   if Pend = ∅ then ∅ else
   // choose a pending task for semi-inversion
   (f,I,O) ∈ Pend;
   // semi-invert all rules of f with index sets I and O
   f-Rules_original  := { ρ | ρ : l → r ⇐ c ∈ R,  root(l) = f };
   f-Rules_inverted  := { localinv(ρ,I,O) | ρ ∈ f-Rules_original };
   // update the pending and done sets
   NewDep := getdep(f-Rules_inverted) \ Done;
   f-Rules_inverted ∪ seminv((Pend ∪ NewDep) \ {(f,I,O)}, Done ∪ {(f,I,O)});
getdep(Rules) =
   { (f,I,O) | l → r ⇐ c ∈ Rules,  l_i → r_i ∈ c,  root(l_i) = f_IO };
```

Fig. 3. Recursive semi-inversion algorithm.

functional program. This is the strength of using conditional term rewriting systems as a foundation for studying semi-inversion: they smoothly model inversion problems across a range of different important programming paradigms.

The algorithm *terminates* for any (f,I,O) because the numbers of function symbols and their possible index sets are finite for any given $\mathcal{R}$. In each recursion, a task is semi-inverted and moved from **Pend** to **Done**. Eventually, no more tasks can be added to **Pend** that are not already in **Done**, and the algorithm terminates.

Invocation of the semi-inverter in Fig. 3 is done by $\mathsf{seminv}(\{(f,I,O)\},\ \emptyset)_{\mathcal{R}}$, where the read-only $\mathcal{R}$ is global for the sake of simplicity. A new system $\underline{\mathcal{R}_{f_{IO}}}$ with all semi-inverted functions *reachable* from the initial task (f,I,O) is returned.

Definition 3 (Semi-inverter). *Given a CCS $\mathcal{R}$, a defined function symbol $f/n/m \in \mathcal{D}$, and two index sets $I \subseteq \{1,\ldots,n\}$ and $O \subseteq \{1,\ldots,m\}$, the semi-inverter in Fig. 3 yields the CCS*

$$\underline{\mathcal{R}_{f_{IO}}} = \mathsf{seminv}(\{(f,I,O)\},\emptyset)_{\mathcal{R}}.$$

Note that if the initial pending set contains two or more tasks, they are semi-inverted together by seminv, which may be useful for practical reasons.

$$\underline{\mathcal{R}_{f_{IO}}} \cup \underline{\mathcal{R}_{g_{I'O'}}} = \mathsf{seminv}(\{(f,I,O)\} \cup \{(g,I',O')\},\emptyset)_{\mathcal{R}}.$$

4.2   Local Semi-inversion of Conditional Rules

The form of the rules with a rule head followed by a sequence of flat conditions considerably simplifies the local inversion. Given the index sets I and O, a rule

$$(l \to r \Leftarrow l_1 \to r_1 \wedge \ldots \wedge l_k \to r_k)$$

is locally semi-inverted into a *left-to-right deterministic* rule

$$(l' \to r' \Leftarrow l'_1 \to r'_1 \wedge \ldots \wedge l'_k \to r'_k),$$

i.e., satisfying $\mathcal{V}ar(l',r'_1,\ldots,r'_{i-1}) \supseteq \mathcal{V}ar(l'_i)$ for all $1 \le i \le k$.

Local inversion (Fig. 4) first generates the new head $l' \to r'$ by rearranging the terms of l and r according to I and O as required for semi-inversion (Def. 2). After heuristic reorders the conditions, localinvc ensures that the new rule is left-to-right deterministic by transforming the conditions $l_1 \to r_1 \wedge \ldots \wedge l_k \to r_k$ from left to right such that all terms in the ith condition $(l_i \to r_i)$ that depend only on the already *known variables* $\mathcal{V}ar(l,r_1,\ldots,r_{i-1})$ are moved to the new left-hand side l'_i and all other terms are moved to the new right-hand side r'_i (ordered by increasing index). Therefore, l'_i contains terms that depend on known variables (including ground terms), and r'_i contains all the other terms. At the same time, the function symbol $\underline{f_i}$ at the root of l'_i is labeled with the corresponding input-output sets. This transformation is repeated recursively from left to right for each condition while updating the set of known variables. In this way, the semi-inverted rule becomes left-to-right deterministic, and each new condition $l'_i \to r'_i$ uses the maximum number of known terms in l'_i. This step is not necessary for correctness but reduces the search space of the intended reduction strategy.

```
localinv(f(p₁,...,pₙ) → ⟨q₁,...,qₘ⟩ ⇐ c, {i₁,...,iₐ}, {o₁,...,o_b}) =
    // semi-invert the rule head and label the function symbol
    {i_{a+1},..., iₙ} := {1,...,n} \ {i₁,...,iₐ}
    {o_{b+1},..., oₘ} := {1,...,m} \ {o₁,...,o_b}
    lhs := f_{i₁,...,iₐ}{o₁,...,o_b}(p_{i₁},...,p_{iₐ},q_{o₁},...,q_{o_b})
    rhs := ⟨p_{i_{a+1}},...,p_{iₙ},q_{o_{b+1}},...,q_{oₘ}⟩
    // locally invert the conditions after reordering
    Var := Var(lhs)
    c'  := heuristic(c, Var)        // reorder conditions of rule
    c'' := localinvc(c',Var)        // local inversion of conditions
    // return the inverted rule
    lhs → rhs ⇐ c''
localinvc(c, Var) = case c of
    // if no condition, then return the empty condition
    ε => ε
    // else invert the left-most condition
    f(p₁,...,pₙ) → ⟨q₁,...,qₘ⟩ ∧ Restc  =>
        // build the index sets
        {i₁,  ..., iₐ} := {i | i ∈ {1,...,n}, Var(pᵢ) ⊆ Var}
        {i_{a+1},..., iₙ} := {1,...,n} \ {i₁,...,iₐ}
        {o₁,  ..., o_b} := {o | o ∈ {1,...,m}, Var(q_o) ⊆ Var}
        {o_{b+1},..., oₘ} := {1,...,m} \ {o₁,...,o_b}
        // locally invert and label the left-most condition
        lhs := f_{i₁,...,iₐ}{o₁,...,o_b}(p_{i₁},...,p_{iₐ},q_{o₁},...,q_{o_b})
        rhs := ⟨p_{i_{a+1}},...,p_{iₙ},q_{o_{b+1}},...,q_{oₘ}⟩
        // return the inverted conditions
        lhs → rhs ∧ localinvc(Restc, Var ∪ Var(rhs))
```

Fig. 4. Local inversion of a conditional rule.

4.3   A Heuristic Approach to Reordering Conditions

We have chosen a greedy heuristic to reorder the conditions in a rule before semi-inverting them, which works surprisingly well. The procedure heuristic (shown in Fig. 5) reorders the conditions according to the *percentages of known parameters* such that the condition with the highest percentage comes first. This procedure dynamically updates the set of known variables each time a condition is moved to the head of the sequence and recursively applies the reordering to the remaining conditions. Clearly, different sets of known variables can lead to different orders of the conditions. The intention with this heuristic is to syntactically exploit as much known information as possible without having to rely on an extra analysis.

Other reordering methods could be used instead. The algorithm by Mogensen [14], which semi-inverts non-overlapping rules in a guarded equational language without extra variables, searches through *all possible semi-inversions* and uses additional semantic information about primitive operators. An exhaustive search will find better orders than a local heuristic, but the search will take more time. This is the familiar trade-off between the accuracy and run time of

```
heuristic(c, KnownVar) = case c of
    // if no condition, then return the empty condition
    ε  =>  ε
    // else find condition with highest percentage of known parameters
    l₁ → r₁ ∧ ...∧ lₖ → rₖ  =>
        // determine percentages
        Percent₁ := percent(l₁ → r₁, KnownVar)
        ...
        Percentₖ := percent(lₖ → rₖ, KnownVar)
        (Pᵢ,i)   := maxPercent((Percent₁,1),...,(Percentₖ,k))

        // select condition, reorder remaining conditions in updated variable set
        lᵢ → rᵢ ∧ heuristic(c \ (lᵢ → rᵢ), KnownVar ∪ Var(lᵢ,rᵢ))

percent(f(p₁, ..., pₙ) → ⟨q₁, ..., qₘ⟩, KnownVar) =
    // determine index sets of known parameters
    I := {i | i ∈ {1, ..., n}, Var(pᵢ) ⊆ KnownVar }
    O := {j | j ∈ {1, ..., m}, Var(qⱼ) ⊆ KnownVar }
    // return percentage of known parameters
    (|I| + |O|)/(m + n)          // known = |I| + |O|, total = m + n
```

Fig. 5. A greedy heuristic for reordering conditions.

a program analysis. The heuristic always finds a reordering (perhaps leading to extra variables), while the semi-inverter [14] may halt with no answer due to the limitations of the language —a later inverter [15] allows functional parameters.

There is no fixed order of conditions that avoids extra variables for all possible semi-inversions of a given rewrite system. Our experiments show that the heuristic usually improves the resulting semi-inversion, but it can also be deceived, as shown in the following example.

Example 6. Given a system consisting of r1–r3, the semi-inversion of test w.r.t. $I = \{1\}$ and $O = \{2\}$ yields the system s1–s3, which has an extra variable in function $\underline{fst}_{\{1\}\{1\}}$, whereas one produced without the heuristic would be EV-free.

$$\text{r1: } test(x,y) \to \langle w,z \rangle \quad \Leftarrow copy(x,y) \to \langle w,z \rangle \wedge fst(x,y) \to \langle z \rangle$$
$$\text{r2: } fst(x,y) \to \langle x \rangle \qquad \text{r3: } copy(x,y) \to \langle x,y \rangle$$
$$\text{s1: } \underline{test}_{\{1\}\{2\}}(x,z) \to \langle y,w \rangle \Leftarrow \underline{fst}_{\{1\}\{1\}}(x,z) \to \langle y \rangle \wedge \underline{copy}_{\{1,2\}\{2\}}(x,y,z) \to \langle w \rangle$$
$$\text{s2: } \underline{fst}_{\{1\}\{1\}}(x,x) \to \langle y \rangle \qquad \text{s3: } \underline{copy}_{\{1,2\}\{2\}}(x,y,y) \to \langle x \rangle$$

4.4   Correctness of the Semi-inversion Algorithm

The correctness of the semi-inversion algorithm is proven by first defining $\underline{\mathcal{R}}_{all}$ by semi-inverting all possible semi-inversion tasks for the function symbols in $\mathcal{R}$.

Definition 4 ($\underline{\mathcal{R}}_{all}$). *Let $\mathcal{R}$ be a CCS, and let $P = \{(f,I,O) \mid f/n/m \in \mathcal{D}, I \subseteq \{1,\ldots,n\}, O \subseteq \{1,\ldots,m\}\}$ be the pending set consisting of all semi-inversion tasks of all function symbols defined in $\mathcal{R}$. Then, we define*

$$\underline{\mathcal{R}}_{all} = \text{seminv}(P,\emptyset)_{\mathcal{R}}.$$

The following theorem can be proven in two steps: First, the rewrite steps of f are in $\mathcal{R}$ if and only if the rewrite steps of its semi-inverse $\underline{f}_{IO}$ are in $\underline{\mathcal{R}}_{all}$, and secondly, the rewrite steps of $\underline{f}_{IO}$ are in $\underline{\mathcal{R}}_{all}$ if and only if they are in $\underline{\mathcal{R}}_{\underline{f}_{IO}}$. The proofs are omitted due to lack of space.

Theorem 1. *Let $\mathcal{R}$ be a CCS, and let $\underline{\mathcal{R}}_{\underline{f}_{IO}} = \mathsf{seminv}(\{(f, I, O)\}, \emptyset)_{\mathcal{R}}$ for a function symbol $f/n/m \in \mathcal{D}$ and index sets $I \subseteq \{1, \ldots, n\}$ and $O \subseteq \{1, \ldots, m\}$. Then, $\underline{\mathcal{R}}_{\underline{f}_{IO}}$ is a semi-inverse of $\mathcal{R}$ w.r.t. f, I, and O.*

5 Application of the Semi-inverter

The semi-inverter has been fully implemented (in Prolog), and in the following, we will present the results: a series of semi-inversions of a discrete simulation of a free fall, each solving a different problem, a decrypter from a simple encrypter, and the inversion of an inverter for a reversible programming language.

5.1 Discrete Simulation of a Free Fall

We consider a discrete simulation of an object that falls through a vacuum [4] and use semi-inversion to generate four new programs, each solving a different aspect. The simulation is defined by the equations $v_t = v_{t-1} + g$ and $h_t = h_{t-1} - v_t + g/2$, where $g \approx 10\,m/s^2$ is the approximate gravitational acceleration. The following system $\mathtt{fall_0}$ yields the object's velocity v_t ($\mathtt{v}$) and height h_t ($\mathtt{h}$) at time t, given t ($\mathtt{t}$) and initial velocity v_0 ($\mathtt{v_0}$) and height h_0 ($\mathtt{h_0}$).

$\mathtt{fall_0(v,h,0)} \rightarrow \langle \mathtt{v,h} \rangle$

$\mathtt{fall_0(v_0,h_0,s(t))} \rightarrow \langle \mathtt{v,h} \rangle \Leftarrow$
  $\mathtt{add(v_0, s^5(0))} \rightarrow \langle \mathtt{v_n} \rangle \wedge$
  $\mathtt{height(h_0, v_n)} \rightarrow \langle \mathtt{h_n} \rangle \wedge$
  $\mathtt{fall_0(v_n, h_n, t)} \rightarrow \langle \mathtt{v,h} \rangle$

$\mathtt{height(h_0, v_n)} \rightarrow \langle \mathtt{h_n} \rangle \Leftarrow$
  $\mathtt{add(h_0, s^5(0))} \rightarrow \langle \mathtt{h_{temp}} \rangle \wedge \mathtt{sub(h_{temp}, v_n)} \rightarrow \langle \mathtt{h_n} \rangle$

Original	$\mathtt{fall_0}$: $(\mathtt{v_0, h_0, t}) \rightarrow (\mathtt{v, h})$
Full inv.	$\mathtt{fall_1}$: $(\mathtt{v, h}) \rightarrow (\mathtt{v_0, h_0, t})$
Partial inv.	$\mathtt{fall_2}$: $(\mathtt{t, v, h}) \rightarrow (\mathtt{v_0, h_0})$
Semi-inv. #1	$\mathtt{fall_3}$: $(\mathtt{v_0, t, h}) \rightarrow (\mathtt{h_0, v})$
Semi-inv. #2	$\mathtt{fall_4}$: $(\mathtt{v_0, t, v}) \rightarrow (\mathtt{h_0, h})$

The system $\mathtt{fall_0}$ is geared towards solving the 'forward' problem, while finding a solution to the 'backward' problem of determining the origin of a fall may be equally interesting, it requires a new set of rules. Full inversion algorithms can transform $\mathtt{fall_0}$ into a new system $\mathtt{fall_1}$ solving the backward problem, while other problems require partial or semi-inversion.

These four programs $\mathtt{fall_1}$ to $\mathtt{fall_4}$ are successfully generated by the semi-inversion algorithm as shown in Fig. 6 (dependency functions are omitted for clarity). The difference between the order of the conditions in the four inversions indicates that the heuristic has taken action.

5.2 Encrypter and Decrypter

The automatic generation of decrypters is fascinating. The following symmetric encrypter is a modification of a simple encryption method suggested by

$$\text{fall}_1(v,h) \to \langle v,h,0 \rangle \qquad\qquad \text{fall}_2(0,v,h) \to \langle v,h \rangle$$

$$\text{fall}_1(v,h) \to \langle v_0,h_0,s(t) \rangle \Leftarrow \quad \text{fall}_2(s(t),v,h) \to \langle v_0,h_0 \rangle \Leftarrow$$

$$\qquad \text{fall}_1(v,h) \to \langle v_n,h_n,t \rangle \wedge \qquad\qquad \text{fall}_2(t,v,h) \to \langle v_n,h_n \rangle \wedge$$

$$\qquad \underline{\text{add}}_{\{2\}\{1\}}(s^{10}(0),v_n) \to \langle v_0 \rangle \wedge \qquad \underline{\text{add}}_{\{2\}\{1\}}(s^{10}(0),v_n) \to \langle v_0 \rangle \wedge$$

$$\qquad \underline{\text{height}}_{\{2\}\{1\}}(v_n,h_n) \to \langle h_0 \rangle \qquad\qquad \underline{\text{height}}_{\{2\}\{1\}}(v_n,h_n) \to \langle h_0 \rangle$$

$$\text{fall}_3(v,0,h) \to \langle h,v \rangle \qquad\qquad \text{fall}_4(v,0,v) \to \langle h,h \rangle$$

$$\text{fall}_3(v_0,s(t),h) \to \langle h_0,v \rangle \Leftarrow \quad \text{fall}_4(v_0,s(t),v) \to \langle h_0,h \rangle \Leftarrow$$

$$\qquad \text{add}(v_0,s^{10}(0)) \to \langle v_n \rangle) \wedge \qquad\qquad \text{add}(v_0,s^{10}(0)) \to \langle v_n \rangle \wedge$$

$$\qquad \text{fall}_3(v_n,t,h) \to \langle h_n,v \rangle \wedge \qquad\qquad \text{fall}_4(v_n,t,v) \to \langle h_n,h \rangle \wedge$$

$$\qquad \underline{\text{height}}_{\{2\}\{1\}}(v_n,h_n) \to \langle h_0 \rangle \qquad\qquad \underline{\text{height}}_{\{2\}\{1\}}(v_n,h_n) \to \langle h_0 \rangle$$

Fig. 6. The fall_0, its full inversion fall_1, the partial inversion fall_2 and the two semi-inversions fall_3 and fall_4.

Mogensen. It produces an encrypted text $z:zs$ given a text formed as an integer list $x:xs$ and a key key. Encryption cleans the key by mod 4, adds the new value to the first character, and repeats the process recursively for the rest of the text (the modification is that we use mod 4 instead of mod 256, as mod 256 consists of 257 rules). The encrypter is given in Fig. 7 (on the left), and the decrypter is a partial inversion of it with respect to $I = \{2\}$ and $O = \{1\}$, as shown in Fig. 7 (on the right). The decrypter ($\underline{\text{encrypt}}_{\{2\}\{1\}}$) produces the decrypted text $x:xs$ given the key key and the encrypted text $z:zs$. Note that mod4 is equivalent to $\underline{\text{mod4}}_{\{1\}\emptyset}$.

Original encrypter:

$$\text{encrypt}(\text{nil},key) \to \langle \text{nil} \rangle$$
$$\text{encrypt}(x:xs,key) \to \langle z:zs \rangle \Leftarrow$$
$$\qquad \text{mod4}(key) \to \langle y \rangle,$$
$$\qquad \text{add}(x,y) \to \langle z \rangle,$$
$$\qquad \text{encrypt}(xs,key) \to \langle zs \rangle$$
$$\text{mod4}(0) \to \langle 0 \rangle$$
$$\text{mod4}(s(0)) \to \langle s(0) \rangle$$
$$\text{mod4}(s^2(0)) \to \langle s^2(0) \rangle$$
$$\text{mod4}(s^3(0)) \to \langle s^3(0) \rangle$$
$$\text{mod4}(s^4(x)) \to \langle w0 \rangle \Leftarrow \text{mod4}(x) \to \langle w0 \rangle$$

Generated decrypter:

$$\underline{\text{encrypt}}_{\{2\}\{1\}}(key,\text{nil}) \to \langle \text{nil} \rangle$$
$$\underline{\text{encrypt}}_{\{2\}\{1\}}(key,z:zs) \to \langle x:xs \rangle \Leftarrow$$
$$\qquad \underline{\text{mod4}}_{\{1\}\emptyset}(key) \to \langle y \rangle,$$
$$\qquad \underline{\text{add}}_{\{2\}\{1\}}(y,z) \to \langle x \rangle,$$
$$\qquad \underline{\text{encrypt}}_{\{2\}\{1\}}(key,zs) \to \langle xs \rangle$$
$$\underline{\text{mod4}}_{\{1\}\emptyset}(0) \to \langle 0 \rangle$$
$$\underline{\text{mod4}}_{\{1\}\emptyset}(s(0)) \to \langle s(0) \rangle$$
$$\underline{\text{mod4}}_{\{1\}\emptyset}(s^2(0)) \to \langle s^2(0) \rangle$$
$$\underline{\text{mod4}}_{\{1\}\emptyset}(s^3(0)) \to \langle s^3(0) \rangle$$
$$\underline{\text{mod4}}_{\{1\}\emptyset}(s^4(x)) \to \langle w0 \rangle \Leftarrow \underline{\text{mod4}}_{\{1\}\emptyset}(x) \to \langle w0 \rangle$$

Fig. 7. Inversion of a simple symmetric encrypter into a decrypter.

5.3   Inverted Inverter

The Janus language is a reversible language [23] where functions can be both called (executed in a forward direction) and uncalled (executed in a backward direction). An inverter for the Janus language creates procedures that are equal to uncalling the original procedure. Since Janus is a reversible language, the full inversion of such a Janus-inverter is equivalent to itself. A Janus-inverter can be described as a left-to-right deterministic EV-free CCS, and in Fig. 8 (on the left), we have given such an inverter for a subset of the language.

A full inversion of the inverter for the reversible Janus language is equivalent to itself. The result of the semi-inversion algorithm is the Janus inverter shown in Fig. 8 (on the right). If we assume that `invName` and its full inversion `invName` are equivalent, then the produced and original rules are equivalent up to the variable naming and order of the parameters.

Janus-Inverter	Fully inverted Janus-inverter
$\text{inv}(\text{proc}(\text{name},\text{progr})) \to \langle\text{proc}(u,v)\rangle \Leftarrow$ $\quad \text{invName}(\text{name}) \to \langle u\rangle \wedge \text{inv}(\text{progr}) \to \langle v\rangle$	$\underline{\text{inv}}(\text{proc}(u,v)) \to \langle\text{proc}(\text{name},\text{progr})\rangle \Leftarrow$ $\quad \underline{\text{invName}}(u) \to \langle\text{name}\rangle \wedge \underline{\text{inv}}(v) \to \langle\text{progr}\rangle$
$\text{inv}(\text{+=}(x,y)) \to \langle\text{-=}(x,y)\rangle$ $\text{inv}(\text{-=}(x,y)) \to \langle\text{+=}(x,y)\rangle$ $\text{inv}(\text{<=>}(x,y)) \to \langle\text{<=>}(x,y)\rangle$	$\underline{\text{inv}}(\text{-=}(x,y)) \to \langle\text{+=}(x,y)\rangle$ $\underline{\text{inv}}(\text{+=}(x,y)) \to \langle\text{-=}(x,y)\rangle$ $\underline{\text{inv}}(\text{<=>}(x,y)) \to \langle\text{<=>}(x,y)\rangle$
$\text{inv}(\text{if}(x_1,y_1,y_2,x_2)) \to \langle\text{if}(x_2,z_1,z_2,x_1)\rangle \Leftarrow$ $\quad \text{inv}(y_1) \to \langle z_1\rangle \wedge \text{inv}(y_2) \to \langle z_2\rangle$ $\text{inv}(\text{loop}(x_1,y_1,y_2,x_2)) \to \langle\text{loop}(x_2,z_1,v_2,x_1)\rangle \Leftarrow$ $\quad \text{inv}(y_1) \to \langle z_1\rangle \wedge \text{inv}(y_2) \to \langle z_2\rangle$	$\underline{\text{inv}}(\text{if}(x_2,z_1,z_2,x_1)) \to \langle\text{if}(x_1,y_1,y_2,x_2)\rangle \Leftarrow$ $\quad \underline{\text{inv}}(z_1) \to \langle y_1\rangle \wedge \underline{\text{inv}}(z_2) \to \langle y_2\rangle$ $\underline{\text{inv}}(\text{loop}(x_2,z_1,z_2,x_1)) \to \langle\text{loop}(x_1,y_1,y_2,x_2)\rangle \Leftarrow$ $\quad \underline{\text{inv}}(z_1) \to \langle y_1\rangle \wedge \underline{\text{inv}}(z_2) \to \langle y_2\rangle$
$\text{inv}(\text{call}(\text{name})) \to \langle\text{call}(u)\rangle \Leftarrow$ $\quad \text{invName}(\text{name}) \to \langle u\rangle$ $\text{inv}(\text{uncall}(\text{name})) \to \langle\text{uncall}(u)\rangle \Leftarrow$ $\quad \text{invName}(\text{name}) \to \langle u\rangle$	$\underline{\text{inv}}(\text{call}(u)) \to \langle\text{call}(\text{name})\rangle \Leftarrow$ $\quad \underline{\text{invName}}(u) \to \langle\text{name}\rangle$ $\underline{\text{inv}}(\text{uncall}(u)) \to \langle\text{uncall}(\text{name})\rangle \Leftarrow$ $\quad \underline{\text{invName}}(u) \to \langle\text{name}\rangle$
$\text{inv}(\text{sequence}(x,y)) \to \langle\text{sequence}(u,v)\rangle \Leftarrow$ $\quad \text{inv}(y) \to \langle u\rangle \wedge \text{inv}(x) \to \langle v\rangle$ $\text{inv}(\text{skip}) \to \langle\text{skip}\rangle$	$\underline{\text{inv}}(\text{sequence}(u,v)) \to \langle\text{sequence}(x,y)\rangle \Leftarrow$ $\quad \underline{\text{inv}}(u) \to \langle y\rangle \wedge \underline{\text{inv}}(v) \to \langle x\rangle$ $\underline{\text{inv}}(\text{skip}) \to \langle\text{skip}\rangle$

Fig. 8. The Janus-inverter `inv` expressed as CCS rules, and its full inverse `inv`.

6   Conclusion

We have shown that polyvariant semi-inversion can be performed for conditional constructor systems (CCSs) that are highly useful for modeling several language paradigms, including logic, functional, and reversible languages. Notably, we have shown that local inversion and a straightforward heuristics suffice for performing the general form of inversion with interesting results. This approach can be used for transformation problems ranging from the inversion of a simple encryption algorithm or a physical discrete-event simulation to a program inverter for a reversible language. We have also implemented the algorithm and shown its correctness. The algorithm makes use of a simple syntactic heuristic that produces good results in our experiments. In full inversion, some auxiliary functions may be partially inverted [17, p. 145], that is, their inversion may also benefit from the algorithm in this paper. Furthermore, the structure of the algorithm is modular such that the heuristic can be easily replaced. In regard to future work, it could be interesting to vary the heuristics with respect to the type of inversion considering that reversing conditions suffices for full inversion; e.g., by parameterization, we might capture other inversion algorithms in this framework.

Acknowledgment. The authors wish to thank German Vidal and the anonymous reviewers. Support by the EU COST Action IC1405 is acknowledged.

References

1. Abramov, S.M., Glück, R.: The universal resolving algorithm and its correctness: inverse computation in a functional language. Sci. Comput. Program. **43**(2–3), 193–229 (2002)
2. Almendros-Jiménez, J.M., Vidal, G.: Automatic partial inversion of inductively sequential functions. In: Horváth, Z., Zsók, V., Butterfield, A. (eds.) IFL 2006. LNCS, vol. 4449, pp. 253–270. Springer, Heidelberg (2007). https://doi.org/10. 1007/978-3-540-74130-5_15
3. Antoy, S.: Programming with narrowing: a tutorial. J. Symb. Comput. **45**(5), 501–522 (2010). (version: June 2017, update)
4. Axelsen, H.B., Glück, R., Yokoyama, T.: Reversible machine code and its abstract processor architecture. In: Diekert, V., Volkov, M.V., Voronkov, A. (eds.) CSR 2007. LNCS, vol. 4649, pp. 56–69. Springer, Heidelberg (2007). https://doi.org/10. 1007/978-3-540-74510-5_9
5. Baader, F., Nipkow, T.: Term Rewriting and All That. Cambridge University Press, Cambridge (1998)
6. Dijkstra, E.W.: Program inversion. In: Bauer, F.L., et al. (eds.) Program Construction. LNCS, vol. 69, pp. 54–57. Springer, Heidelberg (1979). https://doi.org/ 10.1007/BFb0014657
7. Eppstein, D.: A heuristic approach to program inversion. In: Joshi, A.K. (ed.) IJCAI-85. Proceedings, vol. 1, pp. 219–221. Morgan Kaufmann Inc (1985)
8. Glück, R., Kawabe, M.: A program inverter for a functional language with equality and constructors. In: Ohori, A. (ed.) APLAS 2003. LNCS, vol. 2895, pp. 246–264. Springer, Heidelberg (2003). https://doi.org/10.1007/978-3-540-40018-9_17
9. Glück, R., Kawabe, M.: A method for automatic program inversion based on LR(0) parsing. Fundamenta Informaticae **66**, 367–395 (2005)
10. Glück, R., Kawabe, M.: Revisiting an automatic program inverter for Lisp. SIGPLAN Notices **40**(5), 8–17 (2005)
11. Glück, R., Turchin, V.F.: Application of metasystem transition to function inversion and transformation. In: Proceedings of the ISSAC, pp. 286–287. ACM Press (1990)
12. Hanus, M.: The integration of functions into logic programming: from theory to practice. J. Logic Program. **19–20**(Suppl. 1), 583–628 (1994)
13. McCarthy, J.: The inversion of functions defined by Turing machines. In: Shannon, C., McCarthy, J. (eds.) Automata Studies, pp. 177–181. Princeton University Press, Princeton (1956)
14. Mogensen, T.Æ.: Semi-inversion of guarded equations. In: Glück, R., Lowry, M. (eds.) GPCE 2005. LNCS, vol. 3676, pp. 189–204. Springer, Heidelberg (2005). https://doi.org/10.1007/11561347_14
15. Mogensen, T. Æ.: Semi-inversion of functional parameters. In: Proceedings of the PEPM, pp. 21–29. ACM (2008)

16. Nagashima, M., Sakai, M., Sakabe, T.: Determinization of conditional term rewriting systems. Theor. Comput. Sci. **464**, 72–89 (2012)
17. Nishida, N.: Transformational approach to inverse computation in term rewriting. Ph.D. thesis, Graduate School of Engineering, Nagoya University (2004)
18. Nishida, N., Palacios, A., Vidal, G.: Reversible computation in term rewriting. J. Logic. Algebr. Methods Program. **94**, 128–149 (2018)
19. Nishida, N., Sakai, M., Sakabe, T.: Partial inversion of constructor term rewriting systems. In: Giesl, J. (ed.) RTA 2005. LNCS, vol. 3467, pp. 264–278. Springer, Heidelberg (2005). https://doi.org/10.1007/978-3-540-32033-3_20
20. Nishida, N., Vidal, G.: Program inversion for tail recursive functions. In: Proceedings RTA, LIPIcs, vol. 10, pp. 283–298. Schloss Dagstuhl (2011)
21. Ohlebusch, E.: Transforming conditional rewrite systems with extra variables into unconditional systems. In: Ganzinger, H., McAllester, D., Voronkov, A. (eds.) LPAR 1999. LNCS (LNAI), vol. 1705, pp. 111–130. Springer, Heidelberg (1999). https://doi.org/10.1007/3-540-48242-3_8
22. Ohlebusch, E.: Advanced Topics in Term Rewriting. Springer, New York (2002). https://doi.org/10.1007/978-1-4757-3661-8
23. Yokoyama, T., Glück, R.: A reversible programming language and its invertible self-interpreter. In: Proceedings of the PEPM, pp. 144–153. ACM (2007)

Author Index

Printed in the United States
By Bookmasters